In Search of the **Black Panther Party**

In Search of the Black Panther Party

NEW PERSPECTIVES ON A
REVOLUTIONARY MOVEMENT

Jama Lazerow and Yohuru Williams, editors

Duke University Press
Durham and London   2006

2nd printing, 2007

© 2006 Duke University Press

All rights reserved

Printed in the United States of America on acid-free paper ∞

Designed by Heather Hensley

Typeset in Galliard by Keystone Typesetting, Inc.

Library of Congress Cataloging-in-Publication Data appear on the last printed page of this book.

The editors gratefully acknowledge the financial support of Wheelock College.

For Buddy, Max, and Dylan — freethinkers, all!
For Karlyn, Mason, Asa, and Ella

Contents

ix Acknowledgments

xi Editors' Note

1 Introduction: The Black Panthers and Historical Scholarship: Why Now? *Jama Lazerow and Yohuru Williams*

PART ONE The Panthers through the Historian's Lens

15 The Black Panther Party and the Long Civil Rights Era
Robert O. Self

PART TWO The Panthers as American Revolutionaries

59 Introductory Comment: The Panthers and the Question of Violence
Rod Bush

67 In the Shadow of the Gun: The Black Panther Party, the Ninth Amendment, and Discourses of Self-Defense *Bridgette Baldwin*

PART THREE From the Bottom Up and the Top Down: Personal Politics and the Black Panthers

97 Introductory Comment: The Panthers and Local History
James T. Campbell

104 "A Rebel All His Life": The Unexpected Story of Frank "Parky" Grace *Jama Lazerow*

158 WACing Off: Gossip, Sex, Race, and Politics in the World of FBI Special Case Agent William A. Cohendet *Roz Payne*

PART FOUR Coalition Politics: The Panthers as a "Revolutionary Vanguard"

183 Introductory Comment: White Tigers, Brown Berets, Black Panthers, Oh My!   *Yohuru Williams*

191 Invisible Cages: Racialized Politics and the Alliance between the Panthers and the Peace and Freedom Party   *Joel Wilson*

223 Leading the Vanguard: White New Leftists School the Panthers on Black Revolution   *David Barber*

252 Brown Power to Brown People: Radical Ethnic Nationalism, the Black Panthers, and Latino Radicalism, 1967–1973   *Jeffrey O. G. Ogbar*

PART FIVE Revolutionary Politics: The Black Panthers in the American Imagination

289 Introductory Comment: "Culture Is a Weapon in Our Struggle for Liberation": The Black Panther Party and the Cultural Politics of Decolonization   *Davarian L. Baldwin*

306 The Arm(ing) of the Vanguard, Signify(ing), and Performing the Revolution: The Black Panther Party and Pedagogical Strategies for Interpreting a Revolutionary Life   *Tim Lake*

324 Media Culture and the Public Memory of the Black Panther Party   *Edward P. Morgan*

375 Contributors

377 Index

Acknowledgments

This book is the product of many hands, not least of which are the many contributors who endured our repeated requests for more. First, however, we would like to thank Wheelock College—and especially its former president, Marjorie Bakken—for hosting the conference from which the idea for this book is derived ("The Black Panther Party in Historical Perspective," 11–13 June 2003). That idea—to engender a new historical research agenda on a popular but understudied subject—arose well before the conference, and it was only Bakken's unwavering commitment to help us bring the Panthers into the academic historical community as a subject worthy of debate that made possible a book that could stand on its own. It is our hope that this volume, and the spirit that animates it, will be merely a beginning for further work on the Panthers.

The conference itself would not have been possible without the skilled and steady guidance of our assistant, Natalie Levine. As important, though, the book owes its organizational integrity to the technical expertise of Rebecca Zielinski and Sharon Blumenstock, and its bibliographic integrity to our research librarians Amanda Richmond, Carrie Eastman, and especially Lisa Zeidenberg. It also would never have seen the light of day without the generous support of Wheelock's current president, Jackie Jenkins-Scott, and its vice president for academic affairs, Suzanne Pasch, as well as of the College Research and Development Committee. For financial support we also thank Fairfield University.

Most of all, we are indebted to the editorial direction and inspiration of Raphael Allen, who saw from the beginning the value and necessity of bringing the Panthers into the world of historical scholarship. A rarity in the publishing world, he recognized immediately that we were onto something new and significant. For his patient questioning and probing of our ideas, for his pressing us to think more deeply and more broadly about what we were doing, for his insistence that we go beyond the conference and even the book to a larger "research template," and especially for his expert advice on everything from presentation to publication, we are forever in his debt. Also, for his sage advice we thank Chris Rogers, an academic's academic in the world of publishing. Thanks, too, to our editor, Valerie Millholland, who with much on her plate and coming into the project in midstream shepherded the work through its final stages with the aplomb and skill for which she is well known. We also appreciate all the hard work of Valerie's able assistant, Miriam Angress. Finally, we thank Duke University Press for realizing that Panther scholarship deserves the attention of historians.

Editors' Note

Though this book emerged from an academic conference, it is not a book of conference papers and critical comments. The essays here, radically revised from their original forms, have been reshuffled into sections not originally envisioned by the conference coordinators. These sections, though arranged thematically, bring together scholars working from different disciplinary and political perspectives. In addition, the commentaries, whose authors either attended the conference or participated in it, do not conform to the standard scholarly critique of academic papers as such. Rather, they seek to develop a broad context for the reader to think about the essays in each section — essays that are sometimes complimentary to the context and sometimes sharply at odds with it. For that reason, we have placed the commentaries at the beginning rather than at the end of each section.

INTRODUCTION
The Black Panthers and Historical Scholarship: Why Now?

JAMA LAZEROW AND YOHURU WILLIAMS

Eldridge Cleaver was a gifted writer and orator. In his work as a columnist for *Ramparts* magazine after his release from prison in late 1966; as editor of the Black Panther newspaper after he joined the group in the spring of 1967; as author of the instantly acclaimed *Soul on Ice*; as a fiery speaker at Panther rallies; and as an effective spokesman for the Party in interviews with the media, Cleaver was a polemicist whose rhetoric was designed to shock, irritate, cajole, and incite. But he chose his words carefully, and he thought deeply about the revolutionary struggle he embraced in the late 1960s. In the following passage, speaking about the Panthers' recent estrangement from former chairman of the Student Nonviolent Coordinating Committee and former Panther prime minister Stokely Carmichael,[1] Cleaver seeks to distinguish the Black Panther Party (BPP) from the Black Power movement in America:

> Black people have already gained their consciousness; they have a sense of their identity, which was lost in the United States. At the time that this was happening, it was very progressive; it was a very good thing. . . . But after people had assimilated that and were reminded of who they were . . . , to maintain that position and not to go any further becomes reactionary. This is what has happened to Stokely [Carmichael] and a lot of other people, a lot of other people get hung up culturally in that sense, but Stokely has gotten hung up politically in that sense. There's a false distinction people make between culture and politics, and then after making this false distinction, he confuses culture with politics again. So that it's like an error compounded with an error.[2]

The issue, as it had been from the Panthers' earliest days, was how to make revolution, and among the most controversial of the BPP positions on revolution—for black and white radicals alike—was the Party's insistence that coalitions were essential, including coalitions with whites.[3] For Cleaver, as for the Black Panther Party, what had been progressive in 1966—black people gaining a sense of their own identity—had become reactionary in 1969. That is, if cultural revolution was all there was to revolution, then such a view was to make "a false distinction between culture and politics." Carmichael, though, had allowed "being black" to dictate his revolutionary politics. He had compounded an error with an error.

Our interest here is neither in the specifics of Cleaver's problem with Carmichael late in 1969 nor the relative merits of their positions—nor is it to pass judgment on the mercurial and complex Cleaver. Rather, in the metaphor he deployed to clarify what made the Panthers distinctive—in his view, as a dynamic group rather than one frozen in time—we find precisely what we seek to do in offering the essays in this volume. For what Cleaver captured in writing a few short, compelling phrases, typical of his manner of thought, is precisely the problem with our contemporary understanding of the Black Panthers. They have been reconsidered before being fully considered; celebrated and condemned in memory and imagination before historical inquiry has even begun; haunted by the shadow of their failures and resurrected as a legacy for their heroic efforts before being fully appreciated for their uniqueness and their overall significance—"like an error compounded with an error."

In this, the Black Panther Party represents perhaps the most egregious case of a still-problematic 1960s historiography that stubbornly resists the natural process of historical revisionism, despite some important recent attempts at it.[4] Indeed, when John Hope Franklin and Abraham Eisenstadt wrote in their foreword to the American History Series that "every generation writes its own history for it tends to see the past in the foreshortened perspective of its own experience," they inadvertently hit on something that makes historicizing the Panthers especially problematic.[5] And, "like an error compounded with an error," those who have hitherto tried to tell the Panther story have kept the Panthers frozen "between culture and politics," the very phenomenon that Cleaver inveighed against. The BPP remains caught between culture—the popular perception, idealization, and misconception of the Party rooted in the cultural politics of the past and romanticism of the present — and politics — its own politics, sixties politics, black politics, and most especially the politics of historical presentism. The essays and commentary contained in this volume were born out of a conference at Wheelock College — the first conference organized by historians to study the Panthers — in an attempt to put "the Panthers back into history" by first acknowledging and then investigating the complexity of the Party in its sixties "moment."[6] In this aim, we seek ground left barren by those who would only celebrate or vilify, whether inside or outside the academy.

One way to that terrain is by broadening our scholarly horizons to the nexus of culture and politics in American history generally. For example, the historian David Blight, in his prize-winning book *Race and Reunion*, offers a useful interpretation of how a much earlier period in U.S. history — the Civil War and Reconstruction — came to be understood by successive generations of Americans.[7] In making peace with the Civil War, Blight finds, the people of the late nineteenth century constructed a master narrative of the war itself as the struggle between two well-intentioned, if flawed, positions. His book illustrates how white southerners, despite their defeat on the battlefield, nevertheless managed to claim a larger victory over how the war would be remembered. The fruit of their effort was the emergence and general acceptance of the myth of the "Lost Cause." That view then filtered into the academy.

As historians have struggled to come to grips with the 1960s, a similar sort of reunion has taken place. In making peace with the sixties, that reconciliation notably has been at the expense of black militants.[8] All now acknowledge that the southern civil rights movement of 1954–1965 was noble. The movement turned, in the still-standard telling of the story, after it moved north and the radicals took over, plunging the nation into social and political turmoil with urban rioting and calls for "Black Power."[9] The so-called "declension model" of the sixties generally, still popular in the literature of the period, with a "good" early sixties and a "bad" late sixties, offers an equally convenient means of explaining what went wrong in this era. Again, black radicals are typically blamed — this time, though, not black Radical Republicans, but Black Power advocates. The favorite "whipping boys" here are the Black Panther Party and their putative white leftists allies.[10]

But, we stress, the actual history of the Black Panther Party plays a very small role in this historiography. Indeed, the locus of that writing is not among professional historians at all, and, correspondingly, it suffers from a lack of precisely that detachment that gives history its disciplinary power. To be sure, history is not the province of the professional historian alone. As Michel-Rolph Trouillot reminds us, "history reveals itself only through the production (telling, distribution) of specific narratives ... from which [w]e cannot exclude in advance any actors who participate in the production of [it] or any of the sites where the production may occur. Next to professional historians we discover artisans of different kinds, unpaid or unrecognized field laborers who augment, deflect, or reorganize the work of professionals as politicians, students, fiction writers, filmmakers, and participating members of the public."[11] True enough, but in the case of Panther history we have the problem in reverse. Much of what we now call "histories" of the Party are crafted by activist-scholars—former leaders, high-profile members, or supporters—in which recollection collapses into data collection, scholarship into subjective analysis, history into memory. At the same time, there are the scholar-activists who so identify with the subjects of whom they write that the "noble dream" of historical objectivity, however elusive in the first place, has faded entirely.[12] Though activist-scholars rarely produce great works of history, scholar-activists have done so; the Panthers, in any case, have benefited from neither.[13]

Admittedly, part of the problem of Panther scholarship derives from the nature of sources on the Panthers. Take, for example, the question of Party membership. While the Panthers themselves rarely betrayed their actual numbers in print, most estimates in the late sixties and early seventies hovered between 1,500 and 2,000; since those estimates, other sources have suggested figures as high as 5,000. In a recent essay on the Illinois chapter of the Black Panther Party, Jon Rice maintains (based on an interview with one Panther) that in spring 1969 there were 1,000 members of the Party in Chicago alone. If true, then Chicago represented somewhere between one-fifth and three-quarters of the entire national membership of the Party, despite government documents as well as reports in *The Black Panther* that the group established beachheads in most major northern and western cities and even in smaller communities in the South and Midwest.[14]

But, the problem here is more than one of simply accepting at face value the testimony of a single Black Panther thirty-five years later. Rather, it is a failure to address the nexus of culture and politics that Cleaver refers to in his statement quoted above. Lower-class African Americans—or the "lumpen" as the Panthers called them—typically did not express support for an organization by joining its ranks. Politics demanded that the Panthers be counted and that they produce numbers to justify their proclaimed influence, but they were organizing in a street culture in which bourgeois notions about membership were lost on the often poverty-stricken and less-educated individuals they sought to organize. If the Panthers were running for political office or organizing people to vote, then membership made sense; but in the process of community organizing, culture played a far more significant role. What of those who bought (and sold) the Panthers' newspaper, who attended their education classes, who worked in their programs, who gathered at their rallies, who adopted their posture, language, ideology, and who thought of themselves as Panthers?

The same interconnection between their culture and their politics can be seen in how the Panthers moved through this period that Cleaver describes as the moment when black people "gained their consciousness." Just as the Panthers emerged in late 1966, the adoption of African names and cultural symbols represented a rejection of mainstream (white) culture. But unlike the Black Muslims or some other newer Black Nationalist groups, the Panthers generally did not give up their "slave names" or adopt other cultural nationalist trappings.[15] Blacks were united with Third World nations, yet it was a unity not primarily by cultural ties but by political repression—that is, by a common enemy. As Huey Newton observed, the Panther uniform— powder-blue shirt, black leather jacket, and beret—represented a symbolic union of political principles. The Panthers did make a fetish of the gun— an obsession that is obvious in the revolutionary art of Panther minister of culture Emory Douglas. By mid-to-late 1968, however, there was a dramatic increase in the iconography of community service programs, which coexisted for a while in Panther imagery with the weaponry that was there from the beginning. And for those who were watching—the men in law enforcement—the shift was recognizable. As the chief deputy attorney general for California, Charles O'Brien, recalled: "The Panthers seemed to be in deliberate, open, provocative confrontation with police departments in their early period; they used revolutionary language, provocative language, and seemed to be deliberately seeking to confront established authority, particularly police authority. But, then we observed they seemed to have a social side, a concept of doing something beyond these angry confrontations."[16] The FBI was also well aware of the shift, and they took it as an escalation of the threat. If some stressed that the Panthers were black separatists, even as they adopted the slogan "Power to the People," the federal government ramped up its repression of the Party as it showed its "social side." That is, those who were given the task to take the measure of this movement, to contain it, and ultimately to destroy it understood what Cleaver articulated: just as culture was not itself (revolutionary) politics, so Panther Party politics could not be separated from its (revolutionary) culture.

Blinded to this complex and evolving nature of Panther culture in particular historical circumstances, some critics of the Party have dismissed its politics as little more than a front for criminal enterprise. Shortly after the Wheelock conference, for instance, the ex-leftist Kate Coleman, who did not attend the conference, wrote of the proceedings: "It was the same propaganda that old-line Panther veterans — abetted by glam pix in newspapers of good-looking armed blacks with towering afros and guns — had been promulgating from the Party's hey-days beginning in the late 1960s. Despite one organizer's promise that 'We're not out to celebrate the Panthers,' even where the conference backed away from hagiography, the participants seemed so focused on [the] minutia and inconsequentials of smaller Panther chapters in podunk cities, the presentations were irrelevant. And most papers — as well as the audience and panelists — nonetheless were focused on resurrecting the Panthers, this time with academic laurels."[17] Coleman continued by stating, "If the Wheelock College history conference wants to know the real legacy of the Panthers — notwithstanding the organizers' complaints that the media focused on the cocaine and the violence of the Panthers unfairly, they should pore over the cold statistics showing the huge spike in drive-by-shooting deaths and gang warfare that took place in Oakland in the decade following Newton's and the Panthers' demise."[18]

Here, "podunk" cities throughout the nation that produced unique and protean revolutionary formations under the Panther banner are "irrelevant"; all that matters is what happened in Oakland in Huey Newton's later days.[19] The complex individuals like Black Panther Parky Grace of New Bedford, Massachusetts, whose story is told in Jama Lazerow's essay in this volume, or the equally multidimensional FBI agents like Roz Payne's Agent WAC — who in essence became "archivists" of the Party — do not fit Coleman's story or the story of the romanticizers she imagines stalked the Wheelock conference. Neither does the story that Joel Wilson tells in detail here of that early moment when California white radicals and liberals sought alliance with a young Black Panther Party, nor does the arresting case that David

Barber makes for the white revolutionaries in the late sixties saying one thing but doing another when it came to what they hailed as the "vanguard of the revolution," the Black Panther Party. Finally, the complex relations between brown and black at the heart of Jeffrey Ogbar's story of the Panthers and the Latino movement in the late sixties and early seventies is a story, like the others, that simply pales next to what Coleman calls "the cold statistics," because, for her, the "politics" of crime is all that matters.

With the Panthers, of course, the issue to some extent has always been about violence. But their critics make violence the only issue, and they remain frozen in one moment in time. Take David Horowitz, another leftist turned right-winger like his fellow journalist Kate Coleman. Describing a funeral he witnessed of a sixteen-year-old Panther in Oakland in late 1974, Horowitz recalled that he "suddenly . . . saw the real party, to which . . . I had closed my eyes for so long. Of course, the children were there, as were their parents and teachers, but dominating them and everything else physically and symbolically was the honor guard of Panther soldiers in black berets, shotguns alarmingly on display. And added to this spectacle, mingling with the mourners, there were the unmistakable gangster types, whose presence had suddenly become apparent to me after Elaine [Brown] took over the party. . . . They were fitted in shades and Bogarts and pinstripe suits, as though waiting for action on the set of a B crime movie. In their menacing faces there was no reflection of political complexity such as Huey was so adept at projecting, or of the benevolent community efforts like the breakfast for children programs."[20] It was an epiphany: the Panthers were neither benevolent nor thoughtful; they were merely violent black thugs. But what Horowitz really encountered in this instance was the nexus of culture and politics, the stark reality of the street culture where the Panthers were forced to operate, which contrasted to the high-minded idealism with which they sought to imbue their politics. Horowitz had fallen into the same trap described by Cleaver. The self-defense traditions embedded in American life from the inception of the Republic, so intriguingly plumbed by Bridgette Baldwin in her essay, are lost in the one-dimensionality of the great con. The Panthers pretended to be political but they were just gangsters after all.

This is the same essentialist mistake, though of a different stripe, that Alice Walker made in her 1993 review of David Hilliard's autobiography, *This Side of Glory*. In her *New York Times* op-ed piece, the black novelist is obsessed with the machismo male culture of the Party. "All of these men," she proclaimed, referring to the Panthers en masse, "abused women and apparently thought little about it." As she explained in reference to another autobiography by the former Panther Elaine Brown, "[her] book tells what it was like to be a bold, brilliant ambitious black woman in the party. Giving orders when she briefly becomes leader . . . she experiences 'a taste of power.' Other times she is being used sexually by men because that is the way to connect with an unknown and . . . to convince her comrades that she is still 'just a woman.'"[21] Walker's assumptions here deny the agency of women in the Party who were leaders. In any case, if there were a culture of sexism here, it was certainly not limited to the Panthers, or to black militants, or, for that matter, to the Black Power movement, the civil rights movement, or the African American community in general. Walker accurately notes that the word "punk," often used by Panthers, had enormous cultural significance. On the same op-ed page Brown, a product of the Philadelphia streets, explained its significance to the novelist as follows: "Punk, that terrible appellation of the ghetto streets, was a warrior word slung at those who lacked 'manly courage.' Anyone who ever walked the streets knows it addressed not sexuality but power — in the only form it was known and might be claimed by those isolated on the fringes of a society dominated, from without and within, by white men."[22] In short, the matter is inexplicable outside the context of culture and politics.

At the other extreme is the one-dimensional, positive portrait of the Party's history. In grand language, for example, David Hilliard's and Fredrika Newton's Huey P. Newton Foundation proclaims: "The Black Panther Party was a progressive political organization that stood in the vanguard of the most powerful movement for social change in America since the Revolution of 1776 and the Civil War: that dynamic episode generally referred to as The Sixties. It is the sole black organization in the entire history of the black struggle against slavery and oppression in the United States that was armed and promoted a revolutionary agenda, and it represents the last great thrust by the mass of black people for equality, justice and freedom."[23] The scholarly equivalent can be found in *The Black Panther Party [Reconsidered]*, where the political scientist Charles Jones insists that what "drove the men and women in the BPP was a profound sense of commitment to improving the lives of Black and other oppressed people." It was this commitment, he continues, "that undergirded the activism for which some members ultimately lost their lives and others remain incarcerated."[24] In a far more scholarly but no less problematic instance, Jones and his fellow political scientist, Judson Jeffries, emphasize "Panther politics" as the legacy of the Party over its far richer and varied history. For them, the Panther legacy was armed resistance, community service, commitment to the self-determination of all people, and political action for the oppressed—in each instance, however, it is politics that holds center stage.[25]

The emphasis on the political legacy of the Party—perhaps a product of these authors' discipline—is problematic if only because, arguably, Panther reverberations have been greater in terms of culture than politics: the Oakland rapper Paris, who called himself the "Black Panther of Rap"; the late Tupac Shakur, whose parents helped establish the BPP in New York City and who himself quoted from the Panther Platform and Program in some of his raps; and Public Enemy, who made references to Party leaders Huey Newton, Bobby Seale, and Eldridge Cleaver and used the Panther rallying cry, "Power to the People." One of the most engaging commentaries on the Panthers and popular culture was penned by the American studies professor and artist Kali Tal, who recorded her encounter with an advertisement for the Mario Van Peebles Film *Panther* in 1995: "[The ad was about] a contest in which the winner would receive a large reward of money and 'live the Panther dream.' The 'dream' had been distorted into a promise of financial security for a lucky winner, where once it had been a belief in a society where justice and equality were granted [to] all citizens. Presented entirely without irony, the contest promo underlined the complete commercialization and appropriation of Panther history, the revolutionary agenda revised and repackaged to the point where it could be used to promote the very capitalist structures the Panthers sought to destroy. Ideology had, finally and completely, been subsumed by image."[26] Here, Tal opens up the rich avenues for research and analysis that allow Tim Lake in his work in this volume to take us back to the Dadaists and surrealists in search of a way to understand Panther revolutionary "performance." Here, too, is the starting point for Edward Morgan's complex and empirically grounded argument that ends this volume: a mainstream media representing interests truly threatened by the Panther moment tamed the Panther—then and now. Image became reality, regardless of whose hands sought to frame that image. But, the Panthers were real; they have a history.

Historical truth, of course—like the historical moment to which Cleaver referred in 1969—lies somewhere between culture and politics, where, unfortunately, most scholars have thus far feared to tread. Indeed, professional historians are hardly immune to special pleading. Robyn Spencer's short overview of the Oakland Panthers, for example, associates their expressive politics with "Martin Luther King's Beloved Community." Referring to Newton's "substance abuse and criminal activity" only after his return from exile in 1977, she notes that the Panther experiment was "derailed by the cult of personality, lack of accountability of the leadership, breakdown in internal political education, and other flaws . . . long after the juggernaut of political repression had receded into the past." That is, whatever was wrong occurred well into the late stages of the Party's existence.[27]

Such examples might be multiplied; they might well be found within the pages of this collection. This is a matter for the reader to determine. We have brought together in this book an eclectic group of scholars who do not always agree on approach, purpose, or analysis. Our only interest is freshness of perspective, and thus what we offer here — uniquely, we believe — is innovative work that is diverse in discipline, orientation, and argument, which will at long last begin the process of historicizing, not simply judging, the Black Panthers.

Notes

1. For Cleaver's withering attack on Carmichael, whom Cleaver had lionized as a *Ramparts* reporter in 1967, and who resigned from the Party in the early summer of 1969, see "An Open Letter to Stokely Carmichael," in "Eldridge Cleaver Discusses Revolution: An Interview from Exile," Liberation News Service, *The Black Panther*, 19 October 1969, reprinted in Philip S. Foner, ed., *The Black Panthers Speak* (New York: Da Capo Press, 1995 [1970]), 104–8, originally published in *The Black Panther* in July 1969 and reprinted in *Ramparts* the following September. Cleaver's very different view of Carmichael two years earlier can be found in "My Father and Stokely Carmichael," *Ramparts*, April 1967, reprinted in Foner, *The Black Panthers Speak*, 43–56. The question to which Cleaver was responding in the interview was, "What was the situation in America at the time of Stokely Carmichael's split from the Black Panther Party, and how did it contribute to the split?" Carmichael had announced his resignation from his newly adopted home of Conakry, Guinea, denouncing the Panthers' work with whites and endorsing pan-Africanism ("Eldridge Cleaver Discusses Revolution," 279 n.6). *Soul on Ice* was published by McGraw-Hill in early 1968.
2. "Eldridge Cleaver Discusses Revolution," 110.
3. For Newton's retrospective account of the heat that this idea generated among young black radicals in fall 1967—before his fatal encounter with an Oakland police officer led to his arrest, trial, and imprisonment, and thus *before* the national

"Free Huey" campaign in which the Panthers reached out to sympathetic whites—see *Revolutionary Suicide* (New York: Readers and Writers Publishing, Inc., 1995 [1973]), 172. For the complex story of one effort at coalition building in the aftermath of Newton's arrest early in the morning of 28 October 1967, see Joel Wilson's "Invisible Cages" in this volume. For the divergence of rhetoric and behavior on the white radical side of the relationship during the late 1960s in general, see David Barber's "Leading the Vanguard," this volume; and for the view from the Latino perspective, see Jeffrey Ogbar's "Brown Power to Brown People," also in this volume.

4. For a historiographical reflection circa 2000, see Jama Lazerow, "1960–1974," in *A Companion to Twentieth-Century America*, edited by Stephen J. Whitfield (Malden, Mass.: Blackwell, 2004), 87–101. See also, among a now-virtual cottage industry of surveys and monographs, David Farber, *The Age of Great Dreams: America in the 1960s* (New York: Hill and Wang, 1994); Maurice Isserman and Michael Kazin, *America Divided: The Civil War of the Sixties* (New York: Oxford University Press, 2000); and Doug Rossinow, *The Politics of Authenticity: Liberalism, Christianity, and the New Left in America* (New York: Columbia University Press, 1998). For an indication of the state of things, see David Burner's aptly titled *Making Peace with the 60s* (Princeton, N.J.: Princeton University Press, 1996).

5. With dozens of titles, the American History Series is published by Harlan Davidson, Inc.

6. For an attempt to place the Panthers in the sweep of history from the 1930s to the 1970s in the context of the new historical work on the civil rights movement, see Robert Self's "The Black Panther Party and the Long Civil Rights Era," this volume.

7. David W. Blight, *Race and Reunion: The Civil War in American Memory* (Cambridge, Mass.: Belknap Press; Harvard University Press, 2001).

8. We borrow here from the title, though not the analysis, of Burner, *Making Peace with the 60s*.

9. For a corrective to this view, see Jeanne Theoharis's introduction (and especially her source citations) in *Freedom North: Black Freedom Struggles outside the South, 1940–1980*, edited by Jeanne Theoharis and Komozi Woodard (New York: Palgrave Macmillan, 2003), 1–15.

10. For an overview and sources, see Lazerow, "1960–1974."

11. Michel-Rolph Trouillot, *Silencing the Past: Power and the Production of History* (Boston: Beacon Press, 1997), 25.

12. Kathleen Cleaver and George Katsiaficas, eds., *Liberation, Imagination, and the Black Panther Party: A New Look at the Panthers and their Legacy* (New York: Routledge, 2001); and Charles E. Jones, ed., *The Black Panther Party [Reconsidered]* (Baltimore: Black Classic Press, 1998). Note that there are no historians among the nineteen authors in Cleaver and Katsiaficas's collection; of the nineteen authors in Jones's collection there are three historians.

13. For great history by a scholar-activist, see E. P. Thompson, *The Making of the English Working Class* (New York: Pantheon, 1963).

14. Jon Rice, "The World of the Illinois Panthers," in Theoharis and Woodard, eds., *Freedom North*, 56–57, 64 n.93.
15. For the differences within the Party on these issues geographically, see David Hilliard's description of his shock at the dress and cultural style of the New York Panthers when he visited in 1968 (David Hilliard and Lewis Cole, *This Side of Glory: The Autobiography of David Hilliard and the Story of the Black Panther Party* [Boston: Little, Brown, 1993], 168).
16. *Eyes On the Prize. Vol. 1: Power*, video (Boston: Blackside Productions, 1989).
17. For continued distortion of the Wheelock conference by Coleman and her colleagues, see David Horowitz and Peter Collier's new introduction to *Destructive Generation: Second Thoughts about the Sixties* (Los Angeles: Second Thought Books, 1989); reprinted in FrontPageMagazine.com, 6 January 2006.
18. Kate Coleman, "The Panthers for Real," FrontPageMagazine.com, 23 June 2003.
19. For some of the new work on the Panthers beyond Oakland, see our forthcoming collection on Panther local history, to be published by Duke University Press.
20. David Horowitz, "Black Murder Inc.," *Heterodoxy* 1.10 (March 1993): 12.
21. Alice Walker, "They Ran on Empty," *New York Times*, 5 May 1993, A23.
22. Elaine Brown, "Attack Racism, Not Black Men," *New York Times*, 5 May 1993, A23.
23. Statement given on the Web site at http://www.blackpanther.org/legacynew.html.
24. Jones, "Reconsidering Panther History: The Untold Story," in *The Black Panther Party [Reconsidered]*, 8.
25. As Jones and Jeffries explain, "[the BPP] represented one of the rare instances of a successful blend of nationalism and socialist ideals by an independent African-American political organization" ("'Don't Believe the Hype': Debunking the Panther Mythology," in *The Black Panther Party [Reconsidered]*, 27–37).
26. Kali Tal, "From Panther to Monster: Black Popular Culture Representations of Resistance from the Black Power Movement of the 1960s to the *Boyz in the Hood*," in *Innovations in African-American Rhetoric*, edited by Elaine Richards and Ronald Jackson (Urbana: University of Ilinois Press, 2002). This essay is also online at http://www.freshmonsters.com/kalital/Text/Articles/Monster.html.
27. Robyn Ceanne Spencer, "Inside the Panther Revolution: The Black Freedom Movement and the Black Panther Party in Oakland, California," in *Groundwork: Local Black Freedom Movements in America*, edited by Jeanne Theoharis and Komozi Woodard (New York: New York University Press, 2005), 313–14; see Rice, "The World of the Illinois Panthers," 41–64, for another recent example, whose only criticism of the Party is that "some Party members admit . . . that there was an element of male chauvinism that came with the social environment" (57).

PART ONE The Panthers through the Historian's Lens

The Black Panther Party and the Long Civil Rights Era

ROBERT O. SELF

Scholarship on the Black Panther Party is enjoying something of a renaissance. The last decade has seen the publication of two collections of essays about the Party. New books dealing in whole or in part with the Panthers have recently appeared. And a host of dissertations, along with manuscripts in progress, have joined the suddenly rich debate over the meaning and legacy of one of the nation's most conspicuous and controversial political organizations.[1] Alongside this scholarly attention, journalists and former activists, writing from the Left, Right, and positions in between, have advanced their own assessments. Indeed, no single organization stands more prominently than the Panthers at the axis of divergent efforts to claim a usable history of the second half of the 1960s. Many contemporary commentators argue that the Panthers embodied the wrong turn taken by activists after 1965 toward a violence, bravado, and radicalism incapable of redeeming the nation. Others, including many Party memoirists, counter that the Panthers symbolized the joining of Black Power and the antiwar movement in a critique of American imperialism and capitalism whose suppression by the FBI and local police represented a cynical conspiracy of American officialdom in the late sixties and early seventies.[2]

Historians have engaged these sixties-legacy debates in substantive ways, but there is more to assessing the history of the Panthers than locating its valence in contemporary culture wars. Positioning the group to carry the weight of national angst over the fallout of the 1960s forecloses a deeper understanding of black radicalism as an American political tradition and the Panthers' place within the twentieth-century history of that radicalism. As Nikhil Pal Singh has recently reminded us, when Martin Luther King Jr. self-consciously stepped out of the political tradition of liberal "strivers" in the late 1960s to embrace "traditions of black dissidence," he did not move into uncharted territory. He strode into a political space from which black radicals had long inveighed against American racism's dual grounding in ideologies of colonialism and the structures of international capitalism. King and the Panthers were neither ideologically nor temperamentally equivalent, but the dissident positions that each took in the late sixties linked them to a shared black radical tradition that developed in what Singh calls the "long civil rights era," the extended period of struggle over the place of black Americans in national life between the 1930s and the 1970s.[3]

That formulation signals an immense historiographical project: revising the canonized liberal civil rights narrative handed down primarily by sixties-era journalists and validated by the first wave of civil rights historiography.[4] The liberal narrative draws its authority from the power of telegenic events and personalities. It advances an understanding of racism as a primarily psychological and individual phenomenon, and it cultivates a mythology of liberal consensus on racial equality. That familiar narrative begins in 1954 and 1955 with the Supreme Court's decision in *Brown v. Board of Education* and the emergence of Martin Luther King Jr. during the Montgomery bus boycott. It extends through a series of events and places that became iconographic, all of which are located in the South: Greensboro, Birmingham, Washington, Selma, and a handful of other southern cities where movement events captured national television and print media coverage. The movement took aim at the legal architecture of Jim Crow (and its abrogation of *civil* rights) — a system of racial segregation and subordination erected during the last decades of the nineteenth century and the first decade of the twentieth.[5] To press its case, the movement endorsed nonviolent civil disobedience, a philosophy and tactic largely imported into the United States from Mahatma Gandhi's India by Bayard Rustin and A. J. Muste and transformed into a massive popular insurgency by King.[6]

According to the narrative, by judiciously combining nonviolent civil resistance with the Christian fellowship and self-discipline taught by the southern African American church, King and a handful of activists forged a coalition composed of black Americans and white northern liberals, whose political home was the Democratic Party. Propelled by a national mood of liberal optimism, further fueled by John F. Kennedy's election in 1960, that coalition dismantled Jim Crow — a process culminating in the passage of the

Civil Rights Act of 1964 and the Voting Rights Acts of 1965. However, when this triumphant civil rights movement "moved north" between 1965 and 1967, it foundered on the shores of urban rebellions and Black Nationalism. Black rioters in Watts in 1965 and in Detroit and Newark in 1967 accomplished what no southern sheriff or Klan rally could: the rending of the movement itself. Furthermore, Black Power ideology and black militants in the North fueled a white "backlash" and forced sympathetic white liberals to abandon the cause. Narratives of the movement at this point fall back upon a series of familiar oppositions to draw out lessons: South and North, nonviolence and violence, King and Malcolm X / Black Panthers. The South is "the movement." The North is the foil. The South is paradigmatic. The North an aberration.[7]

While this version of history contains a wealth of details that are true, many of its key parameters and assumptions are misleading. Historians since the 1980s have labored in countless archives, recorded thousands of oral histories, and mined hundreds of local case studies to reveal a far more complicated set of stories. These stories do not simply change details in the larger narrative but rather necessitate new paradigms. In their findings historians have shown, for instance, that northern whites were far less supportive of either civil rights or black equality than the traditional narrative holds. White resistance to desegregation was always present; indeed, it was always a fundamental part of the New Deal Democratic coalition. Far from being an innocent bystander in the construction of Jim Crow, or its heroic vanquisher, the federal government through its housing, labor, and welfare policies was a major architect of racial discrimination in the twentieth century. Thus, the federal state itself, not simply a recalcitrant Confederacy, was a target of reform. Moreover, northern segregation was in many places worse than its southern variants, and there were plenty of *southern* militants and *northern* moderates in the civil rights movement. And the movement itself, which began in the 1940s in New York City, was a far more complex assemblage than the Southern Christian Leadership Conference and the Student Nonviolent Coordinating Committee, as important as those organizations were.[8] Despite a generation of academic scholarship advancing these and other arguments, however, the standard narrative continues to dominate high school and college textbooks and, even more substantially, popular memory and its rhetoric of commemoration.

The effort to shoehorn civil rights into the decade between 1955 and 1965 has clear ideological consequences: it minimizes if not silences the movement's long association with radicalism and the critique of American liberalism. By isolating the movement in its most overtly liberal phase, the traditional narrative explicitly positions the *real* civil rights movement in between two forms of discredited radicalism: the communist Left and the Popular Front of the 1930s and 1940s and the Black Power militancy and Maoist internationalism of the late 1960s and early 1970s. According to this view, the movement's essence can only be found in the brief window between the mid-1950s and the mid-1960s, when its dual aims were said to be ending Jim Crow and transforming the hearts and minds of whites. It is perhaps true that only the liberal, moderate dimensions of the movement stood any realistic chance of success within U.S. political culture and institutions.[9] But that cannot foreclose a serious consideration of the movement as a whole, the complicated way the movement was interpreted and understood at the grassroots, and the decisive presence of radical forces pushing from a variety of positions on the Left across the movement's history from the late 1930s through the 1970s. As Robin D. G. Kelley has reminded us, despite the fact that "virtually every radical movement failed," the "alternative visions and dreams" contained within them continue to inspire new generations of activists. Isolating the movement in the decade between *Brown* and Watts risks reducing a complex history to a morality tale of interracial consensus destroyed by intemperate black militancy. It risks reducing that history to a tired American racial trope.[10]

Histories that contextualize rather than marginalize black radicalism, on the other hand, offer greater analytical purchase on the major economic and political questions that black activists confronted between the New Deal in the mid-1930s and the end of the Great Society in the early 1970s. Histories that contextualize black radicalism reveal it to be liberalism's constant companion, sometimes ally and sometimes challenger, rather than its foil or solvent. For my purposes, such histories illuminate two critical dimensions of the Black Panther Party's place within the long civil rights era. First, the Panthers' anticolonial politics emerged as part of a decades-long response on the progressive political Left to the rise of the welfare-warfare state in the context of economic crises at home and geopolitical crises abroad. That state came into being in the 1930s and expanded in scope and power in the postwar decades. Second, the Panthers inherited traditions of black political consciousness that envisioned cities, the *urban*, as both the sites and sources of black liberation in the United States. These two contentions do not constitute a comprehensive explanation of the Party's history or ideology by any means. But they are fundamental to any such explanation, and they are essential to establishing a broader horizon of twentieth-century history in which to understand the Panthers. In the following two sections, I take up each of these dimensions.

The U.S. Welfare State and Global Decolonization

The rise after World War II of the welfare-warfare state married the New Deal to the Cold War. Each half of the marriage represented a modified Keynesianism through which the federal government subsidized an unprecedented expansion of the nation's white middle class. New Deal Keynesianism was a product of the economic crisis of the 1930s and the continuing crises within crucial sectors of the American economy in the postwar period, especially housing. Cold War Keynesianism was a product of the global war of 1939–1945; the withdrawal of Great Britain and France from their imperial holdings in the Middle East, Africa, South Asia, and Southeast Asia; and, most crucially, the confrontation between the United States and the Soviet Union over the political and economic future of Europe between 1947 and the early 1960s. Together, the New Deal and the Cold War produced the largest, most active and interventionist federal state in American history, and in so doing radically remade American cities on the one hand and the nation's political culture on the other. These historical developments represent the critical background to the rise of the Black Panther Party.[11]

Broadly understood, the mid-century U.S. welfare state combined social insurance programs like old-age pensions and direct payments to poor mothers with equally important public subsidies to specific populations and sectors. The public subsidies included: massive federal mortgage and public housing programs; labor law and its attendant collective bargaining apparatus; the G.I. Bill; highway construction; urban renewal; the War on Poverty and other poverty programs; and a variety of additional programs aimed at the labor, housing, and property markets. Together, these shaped the physical and political terrain of urban America between the 1940s and the 1960s, especially in the massive suburbanization of housing and industry and the accompanying forms of racial segregation that brought into being what historian Arnold Hirsch has called the "second ghetto." Federal policy, in short, was a critical handmaiden to the private market's creation of white suburbs and black urban ghettoes. Simultaneously in the postwar decades, the demands of Cold War containment policy and the nation's militarization of its global standoff with the Soviet Union after 1950 produced an enlarged defense sector. Relying on private contractors and public and private universities for materiel as well as for research and development, the federal government helped to bring into being an unprecedented military-industrial-educational complex. The resulting welfare-warfare state that emerged fundamentally shaped the political economy of the nation throughout the whole course of the modern black rights movement, from the 1940s through the 1970s.[12]

Nikhil Pal Singh asserts that "bracketed by Roosevelt's New Deal and Johnson's Great Society, the long civil rights era was a product of a dual phenomenon: the Keynesian transformation of the liberal capitalist state during the 1930s and the emergence of black social movements that were urban, national, and transnational in scope."[13] Singh's joining of civil rights, the rise of the Keynesian state, and urban and transnational politics in the period between the 1930s and the 1970s is precisely the historiographical combination best suited to understanding modern black radicalism. The emergence of the Keynesian state — in both its social welfare and military-industrial guises — raised a central question: How, in the context of the federal government's assertion of broad new powers to shape the domestic economy and to guarantee a social wage, would national citizenship be defined? Not "citizenship" in a narrow, technical sense but what Alice Kessler-Harris has called "economic citizenship . . . the independent status that provides the possibility of full participation in the polity."[14] For African Americans across mid-century America, this notion of citizenship stood at the center of a signal issue: their inclusion in the provisions of the welfare state, constructed in the Jim Crow era, and the necessity that the state itself be leveraged into a vehicle for genuine equity.

As Singh notes, the rise of the Keynesian state interpenetrated with the emergence of the United States as a global superpower. Thus, African Americans were confronted not merely with the existence of the anticolonial struggle in developing nations in Africa and Asia, but with the reality that U.S. policy could decisively shape the timing, nature, and pace of decolonization. That is, black Americans faced simultaneously a struggle to transform the domestic policies of the state and the external reality that the United States could profoundly influence the global color line. To use the "double-V" metaphor of the 1940s, they faced a two-front war. It was not simply that

African Americans expressed sympathy for and symbolic affiliation with independence movements ranging from India to Ghana. It was, more consequentially, that internationalism — anti-colonialism coupled with the strong support of the United Nations and cooperation with Communist states — as a political orientation between the late 1940s and the early 1970s provided fertile ground on which black Americans could criticize American exceptionalism and cold war liberalism. In particular, black internationalism challenged the notion that racism and its attendant forms of subordination were merely flaws within the liberal American political order, flaws whose disappearance over time was assured. By linking the color line in the United States with an international color line — what Richard Wright called the "color curtain" — in the context of anticolonial struggle and the emerging Cold War, black internationalists interpreted racial domination in the United States as part of the history of Western imperialism.[15]

The marriage of New Deal and Cold War thus shaped a fundamental proposition regarding how the *nation-state* at home and abroad framed citizenship and race: how, in effect, the postwar U.S. nation-state defined both inclusion in national citizenship and inclusion in a broader international family of nations. Furthermore, the creation of the United Nations raised the possibility that this international institution might, with appropriate pressure, apply to the United States the same human rights standards the U.N. charter demanded of all member nations; that is, American Jim Crow might become a U.N. human rights issue rather than an "exceptional" case of purely domestic concern. Both contexts, above and beyond the mere existence of anticolonial struggle, made the international context of decolonization of particular weight for black American activists, whether liberal or radical.[16]

Singh's work, along with that of Kelley, Penny Von Eschen, and other historians of black radicalism and internationalism, foregrounds the central tension within black intellectual and political life in the United States between liberalism and radicalism.[17] However, within traditions of the black public sphere, liberalism and radicalism have slightly different valences than they carry in mainstream American political discourses. For black Americans, one of the core political choices has long been between two divergent readings of the legacy of the Declaration of Independence. In the first, liberal, version, the Declaration is understood to be an enunciation of universal human rights to which black people in the United States were denied access because of specific historical circumstances — slavery and Jim Crow. But the Declaration, as both founding document and ideological manifesto, could be *made* to apply to black Americans. Indeed, doing so was understood, especially by the 1940s, to represent the symbolic fulfillment of the national destiny.[18] Black people, once defined out of the national family (for that matter, once defined as the group against which the national family itself was delineated), could be welcomed into a broad liberal-nationalist consensus. Black liberals may have winced a bit more than their white counterparts at imperialist excesses abroad, but this position was essentially invested in an American exceptionalist understanding of the world order of nations. America would lead by example, by the light of the Declaration, as it always had.[19]

In this context, by "American exceptionalism" I mean an ideology through which the United States is understood to represent a unique break with Western European history and thus divorced from Western patterns of racism, colonialism, and class conflict. American exceptionalism has been an exceedingly flexible ideological formation, amendable to liberals and conservatives alike, and it remains deeply embedded in the nation's political culture. Regarding racism and the issue of black American citizenship, both formal and informal, American exceptionalists typically assert that racism has been a "flaw" of, or "diversion" within, the American political economy, rather than a foundational element of liberal capitalism itself. American exceptionalism advocates also tend to claim a monopoly on patriotism, so that to argue, for instance, that American foreign policy objectives are not entirely innocent, or that slavery was central, not peripheral, to the founding of American capitalism, or that Jim Crow might be properly called a form of apartheid is to risk being labeled "anti-American." The fundamental underlying assumption of American exceptionalism, then, is the basic innocence of the nation itself and its historical role as an exemplar of righteousness and democracy.[20]

The radical reading of the Declaration, however, refused to see its promise defined solely by the boundaries of the U.S. nation-state and limited by the tenets of American exceptionalism. Black radicalism instead has long interpreted the color line in the United States as extending outward in an unbroken arc across both the Atlantic and the Pacific, where it joins the racial imperialisms of the European powers. Rather than seeing the United States as a fundamental break with European patterns of racial ideology and domination, radicals have characterized the United States as representing their logical extension. Black radicals have thus interpreted the situation of American blacks as parallel to the colonial subjugation of people of color across the globe. This has required an internationalist framework in which British, European, and U.S. imperialisms have been understood as overlapping (though not always synonymous) forms of economic and political exploitation. The incorporation of black Americans into a liberal nation-state that was simultaneously a global hegemon and a sponsor or defender of imperial projects abroad was both immoral and contradictory. "These colored races," Du Bois wrote in 1949 of the people of Africa, Asia, and the Caribbean, "*with fifteen million Negroes in the United States*—these are the vast majority of mankind whose condition and future are the crucial test of the attitudes of those people who today demand mastery of the world."[21] For black radicals that was the test: how would the U.S. nation-state respond to the rise of the "colored races" at home and abroad?

Thus, a fundamental question that confronted black Americans by the mid-twentieth century was whether the African American liberation movement would become the basis for demands for inclusion in the Cold War nation-state (liberal), or would it call for a larger reimagining of national and global relations of power and racial/class domination (radical)? This was not the only question that activists faced, nor the one always found the most pressing, but in the context of the postwar rise of the United States to global military and economic supremacy, it was inescapable. When the Cold War context of U.S. civil rights is raised by historians or other scholars it is usually to observe that superpower rivalry placed new imperatives on the United States to address domestic racism lest Soviet propaganda reveal American hypocrisy to the world. This imperative was especially strong vis-à-vis the developing world where winning the hearts and minds of Du Bois's "colored races" for American-style liberal capitalism was understood as essential. True, the Cold War gave black Americans some leverage to push for domestic reform, and foreign policy calculations made certain politicians, such as John F. Kennedy and Lyndon B. Johnson, incrementally more likely to at least listen to black leaders (or, as was often the case, *appear* to be listening). The real effects of these calculations can be overstated, however, as pressure from the domestic civil rights movement, not foreign policy tactics, forced the destruction of Jim Crow. Furthermore, focusing exclusively on "Cold War civil rights" obscures the way in which black radicalism's insistence on seeing U.S. racism in a global context was vulnerable to red-baiting. While the Cold War may have proved marginally beneficial to liberal civil rights activists in certain contexts, its far more profound effect was to open fissures within African American intellectual and political circles and to force black radicals on the defensive. Red-baited by liberal whites and blacks alike, black radicals of the early Cold War era found themselves marginalized within the labor movement and civil rights organizations.[22]

Like Singh, Dona Hamilton and Charles Hamilton view the period between the early 1930s and the early 1970s, or what some historians have called the "rise and fall of the New Deal order," as a coherent series of episodes in black political thought and action. They, too, have opened important debates about the relationship between the black rights movement and the liberal state. In their case, though, the focus is on the welfare state rather than Cold War geopolitics. In *The Dual Agenda*, the Hamiltons argue that civil rights groups consistently sought both a traditional civil rights *and* a social welfare agenda at the national level. The latter, they explain, called for a universal social welfare system, full employment, and strong federal control over all welfare programs. The commitment of civil rights groups to the U.S. welfare state remained constant from the 1930s through and beyond the Great Society of the mid-1960s, representing a profound engagement with the modern state apparatus that combined long-standing black political demands (voting and civil rights, anti-lynching legislation, and antidiscrimination legislation covering employment and housing) with calls for expansions of the broader social wage for all Americans. This "dual agenda" arose in large part because the New Deal welfare state not only failed to offer a "new founding" on race, as Singh powerfully argues, but in fact reasserted white supremacy through discriminatory labor, housing, and welfare programs. Civil rights groups sought broad expansions of the social wage in part because blacks remained the group most marginalized from its benefits.[23]

The Hamiltons' work focuses primarily on black liberals within mainline civil rights organizations and labor unions. Faced with the inevitability of a two-tiered welfare system and its creation of vastly unequal forms of economic citizenship, black liberal New Dealers hoped to protect black workers. Civil rights organizations fought to have as many low-paying occupations as possible included in what was labeled Tier 1 welfare benefits — those tied to employment and payroll taxes and widely understood as a right. They feared that Tier 2 of the American welfare state — what became known as "relief" or simply "welfare" — would become a stigmatized system identified in the public mind with the "dole," and even with blackness itself. In keeping their lens focused on civil rights groups and on welfare policy, the Hamiltons are necessarily engaged in a history of liberalism, but, like Singh, they see the relationship between African Americans and the history of the modern welfare state as one of the central pivots of the black rights movement. That movement had to confront the overwhelming power of the state to determine the boundaries of national belonging and the rights, obligations, and privileges of citizenship. The state, in short, was not a neutral arbiter but an active sponsor of segregation at home and problematic policy abroad. The state itself had to be reformed.[24]

Another historian whose recent work draws attention to the relationship between black liberation and the modern state is Martha Biondi. Her compelling volume *To Stand and Fight: The Struggle for Civil Rights in Postwar New York City* makes the case that the movement phase of civil rights politics originated at least a decade before the Montgomery bus boycott, in the period between the end of World War II and the early 1950s. A Popular Front–like alliance of Communist Party activists and other radicals, liberals, labor leaders, and grassroots activists, both black and white, came together in postwar New York to push for fair housing and fair employment laws, massive educational desegregation, colonial freedom abroad, and a host of other laws and measures aimed at racial equality and self-determination. The alliance—in actuality more of a loose network that coalesced in different combinations over different issues—mobilized grassroots support and took to the streets with boycotts, picketing, and marches, and pressed Congress and the New York statehouse with traditional political lobbying. Far from being simply a liberal integrationist exercise, Biondi argues, this movement called for "broad social change, economic empowerment, group advancement, and colonial freedom from the beginning." Thus, she insists, "the traditional narrative omits the [civil rights] movement's full chronology and elides the critically important Black radical tradition." She reclaims that tradition by documenting its centrality to New York politics in the late forties and early fifties, and by demonstrating the extensive influence that New York's movement exerted on virtually every subsequent aspect of the black rights movement in the nation and in every region—South, North, and West.[25]

One of Bondi's signal contributions is to document the centrality of the state to the vision of "another kind of America" advanced by what she calls the "Black World War II generation." Far from merely hoping to transform the hearts and minds of whites, black New Yorkers understood the importance of the state as a guarantor of rights and opportunity. Political power, not moral suasion, would destroy Jim Crow and leverage black Americans out of economic exploitation. New York activists were among those who campaigned to make permanent Roosevelt's Fair Employment Practice Committee (FEPC), a use of the welfare state that neither white southerners nor white northerners were willing to sanction. Many of those same activists played key roles in the passage of New York state's fair employment legislation, the first equal employment law in the nation. In a range of political contests in the late 1940s and early 1950s over labor law, public and private housing, education, and foreign policy, New York's "Negro Rights" movement, as black New Yorkers called their struggle, pushed to make the emerging welfare state (at both federal and state levels) a force for black economic rights and group advancement. Again, the state was central, not incidental, to the creation of a more just and equal world.[26]

Like Singh, the Hamiltons, and Biondi, I have advanced an argument about the long civil rights era that calls for renewed attention to the state, movement politics, urban political economy, and transnationalism. Specifically, I have argued that the postwar black liberation struggle took shape within the shifting patterns of metropolitan geography and economy that accompanied the vast spatial transformation of midcentury urban America. African Americans engaged the processes and institutions responsible for the "second ghetto" and the "urban crisis" as did no other group in American life. Industrial restructuring (including, especially, deindustrialization), redevelopment and urban renewal, highway and rapid transit construction, and suburban city building together became the pivots around which black political organizing turned. These issues were not merely the backdrop to the black liberation struggle; rather, the movement itself was constituted through them. The political discourse and strategies of the long postwar African American rights movement stressed the failure of the urban and metropolitan political economy to secure the promise of democracy and opportunity—activists stressed the failure of the postwar metropolis and the liberal state itself. This required a massive engagement with state power that coincided with, and was propelled by, the largest internal black migration in American history—the movement of four million African Americans from the South to the North and West.[27]

Even as cities and suburbs became battlegrounds over racial segregation and economic power in local places across the country during these years, metropolitan spatial development and the national state shaped one another. After World War II the federal government moved aggressively to define urban and suburban forms, a remarkable turnaround from the minimalist state urban policy of the first half of the century. An enormous array of federal programs, agencies, subsidies, and incentives now played as important a role in metropolitan development as did private corporations and municipal governments. Local politics in places as different as Oakland, Detroit, Cleveland, and Philadelphia thus ultimately became contests over the nature and expression of the American welfare state, in both New Deal and Great Society variants. Across the postwar United States, as cities were remade by two of the most extensive internal migrations in the nation's history—the migration of southern African Americans to the cities of the Northeast, Midwest, and West and the mass suburbanization of whites—the federal government did not stand idly by. Rather, it gave contour and direction to these migrations. Its housing policies helped to develop some places and underdevelop others. Programs like urban renewal subsidized the accumulation of wealth and other resources among some groups, primarily white property-holders, and denied those subsidies and protections to other groups, primarily African American. Further, in the remapping of postwar American capitalism, the commerce and manufacturing that drove consumption grew increasingly mobile, while the nation as a whole gradually shifted toward a service economy. In each of these processes and developments, the federal state exerted a heavier hand than at any other time in the nation's history.[28]

Once we engage this broader, more historical view of the shape of the U.S. welfare-warfare state and the concomitant importance of anticolonial struggle abroad, two developments become clear. First, the long postwar African American struggle for racial equality represented in large part a challenge to the deep racial inequities built into the welfare state and the political coalitions behind it. Black leaders pushed for fair employment and fair housing; for desegregation of the labor movement; for public housing; for an unbiased urban renewal program; for antipoverty efforts far more extensive than those of the Great Society; and, ultimately, for federal investment in urban American on a massive scale, or what the National Urban League called a "Domestic Marshall Plan." All of these efforts were either responses to black exclusion from state programs or calls for shifts in the middle-class bias of the state's supports and subsidies. It is understandable that historical attention has focused on the civil rights struggle against legalized Jim Crow in education, public accommodation, and voting, and that research has concentrated on the principal national organizations, individuals, and places that carried that struggle forward. However, an entire dimension of the postwar black struggle for racial equality has thus been undertheorized— notably its complex, long-term, militant engagement with the national state. That engagement is essential for understanding the black radical tradition inherited by the Black Panther Party.[29]

The second development is that because postwar black radicalism evolved in the context of global struggles by colonized peoples to free themselves of European occupiers, radicals at home could hardly avoid confronting the question of black Americans' relationship to colonialism. Thus black internationalists in the late 1940s and early 1950s asserted a global analysis of the color line and international capitalism. By the 1960s, those assertions led increasingly toward formulations like Frantz Fanon's theory of anticolonial guerrilla struggle set forth in *Wretched of the Earth* or Mao Zedong's notion of a united Third World arrayed against the capitalist-imperialist West. When the writings of Fanon, Che Guevara, Mao, and Malcolm X, among others, made the rounds among black activists and intellectuals in the late 1950s and early 1960s, the project had become finding a domestic analogy for anticolonial struggle. Applying a colonial analysis, even a colonial metaphor, to the status of black Americans was never an easy process, and critics often labeled it a diversion from black politics. But the effort was nonetheless a historically crucial one, because by the 1960s liberal explanations of the causes and remedies of the urban crisis had come to seem insufficient, even hollow. Some aspects of Maoist radicalism and Third World nationalism may have proved to be a dead end for black Americans, but activists nonetheless came by those positions honestly, through an honest assessment of three decades of liberal policy. It is to that subject, the intersection of liberalism and the urban crisis, that I now turn.[30]

Black Political Ideology and Urban America

The urban context decisively influenced the ideological range and political possibilities of 1960s black liberation politics. In this way, what became standard Black Panther discourse emerged from a long history of urban activism, social criticism, and political struggle by African Americans. The ideological tradition inherited by the Panthers was part of the fabric of American urban history from the early twentieth century, forged through the long struggles over housing, jobs, taxes, and political power that shaped the American metropolis across the middle part of the century. That tradition was one in which activists consistently sought an analytical stance outside conventional American liberalism; that is, outside liberalism's presumption of free markets and pluralist social interaction among urban populations. In short, black political ideology in the long civil rights era took shape within, around, and through an existing long-term engagement between African Americans and the American city. Modern black political ideology was, then, in great part an engagement with the nature of American cities.

With its Ten-Point Program, "What We Want, What We Believe," drafted in 1966, the Black Panther Party captured in uncompromising language the collective economic and political grievances articulated by black radicals and many black liberals since the 1930s.[31] Hewn from a longer historical list of demands for black equality in the United States, the particular grievances set forth by the Party centered on the status of black Americans in the urban-industrial political economy of the mid-twentieth century. Black incorporation into that political economy had since World War I virtually guaranteed subordination. Systematic housing and job discrimination as well as exclusion by major labor unions and weak or nonexistent incorporation into urban political machines meant that by the late 1940s the majority of urban African Americans constituted, in effect, a rapidly growing pool of low-skilled, low-wage labor with little collective leverage. In this context, the black rights movement of the World War II era called for economic empowerment, group advancement, and political coalition building, not the individualist-based remedies associated with liberal "integration." The Panthers, then, revived this industrial-era critique of American political economy that the postwar Red Scare marginalized because of its association with radicalism and the Left.[32]

The Party did more than simply rehearse a set of demands from the 1940s, however. Much had changed in urban America by 1966, and the Panthers fashioned their politics in this new context. Rapid postwar suburbanization, accompanied by urban deindustrialization, had diminished the industrial city as a producer of high-wage manufacturing jobs. White flight and its accompanying forms of urban disinvestment, continued housing discrimination, and the physical remaking of cities under federal urban renewal and redevelopment programs together made central cities function even more like collecting points for the economically disenfranchised. Accelerated black migration from the South in this context meant that a generation of urbanizing African Americans encountered the industrial city at or near its vanishing point rather than its historic crest. Together, these factors constitute what has been called the postwar "urban crisis." The Panthers thus combined the radical critique of the World War II generation with the lived urban experiences and politics of the postwar generation. Both had seen the liberal promises of broad opportunity in the industrial city go largely unfulfilled, particularly for the working class.[33]

The postwar city has recently garnered substantial attention among American historians. Joining an earlier urban historical literature on ghetto formation has been new scholarship on the urban crisis and the role that racial segregation and deindustrialization played in deepening that crisis. Both literatures emphasize the hardening of racial segregation in urban America after World War II and the brakes placed on racial liberalism by northern whites in conjunction with federal urban policy in the postwar decades. Extending work begun by, among others, W. E. B. Du Bois, St. Clair Drake, and Charles Abrams, this scholarship offers an important understanding of the relationship between economic restructuring, poverty, race, and the industrial city. But, the standard narrative still marginalizes rather than emphasizes African American politics and self-activity. In our understandable zeal to document the limits whites have placed on liberalism, historians have too often overlooked the fact that white and black Americans alike imagined the city and its possibilities, reacted to urban decline and decay, and fashioned politics and social movements with the ambition of making their neighborhoods and cities better places. Whether they succeeded or failed, these efforts require serious attention. Too often, black self-activity has been reduced to sporadic outbursts of violent rebellion: the "fire" of Watts, Detroit, and Newark.[34]

Histories of the Black Panther Party are especially well positioned to address this problematic in urban history and the strange divorce of black politics and the postwar urban crisis. For, as noted, the Party inherited a tradition of urban social criticism and black political organizing that has consistently read American cities against the dominant mainstream liberal view, which stresses interest-group pluralism, individualism, and assimilation. Sociologists of the Chicago school, under the direction of Robert

Parks, articulated the most influential version of this view of urban America in the 1920s and 1930s, which was based on the laboratory of the city of Chicago itself and its enormous immigrant populations. According to the Chicago school, urban migrants encountered the modern city as individuals, but their experience was mediated through affiliation with larger social and spatial units: ethnic groups, classes, and neighborhoods. Over time, pluralism ensured that competition between groups for space and other resources, while at times fierce, would inevitably result in the democratic assimilation of newcomers. In this view, cities were the essential containers of liberal democracy.[35]

St. Clair Drake and Horace Cayton, in their magisterial 1945 work *Black Metropolis*, used a massive study of the city's South Side to apply Chicago school principles to the circumstances of black Americans. Not since W. E. B. Du Bois's *The Philadelphia Negro* in the late 1890s had social scientists so systematically examined black urban life. But *Black Metropolis* embodied the elisions that rendered liberal pluralism an insufficient explanation for the conditions of black life. Even as Drake and Cayton took great pains to draw a portrait of Chicago's "Bronzeville" on an upward tick toward bourgeois accommodation and assimilation, they could not contain the very different story their subjects told in more than eight hundred pages. *Black Metropolis* concludes (in a section titled "Of Things to Come") that "free competition" and the "bending" and "breaking" of the color line promised black Chicagoans a liberal pluralist future not unlike that offered to the city's European immigrants. But as anyone who has read even parts of *Black Metropolis* understands, this is a decidedly unsatisfying conclusion in light of the overwhelming documentation the authors provide of the deep, structural, and tenacious color line. Drake and Cayton's liberal interpretive framework seemed at war with the history they told.[36]

It was precisely this sort of elision within liberal social science and political economy that black progressives and radicals would seize upon. It was the widening fissure in between the promises of liberal social science and social reform, on the one hand, and the observable material reality, on the other, that led many black intellectuals and activists to insist on seeing cities as constituted by power through race and class, with limited and constrained public spheres, defined by a particular kind of neocolonial exploitation. They insisted on seeing cities not as nodes of free exchange and competition in a capitalist marketplace and a liberal pluralist democracy, but as sites of subjugation and the principal locations of the reproduction of class power and racial privilege in the nation. It would be inaccurate to call this entire tradition "radical," since it was produced by a wide range of figures across the political spectrum. But for my purposes here, the contrast of crucial significance is that between an essentially liberal-pluralist understanding of black people and their relationship to urban life (blacks as an interest group or an ethnic group within pluralist urban America) and a neocolonial understanding in which race is not merely a marker of physical difference but an instrument of exploitation within urban capitalism.

Since the Great Depression, there have been two major periods of intense conflict and debate over the relationship between African Americans and urban America and the relative merits of liberal pluralism in an urban context. The first came between the early 1930s and the late 1940s, and the second came between the late 1950s and the early 1970s. In the first period, which corresponds to the trajectory of the Old Left, black urban critics and activists whose politics ranged from liberal to radical sought to make the Great Migration a foundation of black political liberation in the urban North. Prominent in these efforts, as Jonathan Holloway has demonstrated in *Confronting the Veil*, stood the social science academics Abram Harris Jr., E. Franklin Frazier, and Ralph Bunche, who were leaders among a generation of black intellectuals then emerging to give movement politics new vitality and direction. Harris, Frazier, and Bunche each saw in the Depression-era rise of organized labor the potential for cross-race solidarity among black and white workers, and together they articulated a class-centered view of the fate of urban black Americans. These scholars shared a belief that the color line could be slowly worn away, but they drew more consistently on Marxist analysis than did Drake and Cayton. The integration of black Americans into mainstream urban life, according to Harris, Frazier, and Bunche, would not come through a modernizing process of intergroup struggle followed by accommodation, as described in the Chicago school model. Rather, only class solidarity among all workers and the advance of class-based interests against capital through trade unionism and the reform of the state would finally destroy the color line and its foundation in economic exploitation.[37]

Others in the 1930s saw Black Power less in a democratic politics on the production side than in a politics of consumption. Inspired by the Chicago and Harlem grassroots campaigns "Don't buy where you can't work" and "Spend your money where you can work," Du Bois saw potential power in urban black workers' consumption. He imagined "the two million eight hundred thousand Negro families [that] spend at least two billion dollars a year" as a potent force for political change. On the one hand, these campaigns were broadly liberal. That is, they employed the boycott, a common consumer tactic in American social history, to force changes in hiring practices. Du Bois resisted a liberal reading, however, preferring instead a nationalist take on consumer power. "No group can approach economic independence or a position of self-sustaining inter-dependence unless it is organized as a nation," he argued in 1936.[38] Still others saw in the consumer protests a colonial reading not just of political economy but also of the city itself. White employers and white-owned businesses controlled commerce in black communities, the argument went, and thus the profit generated by these businesses left the community and went elsewhere. When these establishments also refused to hire black workers, the injustice was doubled because wages, too, left. The analysis was clear. Here was a process of capital accumulation with a distinctly one-way trajectory: out of the community. This represented a powerful antecedent to later 1960s colonial analysis of the American city in which the pluralist conception of flawed but ultimately free markets was replaced by a conception of markets as socially concocted artifices that were neither free nor open in any meaningful sense.[39]

The 1930s as a whole was a period of resurgent urban black activism on a variety of fronts. The "Don't buy where you can't work" campaigns spawned black cooperative leagues; Black Nationalists and socialists founded the Provisional Committee to Defend Ethiopia (PCDE); the activist A. Philip Randolph led the triumphant final campaigns of the Brotherhood of Sleeping Car Porters' long struggle for recognition and bargaining power; Bunche, Randolph, Davis, and others founded the National Negro Congress; and a host of black labor activists, Communist Party radicals, and community leaders worked in labor organizing campaigns, consumer boycotts, and local politics. In the decade between the Harlem Renaissance and the flowering of Chicago's South Side black community in the 1920s and the rise of Left politics in the 1930s, a distinct black public sphere took shape. In these years before the Cold War silenced dissent from the Left, black radicals and liberals were engaged in constant conversation and worked in tandem in a broad range of organizing activities. At the core of that conversation and organizing was the belief that the emerging urban black industrial working class represented the critical historical force for change within the African American community.[40]

Activists like Harry Haywood, Benjamin Davis, and other communists, though sympathetic to the labor movement and the strength of black consumer power, emphasized racial self-determination and varieties of nationalism while continuing to work in coalition politics. Davis, for instance, won Adam Clayton Powell's city council seat in 1943 and became what Biondi calls "an architect of Black Popular Front politics in New York." A member of the Communist Party, Davis staked out a broad ideological and programmatic terrain in New York's antiracist struggle. He introduced a range of antidiscrimination bills, called for Negro History Week, and supported rent control and veterans' rights. Though the official position on black Americans changed considerably throughout the late 1930s and early 1940s—first endorsing the Black Belt thesis that emphasized rural blacks in the South, then abandoning it, then reviving it again in 1946—black activists in the Communist Party like Davis were always committed to an urban-centered vision of black liberation. Davis, as well as black radicals like Haywood, were instrumental to civil rights politics in 1940s New York, where protest tactics and political coalition building for black community empowerment were first tested.[41]

As Biondi, Singh, Kelley, Von Eschen, and others have argued, the early Cold War years marked a profound turning point for black radicalism and the larger struggle for black rights. The 1948 Declaration of Negro Voters demonstrated that the black public sphere was considerably to the left of mainstream America, on both domestic and international questions. After 1948, however, cold war anticommunism at home and abroad had begun to sever the broad-based movement, similar to the Popular Front, of the 1930s and the war years when radical and liberals more often than not had worked in relatively spirited cooperation. Black liberals now adopted the anticommunist line, purged radicals from organizations like the NAACP, and quieted their internationalism. Abandoned by the liberals, the anticolonial and internationalist black activists of the mid-1940s and the early 1950s were left unprotected from the depredations of red-baiting opponents and the internal police apparatus of the state. Their trajectory of struggle was cut prematurely short by postwar anticommunism, their potential contributions to American foreign policy were discredited, and their case against American exceptionalism was dismissed.[42]

Despite the strictures imposed by the Cold War, however, black internationalist activists, journalists, and intellectuals created space within the domestic civil rights movement for a pan-African consciousness. The significance of this pan-African internationalism was twofold. First, it offered movement activists an intellectual framework for imagining black America's liberation outside of the dominant liberal paradigm of pluralist integration and assimilation—and, significantly, outside of the dominant discourse of American exceptionalism. Indeed, it challenged American exceptionalism at every turn by insisting that Black liberation with a capital B was a postcolonial project stretching from Birmingham to Dar es Salaam. Second, it drew into the movement a set of texts, a narrative of struggle, and a nondoctrinaire leftism that would shape activists' vision in the 1960s. This movement's figureheads, including Du Bois, Paul Robeson, Alphaeus Hunton, and Charlotta Bass, were marginalized by many African American liberals, but the influence of the movement's figures would be felt strongly by the emerging post–Red Scare generation—the generation of the Panthers. Most significantly, this movement articulated and domesticated an anticolonial model of African American liberation that would in subsequent decades become explicitly urban by drawing the metaphor of colonization and liberation into metropolitan space—and the metropolitan spatial inequalities at the heart of the urban crisis.[43]

The emergence in the mid-1950s of the southern civil rights movement shifted the national focus of movement activism to the fight against Jim Crow in the South. The church-based Southern Christian Leadership Conference (SCLC), along with the Student Nonviolent Coordinating Committee (SNCC) on southern (and some northern) college campuses, took the lead in the early 1960s in defining the struggle primarily as one against the legal architecture of southern segregation. But the political agenda advanced by black radicals and liberals in the urban North, West, and even many places in the South—which included political power at all levels, fair employment and housing laws, reform of police departments to end police brutality, support for labor unions, colonial freedom in Africa and Asia, and expansions of the broader social wage—remained intact, albeit damaged from 1950s red-baiting.

One of the great intellectual and political dramas of the 1960s was the profound revival of the urban-centered vision of black liberation. In city after city, black Americans had arrived as urban migrants from the South in record numbers during the 1950s and 1960s, a population movement that dwarfed the earlier Great Migration. Opportunities for these new migrants, as well as for the millions of blacks who had long been urban dwellers, slammed hard against the persistence of Jim Crow in the private economy, as well as the accelerating pace of deindustrialization, the growing affluence of suburban communities, and the relative disinterest of white urban politicians. In this context, the precepts of liberalism and pluralism began to strike community activists and leaders as not just hollow but perhaps intellectually flawed. Their turn to anticolonial politics from an essentially liberal pluralist vision of the city marked one of the key intellectual developments of the second half of the 1960s. As the urban crisis worsened over the course of the late 1950s and early 1960s, the federal War on Poverty and other Great Society programs seemed to have little impact on urban black poverty, unemployment, and underemployment, while white commitment to black equality waned.[44]

Between 1957 and 1967, a broad strategic and philosophical shift became apparent. The precepts of the black rights movement changed dramatically over those ten years: from faith in law to faith in direct action; from faith in individualist remedies to faith in collective and community-based remedies; and from faith in American pluralism to faith in Black Nationalism and radicalism. Judging liberalism and its promises of inclusion to be a failure, black leaders turned their attention to bringing political and institutional power to African American communities. To remake opportunity was to tackle, and attempt to counter, the social and spatial arrangements of the ghetto and the legacies of both slavery and segregation embedded in it. In doing so, African Americans did more than engage in struggle: they called forth a deep philosophical debate about the meaning of the ghetto and, by extension, the city itself and the place of both African Americans and whites within it. That debate—and the vast grassroots mobilizations behind it—produced an extraordinarily rich intellectual and political ferment among African Americans that would shape the subsequent trajectory of Black Power and black liberation politics in the second half of the 1960s and the first half of the 1970s.[45]

The Black Panther Party in Oakland

In the long sweep of twentieth-century urban history, black self-determination advocates like the Black Panthers articulated a profoundly important reading of the landscape of metropolitan—that is, urban and suburban—America. Oakland, California, the birthplace of the Panthers, stood out in this national context. In 1966, the Panthers defined Oakland's ghetto as a territory, the police as interlopers, and the Panther mission as the defense of community. The use of space in these efforts was not entirely metaphorical, because defense of the community meant driving around West Oakland with rifles, monitoring police. The Panthers' famous "policing of the police" drew attention to the spatial remove that white Americans enjoyed from the state violence that had come to characterize life in black urban communities. But Party activists also defined their anticolonial politics in terms of pushing onto the municipal political agenda the concerns of local residents — who needed jobs, better health care, improved schools, and repaired streets. Again, these common-sense claims that American metropolitan development hinged on the dramatic powerlessness of black communities were not wholly new in the hands of the Panthers. Much less were they necessarily "revolutionary." However, by reclaiming the tradition of black radicalism that the Cold War had suppressed and linking it to the concrete concerns of black communities, the Party joined the black rights struggle in the United States to a global analysis of capitalism and imperialism.

At the heart of the Panthers' anticolonial politics was an analysis of the relationship between urban black communities and the postwar American metropolis, on the one hand, and a critique of the concept of liberal free markets in urban property, employment, and housing, on the other. Unlike most black intellectuals in the 1930s, both radical and liberal, who saw the nation-state as the horizon of class struggle, the Panthers inherited the legacy of those black radical internationalists who, in the 1940s and 1950s, began to see beyond the limits of the nation-state to the capitalist foundations of a global color line. Thus, the Panthers combined an urban-centered critique of U.S. capitalism and racism with a global perspective on postcolonial nationhood. In many instances, the connections drawn by the Panthers between the two were tenuous and, sometimes, hyperbolic. Nevertheless, the mix was powerful and generative, and it was arguably one of the Party's most compelling contributions to American political culture in the 1960s and 1970s.[46]

The Panthers' notions of colonial liberation and resistance to state violence drew from a range of existing political formulations to create a unique politics that subsequently influenced community activists and organizations across the nation. The Revolutionary Action Movement (RAM), founded in the early 1960s, favored a socialist-style state and a Maoist revolutionary politics. Its members were committed to challenging the liberal, desegregationist orientation of groups like SNCC and the Congress of Racial Equality (CORE) by giving voice to the dispossessed and impoverished black residents of the nation's ghettoes. Following the example of the RAM, the Panthers turned to the writings of Mao Zedong for their basic revolutionary lexicon. Mao's notion of a united Third World aligned against the colonial West and his program of moral self-improvement and revolutionary ethics inspired the Panthers' internationalism as well as their internal program of personal discipline. Huey Newton was thus sharply influenced not only by RAM but also by the Black Power turn within SNCC in 1965 and 1966, by the Lowndes County (Alabama) Black Panther Party, and, earlier, by the cultural nationalism of Don Warden's Afro-American Association. By the early 1970s, the Party was also deeply influenced by local Oakland community activists, as well as the Black Convention Movement, an emerging coalition of black political organizations whose meeting in Gary, Indiana, in 1972 set an urban agenda for the black community. Far from being sui generis, then, the Black Panther Party was part of a larger black radical development in the 1960s. At times, the Party seemed to be the leading edge of this development, while at other moments it was quite clearly following the lead of others.

The Party's synthesis of black radicalism and a Maoist critique of capitalism nonetheless took a prominent place alongside the manifestos of SNCC, RAM, and the Students for a Democratic Society (SDS) in the evolution of sixties New Left political discourse. After Newton's arrest for murdering an Oakland policeman, the "Free Huey" campaign made headlines and network television news. Meanwhile, the Panther uniform of leather jackets and black berets redefined black chic. Party boldness in its dealings with police inspired a nationwide movement against police brutality. As inheritors of the discipline, pride, and calm self-assurance preached by Malcolm X, the Panthers became national heroes in African American communities by infusing abstract nationalism with street toughness — by joining the rhythms of black working-class youth culture to the interracial élan and effervescence of Bay Area New Left politics. Black Panther Party chapters opened monthly in city after city during the last years of the decade, thereby producing dozens of local organizations by the late 1960s. They also inspired the formation of other groups like the Puerto Rican organization known as the Young Lords, whose members also defined the ghetto as a territory and thus a space where interlopers monopolized jobs, businesses, and political power. After 1968, letters from African American communities nationwide streamed into Panther headquarters on a scale associated with rock stars. One young follower in Charlotte, North Carolina, wrote to Newton hoping that he "would write back . . . and if you would, send me a picture of you." She concluded her letter by stating "I'm in the eighth grade and very proud that I'm *black* (and I love you too)."[47]

But there was a local meaning, a local story, behind the rise of the Panthers. As much as they operated within the larger national theatrics of the late 1960s, the Panthers emerged out of, and played a critical role in, the milieu of African American struggle in North and West Oakland. Newton and Seale launched the Party in 1966 amid a rich and contentious period of debate and conflict over the direction of the African American community in Oakland, and the city's future hinged on these debates. Over the second half of the 1960s and first half of the 1970s, the city's African Americans from diverse backgrounds and political affiliations were determined that they would shape that future. The Panthers came to play an immensely important role in these efforts, though they were not alone.

Between 1966 and 1972, two principal political strategies evolved in Oakland under the broad rubric of African American community self-determination: Black Panther Third World nationalism and the grassroots community empowerment advocated by the city's War on Poverty activists. Both groups drew for their political language on metaphors of decolonization. Oakland's ghetto stood for "the community" and, more expansively, the black nation. Jobs, political power, and other resources that by right should have been located in the community itself had been stripped from it by outsiders. The answer was liberation. According to this view, the liberal politics of desegregation had advanced the black struggle as far as the logic of those politics allowed—that is, until they came up against the underlying resistance of the white "power structure" and, especially for the Panthers, the structural inequalities and exploitation inherent in capitalist imperialism. Thus, despite their heavy ideological debt to groups like RAM and SNNC, the Panthers were also an important dimension of a local Black Power development in San Francisco's East Bay. Indeed, by the early 1970s, the Party was borrowing heavily from the analysis of Oakland first advanced by community activists in the area. Both groups saw the city's African American community locked in a struggle against Oakland's largely white business and political elite, who dominated the city council and downtown property, as well as what was often called the white suburban "noose." Both strategies politicized, rather than accepted as natural, patterns of East Bay metropolitan development.[48]

Yet most significant was the way that the Panthers deployed an anticolonial analysis to make sense of the specific conditions of the urban United States in the late 1960s. There were three key phases of this radical critique. First, in its initial incarnation, between 1966 and 1970, the Party combined a theatrical performance of radical self-determination—including police patrols; the Party's appearance at the California state capitol in Sacramento; and the early survival programs and liberation schools with their incandescent "Ten-Point Program." The latter was, as suggested above, a resume of demands whose origins dated to earlier expressions of black radical activism. Their calls for "full employment for our people," "decent housing," and "an immediate end to politic brutality," among the first seven demands of the Ten-Point Program, had been central to various Popular Front, labor, radical, and liberal civil rights political platforms in the 1930s and 1940s. The final point—"We want land, bread, housing, education, clothing, justice, and peace," along with their calls for the "power to determine our own destiny" and their later addition of a demand for "a United Nations–supervised plebiscite to be held throughout the black colony"—strongly echoed the internationalist African American Left of the mid-century including men and women like Ben Davis, William Patterson, and Charlotta Bass.

Rejecting the cultural nationalism fashionable at the junior college they attended in Oakland, Newton and Seale, joined subsequently by Eldridge Cleaver, rendered a version of Marxism-Leninism from an eclectic range of sources. Much of the immediate inspiration for and discourse of the early Panthers came from Frantz Fanon's *Wretched of the Earth*, which in 1966 Seale had read and then encouraged Newton to do the same. This treatise on the French colonial regime in Algeria inspired Newton to turn away from strict Black Nationalism to a spatially situated revolutionary community ideology. Behind the guns—literally, as Newton often quoted Mao—lay an elaborate analysis of the black nation as a colony, exploited by an imperialist class system. Colonizers included city hall, white businessmen, the suburbs, and the police, the "pigs of the state." In addition, Mao's notion of a united Third World aligned against the colonial West and his program of moral self-improvement and revolutionary ethics inspired the Panthers' internationalism as well as their internal program of personal discipline. Like Malcolm X, whose legacy the Panthers self-consciously embraced, Panther ideology stressed black self-determination and the necessity of armed resistance to "the brutal force used against us daily." Yet unlike the Nation of Islam, and

Malcolm X until the final months of his life, the Panthers never adopted a separatist language or line, believing that alliances with sympathetic anti-colonial whites, as well as Chicanos, should remain a fixture of the black liberation movement.[49]

In their admittedly raw anticolonial analysis, the Panthers contended that persistent white-enforced segregation had actually delivered to black people a measure of power. That power lay in spatial confinement — the concentration of African Americans in urban centers, where poverty and hopelessness had created a "lumpen proletariat," ignorant but teachable, to develop as the core of a revolutionary movement. This did not excuse segregation. But, like their counterparts in colonial resistance in Africa, the Panthers emphasized that the structures of colonial rule (i.e., the ghetto) could be turned against the imperial nation by creative leaders and appropriate strategy. For the Panthers rose from the crossroads of West and North Oakland, where a particular kind of street culture met Garveyite notions of self-help, the radical internationalist black tradition, the socialist laborite culture of Oakland's waterfront unions, and the armed community-defense strategies of people like Malcolm and Robert F. Williams. This eclectic mix, stirred equally by Newton's idealism and megalomania, emerged in the late 1960s as one of the nation's most elaborate and inspired attempts to reread the nature of American cities and the place of black people within them.

The second phase of Party development, between 1971 and 1973, was marked by the "Base of Operation" campaign in Oakland, when Bobby Seale and Elaine Brown, along with a handful of *Black Panther* journalists, offered a detailed critique of the East Bay metropolis. The culprits were familiar: freeways that tore up and divided traditional black neighborhoods; segregated school systems that funneled money and other resources away from traditionally black high schools and elementary schools; urban renewal that further depopulated black neighborhoods with empty promises of new housing and shopping; a suburban noose of segregated peripheral cities with a solid tax base and white residents who worked in Oakland and spent their money elsewhere. Here was the whole host of urban ills of the 1960s seen not through the exceptionalist prism of Great Society liberalism in which poverty and urban failure were products of community pathology, underpreparation for job market success, and a lack of political power, but through the prism of what many would later call "black political economy" in which the urban crisis was understood as a product of deep structural contradictions within

American urban capitalism and its color-caste-class system. As the historian Carl Nightingale has observed, black political economy in the late 1960s and early 1970s emphasized that "little capital ever accumulated in the archipelago of black urban America," because a neocolonial form of exploitation kept people in "low-paying, low-skill jobs."[50]

This base of operation phase reflected two important branches of the ideological evolution within the Panther Party. The first, intercommunalism, represented subtle but important changes in Party ideology. Intercommunalism defined the world as a collection of communities dominated by the United States and its global allies. The ongoing struggles against oppression worldwide need not be tightly coordinated, because most faced a common set of constraints and enemies. Thus, any liberation anywhere would serve the larger cause. African Americans, in this view, were particularly well placed to lead global opposition to imperialism and neoimperialism because they had more than three hundred years of experience in dealing with European racial oppression and two hundred years of experience with the state apparatus of the United States.[51]

The other branch that the base of operation embodied was the Panthers' notion of advocating practical revolutionary activity. In a long dispute with RAM, Newton and the Panthers insisted that revolutionary action should take place "above ground" in visible public space. The leaders of RAM, on the other hand, argued that revolutionary organization should remain underground and thus beyond the long reach of the state police and surveillance apparatus. But Newton and other Party insiders came to believe that the principal problem with late-twentieth-century radicalism was its abstractness and distance from the material experience of ordinary people. Fomenting violence from "underground," as other groups like the SDS Weatherman faction had begun to do in 1970, only served to alienate any potential revolutionary constituency, because people feared the violence and did not understand its political relevance. The base of operation, launched in conjunction with an expansion of successful local programs, embodied the Party's effort to educate the public in a revolutionary language by developing a practical political agenda that people could find relevant to their daily lives. It was fundamentally about making capital, power, and injustice visible and real—that is, to politicize what most people, ordinary folks both black and white, took for granted as natural: the city as a locus of power.[52]

The base of operation campaign in Oakland, however, signaled more than a turn within the Party to local politics. It came in the midst of a major *national* split within Panther ranks, coupled with internal violence and retribution. In 1971 Newton, acquitted and freed from prison, expelled Eldridge Cleaver and the International Section of the Party, which was based in Algiers, Algeria. The expulsions set off a round of allegedly retaliatory murders that forced branches around the country to choose between Newton and Cleaver. Cleaver and others accused Newton of running the Party through a cohort of sycophants in the service of personal aggrandizement. For his part, Newton directed the Party to focus its energy and resources on Oakland — hence the "base of operation" — a decision that was accompanied by what many called a "reformist" turn in ideology. Admitting that the Party had been wrong to attack the police, Newton announced that the Panthers would henceforth work with black churches, participate in electoral politics, and support black capitalist ventures. In short, the Party seemed poised to work within the system of political pluralism that it had long criticized.[53]

Finally, the third phase in the Panthers' radicalism came in the city council and mayoral campaigns in Oakland in 1973 and 1975, when the Party gave specific programmatic content to an otherwise loose anticolonial critique. Brown and Seale campaigned for a "people's economy" of rearranged political and economic priorities that included major tax reform, massive public-sector investment in urban infrastructure, payroll taxes to deal with suburban income flight, and aggressive affirmative action in public-sector hiring and in public awarding of contracts. It was, in fact, an urban agenda endorsed by a wide range of African American activists and political figures on the progressive Left in the early 1970s, ranging from Amiri Baraka to Whitney Young. In addition to the "base of operation" series in the Party organ, *The Black Panther*, which carefully documented how decisions about economic development in the city had been made, who had benefited, and who had born the costs, the Party now undertook a massive voter registration and grassroots organizing drive: "We must first organize the block, then the neighborhood," the Panthers announced, "gradually expanding to the city." By some estimates, they had registered more than twenty-five thousand new voters by early 1973. During this period, the Panthers forged crucial connections with the Democratic Party through Ronald Dellums, who had been elected to Congress from the Oakland-Berkeley flatlands on an antiwar, Black Power platform in 1970. New connections to white liberals also slowly emerged, as Brown established relationships with progressives who had been working to defeat the Republican "machine" in Oakland since the late 1960s. And, behind it all lay the central platform issues on which Seale and Brown stumped in the first truly grassroots municipal campaign that Oakland had seen since the late 1940s: community control of Oakland's port and City Center; affirmative action; residency requirements for the employees of the city police and fire departments; and a new "revenue-raising, revenue-sharing" plan designed to redistribute the tax burden from the neighborhoods to downtown. Here, in the Panthers' words, lay Oakland's future, "the construction of a people's economy."[54]

At the same time, of course, there is a violent, even criminal aspect to Panther history that cannot be ignored. The political trajectory described above did not take place in a vacuum. Rather, it took shape against the background of an ongoing war with the police coupled to other instances of Panther-inspired violence, both within and outside the Party. Panther memoirs offer compelling testimony to the complicated layering of violence within the group's milieu, a violence that should neither be ignored nor romanticized. The Party issued a rallying cry for a generation of street toughs as well as for young black intellectuals and political figures. After summer 1966, on occasion the street violence that had shaped the background of many members blurred the line between radical nationalism and extortion. When local stores refused to donate food and other resources to Panther social programs, Party members often threatened violent retaliation. On 10 May 1969, for example, a group of Panthers firebombed a convenience store on San Pablo Avenue in North Oakland because the store owner refused to donate more than a dozen eggs to a breakfast program. In 1971, the Panthers staged a massive boycott of California's largest black-owned liquor distribution network, Cal-Pak, to force its members to make cash donations to the party. "I was angered and amazed because I had never heard anybody publicly threatened like this," stated Albert KcKee, a black real estate broker, in reference to Newton's behavior at one of the Cal-Pak meetings. "Some of us were fighting against racial injustice when Newton was running around barefoot," McKee added. Accused in dozens of other incidents, by the 1970s the Party faced increasing criticism from both white and black leaders for its alleged involvement in illegal markets in weapons and drugs. For Newton, Fanon's *Wretched of the Earth* provided the final justification for translating the street violence and the underground economic entrepreneurship of his adolescence into political resistance: the proletariat was the legitimate agent of revolution in anticolonial struggle. In their hands, guns were justified. Newton deployed Fanon's notion of a revolutionary colonized proletariat to explain organizing "the brothers on the block" rather than the black bourgeoisie. Yet these "brothers" included some of Oakland's most alienated youth, whose inclinations ran more toward firebombing than building an alternative vision of African American progress. The question remained whether these so-called brothers inspired or repulsed the Party's potential base in the black community.[55]

The Party also indulged in inflammatory speeches and offered cover for a violence clearly unrelated to the legitimate defense of community. But such judgments are applicable to the white-led police and FBI COINTELPRO operatives as well, who met the Panthers with their own brand of violence and subterfuge that crossed both legal and moral boundaries. The Panthers' alleged and proven connections to illegal activities called forth a swift and terrible repression. The Oakland police department, long a bastion of both racial paternalism and virulent racism, responded to the Panthers with nothing short of guerrilla warfare—no less than three black men were killed by Oakland police in spring 1968 alone. For his part, FBI director J. Edgar Hoover called the Party "the greatest threat to the internal security of the country," and he supervised an extensive program of counterorganizing that included surveillance and eavesdropping, infiltration, harassment, false testimony, and a laundry list of other tactics designed to jail Party members and drain the organization of resources. In 1976, a Senate report on FBI COINTELPRO operations charged that the bureau had "engaged in lawless tactics and responded to deep-seated social problems by fomenting violence and unrest." In the late 1960s and early 1970s, 233 out of 295 total FBI counterintelligence operations directed against black liberation groups across the nation had been aimed at the Black Panther Party. The slaying by the Chicago police of Fred Hampton, leader of the Illinois branch of the Party, remains one of the signature political assassinations of the decade, but it was only the most extreme example of systematic efforts by local cops and federal agencies to harass and disrupt the Party. The state repression of the Panthers, along with the long FBI campaign against Martin Luther King Jr., surely stands as one of the darkest and most cynical acts of American officialdom in the 1960s.[56]

At the same time, at some remove from these struggles, grassroots Panther activists brought a romantic idealism and practical agenda to their work in Oakland. As the Party's leadership battled the city of Oakland in the courts and newspapers; fought a near-constant war with the FBI; and watched many of its principal figureheads — including Newton, Seale, and its chief of staff David Hilliard — go to prison, Panther recruits established a host of social programs for the East Bay's poorest African Americans. Beginning with their free breakfast for schoolchildren program in 1968 and stretching through its free ambulance program of 1974, the Party introduced to Oakland some of the most interesting and audacious community welfare experiments of the era. The free breakfast program was followed in 1969 by the founding of the liberation schools, which taught children "about the class struggle in terms of black history." The Intercommunal Youth Institute and the People's Free Medical Research Health Institute were also founded that same year. A free clothing program followed in 1970, and the Sickle Cell Anemia Research Foundation, which provided free sickle cell anemia testing, came after that. By 1972, when Panther rallies at DeFremery Park became larger and more numerous as components of their various political campaigns, a free food program was added, in which bags of groceries were given away. While some of these programs were conceived and directed from the top of the Panther hierarchy, others, such as the liberation schools, were initiated by rank-and-file members, thereby testifying to the relative openness and degree of experimentation possible within the interstices of an otherwise centrally directed organization.[57]

The breakfasts in particular embodied the Panthers' notion of practical revolutionary activity. Along with free sickle cell anemia testing and other periodic food giveaways, the breakfasts formed the core of what became known as the Party's survival programs. By "helping the people survive," the breakfast program allowed the children of West Oakland's poorest neighborhoods to eat a healthy meal in a safe, supportive environment. Those Panthers who worked in the program, particularly women, made sure that the free breakfasts offered concrete assistance to the city's poor while dramatizing a powerful symbol of racial injustice and ghetto marginalization in America: childhood hunger. Free breakfasts were both practical and idealistic in the Panther commitment to ameliorating this social wrong. As an important historical companion to Head Start, initiated by the federal government in 1965, the free breakfast program also stood as a powerful reminder that Title I funding under the 1965 Education Act should directly benefit poor schoolchildren, not middle-class school districts. It would be a decade or more before free breakfasts would become almost universally available to poor children — in no small part because of the Party's ambitious example.[58]

Beyond their immediate material impact, though, the survival programs aimed at deeper spiritual and ideological transformations among the neighborhood men and women whom the Party hoped to mobilize. As models of black self-determination and pride, the programs combined self-help and education in revolutionary diction with the free-spirited, animated public displays of political commitment that had become the *sine qua non* of Left culture in the Bay Area. Schoolchildren at Party breakfasts sang in uproarious tones, often with their female teachers, "Black is beautiful, Free Huey!" The events for grocery giveaways and for sickle cell anemia testing attracted large crowds to DeFremery Park in West Oakland, where Party stalwarts gave speeches about black pride. Like "patrolling the pigs," which Seale described as "bringing [local residents] basic things in everyday life about the law," the survival programs positioned the Panthers as a vanguard party and vehicle of consciousness raising. The Party held that "the people can't understand and progress to the stage of communists right away because of abstract arguments." Community programs, rather than the elusive grammar of radical politics, would win broad grassroots support for the Party's political objectives. At the same time, the survival programs solidified the Panthers' standing in the larger community. Many people in West and North Oakland, especially older adults, knew Newton when he was a "C" student and a bully. The Party's daily presence by way of those neighborhood programs changed this impression among people who knew him and, among those who did not, raised the Panthers' profile as community leaders not gangsters.[59]

Nevertheless, the violence and criminality, both real and alleged, provided ammunition to people who sought to discredit the Panthers, both inside and outside the black community. Indeed, as many Panthers later admitted, the period of the worst violence between Panthers and police, 1967–1970, did alienate them from much of their potential base in the black community. Part of Newton's justification for closing far-flung Party chapters beginning in 1971 to concentrate energy on Oakland was, he said, the need to cultivate a "base" of support in order to foreground the Party's politics and vision rather than its clashes with police.

Both the violent acts by Panthers and their Marxist-Leninist-Maoist ideology have continued to raise questions about their place within the larger constellation of black politics in the late sixties and early seventies. One of the most important criticisms of the Party, and of the tendencies within sixties black radicalism more generally, has come from the political theorist Adolph Reed. Reed argues that the Party's violent entanglements in the "late sixties," along with its preoccupation with the antiwar movement and the white Left, prevented it from becoming a serious contender for leading black radical politics. Furthermore, Reed observes, the broader trajectory of black radicalism in the 1968–1972 period toward Marxist-Leninist variants represented a disengagement with the majority of the black community and from a black political project capable of "energizing radical alternatives." The essays in this volume will go a long way toward determining the validity of that claim, but it must be noted that by the early 1970s many in the Party, including Seale and Brown, recognized the perils of the disengagement that Reed criticizes. The turn to electoral politics in Oakland reflected the Panthers' recognition, however belated, that reenergizing a black political movement realistically capable of achieving power should take precedence over positioning a small cadre of "revolutionaries" as a political "vanguard."[60]

This reorientation of Panther politics returns us to the urban crisis of the 1960s and to the relationship between urban historiography and the historiography of the Black Panther Party. To comprehend fully the nature and extent of the multiple crises in American cities during the 1960s and 1970s, we must position the history of civil rights, Black Power, and black radicalism within longer traditions of urban American politics and social activism. The urban crisis literature is correct to emphasize discriminatory federal urban housing policy, white racism, and deindustrialization as overwhelmingly the cause of whatever we may think of as the "urban crisis," but there was equal political drama in the imagining of remedies. The real drama lay in the political battles to determine whose path *out* of the crisis would gain purchase. African American radicals and liberals alike spent most of the twentieth century in an extended ideological and philosophical quest for this purchase. In doing so, they offered to American political culture multiple readings of the urban landscape that diverged in crucial ways from the liberal pluralist, free-competition models celebrated by the white majority. That the political objectives to emerge from these readings of the American city were eventually either defeated from the right or absorbed and refracted through liberalism should neither obscure their importance nor encourage us to dismiss them. Indeed, historians must pursue even more aggressively the comparisons between black radicalism in the 1940s/1950s period and that in the 1960s/1970s period, while continuing to assess black radicalism in the context of twentieth-century urban history.

African American activists like the Panthers, in Oakland and across the nation, fought to secure a place for black communities in the shifting patterns of metropolitan geography and economy that accompanied the vast spatial transformation of American cities at mid-century. They engaged the institutions responsible for erecting the "second ghetto" and for the urban crisis as few groups in American society did. Industrial restructuring, redevelopment, highway and rapid transit construction, and suburbanization together became the pivots around which black politics turned. These issues were not merely backdrops to the black liberation struggle; rather, it was through them that the movement itself was constituted. When Eldridge Cleaver said, "If we give freedom to ourselves right here in Babylon, we will give freedom to the world," he was in part speaking about what the twentieth-century American city had become: the place that both provided the conditions for liberation and made that liberation all but essential. And though Cleaver himself would prove to be a fickle, arbitrary, and ultimately frustrating guide through postwar black politics and political economy, he does here what he did best in his era, which is point us toward something interesting—in this case the fertile meeting ground for urban and African American historiography. For, where we find the politics and ideology of the city, we find the place where segregated urban America meets long traditions of black radicalism and movement politics within the black public sphere. It is at that juncture that we must situate any serious historical consideration of the Black Panther Party.

Notes

1. Charles E. Jones, ed., *The Black Panther Party [Reconsidered]* (Baltimore: Black Classic Press, 1998); Kathleen Cleaver and George Katsiaficas, eds., *Liberation, Imagination, and the Black Panther Party: A New Look at the Panthers and their Legacy* (New York: Routledge, 2001); Jennifer Smith, *An International History of the Black Panther Party* (New York: Garland, 1999); Yohuru Williams, *Black Politics/White Power: Civil Rights, Black Power, and the Black Panthers in New Haven* (St. James, N.Y.: Brandywine Press, 2000); Robert Self, *American Babylon: Race and the Struggle for Postwar Oakland* (Princeton, N.J.: Princeton University Press, 2003); Paul Alkebulan, "The Role of Ideology in the Growth, Establishment, and Decline of the Black Panther Party, 1966 to 1982" (Ph.D. diss., University of California, Berkeley, 2003); Rose Thevenin, "'The Greatest Single Threat': A Study of the Black Panther

Party, 1966–1971" (Ph.D. diss., Michigan State University, 2003); Robyn Spencer, "Repression Breeds Resistance: The Rise and Fall of the Black Panther Party in Oakland, California, 1966–1982" (Ph.D. diss., Columbia University, 2001); Craig Peck, "Educate to Liberate: The Black Panther Party and Political Education" (Ph.D. diss., Stanford University, 2001); Tracye Matthews, "No One Ever Asks What a Man's Place in the Revolution Is: Gender and Sexual Politics in the Black Panther Party, 1966–1971" (Ph.D. diss., University of Michigan, 1998).

2. Among Panther critics, see Hugh Pearson, *The Shadow of the Panther: Huey Newton and the Price of Black Power in America* (Reading, Mass.: Addison-Wesley, 1994); and Peter Collier and David Horowitz, *Destructive Generation: Second Thoughts about the Sixties* (New York: Summit, 1989). More sympathetic accounts include Ward Churchill and Jim Vander Wall, *Agents of Repression: The FBI's Secret War Against the Black Panther Party and the American Indian Movement* (Boston: South End Press, 1988); and Judson Jeffries, *Huey P. Newton: The Radical Theorist* (Jackson: University Press of Mississippi, 2002). For Panther memoirs, see Huey P. Newton, *Revolutionary Suicide* (New York: Harcourt Brace, 1973); Bobby Seale, *Seize the Time: The Story of the Black Panther Party* (New York: Vintage, 1970); David Hilliard and Lewis Cole, *This Side of Glory: The Autobiography of David Hilliard and the Story of the Black Panther Party* (Boston: Little, Brown, 1993); Elaine Brown, *A Taste of Power: A Black Woman's Story* (New York: Doubleday, 1992); and Earl Anthony, *Spitting in the Wind: The True Story Behind the Violent Legacy of the Black Panther Party* (Malibu, Calif.: Roundtable, 1990).

3. Nikhil Pal Singh, *Black Is a Country: Race and the Unfinished Struggle for Democracy* (Cambridge, Mass.: Harvard University Press, 2004), 2. On black radicalism, see Robin D. G. Kelley, *Freedom Dreams: The Black Radical Imagination* (Boston: Beacon, 2002); Robin D. G. Kelley, "'But a Local Phase of a World Problem': Black History's Global Vision, 1883–1950," *Journal of American History* (December 1999), 1045–77; Cedric Robinson, *Black Marxism: The Making of the Black Radical Tradition* (London: Zed, 1983); and Jonathan Scott Holloway, *Confronting the Veil: Abram Harris Jr., E. Franklin Frazier, and Ralph Bunche, 1919–1941* (Chapel Hill: University of North Carolina Press, 2002).

4. Kevin Gaines, "The Historiography of the Struggle for Black Equality Since 1945," in *A Companion to Post-1945 America*, edited by Jean-Christophe Agnew and Roy Rosenzweig (Malden, Mass.: Blackwell, 2002); Peniel Joseph, "Black Liberation without Apology: Reconceptualizing the Black Power Movement," *The Black Scholar: Journal of Black Studies and Research* 31 (fall/winter): 3–20; Jeanne Theoharris and Komozi Woodard, eds., *Freedom North: Black Freedom Struggles outside the South* (New York: Palgrave Macmillan, 2003); Barbara Ransby, *Ella Baker and the Black Freedom Movement: A Radical Democratic Vision* (Chapel Hill: University of North Carolina Press, 2003); Charles M. Payne, *I've Got the Light of Freedom: The Organizing Tradition and the Mississippi Freedom Struggle* (Berkeley: University of California Press, 1995); Robin D. G. Kelley, *Race Rebels: Culture, Politics, and the Black Working Class* (New York: Free Press, 1994); Michael Dawson, *Black Visions: The Roots of Contemporary African-American Political Ideologies* (Chicago:

University of Chicago Press, 2001); Timothy Tyson, *Radio Free Dixie: Robert F. Williams and the Roots of Black Power* (Chapel Hill: University of North Carolina Press, 1999).

5. I emphasize the word *civil* to contrast with other sorts of rights, especially economic.

6. Harvard Sitkoff, *The Struggle for Black Equality, 1954–1980* (New York: Hill and Wang, 1981); Clayborne Carson, *In Struggle: SNCC and the Black Awakening of the 1960s* (Cambridge, Mass.: Harvard University Press, 1981); Jack M. Bloom, *Class, Race, and the Civil Rights Movement* (Bloomington: Indiana University Press, 1987); Taylor Branch, *Pillar of Fire: America in the King Years, 1963–65* (New York: Simon and Schuster, 1998).

7. Todd Gitlin, *The Whole World Is Watching: Mass Media in the Making and Unmaking of the New Left* (Berkeley: University of California Press, 1980); August Meier et al., eds., *Black Protest in the Sixties: Articles from the New York Times* (New York: Markus Wiener Publishing, 1991).

8. See notes 1–4, above, and Doug McAdam, *Political Process and the Development of Black Insurgency, 1930–1970* (Chicago: University of Chicago Press, 1982); Aldon Morris, *The Origins of the Civil Rights Movement: Black Communities Organizing for Change* (New York: Free Press, 1984); Robin D. G. Kelley, *Hammer and Hoe: Alabama Communists during the Great Depression* (Chapel Hill: University of North Carolina Press, 1990); Michael Honey, *Southern Labor and Black Civil Rights: Organizing Memphis Workers* (Urbana: University of Illinois Press, 1993); Glen T. Eskew, *But for Birmingham: The Local and National Movements in the Civil Rights Struggle* (Chapel Hill: University of North Carolina Press, 1997); Mary Pattillo-McCoy, *Black Picket Fences: Privilege and Peril among the Black Middle Class* (Chicago: University of Chicago Press, 1999); Mary Dudziak, *Cold War Civil Rights: Race and the Image of American Democracy* (Princeton, N.J.: Princeton University Press, 2000); Amy Bass, *Not the Triumph but the Struggle: The 1968 Olympics and the Making of the Black Athlete* (Minneapolis: University of Minnesota Press, 2002); Robert Korstad, *Civil Rights Unionism: Tobacco Workers and the Struggle for Democracy in the Mid-Twentieth-Century South* (Chapel Hill: University of North Carolina Press, 2003).

9. Here I refer to the U.S. Senate, where power was disproportionately invested in a minority (southern defenders of Jim Crow); other constitutional and electoral arrangements that make third parties untenable; the generally conservative nature of the American electorate, especially on racial matters; and what Thomas Sugrue has called the "persistence of localism" in U.S. politics. See Robert A. Dahl, *How Democratic is the American Constitution?* (New Haven, Conn.: Yale University Press, 2002); and Thomas J. Sugrue, "The Persistence of Localism in Twentieth-Century America," in *The Democratic Experiment: New Directions in American Political History*, edited by Meg Jacobs et al. (Princeton, N.J.: Princeton University Press, 2003).

10. Kelley, *Freedom Dreams*, ix.

11. William Keylor, *The Twentieth-Century World: An International History*, 4th ed. (New York: Oxford University Press, 2001); Alan Brinkley, *The End of Reform: New Deal Liberalism in Recession and War* (New York: Knopf, 1995).

12. Roger Lotchin, *Fortress California, 1910–1961: From Warfare to Welfare* (New York: Oxford University Press, 1992); Bruce Schulman, *From Cotton Belt to Sunbelt: Federal Policy, Economic Development, and the Transformation of the South, 1938–1980* (Durham, N.C.: Duke University Press, 1994); Diane B. Kunz, *Butter and Guns: America's Cold War Economic Diplomacy* (New York: Free Press, 1997).
13. Singh, *Black Is a Country*, 6.
14. Alice Kessler-Harris, *In Pursuit of Equity: Men, Women, and the Quest for Economic Citizenship in Twentieth-Century America* (New York: Oxford University Press, 2001), 5.
15. *The Color Curtain: A Report on the Bandung Conference* (Cleveland: World Publishing, 1956).
16. Singh, *Black Is a Country*; Singh, "Culture/Wars: Recoding Empire In an Age of Democracy," *American Quarterly* 50.3 (1998): 471–522.
17. Von Eschen, *Race against Empire: Black Americans and Anticolonialism, 1937–1957* (Ithaca, N.Y.: Cornell University Press, 1997); Singh, *Black Is a Country*; Kelley, *Freedom Dreams*.
18. This was especially the framework articulated by the two most influential documents of what might be called official midcentury liberal civil rights philosophy. Both were products of either black scholarship or black political activism filtered through white-dominated perspectives and institutions. See Gunnar Myrdal, *An American Dilemma: The Negro Problem in American Democracy* (New York: Harper and Row, 1962 [1944]); President's Committee on Civil Rights, *To Secure These Rights: The Report of the President's Committee on Civil Rights* (New York: Simon and Schuster, 1947).
19. Again, see Singh's *Black Is a Country*.
20. Scholarly treatments of American exceptionalism include Charles Bergquist, *Labor and the Course of American Democracy: U.S. History in Latin American Perspective* (London: Verso, 1996); Deborah Madsen, *American Exceptionalism* (Jackson: University Press of Mississippi, 1998); and Singh, *Black Is a Country*.
21. W. E. B. Du Bois, "Peace: Freedom's Road for Oppressed People," in *W. E. B. DuBois: A Reader*, edited by David Levering Lewis (New York: Henry Holt, 1995), 752.
22. Mary L. Dudziak, *Cold War Civil Rights: Race and the Image of American Democracy* (Princeton, N.J.: Princeton University Press, 2000); Thomas Borstelmann, *The Cold War and the Color Line: American Race Relations and the Global Arena* (Cambridge, Mass.: Harvard University Press, 2001).
23. Dona Cooper Hamilton and Charles V. Hamilton, *The Dual Agenda: The African American Struggle for Civil and Economic Equality* (New York: Columbia University Press, 1997).
24. On the welfare state, see Michael K. Brown, *Race, Money, and the American Welfare State* (Ithaca, N.Y.: Cornell University Press, 1999); Adolph Reed Jr., ed., *Without Justice for All: The New Liberalism and Our Retreat from Racial Equality* (Boulder, Colo.: Westview Press, 1999); Mark Gelfand, *A Nation of Cities: The Federal Government and Urban America, 1933–1965* (New York: Oxford University Press, 1975);

and Thomas F. Jackson, "The State, the Movement, and the Urban Poor: The War on Poverty and Political Mobilization in the 1960s," in *The "Underclass" Debate: Views from History*, edited by Michael Katz (Princeton, N.J.: Princeton University Press, 1993), 403–39. On independence movements and U.S. civil rights, see Von Eschen, *Race against Empire*; Carol Anderson, *Eyes Off the Prize: The United Nations and the African American Struggle for Human Rights, 1944–1955* (New York: Cambridge University Press, 2003); James H. Meriwether, *Proudly We Can Be Africans: Black Americans and Africa, 1935–1961* (Chapel Hill: University of North Carolina Press, 2002); Brenda Gayle Plummer, *Rising Wind: Black Americans and U.S. Foreign Affairs, 1935–1960* (Chapel Hill: University of North Carolina Press, 1996), and *Window on Freedom: Race, Civil Rights, and Foreign Affairs, 1945–1988* (Chapel Hill: University of North Carolina Press, 2003); and Thomas Borstelmann, *Apartheid's Reluctant Uncle: The United States and Southern Africa in the Early Cold War* (New York: Oxford University Press, 1993).

25. Martha Biondi, *To Stand and Fight: The Struggle for Civil Rights in Postwar New York City* (Cambridge, Mass.: Harvard University Press, 2003), 272–73.

26. Ibid., 9, 12, 18, 117–18, 272–73.

27. Self, *American Babylon*, 10–14.

28. Gelfand, *A Nation of Cities*; Barry Bluestone and Bennett Harrison, *The Deindustrialization of America: Plant Closings, Community Abandonment, and the Dismantling of Basic Industry* (New York: Basic Books, 1982); Susan S. Fainstein and Norman I. Fainstein, "Economic Change, National Policy, and the System of Cities," in *Restructuring the City: The Political Economy of Urban Redevelopment*, edited by Susan S. Fainstein et al. (New York: Longman, 1983); Robert O. Self and Thomas J. Sugrue, "The Power of Place: Race, Political Economy, and Identity in the Postwar Metropolis," in Rosenzweig and Agnew, eds., *Companion to Post-1945 America*.

29. Brown, *Race, Money, and the American Welfare State*; Hamilton and Hamilton, *The Dual Agenda*; Self, *American Babylon*.

30. Robin D. G. Kelley and Betsy Esch, "Black Like Mao: Red China and the Black Revolution," *Souls* (fall 1999): 6–41.

31. Johanna Fernandez, "Between Social Service Reform and Revolutionary Politics: The Young Lords, Late Sixties Radicalism, and Community Organizing in New York City," in Theoharis and Woodard, eds., *Freedom North*, 255.

32. Bluestone and Harrison, *The Deindustrialization of America*; John T. Cumbler, *A Social History of Economic Decline: Business, Politics, and Work in Trenton* (New Brunswick, N.J.: Rutgers University Press, 1989); Douglas Massey and Nancy Denton, *American Apartheid: Segregation and the Making of the Underclass* (Cambridge, Mass.: Harvard University Press, 1993); Robin D. G. Kelley, *Yo' Mama's Disfunktional! Fighting the Culture Wars in Urban America* (Boston: Beacon Press, 1997); Thomas J. Sugrue, *Origins of the Urban Crisis: Race and Inequality in Postwar Detroit* (Princeton, N.J.: Princeton University Press, 1996); Stephen Gregory, *Black Corona: Race and the Politics of Place in an Urban Community* (Princeton, N.J.: Princeton University Press, 1998).

33. Thomas J. Sugrue, "The Structures of Urban Poverty: The Reorganization of Space

and Work in Three Periods of American History," in Katz, ed., *The "Underclass" Debates: View from History*; Wendell Pritchett, *Brownsville, Brooklyn: Blacks, Jews, and the Changing Face of the Ghetto* (Chicago: University of Chicago Press, 2002); Heather Ann Thompson, *Whose Detroit? Politics, Labor, and Race in a Modern American City* (Ithaca, N.Y.: Cornell University Press, 2001); Edward Banfield, *The Unheavenly City: The Nature and Future of Our Urban Crisis* (Boston: Little, Brown, 1968).

34. Arnold Hirsch, *Making the Second Ghetto: Race and Housing in Chicago, 1940–1960* (New York: Cambridge University Press, 1983); Sugrue, *Origins of the Urban Crisis*; Jon Teaford, *The Rough Road to Renaissance: Urban Revitalization in America, 1940–1985* (Baltimore: Johns Hopkins University Press, 1990); Lisa McGirr, *Suburban Warriors: The Origins of the New American Right* (Princeton, N.J.: Princeton University Press, 2001); Becky Nicolaides, *My Blue Heaven: Life and Politics in the Working-Class Suburbs of Los Angeles, 1920–1965* (Chicago: University of Chicago Press, 2002); Kenneth D. Durr, *Behind the Backlash: White Working-Class Politics in Baltimore, 1940–1980* (Chapel Hill: University of North Carolina Press, 2003).

35. Alice O'Connor, *Poverty Knowledge: Social Science, Social Policy, and the Poor in Twentieth-Century U.S. History* (Princeton, N.J.: Princeton University Press, 2001); Stow Persons, *Ethnic Studies at Chicago, 1905–1945* (Urbana: University of Illinois Press, 1987).

36. St. Clair Drake and Horace Cayton, *Black Metropolis: A Study of Negro Life in a Northern City* (Chicago: University of Chicago Press, 1993 [1945]); O'Connor, *Poverty Knowledge*.

37. Holloway, *Confronting the Veil*.

38. Du Bois quoted in Singh, *Black Is a Country*, 74.

39. Singh, *Black Is a Country*, 74; Cheryl Lynn Greenberg, *"Or Does It Explode?" Black Harlem in the Great Depression* (New York: Oxford University Press, 1991); Davarian Baldwin, "Chicago's New Negroes: Race, Class and Respectability in the Midwestern Black Metropolis, 1915–1935" (Ph.D. diss., New York University, 2002).

40. Singh, *Black Is a Country*, 63–66.

41. Biondi, *To Stand and Fight*, 43–47.

42. Von Eschen, *Race against Empire*; Singh, *Black Is a Country*; Biondi, *To Stand and Fight*.

43. Von Eschen, *Race against Empire*; Meriwether, *Proudly We Can Be Africans*.

44. Robert O. Self, "'To Plan Our Liberation': Black Power and the Politics of Place in Oakland, California, 1965–1977," *Journal of Urban History* 26.6 (September 2000): 759–92; Carl Nightingale, "The Global Inner City: Toward a Historical Analysis," in *W. E. B. DuBois, Race, and the City: The Philadelphia Negro and Its Legacy*, edited by Michael Katz and Thomas Sugrue (Philadelphia: University of Pennsylvania Press, 1998), 217–58.

45. See, for instance, Floyd Barber, ed., *The Black Power Revolt* (Boston: Extending Horizons Books, 1968); Robert L. Allen, *A Guide to Black Power in America: An Historical Analysis* (London: Doubleday, 1969); and Whitney Young, *Beyond Racism: Building an Open Society* (New York: McGraw-Hill, 1969).

46. Singh, *Black Is a Country*, 85.
47. Letter dated 22 January 1976, Huey P. Newton Collection, Series 2, Box 41, Folder 5, Green Library, Stanford University (emphasis in original).
48. Self, *American Babylon*, 217–30.
49. Newton, *Revolutionary Suicide*, 73–74; Judith May, "Black Panthers," unpublished report, 8 May 1968, Oakland Project Interviews, Vol. 4, Institute for Government Studies, University of California, Berkeley (IGS); Kelley and Esch, "Black Like Mao"; Allen, *Guide to Black Power*.
50. Nightingale, "The Global Inner City," 218.
51. Newton, "Uniting against a Common Enemy" (23 October 1971), in *The Huey P. Newton Reader*, edited by David Hilliard and Donald Weise (New York: Seven Stories Press, 2001), 234–40.
52. Peck, "'Educate to Liberate.'"
53. Kathleen Neal Cleaver, "Back to Africa: The Evolution of the International Section of the Black Panther Party," in Jones, ed., *The Black Panther Party*, 211–51.
54. *The Black Panther*, 30 September 1972.
55. Pearson, *Shadow of the Panther*, 93–110; McKee quoted in the *San Francisco Chronicle*, 26 September 1971.
56. Hoover quoted in *Book III: Final Report of the Select Committee to Study Government Operations with Respect to Intelligence Activities*, S.R. No. 94–755, 94th Congress, 2d Sess., 1976, p. 188. The literature on the repression by the police and the FBI of the Black Panther Party is extensive. See Ward Churchill and Jim Vander Wall, *Agents of Repression*; Charles E. Jones, "The Political Repression of the Black Panther Party, 1966–1971: The Case of the Oakland Bay Area," *Journal of Black Studies* (June 1988): 415–21; Roy Wilkins and Ramsey Clark, *Search and Destroy: A Report by the Commission of Inquiry into the Black Panthers and the Police* (New York: Metropolitan Applied Research Center, 1973); and Winston A. Grady-Willis, "The Black Panther Party: State Repression and Political Prisoners," in Jones, ed., *The Black Panther Party*, 363–90.
57. JoNina Abron, "'Serving the People': The Survival Programs of the Black Panther Party," in Jones, ed., *The Black Panther Party*, 177–92.
58. Ibid.
59. Seale, *Seize the Time*, 86; *The Black Panther*, 3 January 1970; Pearson, *Shadow of the Panther*, 197–200; Hilliard, *This Side of Glory*, 182; Brown, *Taste of Power*. On survival programs in New Haven, see Williams, *Black Politics/White Power*; on the survival programs and gender in the Party, see the essays by JoNina M. Abron, Regina Jennings, Tracye Matthews, and Angela LeBlanc-Ernest in Jones, ed., *The Black Panther Party*; and Adolph Reed Jr., "Response to Eric Arneson," *International Labor and Working-Class History* (fall 2001): 69–80.
60. Reed, *Stirrings in the Jug: Black Politics in the Post-Segregation Era* (Minneapolis: University of Minnesota Press, 1999), 277–78.

PART TWO The Panthers as American Revolutionaries

Introductory Comment

The Panthers and the Question of Violence

ROD BUSH

We tend to forget how deeply we are influenced by our biographies. However, too often our historical reflections are colored by our present preoccupations. In light of this, the post-1960s conservative "backlash" should not be allowed to expunge the context within which the Black Panther Party (BPP) operated. Only by grasping the drama of that historical moment can we understand the role that violence played in the origins, nature, and development of one of the most misunderstood movements of modern times.

The 1960s was a period of world revolution. The insurrectionary mood among common people tempered the corrosive and socially degrading power of corporate capitalism and boldly challenged the presumptions of global white supremacy. People of color all over the world rose up to claim their place in the human family as full and respected members of the world community. Malcolm X heralded this rising — of what was called the "dark world" — as "the end of white world supremacy."[1] He pointed out that the black revolution in the United States was not the rebellion of a minority but rather a part of the worldwide struggle of the oppressed against the oppressor. The great Chinese revolutionary Mao Zedong agreed with this view. He argued that the evil system of imperialism began with the enslavement of African Americans, and it would surely end with their complete liberation.[2] The Black Panther Party was thus part of a larger movement that illuminated the landscape with its fresh understanding of the world and its vision that ordinary people who had been victims of the most ruthless exploitation and degradation could collectively create a world that was egalitarian, democratic, and just. However, the Panthers' heroic and sometimes foolish actions brought down on their collective necks the full power of the iron fist of American imperialism, while their more moderate cohorts were courted and seduced into working at integrating black people into the system.

Of course, the Panthers worked "within the system" from the very beginning: lawfully carrying guns as they "patrolled the police"; lobbying for street lights at dangerous intersections; running for state and national office on the Peace and Freedom Party ticket; organizing "survival programs pending revolution"; and registering black people to vote. Indeed, their electoral strategy in Oakland in the 1970s would culminate in the election of the first black mayor in the city's history.[3] But, again, this must be seen within the proper historical context in what Henry Luce dubbed the American Century, which was characterized in part by a mature global liberalism that promised the spread of the Good Society followed by the Great Society to all Americans and eventually to all in the world who followed America's example and direction. At the same time, the civil rights movement sounded the central themes of democratization, equal rights, and social justice. Martin Luther King Jr., for example, skillfully articulated a vision of the American Dream that captured the imaginations of tens of millions of Americans of all colors and creeds. His challenge that America should work to live up to what it professed was thus viewed by many as a call to complete the great unfinished American Revolution. Malcolm X for his part was skeptical; he had listened carefully to the voices of millions of black people who lived outside the Jim Crow South yet were deeply alienated from the white mainstream. He helped to call the nation's attention to these marginalized masses by speaking in their voice and by helping them to do the same. The consequent eloquence, with that of "the barefoot people in the jungles of Vietnam," drew King closer to Malcolm's view. By the end of his life, King would say that American power constituted a nightmarish ordeal for the world's have-nots and for many of the most disadvantaged people of color within America's national borders.[4]

Meanwhile even in the early 1960s, during the most idealistic period of America's global liberalism, the youthful rebels of the Students for a Democratic Society (SDS) were arguing for a radical democratization of society. Then, the rebellion against American hegemony, manifested in struggles in Vietnam, Algeria, Cuba, China, Ghana, Guinea, and other parts of three continents, combined with the struggle of oppressed strata within the United States to undermine the largesse of the liberal state. The *rapports de force* had shifted decisively in favor of the colonized, semicolonized, and dependent zones of the world economy occupied in the main by people of color. Not only did Malcolm and SDS call for solidarity with the revolutionaries of the three continents, but they were joined by the Student Nonviolent Coordinating Committee (SNCC), the Congress of Racial Equality (CORE), and King himself, along with a host of other activist organizations and leaders. And, furthermore, they urged Americans themselves to become a part of this elemental rebellion.

In the more conservative twenty-first century atmosphere of neoliberal globalization and the neoconservative Project for a New American Century, it is easy to forget (and even difficult to comprehend) a time when subaltern groups across the globe challenged American hegemony, with many by the late sixties believing victory was within sight. Yet what was truly remarkable about this period was the depth of support within the United States for these movements as arrayed in opposition to the nation's own ruling class. This kind of internationalism had been a regular feature of large sections of the black freedom struggle and of the world socialist movement throughout the century. But, now it was the dominant position of large sections of the population of the hegemonic power.

Max Elbaum, in the opening pages of his *Revolution in the Air*, describes this moment as one in which "all society was a battleground."[5] Here, he captures the essence of this period by pointing out that the power of the post-1968 New Left stemmed in part from its all-important recognition "that the power of the oppressed was on the rise and the strength of the status quo was on the wane."[6] By fall 1968, one million students saw themselves as part of the Left and many longed for a mass revolutionary party. Among African Americans, revolutionary sentiments contended not just for influence but for preeminence, especially among those under the age of thirty, as more than three hundred rebellions flared up among inner-city blacks from 1964 to 1968. Then, with Richard Nixon's brutal invasion of Cambodia in April 1970 came the largest explosion of protest on college campuses in the nation's history. As *Business Week* lamented at the time, "the invasion of Cambodia and the senseless shooting of four students at Kent State University in Ohio have consolidated the academic community against the war, against business, and against government. This is a dangerous situation. It threatens the whole economic and social structure of the nation."[7] By the early 1970s, polls reported that upward of 40 percent of college students

—nearly three million of them—and a majority of young blacks thought that a revolution was necessary in the United States.

The background of the period's tenor of revolution is necessary to understand the meaning and significance of the work of the lawyer-turned-professor Bridgette Baldwin in her chapter "In the Shadow of the Gun." By turning traditional interpretations upside down—that is, by seeing the Panthers as either a self-defense group that became revolutionary or, more commonly, as a violent criminal gang from the beginning—Baldwin places the group squarely in the tradition of American revolutionary self-defense of rights raised by those who broke away from England in the late eighteenth century. That is, she rejects the commonsense distinction between admissible "defensive" strategy and unacceptable "offensive strategy" (which risks losing sight of what Fernand Braudel calls "social time") and places the Panthers squarely in the American grain. In working in this manner, Baldwin's thesis mirrors the Panthers' own originality and daring.[8]

Baldwin's essay skillfully documents how the Party built its case for the "right of revolution" on the basis of the anticolonial struggle waged against the British, as well as on what she views as the Constitutional guarantee to the right of self-defense. But her evidence and argument go further to suggest that when the Panthers undertook a revolutionary struggle on behalf of an aggrieved African American population, they did so on Constitutional grounds. Baldwin supports this striking thesis by looking broadly at the BPP program in the context of the conditions under which African American people lived during the 1960s and 1970s. Her argument that the period between 1967 and 1970 was one of intense repression of black communities in which the Panthers legitimately exercised their right to defend those communities illuminates how they operated solidly within the American mode while adding to it a vibrant and transformative element. Their demands included those "inalienable rights" articulated in the Declaration of Independence, and only when oppressed groups have fought for them have these rights been achieved.

Baldwin thus captures a crucial dimension of the Panthers' self-defense activities: they sought street credibility with urban black youth and later with Third World revolutionaries. While Baldwin recognizes that such activities carried a cost—for example, the view held by the white mainstream of the Panthers obsessed with irrational violence—she also notes that the Panther leadership had adopted weapons in part as an organizing strategy. Thus, she quotes Panther Chairman Bobby Seale on the relationship between picking up the gun and social revolution: "We knew that at first the guns would be more valuable and more meaningful to the brothers on the block, for drawing them into the organization."[9]

Baldwin's close attention to the BPP's arsenal of strategy and tactics allows her to point out that the Panthers used pragmatic and individualistic rhetoric that both accessed and critiqued the language of the Constitution. Thus, as she reminds us, they considered their approach to U.S. and local governing authorities as "absolutely legal." Indeed, the BPP legal framework must be understood as but one component of their overarching goal of anticolonial revolution, a revolution portrayed as one that closely tracked the American Revolution itself. For, though the American resistance to British colonialism often took the form of nonviolent resistance, "they also engaged in acts of violent resistance, explicitly understood as self-defense."

While some argue that the Panthers became more reformist after they dropped "Self-Defense" from their organizational name, Baldwin insists that the concept of self-defense was expanded in the process of doing so. In this context, the so-called survival programs could be seen as a defense against various kinds of violence, such as massive black unemployment or inadequate health care. The Revolutionary People's Constitutional Convention (RPCC) was set in Philadelphia in 1970 deliberately as a symbolic return to the scene of the original sanctioning of the second-class citizenship of African American people. Although the RPCC did not succeed in altering the Constitution, it did set the stage for subsequent strategies for fundamental change within the nation. The efforts of the BPP, like no other organization, thus revealed the contradictory status of democracy within the United States during the 1960s and 1970s. But what is most remarkable and revealing about Baldwin's thesis is that the BPP participated legally in the system, leaving a critical legacy for black people and for Americans more generally.[10]

The brutality of Jim Crow as a system of social control of African Americans caused both resistance (the civil rights movement) and flight (migration to the North, the Midwest, and the West Coast). At the end of their journey, however, the migrants did not reach the Promised Land but rather another system of social control: the black ghetto.[11] Although the ghetto was less rigid than the Jim Crow South, it was no less constricting and all-encompassing. But the ghetto proved to be a double-edged sword, for while it constrained those southerners of African descent who migrated, it also concentrated them in such a way that forced them to build their own institutions much more broadly and enhanced their sense of being a "nation within a nation." It was this social situation that fostered the historical evolution of the New Negro Movement, which gave us the Garvey movement, the African Blood Brotherhood (a group much like the BPP), the *Messenger*, the Harlem Renaissance, and the Nation of Islam. Later, the southern civil rights movement would emerge and capture the support and imaginations of people around the nation as well as in many other parts of the world. The southern movement also dramatically altered the *rapports de force* within the United States in favor of an insurgent black population whose radicalism deepened with a revival of the radical nationalist movements that had so often inhabited the black ghetto. At the same time, the two most prestigious leaders of Afro-America, Malcolm and King, articulated revolutionary solidarity with the oppressed of the three continents.

This created a unique historical conjuncture similar in many ways to the New Negro Movement of the post–World War I period and the Popular Front movements of the 1930s and 1940s (e.g., the Negro National Congress and the Council on African Affairs), but one in which the rearrangement of power relations favorable to the disadvantaged appeared to be stronger than ever before in American history. Because of America's preeminent world position, the movements of the 1960s seemed to be a prelude to the redistribution of global power called for by Malcolm and King, SNCC, and the Revolutionary Action Movement. At the center of this, for a time, was the Black Panther Party, which came of age precisely as the rebellion of the masses crested in the black urban ghettos of the North, Midwest, and along the Pacific Coast. Further, oppressed people from all walks of life began to seek entry into this coalition. In the meantime, FBI director J. Edgar Hoover argued that the civil rights movement was the leading edge of a social revolution and thus had to be destroyed.[12] By late 1968, he would place the Panthers at the top of his list of targets.[13]

The liberal establishment that had supported a moderate civil rights agenda to that moment was politically marginalized as the ruling class responded to this threat. The right came to power under a racist law-and-order doctrine because the ghettos were no longer able to contain their inhabitants of color. The story of the rise and fall of the Black Panther Party was a part of the rise of this moment of revolution and repression—the sharpest such moment in American history. The power of the people seemed everywhere on the rise, and the power of established social groups was under challenge. The Panther story was inextricably intertwined with the beginning of this structural crisis of world capitalism. To their credit, they attempted to prepare oppressed strata to wage the struggle for a new historical system. That such a struggle would be a long one the Panther leadership seemed to know well, though the rapid pace of events during the revolution of 1968 could have led them to believe that the revolutionary seizure of power might come sooner rather than later. But, those were heady days, and in other historical periods revolutionary forces have been fooled by the pace of events. Indeed, Marx, Engels, and Lenin all foretold the obsolescence of capitalism during their own times.

The current ongoing counterrevolution of the conservative forces does not lessen the historical significance of this revolutionary period — or of the Panthers who were at the center of it — although it has dramatically altered the momentum of the movement more generally. In this context, the tendency is to remember, and exaggerate, the mistakes made; but we should beware of assuming that we are in the midst of a long-term conservative hegemony. The disputed outcomes of both the 2000 and 2004 presidential elections, the terrorist attack of September 11, 2001, and the launching of several preemptive wars all serve as symbols of the long-term decline of U.S. power. And, though I write in the immediate aftermath of the controversial 2004 presidential election, the controversy itself is indicative that we are on the cusp of a new day. The massive activation of the electorate on both sides, and the social and demographic trends that in fact are moving away from the base of the conservative faction, eventually will return us to the ground laid by the Black Panther Party.

While the BPP talked about the need for self-defense, we should beware of overemphasizing the role of violence, even "revolutionary violence," in the Panther program. While the willingness to use violence to defend the black community against attacks by the local police forces was important in reinforcing the notion that black people had the right to defend themselves against authorities who had a monopoly on the legitimate use of force, bringing to a halt the violent acts of local law enforcement agencies was in the final analysis to be achieved by political means and not by military means. For it was not military struggle that was the main goal of the BPP's revolutionary program, rather it was to promote the power of the people; the ability of black communities to fight on their own behalf and to unify with other social forces. This is a lesson that we should take from the experience of the Black Panther Party into this period of transition where our efforts will be key to constructing a new historical system. With this view as our lodestar, we can build the economic, political, cultural, and social institutions that will manifest our commitment to a society that places in the center of its efforts the attempt to grant "All Power to the People."

Notes

1. Malcom X, *The End of White World Supremacy* (New York: Merlin House, 1971), 130.
2. Mao Zedong, "Oppose Racial Discrimination by U.S. Imperialism," in *The Political Thought of Mao Tse Tung*, edited by Stuart Schram (New York: Praeger, 1969), 409–12.
3. Rod Bush, "Oakland: Grassroots Organizing against Reagan," in *The New Black Vote: Politics and Power in Four American Cities*, edited by Rod Bush (San Francisco: Synthesis Publications, 1984), 315–74.
4. Vincent Harding, *Martin Luther King: The Inconvenient Hero* (New York: Orbis Books, 1996), 18–21.
5. Max Elbaum, *Revolution in the Air: Sixties Radicals Turn to Lenin, Mao and Che* (London: Verso, 2002).
6. Ibid., 2.
7. Quoted in ibid., 18–19.
8. Fernand Braudel, "History and the Social Sciences: The *longue duree*," in *Economy and Society in Early Modern Europe*, edited by Peter Burke (London: Routledge, 1972).
9. Baldwin, "In the Shadow of the Gun," this volume.
10. Baldwin here is reminiscent of another lawyer/scholar/activist from this period—namely, Kenneth Cockrel of the Dodge Revolutionary Union Movement and the League of Revolutionary Black Workers. Cockrel took the same kind of macrosociological approach to analyzing the legal system, which resonated brilliantly with the juries of the peers of the accused. His record of success in trial was therefore nothing short of astounding. Baldwin's contribution seems to indicate promise for the rise of another such great scholar/lawyer/activist.
11. Loic Wacquant, "Slavery to Mass Incarceration," *New Left Review* 52 (January/February 2002): 13, 33–40, 41–60.
12. Kenneth O'Reilly, *"Racial Matters": The FBI's Secret File on Black America, 1960–1972* (New York: Free Press, 1989), 125–55, 355–59; U.S. Senate, 94th Congress, 2d Session, *Supplementary Detailed Staff Reports on Intelligence Activities and the Rights of Americans. Book III: Final Report of the Select Committee to Study Governmental Operations with Respect to Intelligence Activities* (Washington, D.C.: U.S. Government Printing Office, 1976), 81–184.
13. U.S. Senate, 94th Congress, 2d Session, *Supplementary Detailed Staff Reports*, 187–88.

In the Shadow of the Gun: The Black Panther Party, the Ninth Amendment, and Discourses of Self-Defense

BRIDGETTE BALDWIN

In spite of the British conviction that Americans had no right to establish their own laws to promote the general welfare of the people living here in America, the colonized immigrant felt he had no choice but to raise the gun to defend his welfare. . . . Now these same colonized White people, these bondsmen, paupers, and thieves, deny the colonized Black man not only the right to abolish this oppressive system, but to even speak of abolishing it.

— Huey P. Newton, "In Defense of Self-Defense"

I say violence is necessary. It is as American as cherry pie.

— H. Rap Brown, press conference, 27 July 1967

Even in the newly emerging scholarship on the Black Panther Party (BPP) most accounts begin and end with the standard portrait of an organization of angry and violent black revolutionaries. Interspersed between descriptions of their official uniform—"black berets, black leather jackets, black trousers, and shiny black shoes"—and their penchant for back talk in interacting with white authority, looms the most common symbol associated with the Panthers: their supposed fetish for the gun. Even journalist Gene Marine's sympathetic early account, *The Black Panthers*, sensationally advertised the Panthers' supposed agenda as "UNIFORMED, ARMED MEN IN AMERICA! BLACK MEN WHO TALK BACK—AND SHOOT BACK!"[1] However, this one-dimensional portrait tells only half the story of the paradoxically street conscious and yet "book smart" "Bad Niggas." In their decision to pick up the gun, they simultaneously waged both legal and street battles for the control and self-defense of black communities; battles that extended beyond a simple debate on the right to bear arms guaranteed in the Second Amendment.[2]

Disentangling the Panthers' image from the substantive legal issues raised by their efforts is a troublesome business, precisely because of how deeply that image is imbedded in both public and historical memory. Alongside figures ranging from Stagolee to Muhammad Ali, the pantheon of "Bad Nigga" black heroes includes Huey Newton, who combined both pimp and paramilitary imagery in his infamous photo in a high-back wicker chair, brandishing an African spear in one hand and a rifle in the other — the iconographic metaphor for armed black self-determination in the late 1960s and early 1970s. In particular, this BPP image in the white mind foregrounds memories of that "fateful" day in 1967 when armed male and female Black Panthers ascended the steps of the California state capitol building in Sacramento to protest a bill aimed directly at their constitutional right to bear arms. With the fully repressed reportage of white gun lobbyists who were also there in protest, the mainstream media created a national imagined community of racial fear with headlines like "Blacks with guns invading the legislature."[3] To be sure, the Party's fight for the right to possess firearms was not mere performative protest or political principle alone. Armed confrontations took place throughout the nation, with police but also with Black Nationalists like Maulana Karenga's Us. At the same time, the national spotlight that shone down on those Sacramento steps also created sympathy for, and even allegiance with, the BPP's fight for equal protection under the law, especially among those engaged in parallel struggles for black and working-class self-determination.

From the outset, as well as in retrospect, the Panthers' conscious posture and performance of armed self-defense garnered both positive outcomes (street credibility with urban black youth and, later, Third World revolutionaries) and negative consequences (a distorted image of the BPP as a revolutionary "gang" obsessed with irrational violence).[4] However, historical memory and scholarship are just beginning to open wide enough to locate the Panthers within the more complex social context and theoretical frameworks in which they actually existed and, most important, helped to create.[5] Unbeknownst to many, the BPP's more comprehensive discourse of self-defense, including armed resistance and community "survival programs," were derived from both an international Third World anticolonial context and a national American constitutional one. Although the Panthers did not directly argue their case along such lines, they employed a language as much in line with the Ninth Amendment's preservation of inalienable rights as they did with the more celebrated rhetoric, "By any means necessary." A close analysis of the Panther argument for self-defense reveals one of the clearest articulations in the history of American radicalism of the inalienable "other rights" referred to in that amendment.

The Panthers and the U.S. Constitution: The Legal Theory

Though BPP members may not have thought about the Ninth Amendment as legal justification for their acts of self-defense, they did read, use, and work within the bounds of the U.S. Constitution as a weapon equal to the gun. They brandished both firearms and copies of the Bill of Rights on police patrol. The Declaration of Independence is liberally quoted in their Ten-Point Platform and Program, "What We Want, What We Believe." And, their People's Constitutional Convention of 1970 was a direct attempt to remake the Constitution itself. In the end, their persistent use of the "mother country-colony" metaphor helped structure their vision of black communities under siege and in need of armed self-defense as one part of their larger program for self-determination. Such an approach aligned them with and drew from Third World revolutionary struggles against white nationalist colonialism, but it also tested the limits of the right of black people to an American legacy of armed resistance against despotism that established socio-legal parameters for the U.S. Constitution.

To be sure, within the Party there was no unified position on the means and meanings of self-defense, as demonstrated by the rift between Huey Newton and Eldridge Cleaver that broke into the open in early 1971. For that rift occurred precisely over self-defense as community protection and development versus self-defense as guerrilla warfare.[6] Still, the Panthers' conscious theorizing and application of self-defense, no matter how sensationally represented or vigorously debated internally, remains an important legacy: a politically radical organization attempted to access constitutionally protected rights to forge community autonomy, seek self-determination, and even bear arms in the face of legally sanctioned injustice. Moreover, the Panthers' deliberate use of the Constitution offers an important starting point for reconsidering the Ninth Amendment as a viable resource for resistance in general terms. It is indeed striking that both the American revolutionaries of the late eighteenth century and the Black Panther revolutionaries of the late twentieth emerged within a context of "colonial" occupation and, from there, devised similar theories of armed self-defense as an expression of self-determination and governance. Through the specific lens of the Ninth Amendment, even the BPP's most controversial acts of armed self-defense were not simply rational or morally justified but constitutionally legal.

In his first of many treatises, Huey Newton's "In Defense of Self-Defense" drew directly from the language and laws of the newly formed United States of America in formulating the program he and Bobby Seale devised almost exactly two hundred years later.[7] The historiography of the American Revolutionary period may be complex and contested, but the Panthers understood it elementally as an era of vigorous struggle between the British mother country and its American colonial outpost. American colonists faced restricted political representation in decision-making about their lives and property and were subjected to legal acts that sanctioned what they perceived as unjust and excessive economic taxation. The founding father John Hancock summarized such one-sided government when he proclaimed, "They have undertaken to give and grant our money without our consent."[8] The colonists responded with nonviolent protest but also engaged in acts of violent resistance, explicitly understood as self-defense. In the face of colonial occupation, Samuel Adams wrote, "If existence . . . is at stake, it is lawful to resist the highest authority."[9] His cousin and the future president, John Adams, concluded that "insurrection is always due to despotism from the government" and, further, that it served as legitimate resistance against a colonial regime.[10] In the words of the modern constitutional historian A. J. Langguth, Revolutionary-era boycotts, riots, looting, and other acts of violent self-defense of the era were "legitimate . . . protest by an oppressed people."[11] The BPP would have agreed, noting in 1967 that "the colonized immigrant felt he had no choice but to raise the gun to defend his welfare. Simultaneously he made certain laws to ensure his protection from external and internal aggressions."[12]

The BPP, then, understood that the revolutionary ideas embodied in the Declaration of Independence and the Constitution emerged out of a larger moment of colonial oppression and resistance. During the writing of the Constitution, the thirteen colonies generally shared the goal of creating a united front. Yet, many were not willing to give over complete control to a new "federal" government. Some argued that if individual rights were not spelled out, they could be subjected to unfettered abuse by that government, while others feared that spelling out specific rights could imply that the states had fewer rights against the federal government than actually had been intended. To resolve the issue the Virginian delegate James Madison, who had initially opposed the addition of the amendments that would be called the Bill of Rights, suggested the addition of a clause dispelling the notion that states had given up any rights other than those specifically delegated to the new federal government. His proposal, later ratified in the form, "The enumeration . . . of certain rights, shall not be construed to deny . . . others retained by the people," became the Ninth Amendment.[13]

Indeed, that amendment was a key result of colonial resistance to British occupation. For both the context and language of this part of the Constitution rationalized the resistance of the 1760s and 1770s, and further "legalized" resistance on the very same grounds for any other citizen bound by its constitutionality. And, while legal scholars consider the Ninth Amendment a recent rediscovery, it has been an essential part of the Constitution since the ratification of the Bill of Rights in 1791.[14] Included in the first of those eight amendments were specific rights that the founding fathers believed were fundamental to humanity according to natural law. However, the history and text of the Ninth Amendment suggest that there were more rights reserved to the people than those articulated in Amendments one through eight. The very language used in the document — "certain rights, shall not be construed to deny or disparage others retained by the people" — made clear that the list in the other amendments was not exhaustive.[15] But, the language of the Ninth Amendment serves only as the *source* for these "other rights," leaving no clue as to what these rights might be.[16] Nevertheless, the existence of these "other rights" *preceded* the establishment of the new federal government.[17] Accordingly, many have argued (albeit unsuccessfully), under the Ninth Amendment certain "other rights" exist that not only prevent the federal government from infringing on states' rights, but also all other forms of government from usurping citizens' personal freedoms.[18]

In his essay I take the same theoretical ground in applying the argument to the history — in words and deed — of the Black Panther Party.[19] I do not, however, suggest that the Ninth Amendment "creates" enforceable constitutional rights.[20] Rather, I merely seek to illuminate the existence of these "other rights" deemed fundamental, now protected from state intrusion.[21] While the Bill of Rights originally applied restrictions on the federal government's power, the subsequent enactment of the Reconstruction amendments, particularly the Fourteenth Amendment, also prohibited the states from abridging inherent fundamental personal liberties.[22] To the extent that the Fourteenth Amendment incorporated the Bill of Rights, the "other rights" in the Ninth Amendment are not only applicable to the federal government but also to state police power.[23] Such rights exist within the "customary, traditional, and time-honored rights, amenities, privileges, and immunities . . . , which come within the meaning of the term 'liberty' as used in the Fourteenth Amendment."[24]

Again, there has been very little discussion about what "other rights" are guaranteed in the Ninth Amendment, and, in fact, the United States Supreme Court has never delivered a majority opinion based exclusively on the text of the Ninth Amendment.[25] Yet in some court cases the amendment has been considered to confirm the existence of rights that are not provided in the first eight amendments. Justice Goldberg, concurring in *Griswold v. Connecticut*, for example, devoted several pages to the Ninth Amendment: "The language and history of the Ninth Amendment reveal that the Framers of the Constitution believed that there are additional fundamental rights, protected from governmental infringement, which exist alongside those fundamental rights specifically mentioned in the first eight constitutional amendments. . . . The Ninth Amendment shows a belief of the Constitution's authors that fundamental rights exist that are not expressly enumerated in the first eight amendments and an intent that the list of rights included there not be deemed exhaustive."[26] The Ninth Amendment has also emerged as a new textual source for other constitutional rights. By example, it has been used to argue for equal treatment for gays and lesbians,[27] rights to employment,[28] visitation rights for children,[29] and the right to transport "obscene materials" for private use.[30]

Most notably, in *Griswold* Justice Douglas used the Ninth Amendment to grant the right to marital privacy.[31] Douglas opined that "specific guarantees in the Bill of Rights have penumbras, formed by emanations from those guarantees that help give them life and substance."[32] Indeed, he used the Ninth Amendment to advance the idea that fundamental rights are protected by an indefinite source of constitutional provisions, despite the absence of any specific reference to these in the document itself. Still, thus far the Ninth

Amendment has never been used to justify what might be considered "acts of violence." However, locating such acts within their social and historical context, as in the case of the BPP and much like the case of the framers of the Constitution, forces a reconsideration of traditional understandings of the Ninth Amendment. It also throws the Panthers and their historical moment into a new light.

Critically, the constitutional protection against the newly established government of the late eighteenth century through "other rights" not found in the first eight amendments is not a gift offered by the Ninth Amendment. Rather, it serves as recognition of the existence of other fundamental and inalienable rights. For this reason, the Ninth Amendment's conception — and its social and legislative context — did become a source of inspiration for later anticolonial struggles. Further, even if it were not referred to directly, the meaning embodied in the amendment offered legal precedent for later acts of self-defense and demands for self-determination. For example, there are striking similarities between the Revolutionary period and what, almost exactly two hundred years later, would be called the Black Power era. Appropriately, in the late 1960s BPP leader Eldridge Cleaver suggested that "there are two things happening in this country. You have a black colony and you have a white mother country and you have two different sets of political dynamics. . . . What's called for in the mother country is a revolution and there's a black liberation called for in the black colony."[33] When 1960s colonial occupants within the United States interpreted struggles and devised solutions for freedom, they did so at least partly in the language of America's own anticolonial Revolutionary moment.

The BPP emerged during a watershed moment of mass violence — a period of mass violence coming on the heels of centuries of racial violence enacted by state agents and private citizens against communities of color. These acts in turn inspired more-pronounced arguments for black self-determination through armed self-defense. Such arguments not only encompassed but also extended beyond the philosophies generated in late-eighteenth-century colonial America. In the 1960s, black communities across America faced the combined violent forces of lynching, police brutality, unemployment, substandard housing, and inferior social services and educational facilities. Protests for justice and the simple right to life during the southern phase of the freedom struggle met dramatic forms of white retaliation — bombings, arson, beatings, murder. These violent responses were matched in force and effect by countless acts of state-sanctioned violence in the form of police brutality in appropriately described "war zones" during urban riots of the mid-1960s. The BPP's harnessing and reconceptualization of the Constitution, then, was sharpened by insights drawn from social movements that had already made connections between resistance struggles against open racist violence in the United States and colonialism in Africa, Asia, and Latin America. Local demands for an end to police brutality and an increase in social services, for example, were interpreted through Third World philosophies of self-determination in the creation of a more comprehensive project of self-defense against violence and structural abuse.[34]

The 1955 Bandung Conference of nonaligned nations set the stage for an alternative worldview outside a mode of strict Western capitalism or Eurocentric communism, and it would directly influence the BPP's notion of self-defense as explicitly anticolonial. Those in the so-called Third World had begun to make alliances among themselves, creating visions of liberation to combat colonialism and the fight against racism in overdeveloped countries like the United States. Mao Zedong's notion of abolishing the gun by picking it up, the revolutionary violence theories of Che Guevara and Frantz Fanon, and the actual armed revolutions in China, Cuba, and Africa offered activists a solution outside the purview of the emerging nonviolent hegemony taking hold in the United States. However, more popular memories of passive resistance had always existed uneasily alongside the realities of armed groups—including the Deacons for Defense and Justice in the Deep South and the Cambridge movement in the Chesapeake region—which had protected even the most nonviolent of protestors in such a violent world.[35]

At the same time, Robert Williams's organizing of armed self-defense groups in North Carolina against the Ku Klux Klan and the police was immortalized in black radical circles through his essays and his book *Negroes with Guns*. Williams eventually fled to Cuba for political asylum, where he developed an ideology of Black Nationalism and Third World internationalism and was elected provisional president of the Republic of New Africa. Finally, Malcolm X's self-defense ideology, "By any means necessary," his travels throughout the Third World, and his appeals to the United Nations to intervene on behalf of black people in the United States consolidated the American history of black armed resistance and anticolonial self-determination. Malcolm was especially appealing to the BPP because he embraced Fanon's idea of organizing the "lumpen proletariat" into revolutionaries through his more vernacular style of address, which was aimed directly at the so-called street brothers in the community. Moreover, all of these tendencies had made direct links between conditions in the United States and Third World. Foreshadowed by the Revolutionary Action Movement and echoed by the Dodge Revolutionary Union Movement in Detroit, the BPP's comprehensive strategy of self-defense grew out of this larger international revolutionary context. Black struggles for self-determination against racist community control in the United States were thus envisioned as but one plank of the larger platform of "decolonization" taking place throughout the world.[36]

By applying the "mother country/colony" or "internal colony" metaphor to black living conditions in U.S. cities, activists glimpsed the international proletarian likeness between, for example, Saigon and South Central (Los Angeles). For, as Newton acutely observed, "as the aggression of the racist American government escalates in Vietnam, the police agencies of America escalate the repression of Black people throughout the ghettos of America."[37] Urban conditions and race relations had been reimagined within a global context. Kwame Ture (né Stokely Carmichael) and Charles Hamilton's *Black Power* offered a conceptual structure to this more general analysis of U.S. urban "colonial" conditions by asserting that "exorbitant rents," police brutality, "uncollected garbage," and overall neglect in black communities were products of the "white power structure." From these conditions, they concluded, "Black people are legal citizens of the United States with, for the most part, the same *legal* rights as other citizens. Yet they stand as colonial subjects in relation to white society. Thus institutional racism has another name: colonialism."[38] This approach complicated inherent distinctions between the spatially demarcated race relations among "chocolate cities" and "vanilla suburbs" in the United States and the struggles between Third World colonies of color and European nations, as it sought a wider Third World solidarity. Most important, seeing black urban communities as internal colonies helped to make clear that the only response to systemic and state-sponsored neglect and attack was a comprehensive platform and program of self-determination. This larger anticolonial vision would have a direct impact on the Panthers' interpretation of the U.S. Constitution in the defense of these same black communities.

The revolutionary nationalist "internal colony" vision of the BPP, of course, was also descriptive of contemporary black-white relations in the United States — without, however, the demand for black secession.[39] Whereas the prescriptive approach of early American Revolutionaries and twentieth-century Third World anticolonial activists sought autonomy, the Panthers' internal colony metaphor illuminated actually existing relations in an attempt to gain proportionate representation and equal protection from *within* the nation-state. Thus, even their early armed police patrols were conceived, according to Newton, "within legal bounds."[40] Again, the BPP's application of an anticolonial critique to black urban conditions specified their larger program of self-determination as protection from governmental infringement as outlined in the Constitution. Specifically, their language and approach to armed self-defense, even if unintentional, was rooted in the language and history of the Ninth Amendment.

To grasp the theory behind the BPP's employment of constitutional rights generally, we must reconsider the meaning of, and guarantees in, the Ninth Amendment in the context of late-sixties America. The right to self-defense/preservation is, of course, an integral part of any notion of freedom in the United States, as outlined in the Declaration of Independence. This right, however, was not included in the language of the first eight amendments, even though it should be a constitutionally protected right.[41] In fact, scholars as early as Locke, Pufendorf, and Hobbes made arguments that self-defense is the "ultimate natural right."[42] Some have even asserted that it is a natural right that "might be used as evidence of" the type of right "originally understood to exist when the Ninth and Tenth Amendments were adopted."[43] Moreover, this argument runs, in order to determine which rights are fundamental, judges must look to the "traditions and conscience of our people" to determine whether a right is "so rooted . . . as to be ranked as fundamental."[44] The key issue, from this perspective, is whether a right "is of such a character that it cannot be denied without violating those 'fundamental principles of liberty and justice which lie at the base of all our civil and political institutions.'"[45] A reconsideration of the Ninth Amendment, then, offers constitutional appeal for the self-defense discourse of groups like the Black Panthers precisely because of their particular demand for individual rights and their desire to limit the exercise of abusive government power in the black community.

As noted above, according to the Ninth Amendment no state or federal government can deny constitutionally protected rights, even if these rights are not specifically mentioned in the Constitution. Legal scholars such as Thomas McAfee have argued that the Ninth Amendment was only meant to allow states to trump the federal government's authority and not individuals to trump state power.[46] But the amendment has a more expansive reach. It seems implausible that the founding fathers contemplated the unfettered abuse of citizens' rights by state officials while simultaneously prohibiting governmental infringement by federal officials. Any such interpretation would provide a constricted and limited interpretation of intent, as well as severely circumscribing the Fourteenth Amendment.[47]

While there is, of course, no other constitutional provision allowing individuals to defend against identified enemies, that right, like the right to marital privacy, might be considered fundamental and thus retained by the people under the Ninth Amendment.[48] The Constitution was founded on principles that were dedicated to the basic "rights of men." Clearly, in that document, slaves were not men with those basic rights. And yet it is also clear that "man" is a term that has been reinterpreted under the law over time. The "rights of man" rhetoric of the eighteenth century has been the ground on which many oppressed groups (including groups of women) have fought for inclusion in the American Republic. As such, black people might lay claim to the same rights and privileges in the Constitution as those for whites and not simply wait to see which rights whites were willing to give them.[49] In this same vein, the Ninth Amendment reference to "other rights" might indeed be wide enough to include self-defense. This plausible interpretation would reclassify many acts of self-defense deployed by the BPP as not only necessary but also constitutional. Further, if a reasonable understanding of the Ninth Amendment illustrates that self-defense is constitutionally sound, it might be said that, as the ex-Panther Sundiata Acoli states, "it also makes common sense."[50]

Of course, if we focus solely on Panther acts of armed self-defense, then the argument for a reconsideration of the meaning of the Ninth Amendment will appear displaced or even as a justification for random acts of violence. Yet the Panthers consistently regarded armed resistance as merely one part of their larger discourse of self-defense. When in 1971 Newton offered a critique of what he considered Cleaver's obsession with the gun, he emphatically stated that the BPP understood the need for self-defense in the face of a number of oppressing agents, "from armed police to capitalist exploiters."[51] By examining the relationship between the many components of the BPP's larger revolutionary project of self-defense, we will find them commensurate with the strategies and aims of the Constitution — its rights, justice, liberties, and freedoms.[52] Accordingly, a reconsideration of the meaning and significance of the Ninth Amendment suggests a striking paradox: the militant actions and revolutionary demands of the Black Panther Party were legitimate, reasonable, and within the bounds of the U.S. Constitution.

The Panthers and the Constitution: The History

While defenders of capitalism celebrated their system with the symbols of individualism and freedom, the Panthers condemned that system as a mode of production that reinforced what they called "community imperialism." For the economic structure that systematically violated individual rights in ways that specifically oppressed and targeted black communities needed dismantling. In the Panthers' vision, that would happen through a program of revolutionary nationalism in which economic wealth, social services, and political power were deployed in the people's interest. Their socialist political agenda demanded that the government allow black people to control the key institutions both affected by and located within their communities. Thus, the Panthers did not embrace black cultural nationalism because they insisted that integrating black faces or cultural styles into capitalist institutions would not alter the power relations of a socioeconomic system that prized private property and gross accumulation over the well-being of the citizenry.[53] At the same time, the BPP remained both politically idealistic and strategically practical. An often-overlooked aspect of its history is the use of a pragmatic individualist rhetoric that both accessed and critiqued the language of the Constitution. While socialist, the Party program, with its reprinting of the preamble to the Declaration of Independence, represented the group's commitment to the perhaps problematic preservation of individual natural rights in the black community. Moreover, a landmark intervention in political philosophy and policy on the part of oppressed people in the overdeveloped world — even if in style and substance indebted to other black groups — the program set the tone for a comprehensive vision of self-defense that was at its foundation. But, though pulling from Third World anticolonial struggles, as it was part of a larger appeal to the American state for self-determination from "community imperialism," it was self-consciously constitutionalist and conceived as perfectly legal.[54] Here, then, on the home front of a wider revolution, the Panthers sought the protection of individual natural rights defense from racially unequal surveillance and the suppression of livelihood in black communities.

The BPP addressed the fundamental needs of black people and demanded power to determine their own fate, full and meaningful employment, an end to exploitation, decent housing and education, exemption from military service for all black men, and freedom for all black "political" prisoners.[55] It also demanded an "education [for black people] that exposes the true nature of this decadent American Society. . . . [an] education that teaches [black people their] . . . true history and role in the present-day society." In addition, the BPP sought basic human resources, making it clear that those resources should be taken from the capitalists and controlled by black people within the black community. Finally, in insisting that oppression end immediately, the platform served as the basis for a course of action. As such, the Panther program embodied revolutionary ideology rooted in black political traditions and committed the Party to establishing fundamental change—within the legacy of the American Revolution.

When Newton and Seale substantiated their anticolonial demands, both legally and historically, by ending their platform with a long excerpt from the opening lines of the Declaration of Independence, they emphasized the words, "whenever any form of government becomes destructive . . . it is the right of the people to alter or to abolish it, and to institute a new government." Eighteenth-century colonial rebels and their crafting of a document that spoke of "abuses and usurpations" under "absolute despotism" thus resonated with what these twentieth-century black citizens saw in their urban communities on a daily basis. Importantly, the Declaration's discussion of "inalienable rights" also echoed the Ninth Amendment's language of the unenumerated "other rights" with which American citizens were to maintain individual rights in the face of encroaching governmental power. The American solution to "throw off such government" and "provide new guards for" the people's "security" provided the BPP with a foundation on which to act that was directly relevant to the issue of platform point seven: "An immediate end to POLICE BRUTALITY and MURDER of black people."

The clearest example of colonial-like racial inequality and unequal protection was state-sanctioned racial violence and, particularly in urban locales, police brutality. Thus, in using the internal colony metaphor, the BPP denounced "the racist police who come into our communities from outside and occupy them, patrolling, terrorizing, and brutalizing our people like a foreign army in a conquered land."[56] Accordingly, countless BPP posters and speeches made parallel demands for the United States, typically represented as a pig, to "get out of" Asia, Africa, Latin America, and the ghetto.[57] Thus, point seven was the first issue acted on by the Party. Newton and Seale well understood that police brutality in black communities constituted the clearest example of unequal protection under the law and exposed a fundamental opposition between the needs of the people and the interests of the state.

One of the most astute constitutional critiques of police occupation and practice appeared in the Party organ, the *Black Panther*, in late 1969.[58] Written by an apparent rank-and-file member under the byline "Candy," the essay, titled "Pigs-Panthers," refers directly to the Constitution and excerpts the language of the Declaration to insist that the people possess certain "inalienable rights." The combined use of America's founding documents in fact resonates with the language of the Ninth Amendment and its protection of rights that either preceded or were given in the Constitution. In fact, the only place in the Constitution with phrasing similar to the expression of inalienable rights outlined in the Declaration of Independence is in the Ninth Amendment. Candy notes that if as specified in the Constitution the people direct the actions of the government and "sanction its authority," then the police as the military arm of a governing few "have no right in our community." She charges the police with failing to live up to the Constitution, concluding that the BPP phrase "All Power to the People" was the conceptual basis on which America's founding fathers had built the Constitution.[59] In this way, Panther police patrols were a means of carrying a living Constitution — in defense of the people — out into the streets.

The BPP solution to state violence was the organization of "black self-defense groups" — police patrols — that would survey the (mis)conduct of police officers. The most controversial aspect of these patrols, and what is remembered most about them, is that those on patrol openly carried loaded weapons. While the idea of "niggers with guns" was seen as simply the opportunity to retaliate against unlawful police brutality, again this vision of armed self-defense was not divorced from a larger political philosophy.[60] Newton reasoned that because black people did not own the means of production (land or industrial power), they could not generate what he called a "political consequence" when their desires went unmet. In essence, they had political representatives but no power. The political consequence for an otherwise defenseless people, then, was what Newton called "Self-Defense Power."[61]

This threatening language sounded ominous, retaliatory, even vengeful, but in reality political action committees, like nation-states, can exact consequences. Moreover, the BPP "never used [their] guns to go into the white community to shoot up white people," or "claimed the right to indiscriminate violence."[62] Indeed, the Panthers criticized what they called the "traditional riots and insurrections" of the mid-1960s as antagonistic to the program of organized and systemic self-defense.[63] Picking up the gun was consistently presented as a revolutionary but defensive action in the face of police as an occupying imperial force, who claimed "the right to indiscriminate violence and practice[d] it everyday."[64]

In keeping with their political approach to armed self-defense, the Panthers consistently grounded in the Second Amendment and the California Constitution their critiques of the police and their right to create armed patrols.[65] On patrol, the Panthers carried more than just guns, despite what the media may have reported. They also had law books, cameras, and tape recorders. As important, perhaps, the meaning of the gun for these activists was complex. Drawing on the teachings of Mao, Newton consistently argued that "in order to get rid of the gun, it is necessary to take up the gun."[66] Simply put, black people had to create a *"community structure"* where "the people" had control of all local institutions, including law enforcement, whereas presently they were victims of all local institutions, most visibly the police.[67] At the same time, as an advertising, recruiting, and teaching tool, as well as an actual weapon, the gun was strategically central to what might be called the BPP's discourse of self-defense.

Even beneath the provocative "kill the pig" rhetoric, Cleaver, for example, maintained the language of the American Revolution in arguing that "black men know that they must pick up the gun, they must arm black people to the teeth, they must organize an army and confront the mother country with a most drastic consequence if she attempts to assert police power over the colony."[68] Standoffs between "a cadre of disciplined and armed Black men" and the police over their conduct endeared the Party to local black communities and attracted the so-called street brothers to a politically engaged vision of revolutionary violence and defiance of authority.[69] However, in advocating the propaganda of the gun, the BPP's primary goal was to teach black people that they had to defend themselves and their legal rights in the face of governmental abuse. Even the term "pig," which was thought to mean the police exclusively, actually referred to, according to Bobby Seale, anyone who "violate[s] people's constitutional rights."[70]

The public display of armed Panther patrols, then, served as a weapon against police violence. Further, the patroller's recitation of the Bill of Rights or the appropriate penal code served as a teaching tool so that community members could learn to defend themselves. The arrests of armed BPP members who acted fully within their constitutional right to bear arms served to "educate the masses," according to David Hilliard, who notes that "Black people did not have their rights guaranteed by the constitution to bear arms in defense of their lives against racist mobs of fascists in and out of uniform."[71] That patrols were required to stay within legal bounds — refrain from cursing, keep guns always visible, and read the law — undermines the image of the Panthers as purveyors of random and irrational violence, Panther scholarship stressing the travails of black underclass culture, or purely psychoanalytic readings of the violent upbringings of individual Panther members. When patrol members read the law out loud to police officers, most pointedly on capitol building steps while obeying the legal right to bear arms, and were then still harassed and arrested, the scene served as important street theater and instruction to black people and white state agents alike about unequal protection under the law. Moreover, if Huey Newton's retrospective account can be believed, the Panthers' patrols helped to decrease acts of police brutality, bringing in more recruits while helping black people perceive the Party as a community not an outside entity.[72]

A point that is frequently missed about the BPP's discourse of self-defense was that for many in the organization, protecting the right to self-defense and to bear arms in particular was as important as the actual use of arms. In Seale's account of one exchange between Newton and a police officer over the right to bear arms, Newton is portrayed as seeing the exchange itself — the spectacle of a black man using the law to his advantage and in defiance against a state agent — as a recruiting tool.[73] At the same time, his declaration to the officer that he not only had the legal right to bear arms but that he would open fire if the police should draw their guns or try to disarm him illegally arguably exceeded the bounds of the Second Amendment. But in the expression of his intentions Newton legitimately exercised his constitutional rights, specifically his right of self-defense. And one could argue that Newton's exchange with that police officer did not exceed the inalienable "other rights" protected by the Ninth Amendment. It is also revealing that the police officer allegedly accused Newton of trying to "turn the Constitution around."[74] Yet such a charge of legal perversion, or anarchy against the law, must be read against the Panther leader's consistent adherence to the law: once the California legislature in mid-1967 passed the bill against carrying loaded firearms within city limits, the BPP put down the gun.

Shortly after this critical moment in its political development, the Panthers underwent an important philosophical shift marked by the change of their name from the Black Panther Party for Self-Defense to simply the Black Panther Party. Some scholars, as well as some of the Panthers' contemporaries, view this name change—followed shortly by an increased focus on survival programs over armed self-defense—as evidence that the BPP was "more reformist than revolutionary."[75] However, when the Panthers changed their name it was not an expression of a weakening of their self-defense vision; rather, it signaled an expanded notion of self-defense based on "a deeper, richer discussion of what the party's vision for the future might entail."[76] In line with the internal colony thesis, the BPP saw that spatially and politically marginalized communities needed a wider array of defense mechanisms and that too many people both inside and outside the Party were focusing on what Panther Captain Crutch called "the purely military viewpoint."[77] Newton tried later to make clear that gun violence was simply the "*coup de grace*" of what black working-class people needed defense against. He added that there were "other kinds of violence poor people suffered—unemployment, poor housing, inferior education, lack of public facilities, the inequity of the draft"—all as "part of the same fabric."[78] Through the survival programs, the BPP's dedication and service to the black community, through a program of defense against these various forms of violence, helped them embark on a new meaning of "inalienable," or, in the words of the Ninth Amendment, unenumerated rights.

The BPP's survival programs in fact enacted a defense system against black hunger, a corrupt legal system, inadequate health care, and extreme unemployment.[79] Under siege by police and internal dissent in 1971, Newton argued that the survival programs were the "only reason that the Party is still in existence," because they served the community and addressed its needs.[80] As part of the "process" of revolution, the first front of attack against a racist, capitalist regime was attacking substandard housing conditions, poor health care facilities, and an indifferent criminal justice system.[81] For example, consider the following excerpt from the diary of a former Panther member: "Poverty and people everywhere. Haven't seen this kind of mistreatment, poor conditions ever before . . . Black people need the party to do something . . . The pigs came for us again. Trapped us coming from the park on our way back to [the] office. . . . Said we had failed to appear for court and had a bench warrant out for us . . . They kept us at the . . . station until the following day then took us to the . . . city jail . . . No arraignment or anything just tossed inside and left. No bail on a damn disorderly conduct and failure to appear."[82] In response to such conditions, the BPP established social policy programs to improve black urban life.[83] Under these auspices, its community programs focused on the prolonged and detrimental effects of racism and capitalism in the black community.

These community programs fed thousands of hungry children, established free health care clinics, which included free sickle cell testing, and provided moral support and attorney referrals to black people and their families who were "caught up" in the criminal justice system.[84] Often, however, the history of these community programs lies in the shadow of the notorious gunfights between the BPP and "the pig." Moreover, present-day social welfare programs that stem directly from the Panthers and their era remain under siege, especially those serving oppressed communities; ironically, those attacking such programs construct them as antithetical to the democratic spirit. The Panthers, though, insisted that a fully functional sociopolitical system required at its foundation that citizens be defended from illiteracy, homelessness, disease, and other forms of social inequality. It was in the spirit of this novel political philosophy, as noted earlier, that the BPP joined forces with other radical organizations in late 1970 in the hope of writing such a vision directly into the U.S. Constitution.

The BPP's convening of the Revolutionary People's Constitutional Convention (RPCC) is significant on both symbolic and structural grounds. It was purposefully staged in Philadelphia because, in the words of Panther Chief of Staff David Hilliard, it was "the same place the pigs had theirs."[85] Against the backdrop of local Panther surveillance and bloody police violence, the RPCC brought together approximately six thousand people from a cross-section of progressive organizations representing Third World liberation groups, welfare mothers, high school and college students, gay liberation activists, tenant farmers, and professionals. According to George Katsiaficas, who participated in the convention, instead of meeting the expected police terror, delegates were welcomed into local African American homes and churches. Moreover, once the delegates began to draft reforms, they utilized the model of self-defense made popular by the BPP Ten-Point

Program and Platform. One of the major legislative aims of the Convention —in line with the Ninth Amendment—was to limit government intrusion by allocating only 10 percent of the national budget for the military and police, and to "guarantee and deliver to every American citizen the inviolable rights to life, liberty and pursuit of happiness."[86] Though the RPCC project quickly collapsed, it set the tone for later progressive initiatives for equal rights among men and women, bans on the manufacture of genocidal weapons, and the currently powerful prison abolition movement. Most significant, the RPCC put into action the constitutional theory that "the people" possessed "other rights" that could not be trampled upon, and, if those rights were violated, they had the power to create a new government.

The comprehensive discourse of self-defense generated by the BPP, then, revealed the contradictory status of democracy in America in the 1960s and 1970s. Its political philosophy suggested that laws were enforced for the benefit of the powerful. Generally, those in power did not act on behalf of all Americans, most especially the poor and the oppressed. The history of the American Revolution, the establishment of the federal government, and the writing of and subsequent appendage to the Ninth Amendment clearly show that this type of oppressive power was exactly what those who wrote the Constitution sought to prevent. To be sure, there are those who have argued that the framers, including Madison, intended the text of the Ninth Amendment to be merely "a truism"[87] by only stating the already self-evident limited powers granted to the new federal government. Although that may be the case in theory, in reality what the Ninth Amendment leaves open is the relationship between individual rights and government officials. Instead of interpreting the Ninth Amendment as merely a construction of the limiting power of the federal government, it might instead be seen as the source for a range of freedoms for all individuals against state-sponsored benign neglect or direct forms of coercion.

Conclusion

The Ninth Amendment stands as a bulwark against implied federal government powers and, most important, the implication that the first eight amendments were the only basic and fundamental rights guaranteed to the people. Although it can be argued that it was the intent of Madison and the other delegates to insert the Ninth Amendment "merely for greater caution," it serves as much more than that. Thomas McAfee summarizes well the magnitude of the amendment's significance, when he states: "What is ultimately at stake is the appropriate foundational account of our constitutional order. Proponents of the more expansive reading of the amendment ultimately ground their reading in the view that, for the founding generation at least, the inalienable rights held an inherent constitutional status because they were rooted in a natural law that was binding over all positive law. The most fundamental rights were withheld from the government, not because the people made that decision, but because God or nature had decreed it, and because such rights were the very basis of the social contract. Because of this, the foundation of American constitutionalism is the very idea of natural rights."[88] The Ninth Amendment represents the recognition of an infinite source of additional "other rights," which are not listed but nonetheless are protected by the Constitution. It was that reservoir of rights that the Black Panther Party tapped in the 1960s and 1970s.

While the knee-jerk response to such an argument might be to associate the revolutionary actions of the BPP with present-day white militia groups, it must be stressed — against the prevailing view — that violence was not the first option advocated by the Party. Instead, the group developed a program of self-defense in response to an oppressive state. Thus, it is important to stress that "self-defense" took on a broad form with violence as only one component in resisting state oppression. This contextual distinction helps to clarify a use of the Ninth Amendment in the cause of progressive change, both historically and in the future. A litmus test for its application would be the conditions of the community from which social movements emerge. In the case of BPP activities, self-defense was not an act of choice to opt out of the nation-state but rather a response to state exclusion from its goods and services. In the case of communities under siege, self-defense was a desire for inclusion and equal protection and an act of supplementary social development.[89]

The communities from which white militia groups and other conservative social movements emerge are not surveyed by the police or denied states' rights simply because of their race; rather, they are targeted because of their disdain for equal protection under the law. Their desire to "take back the country" is predicated on a demand for a racially pure nation-state, while the BPP sought a more equal distribution of wealth and power in a racially mixed, if revolutionary, nation-state. The constitutional idea of equal protection thus runs directly counter to the vision of white militias and hence would not be covered under the Ninth Amendment.

Black communities were truly under siege in the 1960s, and the Panthers sought out community restructuring through police patrols, free health and legal clinics, and breakfast programs for children. If we are ever to understand that combination of activities, there must be an expanded understanding of the historical significance of the Party through more critical analysis of the relationship between constitutional law and such social movements. Such critical analysis will likely lead to the conclusion that, overall, the BPP participated legally within the system, and they should be remembered as an important freedom organization for the black community and for America as a whole. In this light, as a case study, the Black Panther Party offers an example of an attempted reconstruction of jurisprudence that directly reflects the actual needs of the citizenry for whom the law—like the Ninth Amendment to the U.S. Constitution—was written in the first place.

Notes

I would like to thank Wallace Sherwood, Sean Varano, Soffiyah Elijah, and Jen Balboni for their insightful comments and helpful criticism on early drafts of this essay. I also want to thank Jama Lazerow and Yohuru Williams for their invitation to contribute this essay to the anthology. And, along with them, I greatly appreciate the helpful insights from Rod Bush and the anonymous readers from Duke University Press. Finally a very special thank you to Davarian Baldwin for numerous draft readings and late nights of chai tea.

1. Gene Marine, *The Black Panthers* (New York: Signet Press, 1969), back cover.
2. Eldridge Cleaver, "The Courage to Kill: Meeting the Panthers," in *Post-Prison Writings and Speeches*, edited by Robert Scheer (New York: Random House, 1969), esp. 29.
3. Philip S. Foner, "Introduction," in *The Black Panthers Speak*, edited by Philip S. Foner (New York: Da Capo Press, 1995 [1970]), xxxi.
4. Bobby Seale, *Seize the Time: The Story of the Black Panther Party and Huey P. Newton* (New York: Vintage, 1970), 83.
5. See Kathleen Cleaver and George Katsiaficas, eds., *Liberation, Imagination and the Black Panther Party: A New Look at the Panthers and Their Legacy* (New York: Routledge, 2001); Charles E. Jones, ed., *The Black Panther Party [Reconsidered]* (Baltimore: Black Classic Press, 1998); and, earlier, Kim Kit Holder, "The History of the Black Panther Party, 1966–1972: A Curriculum Tool for Afrikan-American Studies" (Ph.D. diss., University of Massachusetts, 1990).
6. Newton, "'On the Defection of Eldridge Cleaver from the Black Panther Party and the Defection of the Black Panther Party from the Black Community': 17 April 1971," in *The Huey P. Newton Reader*, edited by David Hilliard and Donald Weise (New York: Seven Stories Press, 2002), 200–8.
7. Newton, "In Defense of Self-Defense: Executive Mandate Number One," *The Black Panther*, 2 June 1967.

8. Quoted from online source at www.historyplace.com/unitedstates/revolution/causes.htm.
9. Quoted in A. J. Langguth, *Patriots: The Men Who Started the American Revolution* (New York: Touchstone, 1988), 32.
10. Ibid., 159.
11. Ibid., 56.
12. Newton, "In Defense of Self-Defense," in Hilliard and Weise, eds., *The Huey P. Newton Reader,* 134.
13. Alexander Hamilton, James Madison, and John Jay, *The Federalist Papers,* edited by Clinton Rossiter (New York: Mentor, 1999), 478–88. See also Langguth, *Patriots.*
14. Bennett B. Patterson, *The Forgotten Amendment: A Call for Legislative and Judicial Recognition of Rights under Social Conditions of Today* (Indianapolis: Bobbs-Merrill Co., 1955); Calvin R. Massey, *Silent Rights: The Ninth Amendment and the Constitution's Unenumerated Rights* (Philadelphia: Temple University Press, 1995).
15. Patterson, *The Forgotten Amendment.*
16. Charles Black, *Decision According to Law: The 1979 Holmes Lectures* (New York: Norton, 1981), 46; Mark N. Goodman, *The Ninth Amendment: History, Interpretation, and Meaning* (Smithtown, New York: Exposition Press, 1981), 1; *United Public Workers v. Mitchell*, 330 U.S. 75, 94–95 (1947); *Calder v. Bull*, 3 U.S. (3 Dall), 386, 388 (1798); *Loan Ass'n v. Topeka*, 87 U.S. 655, 662–63 (1875); *Ashwander v. TVA*, 297 U.S. 288, 330–31 (1936); *Tennessee Electric Power Co. v. TVA*, 306 U.S. 118, 143–44 (1939).
17. John Choon Yoo, "Our Declaratory Ninth Amendment," *Emory Law Journal* 42 (1993): 967–1043.
18. Some scholars have argued that the Ninth Amendment was not intended to limit state power but to serve only as a rule of construction regarding the extent of the Constitution's enumerated powers. Thomas McAfee, "The Original Meaning of the Ninth Amendment," *Columbia Law Review* 90 (1990): 1215–1305; Massey, *Silent Rights*; Charles J. Cooper, "Limited Government and Individual Liberty: The Ninth Amendment's Forgotten Lessons," in *The Bill of Rights: Original Meaning and Current Understanding*, edited by Eugene J. Hickok (Charlottesville: University Press of Virginia, 1991).
19. The position taken here—that the Ninth Amendment is enforceable against state and federal government officials—can be found in numerous works, including Yoo, "Our Declaratory Ninth Amendment"; Charles Black, *A New Birth of Freedom: Human Rights, Named and Unnamed* (New York: Putnam, 1997); Mark C. Niles, "Ninth Amendment Adjudication: An Alternative to Substantive Due Process Analysis of Person Autonomy Rights," *UCLA Law Review* 48 (2000): 85–157.
20. Laurence H. Tribe and Michael C. Dorf, *On Reading the Constitution* (Cambridge, Mass.: Harvard University Press, 1991), 54.
21. See *Planned Parenthood v. Casey*, 505 U.S. 833, 848 (1992); Yoo, "Our Declaratory Ninth Amendment," 1009.
22. Ibid.

23. Although the current trend is to absorb a few of the Bill of Rights into the Fourteenth Amendment's Due Process Clause, case law has clearly established that the court will look at rights considered "fundamental principles of liberty and justice which lie at the base of all our civil and political institutions" (*Palko v. Connecticut*, 302 U.S. 319, 328 [1937]). As stated in *Planned Parenthood v. Casey*, 505 U.S. 833, 834 (1992): "Neither the Bill of Rights nor the specific practices of States at the time of the adoption of the Fourteenth Amendment marks the *outer limits* of the substantive sphere of liberty which the Fourteenth Amendment protects. See U.S. Const., Amdt 9" (emphasis mine).
24. *Doe v. Bolton*, 410 U.S. 179, 210–11 (1973).
25. Tribe and Dorf, *Reading the Constitution*, 55. Although the courts have had little occasion to interpret the Ninth Amendment, see *Marbury v. Madison*, 5 U.S. 137, 174 (1803): "It cannot be presumed that any clause in the Constitution is intended to be without effect." In interpreting the Constitution, "real effect should be given to all the words [the Constitution] uses" (*Myers v. United States*, 272 U.S. 52, 151 [1926]).
26. 381 U.S. 479, 488, 491, 492 (1965).
27. *Bowers v. Hardwick*, 478 U.S. 186 (1986).
28. *Webster v. Doe*, 486 U.S. 592 (1988).
29. *Troxel v. Granville*, 530 U.S. 57 (2000).
30. *United States v. Orito*, 413 U.S. 139 (1972).
31. *Griswold v Connecticut*, 381 U.S. 479 (1965).
32. Ibid., 484.
33. Quoted in Foner, *The Black Panthers Speak*, xxxi. See also Cleaver, "The Land Question and Black Liberation" (April/May 1968), in *Post-Prison Writings and Speeches*, 57–72.
34. The literature on this topic is immense and still growing. For examples from the last decade, see Nikhil Pal Singh, *Black Is a Country: Race and the Unfinished Struggle for Democracy* (Cambridge, Mass.: Harvard University Press, 2004); Barbara Ransby, *Ella Baker and the Black Freedom Movement: A Radical Democratic Vision* (Chapel Hill: University of North Carolina Press, 2003); Martha Biondi, *To Stand and Fight: The Struggle for Civil Rights in Postwar New York City* (Cambridge, Mass.: Harvard University Press, 2003); Gail Williams O'Brien, *The Color of Law: Race, Violence, and Justice in the Post–World War II South* (Chapel Hill: University of North Carolina Press, 1999); Leon Litwack, *Trouble in Mind: Black Southerners in the Age of Jim Crow* (New York: Knopf, 1998); Fitzhugh Brundage, *Under Sentence of Death: Lynching in the South* (Chapel Hill: University of North Carolina Press, 1997); Joy James, *Resisting State Violence: Radicalism, Gender, and Race in U.S. Culture* (Minneapolis: University of Minnesota Press, 1996); Charles M. Payne, *I've Got the Light of Freedom: The Organizing Tradition and the Mississippi Freedom Struggle* (Berkeley: University of California Press, 1995); Gerald Horne, *The Fire This Time: The Watts Uprising and the 1960s* (Charlottesville: University of Virginia Press, 1995).

35. Singh, "The Black Panthers and the 'Undeveloped Country' of the Left," in Jones, ed., *The Black Panther Party;* Robin D. G. Kelley, "Roaring from the East: Third World Dreaming," in *Freedom Dreams: The Black Radical Imagination* (Boston: Beacon, 2002); Robin D. G. Kelley and Betsy Esch, "Black Like Mao: Red China and Black Liberation," *Souls* 1 (fall 1999): 6–41; Vijay Prashad, *Everybody Was Kung Fu Fighting* (Boston: Beacon, 2000); Lisa Brock and Digna Castaneda Fuertes, eds., *Between Race and Empire: African-Americans and Cubans before the Cuban Revolution* (Philadelphia: Temple University Press, 1998); Van Gosse, *Where the Boys Are: Cuba, Cold War America, and the Making of a New Left* (London: Verso, 1993); Frantz Fanon, *The Wretched of the Earth* (New York: Grove, 1967); Mao Tse-tung [Zedong], *Quotations from Chairman Mao Tse-tung* (Peking [Beijing]: Foreign Languages Press, 1966); Rolland Snellings [Askia Muhammad Toure], "Afro American Youth and the Bandung World," *Liberator* 5 (January 1965).

36. Rod Bush, *We Are Not What We Seem: Black Nationalism and Class Struggle in the American Century* (New York: New York University Press, 1999); Timothy Tyson, *Radio Free Dixie: Robert Williams and the Roots of Black Power* (Chapel Hill: University of North Carolina Press, 1999); Komozi Woodard, *A Nation within a Nation: Amiri Baraka (LeRoi Jones) and Black Power Politics* (Chapel Hill: University of North Carolina Press, 1998); Grace Lee Boggs, *Living for Change* (Minneapolis: University of Minnesota Press, 1998); Williams Sales Jr., *From Civil Rights to Black Liberation: Malcolm X and the Organization of Afro-American Unity* (Boston: South End Press, 1994); Ferruccio Gambino, "The Transgression of a Laborer: Malcolm X in the Wilderness of America," *Radical History Review* (winter 1993): 7–31; William Van Deburg, *A New Day in Babylon: The Black Power Movement and American Culture, 1965–1975* (Chicago: University of Chicago Press, 1992); Joe Wood, ed., *Malcolm X: In Our Own Image* (New York: St. Martin's Press, 1992); James Cone, *Martin or Malcolm and America: A Dream or a Nightmare?* (Maryknoll, N.Y.: Orbis Books, 1991); Maxwell Stanford, "Revolutionary Action Movement: A Case Study of an Urban Revolutionary Movement in Western Capitalist Society" (MA thesis, Atlanta University, 1986); Marcellus Barksdale, "Robert Williams and the Indigenous Civil Rights Movement in Monroe, North Carolina, 1961," *Journal of Negro History* 69 (spring 1984): 73–89; Kalamu ya Salaam, "Robert Williams: Crusader for International Solidarity," *Black Collegian* 8.3 (January/February 1978): 53–60; Malcolm X, with Alex Haley, *The Autobiography of Malcolm X* (New York: Grove Press, 1965); Robert Williams, *Negroes with Guns* (New York: Marzani and Munsell, 1962).

37. Newton, "In Defense of Self-Defense," in Foner, ed., *The Black Panthers Speak*, 40.

38. Kwame Ture and Charles Hamilton, *Black Power: The Politics of Liberation* (New York: Vintage, 1992), 9, 5.

39. At Cleaver's behest, the BPP added a plank to their original platform and program, calling for a United Nations plebiscite allowing black citizens the right to decide on national inclusion or independence. For that amended version, see "What We Want, What We Believe," mislabeled as the "October 1966 Black Panther Party

Platform and Program," in Foner, ed., *The Black Panthers Speak*, 2–4. See also Cleaver, "The Land Question."

40. "Patrolling," excerpted from Newton's autobiography, *Revolutionary Suicide*, in Hilliard and Weise, eds., *The Huey P. Newton Reader*, 60.
41. See, for example, *Snyder v. Massachusetts*, 291 U.S. 97, 105 (1934); *Powell v. Alabama*, 287 U.S. 45, 67 (1932) (quoting *Herbert v. Louisiana* 272 U.S. 312, 316 [1926]).
42. See John Locke, *Second Treatise of Government*, edited by C. B. Macpherson (Cambridge, Mass.: Hackett Publishing, 1980 [1690]); Samuel Pufendorf, *De jure naturae et gentium libri octo* [The Law of Nature and Nations], vol. 2., translated by C. H. Oldfather and W. A. Oldfather (Dobbs Ferry, N.Y.: Oceana Publications, 1964 [1688]), 264; Thomas Hobbes, *Leviathan*, edited by Michael Oakeshott (Oxford: Basil Blackwell, 1957 [1651]), 103.
43. J. D. Droddy, "Originalist Justification and Methodology of Unenumerated Rights," *Michigan State University–Detroit College of Law Law Review* 199 (1999): 831.
44. *Snyder v. Massachusetts*, 291 U.S. 97, 105 (1934).
45. *Powell v. Alabama*, 287 U.S. 45, 67 (1932) (quoting *Herbert v. Louisiana*, 272 U.S. 312, 316 [1926]).
46. McAfee, "The Original Meaning of the Ninth Amendment,"
47. Patterson, *The Forgotten Amendment*, 36–43; Black, *A New Birth of Freedom*, 47.
48. Knowlton H. Kelsey, "The Ninth Amendment of the Federal Constitution," in *The Rights Retained by the People*, edited by Randy Barnett (Fairfax, Va.: George Mason Press, 1989), 96–99; see also Patterson, *The Forgotten Amendment*, 107.
49. For example, in the Civil Rights Act of 1964 and the Voting Rights Act of 1965.
50. Sundiata Acoli [né Clark Squire], "A Brief History of the Black Panther Party: Its Place in the Black Liberation Movement," from the Sundiata Acoli Freedom Campaign 1995, Marion Penitentiary, 4/2/85, online at http://www.afrikan.identity.com/sundiata/sun04.html.
51. Newton, "On the Defection of Eldridge Cleaver," in Hilliard and Weise, eds., *The Huey P. Newton Reader*, 201.
52. Hence the BPP-organized Revolutionary People's Constitutional Convention, which proposed a new Constitution with expanded individual rights and limited government intrusion. George Katsiaficas, "Organization and Movement: The Case of the Black Panther Party and the Revolutionary People's Constitutional Convention of 1970," in Cleaver and Katsiaficas, eds., *Liberation, Imagination, and the Black Panther Party*, 141–55.
53. Newton, "Huey Newton Talks to the Movement about the Black Panther Party, Cultural Nationalism, SNCC, Liberals and White Revolutionaries," in Foner, ed., *The Black Panthers Speak*, 50. Cf. Scot Brown, *Fighting for US: Maulana Karenga, the US Organization, and Black Cultural Nationalism* (New York: New York University Press, 2003), 115–19.
54. Seale, "The Ten-Point Platform," 78, and "Defend the Ghetto," (Brooklyn Panther leaflet), 180, in Foner, ed., *The Black Panthers Speak*.

55. The rationale is offered by Seale, in *Seize the Time*, and by Huey Newton (with the assistance of J. Herman Blake, in *Revolutionary Suicide* (New York: Writers and Readers Publishing, 1995 [1973]), 114–27.
56. Seale, "Defend the Ghetto"; Newton, "Functional Definition of Politics," *The Black Panther*, 17 January 1969, and Hilliard, "If You Want Peace You Got to Fight for It," *The Black Panther*, 19 November 1969, in Foner, ed., *The Black Panthers Speak*, 44–47, 128–30, respectively.
57. Fliers/posters in Foner, ed., *The Black Panthers Speak*, 53, 180, 221.
58. Candy, "Pigs-Panthers," *The Black Panther*, 22 November 1969, in Foner, ed., *The Black Panthers Speak*, 35–37.
59. The fundamental power of "the people," of course, is embodied in the Tenth Amendment: "The powers not delegated to the United States by the Constitution, nor prohibited by it to the States, are reserved to the States respectively, *Or to the People*" (emphasis mine).
60. Seale, *Seize the Time*, 157.
61. Newton, "A Functional Definition of Politics," *The Black Panther*, 17 January 1969, in Hilliard and Weise, eds., *The Huey P. Newton Reader*, 148.
62. Seale, *Seize the Time*, 71; Newton, "Violence," *The Black Panther*, 23 March 1968, in Foner, ed., *The Black Panthers Speak*, 19.
63. Newton, "Huey Newton Talks to the Movement," in Foner, ed., *The Black Panthers Speak*, 62.
64. Newton, "Violence," in Foner, ed., *The Black Panthers Speak*, 19.
65. The Second Amendment states: "A well regulated Militia, being necessary to the security of a free State, the right of the people to keep and bear Arms, shall not be infringed."
66. Newton, "On the Defection of Eldridge Cleaver," in Hilliard and Weise, eds., *The Huey P. Newton Reader*, 204.
67. Ibid., 207.
68. Cleaver, "The Land Question," in *Post-Prison Writings and Speeches*, 72.
69. Newton, "Patrolling," in Hilliard and Weise, eds., *The Huey P. Newton Reader*, 60.
70. "Bobby Seale Explains Panther Politics: An Interview," *Guardian* (January 1970), in Foner, ed., *The Black Panthers Speak*, 82; further explication of this position can be found on page xxx. For a retrospective explication of how and why the Panthers adopted the term "pig," see Newton, *Revolutionary Suicide*, 165–66.
71. David Hilliard, "The Ideology of the Black Panther Party," *The Black Panther*, 8 November 1969, in Foner, ed., *The Black Panthers Speak*, 122.
72. See Newton, *Revolutionary Suicide*.
73. Seale, *Seize the Time*, 85–99.
74. Quoted in Michael Newton, *Bitter Grain: Huey Newton and the Black Panther Party* (Los Angeles: Holloway House, 1991), 19.
75. Floyd Hayes III and Francis Kiene III, "'All Power to the People': The Political Thought of Huey P. Newton and the Black Panther Party," in Jones, ed., *The Black Panther Party*, 161; Newton, "On the Defection of Eldridge Cleaver," in Hilliard and Weise, eds., *The Huey P. Newton Reader*, 203.

76. Kelley, *Freedom Dreams*, 95–96.
77. "Correcting Mistaken Ideas," *The Black Panther*, 26 October 1968, in Foner, ed., *The Black Panthers Speak*, 23.
78. Newton, *Revolutionary Suicide*, 188–89.
79. See Acoli, http://www.afrikan.i-entity.com/sundiata/sun04.html.
80. Newton, "On the Defection of Eldridge Cleaver," in Hilliard and Weise, eds., *The Huey P. Newton Reader*, 201.
81. Ibid, 203; *The Black Panther*, 4 August and 5 October 1969.
82. Steve McCutchen, "Selections from a Panther Diary," in Jones, ed., *The Black Panther Party*, 119, 121.
83. Abron, "'Serving the People': The Survival Programs of the Black Panther Party," in Jones, ed., *The Black Panther Party*, 177–92.
84. Through the prison bus rides, for example, families could visit family members incarcerated in a far-flung state prison system.
85. "Black Panthers: Panthers Plan New 'Constitution,'" *Facts on File World News Digest*, 15 July 1970, online at http://www.2facts.com.
86. Ibid. See also Katsiaficas, "Organization and Movement."
87. *Griswold v. Connecticut*, 381 U.S. 479, 529 (1965) (Stewart's dissent).
88. Thomas McAfee, "A Critical Guide to the Ninth Amendment," *Temple Law Review* 69 (1996): 91–92.
89. For the contrary view, see John A. Wood, *Panthers and the Militias: Brothers Under the Skin?* (Lanham, Md.: University Press of America, 2002).

PART THREE From the Bottom Up and the Top Down:
Personal Politics and the Black Panthers

Introductory Comment

The Panthers and Local History

JAMES T. CAMPBELL

It is by now a truism that history is political; that the past can be retailed in different ways and to different political ends. The history of the so-called sixties represents an obvious case in point. Just as American politics in the late nineteenth century and early twentieth turned on the alleged "lessons" of Reconstruction, so have the politics of our own time come to hinge on competing interpretations of the tumultuous decade that gave us an expanding war in Southeast Asia and a burgeoning antiwar movement at home; Lyndon Johnson's Great Society and Richard Nixon's "Southern Strategy"; the uplifting rhetoric of Martin Luther King Jr.'s "I Have a Dream" speech and the smoke and ashes of burning ghettos. Amid this welter of competing images and ideas, the Black Panther Party (BPP) stands out as perhaps the single most contentious symbol. Decades after its meteoric rise and fall, the BPP has become a kind of historical Rorschach test, an inkblot on a white screen that seemingly represents nothing in itself yet somehow elicits observers' deepest assumptions, yearnings, and fears.

Today, as in the Party's heyday, interpretations of the Panther phenomenon generally fall within two opposing camps. In the first, the Panthers appear as "the vanguard of the Third World Revolution," an insurgent movement that challenged American hegemony abroad and the brutal forces of colonial occupation at home before being smashed by a concerted campaign of violent repression by local, state, and federal authorities. Commentators working in this tradition often emphasize the Panthers' community-based "survival programs"—not only the celebrated free breakfast program but also the programs for clothing and shoe distribution, sickle cell anemia screening, escorts for the elderly, free transportation to visit relatives in prison, and so forth—all of which helped the Party to build a broad grassroots constituency in dozens of American cities. In the opposing (and far more popular) version, the Panthers appear as a group of cartoonish, pseudorevolutionary thugs, who earned a brief notoriety with their black berets and militant posturing before collapsing into internecine conflict, violence, and criminality. If the free breakfast program enjoys pride of place in the Panther defense, Exhibit A for the prosecution is Huey Newton, whose descent into drug addiction and violent psychosis is presented as emblematic of the Party as a whole.

Both narratives contain elements of truth. At the same time both are caricatures, simple stories of complex events, intended to inculcate this or that political "moral." As Nikhil Singh has noted, denigrating the Panthers has become a means to demean and discredit other expressions of black radicalism, and indeed any movement or discourse that does not "conform, in one way or another, to the dictates of American universalism, populism, and patriotism."[1] Not coincidentally, this approach conveniently obscures the illegal, violent, and in some instances literally murderous war waged against the Party under the auspices of the FBI's COINTELPRO program. The alternative, sympathetic version of Panther history, while less obviously poisonous, is similarly partial and self-serving. Portraying the Panthers as romantic revolutionaries cut down by a reactionary state neglects many of the Party's own substantial internal flaws, a roster that would include, at a minimum, authoritarianism, intolerance of dissent, and a valorization of violence as an end in itself. While these qualities helped to make the Panthers media celebrities, in the end they promoted factionalism and a pervasive climate of suspicion, leaving the organization peculiarly vulnerable to COINTELPRO operations.

For all their differences, these two caricatured accounts of the Panther's rise and fall have collaborated in preventing any balanced assessment of the Party's origins, achievements, limitations, and legacy—all of which makes the June 2003 conference at Wheelock College, from which the papers in this volume are assembled, such a signal event. The conference, the first gathering organized by professional historians on the BPP and its legacy, brought together veterans of the movement, students, and over fifty university-based scholars, many of whom had personal memories of the events they described. While panelists discussed the now-canonical works in Panther history—*Soul on Ice, Revolutionary Suicide, Seize the Day, Assata, A Taste of Power*—they also drew on a much broader archive, including internal Party documents, court records, private letters, police and FBI reports, and extensive oral interviews with former Panthers (and, in a few cases, with the police and FBI agents who ran operations against them). Needless to say, the resulting papers varied considerably, but together they expressed a determination to push beyond the shibboleths in order to produce a balanced, empirically grounded understanding of the Panther phenomenon.

The possibilities of this new research were perhaps best revealed in a series of panels dedicated to "the local perspective." With some conspicuous exceptions, most of what we know (or think we know) about the Black Panther Party refers to the history of the Party's Oakland chapter. As the founding branch and its headquarters, Oakland is obviously important, but what was happening there did not necessarily dictate what occurred in New Orleans or New Bedford, Bridgeport, or Birmingham. On paper, the Party was an extremely hierarchical organization (what other group called their leaders "Field Marshals" or described their policy papers as "Executive Mandates"?) but in practice it remained highly decentralized, not to say disorganized, especially as state repression intensified. Many chapters grew up more or less spontaneously, as groups of local activists decided to affiliate themselves with the Party after reading about it or seeing reports on television. In Kansas City, for example, the Panthers got their start by absorbing the Black Vigilantes, which had emerged in the aftermath of the King assassination. In New Orleans, the Party operated through an affiliate, the National Committee to Combat Fascism, which was based in the city's massive Desire housing project.[2] Other cities had similarly unique experiences.

Perhaps not surprisingly, the links between local chapters and national Party headquarters in Oakland were tenuous, often contentious, and sometimes purely notional. The weekly appearance of the *Black Panther* gave the movement a certain institutional and ideological coherence—for ten years, between 1967 and 1977, the paper never missed an issue, an extraordinary achievement given the pressures on the Party—but it is an open question how closely the various theoretical postures and policy shifts announced in the paper were followed by local branches. (In some instances, the paper may actually have provoked disunity, with the national organization and local branches battling over the control of proceeds from selling the paper.) At the risk of stretching the point, the BPP may not have been a single national movement at all but rather a congeries of local movements, bound together by certain core issues (preeminently the conduct of police in black communities), a revolutionary argot, and a distinctive cultural and political style, including signature forms of dress and deportment.

In the short term, the lack of institutional rigor may have been an asset, enabling the BPP to sprout in different settings and to accommodate a range of locally specific grievances and experiences. Yet this same characteristic magnified problems of indiscipline and factionalism, contributing directly to the violent split between the Cleaver and Newton factions of the Party. These qualities, in turn, made the Party easy prey for the FBI, which was always on the lookout for opportunities (in J. Edgar Hoover's words) "to further plant the seeds of suspicion" within the Party.[3] Declassified records from the COINTELPRO program reveal more than two hundred such operations, including the use of agents provocateur, planting false news releases, and "bad jacketing" Party members (that is, circulating information to give the impression that an individual was an informer).

All of these issues made for a combustible combination, which the merest spark could set ablaze. Take, for example, the 1969 murder of Alex Rackley, an episode that is examined in detail in Yohuru Williams's study of the Party's New Haven branch.[4] At the center of the tale is George Sams, who arrived in New York representing himself as a security officer dispatched from national headquarters. Sams (whose nom de guerre, "Crazy George," reflected a prior stint in a mental institution) had in fact been purged from the Party by Bobby Seale, but in the roiled circumstances of the time no one challenged his credentials. After a short stay in New York, Sams proceeded to New Haven, accompanied by Alex Rackley, the twenty-four-year-old security officer for the Panthers' Harlem chapter. On arrival, Sams denounced his unwitting companion as a police informer and ordered his detainment and interrogation. For the next three days, Rackley was tortured by members of the New Haven chapter, with Sams presiding. The torturers recorded the "interrogation" on audiotape, but they need not have bothered to do so because the New Haven police were already recording it, thanks to an illegal wiretap of Panther headquarters. (The police, who regularly shared with the FBI the fruits of the wiretap, did not intervene to stop the torture.) At the end of the third day, Rackley, still bound, was loaded into a car with Sams and two other chapter members, at least one of whom, according to Williams, was an FBI informant. His beaten, bullet-riddled body was recovered the following morning.[5]

The murder proved to be a watershed in Panther history, providing the authorities with the pretext they needed to act forcefully against the Party. All over the country BPP chapters were raided and over thirty people were arrested, eight of whom were charged with Rackley's murder (including Bobby Seale, who was in New Haven at the time on a speaking engagement at Yale University). Ironically, the only people to escape more or less unscathed were Sams and Kimbro, both of whom turned state's evidence and served only short sentences.

The purpose of this account is not to rehash old horrors but to highlight the value of the kind of close, locally focused research that Yohuru Williams and other historians have begun to do. At the same time, the story suggests again the dangers of the one-sided portrayals that have prevailed in much of the popular and scholarly writing about the Panthers. Alex Rackley's fate starkly reveals the destructive impact—and utter cynicism—of the wars by local, state, and federal authorities against the BPP. At the same time, something was clearly amiss in the political culture of an organization whose members would willingly torture a man they had just met based solely on the testimony of another complete stranger. In this instance at least, the two interpretations counterposed in the historiography are not alternatives at all but two sides of the same coin.

The possibilities of this new generation of Panther scholarship are limpidly displayed in the two essays that constitute this section of this book. Jama Lazerow's essay recounts the "unexpected story" of Frank "Parky" Grace, a one-time Panther who spent a decade in prison for a murder that he did not commit. Friends and adversaries alike remember Grace as an "enigma," at once a "natural leader" of "great dignity" and a violent "sociopath" with a lifelong penchant for thuggery. Born in New Bedford, Massachusetts, Grace was in some ways an unlikely Panther, having grown up in a Cape Verdean community whose members typically did not regard themselves as "black." In other ways, however, he had the classic Party resume: a youth spent in poverty in a declining industrial city, membership in a street gang, frequent confrontations with the police, and a harrowing tour of duty in Vietnam, followed by a rocky reentry into a civilian world transformed by the War on Poverty and a burgeoning antiwar movement. When precisely Grace joined the BPP and how long he remained a member are difficult to establish; for a time, even while a Panther, he was also a charter member of the Black Brothers, a local veterans group. But he clearly played a pivotal role in introducing the Panthers to New Bedford, and it was his association with the Party that first brought him to the attention of federal authorities. Lazerow uses oral testimony and a previously untapped collection of prison letters to reconstruct Grace's career, from his childhood in New Bedford to his vain attempts to reconstruct his life after his release from prison. In the process, Lazerow illuminates not only Grace's own character but also the complex character of black radical politics in an unexpected locale.

William A. Cohendet, the FBI agent who is the subject of Roz Payne's essay, is in some ways an even more perplexing figure: a seemingly decent, wry, reflective man, whose biweekly "air-tels" on the activities of the BPP's Oakland branch found their way directly to the desk of J. Edgar Hoover. Payne encountered Cohendet in the most unlikely of ways, while working as a researcher for attorneys representing Dhoruba Bin Wahad (né Richard Moore), one of the (New York) Panther 21. In the course of slogging through the more than three hundred thousand documents released to the defense by court order, Payne and her colleagues were struck not only by the FBI's role as unwitting Party archivist, but also by a San Francisco special agent identified simply as "WAC," whose felicitously written, mordantly funny intelligence reports offered an occasional respite from an otherwise grim and grueling task. Whether Cohendet, whom she subsequently met and interviewed, was as blithely innocent as he presents himself to be is an open question; as Payne notes, it is virtually impossible to reconcile his account of his activities with what we know about the FBI campaign against the Panthers. At the very least, however, the essay opens up an important, if inherently problematic, archive, while posing new questions about the operation of the state apparatus, which may have been less monolithic than most scholars assume.

Obviously, William Cohendet was not a "typical" FBI agent any more than Parky Grace was a typical Panther. Yet it is precisely for this reason that their stories should command our attention. Such careful, empirically grounded case studies promise to complicate our understanding by raising new questions while rendering untenable the caricatures and self-serving simplifications of so much contemporary writing about the Panthers. Clearly, the national story remains important, but we will never be able to tell it persuasively until we know more about the myriad ways in which local chapters took root, struggled, fractured, and died. And, this research needs to be done sooner rather than later, before the generation of activists touched by the Party passes.

There are, needless to say, limits to such an approach. There is a danger (to return to the original metaphor) of replacing the inkblot version of Panther history with a kind of academic pointillism, in which any sense of pattern is lost amid an infinity of individual data points. Ultimately, historians need to generalize in order to focus (as pointillists do, after all) on the big picture. All the "big questions" that have heretofore preoccupied scholars of the BPP — questions about the Party's relationship with the white Left and with other insurgent movements, the impact of the War on Poverty, gender ideology, violence, COINTELPRO, and so forth — remain not simply valid but vital. The point is not to reject synthesis but rather to suggest how much richer our syntheses will be when they are grounded in an empirically rich, nuanced understanding of what the Panthers meant in particular places and times. And when we have that complex understanding of the past, we may perhaps be better able to assess the meaning of the Black Panther Party in our own time.

Notes

1. Nikhil Pal Singh, "The Black Panthers and the 'Undeveloped Country' of the Left," in *The Black Panther Party [Reconsidered]*, edited by Charles E. Jones (Baltimore: Black Classic Press, 1998), 59.
2. Reynaldo Anderson, "The Black Panther Party in Kansas City, Des Moines, and Omaha," and Carolyn Kolb, "Exceptional Incidents: The Black Panthers in New Orleans, 1970–71" presented at The Black Panther Party in Historical Perspective conference, Wheelock College, Boston, 11–13 June 2003.
3. Director of FBI to SAC, Albany, NY, Re: Buelet to Baltimore dated 11/25/68, 1 January 1969, File number 100-448006 Subject (BPP), Freedom of Information Act Reading Room, FBI Headquarters, Washington, D.C.
4. Yohuru Williams, *Black Politics/White Power: Civil Rights, Black Power, and the Black Panthers in New Haven* (St. James: Brandywine Press, 2000).
5. In a forthcoming book on the Rackley affair, authors Paul Bass and Douglas W. Rae argue that the local Panthers had several, perhaps a dozen, informants in their midst — and that Kimbro was not among them. One of these informants, according to Bass and Rae, was an aspiring police officer named Kelly Moye, who actually lent the Panthers the car in which they drove Alex Rackley to his death on the night of the murder. As for Sams, it is unclear if he was an agent provocateur, or simply an unbalanced, violent individual whose actions just happened to dovetail with the stated goal of COINTELPRO. In their work Bass and Rae note the existence of evidence supporting both scenarios.

"A Rebel All His Life":
The Unexpected Story of Frank "Parky" Grace

JAMA LAZEROW

He was a Panther, a political prisoner "railroaded" to jail for a crime he did not commit, and the struggle to free him took far longer than the years he spent in the Party. Among his friends and comrades, he was known not by his given name but by his nickname. His heritage mixed religions, ethnicities, and colors, but the message of his tutors was consistent: he was raised "not to take anybody's crap." He learned of politics from his grandmother and mother, he would later claim, and especially from the town elders who talked politics at the local barbershop. In 1965, he joined the army and went to Vietnam, where he saw a lot of action, including things "I don't want to remember." While in Vietnam, he heard about a group called the Black Panther Party for Self-Defense. And, when he returned home in 1968, he entered college and soon became a Panther himself. As a "natural leader," he rose quickly in the Party to a leadership position in the city where he lived. He would train others in the art of war; he would be dogged by the police and FBI for his activities; and he would be arrested in a predawn raid that netted about twenty others who were charged with, among other things, conspiracy to commit murder and "armed anarchy." He would eventually be accused, tried, and convicted of a street crime—murder—unrelated to his political work as a radical, and then sentenced to life. Although many local residents could testify he was in another place that night, informer testimony tainted the evidence. But there were eyewitnesses, and the now-former Panther—after an outburst of disbelief at the reading of the guilty verdict—languished in prison for years, where he was moved from place to place and held in solitary because of his reputation as a leader. He was finally exonerated, crucially with the help of a young white attorney who made the case his own crusade.

This is, in each particular, the saga of the famed Panther Elmer "Geronimo" Pratt (Geronimo ji Jaga), who by the 1990s had become a national, even international, cause celebre.[1] But, it is also, in each particular, the story of Frank "Parky" Grace, the founder of the Black Panther Party in a place where most do not even know a Panther Party existed — New Bedford, Massachusetts.[2] His is an untold story because historians have too often followed the media-driven narrative of the Black Panthers. This larger narrative is the tale of Huey Newton and Bobby Seale founding the Party in October 1966 at an Oakland antipoverty agency. It is the story of Eldridge Cleaver, the author of the instantly acclaimed *Soul on Ice*, the presidential candidate of the Peace and Freedom Party, and the revolutionary exile in Algiers. It is the saga of Panthers on trial in San Francisco, Los Angeles, Chicago, New York, and New Haven. Fortunately, historiographical trends that have become dominant in civil rights studies over the last generation offer hope that we might revisit the Panther story in a way that is "shaped by the new history developed in the 1960s" — namely, "history from the bottom up."[3] Inevitably, such a history will be about particular communities, and, while chronicling the origins, nature, development, and legacy of an organization, it must at the same time be rooted in the complex, messy, even contradictory lives of the individuals who composed that organization.[4] Neither hagiographic nor demonologic, neither simple nor straightforward, that new history will have to account for personalities and historical context, and for human nature and individual evolution.[5] Parky Grace's story, which ended with his death in fall 2001, can be told in such rich detail that it provides a rare opportunity to glimpse the Panthers as more than the standard one-dimensional tale.

Indeed, Grace's life reveals five paradoxical themes that dramatically underscore the many dimensions of his life as a rebel. First, he developed a defiant personality at an early age, which combined criminal activity with a fierce, if complicated, sense of social justice. Second, he was the product of Cape Verdean immigration — the only mass voluntary migration of West Africans to the United States — and thus the product of an island population produced by Portuguese colonialism and centuries of interaction with people from all over the world. His radical politics thus developed in an ethnic and racial milieu where the lines between "black" and "white" were at once stark and blurred. Third, his path to the Panther movement led first from

Vietnam, where he connected with black soldiers and clashed with white soldiers, and then from college, where he connected with white antiwar activists and sometimes clashed with black activists. Fourth, his bringing the Panthers to New Bedford demonstrates that they frequently emerged from within (spreading, often, through family connections) and yet were significantly influenced from without (in this case principally by Panthers from nearby Boston). Fifth, in the aftermath of the Panther "moment," on the streets of New Bedford, in prison, and then back on the streets again — until his death — Grace maintained his politics *and* his life outside the law.

Because his personality so clearly shaped his politics — and because the best available evidence, both oral and written, is of that complex personality — I begin this essay with him fully formed. In doing so, I seek him first through the eyes of those who knew him as an adult, and then by listening to him in his own voice, which is revealed in a remarkable set of letters he wrote while serving his life sentence during the late 1970s and early 1980s. In the second section I return to his beginnings in New Bedford, carrying the story forward to his days as a Panther in the late 1960s and early 1970s. In the third section I closely examine the case that sent him to prison — the 1972 shooting death of a drug dealer named Marvin Morgan — by tracing that story from his trial and conviction to his release in 1985. Finally, I end the essay with a few observations about Grace's days after prison, suggesting some alternative ways of seeing the Panthers through this one individual who, toward the end of his life, said "I go down Panther."

"Parky Was a *Thing*"

The rich body of evidence about Parky Grace's life does not necessarily make reconstructing his story an easy task, if only because, like Huey Newton, Grace gained legendary status, and it is thus sometimes hard to separate fact from fiction. In part, the problem arises from the tales he spun about himself as a gang member, a combat soldier, and a revolutionary.[6] But, more important (and again like the more famous Newton) was his volatile and complex personality, interpreted in radically different, and sometimes surprising, ways by the people who knew him. Strikingly, one sixties activist who had lived in New Bedford all his life was moved to ask recently, "What *was* the deal with Parky, anyway?"[7] Another activist, closer to the street, offered this: "He was a friend of mine, but Parky was a thug."[8] Many in the police department and city government, as well as many community residents, agree with that assessment. After all, by the time he was twenty-one and entered the army he had been arrested a dozen times, and the arrests continued almost immediately upon his return in early 1969.[9] Then, in the early 1970s, he was convicted of murdering an eighteen-year-old Providence heroin dealer, Marvin Morgan (in a manner characterized by the police as "execution style"), for which he served eleven years of a life-without-parole sentence before the conviction was vacated on appeal in 1985.[10] And there is no dispute about Grace's fierceness as a street fighter, for which he was often arrested.[11] Still, it was his confrontational manner — especially when he became politically radical from 1969 onward — that frequently emerged in his relations with local police and thus made him a target; his arrest record represents something more than a simple reflection of his criminal activity.

A key witness to the complexities of Grace's personality comes from an unlikely source — Jibreel Khazan (né Ezell Blair Jr.), who was one of the Greensboro Four and an advocate of nonviolence all his adult life. Five years after having helped launch the civil rights sit-in movement in February 1960, Khazan came to New Bedford to work in the Job Corps program of the War on Poverty. One night shortly after arriving in town and locked out of his apartment, Khazan claims, he happened onto Grace's turf.

> I knew that he and his gang, the West End Gang, had been watching me.[12] And what happened was, I picked up a black cat. I think I fed the cat . . . and he came out of the shadows. He was walking east on Kempton Street and I was walking west. He said, "Hey Cuz, where're you from?" I said, "My name is Ezell Blair Jr.; you can call me 'Easy.'" [He] said, "My name is Frank Parky Grace; they call me 'Parky.'" He said, "Where you all from, Cousin?" I say, "Greensboro, North Carolina." He said, "You're all right with me; you're green people."[13] That's what he said. He said, "What's the problem?" I said, "I got locked out o' my apartment." He said, "Hey, man, you can sleep in the Gang House tonight." . . .
>
> Later, he told me . . . that the gang had been watching me, and had I mistreated the cat, then he was going to let the guys beat me up. But, he said — he was clearly the leader — "because you treated this cat well," he said, "your life was, you know, we let you; I told them, don't touch him." I said, this is a good man.

Switching to the present tense, and reflecting the diversity of opinion about Grace in New Bedford, Khazan continues,

> Parky has a sense of great dignity, but some also — some people want to call him a sociopath — [but] Parky is a natural leader.

Then, back to the past tense.

> Some people in the community, they said that Parky could be a troublemaker. They said he was always a troublemaker. He had a split personality.

Reflecting on Grace's years in prison for murder, Khazan says about his friend,

> But he carried through; he's a warrior; he's not afraid to fight anyone. And he'd take him on, 'cause, he said, "A man's afraid to die, he's got nothing to live for." He said, "I haven't died already, man. Death — I ain't afraid of death," he said, "it's the livin' part." He said, "nothing worse than livin', suffering, and being oppressed." He said, "to die is easy; to live is what's hard."

In a telephone conversation with Parky about a year before Grace's death, Khazan says he told his friend:

> "Parky, you know what?" . . . "You got more heart than I could ever have." . . . "I come from the South, man, but . . . when it comes to heart . . . you cross the dimensions that I have not crossed. . . . You are a living hero. A living witness." . . . "I wish I had a heart like you," I said, "I really admire you greatly"; which I do. . . . And I don't care which side of the fence you may be on. I have to give this man all due respect that he lived to tell the story; he's still walkin' the street.[14]

Perhaps the most accurate description of Parky Grace was captured by one of his life-long friends, his fellow Vietnam veteran and sixties street activist Ronnie Cruz, who said simply, "Parky was a *thing*" — by which he meant someone too complex, too contradictory, and too larger-than-life to be defined by any one label.[15] Even Parky's younger brother, Ross, a New Bedford Panther activist who idolized Parky all of his life, remembers him today as "an enigma."[16] But, in this, Grace's life also helps to provide a glimpse of the broader meaning of the Panther "moment," especially in light of contemporary New Bedford's favorite way to describe him: "Parky," they say, "was stuck in the sixties."[17] As Ross put it, even after Parky left the Party (he joined in late 1969), "He was a Panther all his life" — a phrase Ross used repeatedly in explaining his brother's lifelong political commitment.[18]

Some measure of this reality — and of the man himself — can be glimpsed in the letters Grace wrote to his friend and radical compatriot, Gloria Clark, while in the State Correctional Institution at Walpole, Massachusetts, during the late 1970s.[19] The letters reveal someone who wielded power within the institution—a picture verified by those on both sides of institutional divide—and who was often a target of the prison authorities. For example, Ernie Santos, Parky's friend and one-time fellow street militant, ended up in the late 1970s as a corrections officer in Walpole, where he found in Parky a protector in a strange and dangerous environment.[20] Vern Rudolph, another friend and political ally in earlier years, ended up in Walpole in the same period as a prisoner, and he also found that Parky seemed to have had the run of the place.[21] Still, Grace was a recalcitrant jailhouse presence, for which he would suffer repeated periods of isolation along with transparently punitive transfers to federal penitentiaries outside the state and even an unsuccessful attempt to frame him for stabbing a prison guard. Most portentous of his formal activities, apparently, was his involvement in cofounding the interracial Association for the Reduction of Violence (ARV), a group that sponsored lectures by local professors, counseled young people, and most crucially sought to reduce violence among prisoners and redirect their energy against the prison administration. In late 1978, following a five-week "lockup" of prisoners, the Walpole warden shut down the ARV. In response, the prisoners sued in federal court, which appointed to represent them the prestigious law firm of Hale and Dorr (the lawyers for Richard Nixon in the Watergate tapes case). This was a fortuitous event, as it would turn out, because it was Bob Thuotte, a young recruit to the firm who, six years later, would press the partners to take on Grace's case. And in 1985, with the help of a small but dedicated band of activists in New Bedford, Hale and Dorr would secure Parky's release and a measure of exoneration. In the aftermath, and until his death—now with the trademark dreadlocks he grew in prison in solidarity with another prisoner harassed for his hairstyle—he "maintained his militancy and Left politics."[22]

In his prison letters, Grace called his new home "Madpole," a "lunatic convict factory," the "inside of a garbage can—literally." He wrote to Gloria Clark in late 1976 that after three years of prison life, things were "getting harder by the minute." "The time has taken its toll on my mind, and it promises to take more," he observed.[23] "At times," he acknowledged, "I know I'm going to blow," and he admitted to being "pissed off all the time."[24] In lamenting living "in this madness all day"—a situation that helped produce the ARV that year—he reminded his correspondent, "I'm a hard dude" ("I can't even take myself for three minutes"), but then he added quickly, "It hurts . . . This whole situation hurts." A year later, he referred to his "living a

A Rebel All His Life

life of death," even admitting during a lockup and shakedown in early 1978 that he "sat here scared shitless" ("Yea, that's the truth"), thinking about how to take this "ass whipping that's coming."[25] The admission was significant: three months earlier, in response to Clark's request that he put his feelings down on paper, he reminded her, "You know that I've got a heavy case of Macho. Got to keep up that front (smile)."[26] A year later, now in Walpole's notorious 10 Block, he confided,

> We try not to show our fear to our visits or each other but it's there, here. Some men may not have long to live and if they do live the administration will make [them] wish they were dead. I've resigned myself to the fact that there is a strong possibility that I will die in here.[27]

At the same time, Parky had more than one audience — his letters were censored, and he knew it — and he was fighting a psychological as well as a physical war. He wanted the guards to know, he told Clark, that if they "fuck with me that they will not come back to work." "And you know something G, I'm good at the [martial] arts. I know it, and they know it. They go around bullying people and I go around intimidating them. You could say I'm at war with these folks."[28]

As elsewhere throughout these letters, however, his reference to being at "war" with prison administrators marked him as a political animal. In reaching for some analogy that Clark would understand, he reminded her of "the feeling you had in D.C." during a 1969 antiwar demonstration. Only here there's no retreat."[29] Similarly, with his anger in late 1976, he wrote:

> I sit here and get mad because I know it's the system that causes not only my misery but the misery and death of countless others. I see this system destroys guards and prisoners alike. It's like the Vietnam War all over again, people versus people. I try to educate the men here to what I believe is wrong with the system. I talk to cons and the guards. Every once in awhile I even talk with someone from the administration.[30]

Two years later, he referred to the disciplinary "tickets" he received as something that "takes you back to the Vietnam era" of "body counts." And, just as in Vietnam, these punishments — "the master's mental whip" — fell most heavily on "us, we niggers!"[31] The previous month, he compared prison conditions to ghetto conditions, and the violence at Walpole to the riots of the 1960s and early 1970s.[32] In all of this it is difficult to disentangle the political organizing — one might even call it community service work —

from the self-defense posture that involved the ever-present threat of violence, from both sides. Drawing on language that connected him to a history of oppression in the United States that his Cape Verdean ancestors, singularly, had not experienced, he wrote in early 1977:

> I'm a good slave. I attend school, doing as poorly as ever (smile). I also belong to . . . a drug program in which I'm a counselor. I am working in the metal shop but they had a strike and I was charged with mutiny and inciting a riot. Since that time I have not been allowed back to the slave shop. I'm also with a group of big brothers. We have rap sessions with so-called troubled youth.[33]

And, again, the following October, he spoke of "seeing men driven mad, living with rats and roaches, suffering daily from ulcer attacks, headaches, mental and physical abuse," and then claimed to have all the while tried to teach "love for the people," pledging, "I don't want to hate, not people. I want to love and fight for the people."[34]

"I guess it was love and spite that kept me going," he wrote Clark five years later, in celebration of having survived eight years in the system ("I sit here smiling, saying to myself, 'well you ain't been broke yet'"). In his rendition, he had always been engaged in a political struggle.

> I always looked at myself as the people's soldier and I wouldn't let them punks break the people's soldier. Time's I had words with 'one pig or another,' and told them, 'you and a million mother f— like you ain't gonna break me punk, I'm people's liberation army!!'

"The spite and hate I have for some of these dogs and my love for people has kept me going," he concluded.[35] At the time of his exit from prison in 1985, he said essentially the same thing to Michael Matza of the alternative newsweekly the *Phoenix*:

> I always considered myself a soldier. . . . And being a soldier, POW, prisoner of war, I had to conduct myself in a special way, you know? Because I hold a special position, you know? Other people coming in here know I'm a political prisoner, right? So, I have to carry myself where I'm beyond reproach. And I have to be strong and I have to be an example to other prisoners. When I went in there, it was with a sense of mission. Like a soldier into a new field. And I was angry. I was very, very angry.[36]

Though not always, apparently. In 1982, in a card bearing an imprint of a Van Gogh painting, he wrote of the year ending—a good one "on the whole" for me, hoping the next will be "better for all of us." In closing, he proclaimed. "I just have faith in the people and I know tomorrow will be brighter. . . . I send you smiles, strength, and revolutionary love."[37]

Here is the most consistent theme of Parky's letters to Gloria Clark—and, indeed, of his life as early as his teen years: the commitment to transcending divisions, especially of race (something that made him a natural recruit for the Panthers, especially the post-April 1969 Boston Panthers, with whom he would made contact later that fall).[38] In late 1977, speaking of his own case, he argued for a political effort to free him—one that went beyond legal considerations—because the "community, particularly the Black and Cape Verdean and Puerto Rican peoples would get a boost out of something like this." "That," he confided, "would be the ultimate high for me."[39] Early the following year, during the lockup that he had admitted "scared the hell out of me," he claimed he had been training in the martial arts with a number of "white brothers" for several months. It was now, "black and white together," he wrote, and they had proclaimed, " 'No More!' "—an obvious reference to the ARV. Black, white, Puerto Rican, Cape Verdean, everybody "fighting for human rights."[40]

That summer, Parky wrote of a "lumpen brother" who, "not long ago, hated honkeys," but now "talks to white dudes and addresses them as brother." "He was a reactionary," Parky wrote, "now he's becoming something different."[41] And, describing his involvement with the ARV as a "personal-political decision," Grace spoke of educating youth to "racism and alternatives to violence."[42] He also noted the "divide and conquer" tactics used by the Walpole administration, as well as insisted that he was a particular target of prison guards because he was married to a white woman, Lynette Bingham.[43]

In still another letter to Clark in 1978 he noted his stance against "authority, reactionary, negative, ill-gotten authority." "It's hard for me to compromise," he wrote. "I don't like to give an inch. I've been that way most of my life, for as long as I can remember."[44] From Memphis, Tennessee, where he had been transferred for his role in the ARV, he wrote:

> Jails, prisons, houses of correction, etc., they all suck!—dehumanize, hurt and kill, spiritually and mentally—everyday died a little more! So before I lose to (*sic*) much[,] steps will have to be taken. I might have to say fuck it to the freedom which might be lurking down the rode (*sic*). It's not that I don't want to be free of that I won't compromise. It's just that I won't let them take everything. I'd rather be dead. After all, G., I've got to live with me.[45]

Finally, there is in these letters evidence of Grace's wit. On his release from "the hole" in late summer 1978, for example, he wrote, "things here seem to be the same, still locked up. Damn, I get out of isolation and they lock the whole joint up. All I can say is 'This is a great country.'"[46] During a previous lockup in late 1977, which he had referred to as a "horror show," he told Clark that, amidst the garbage and rodents, he walked up and down, yelling, "'This is a good country!'" People would smile, laugh, and "I feel better." Combining his politics with that same sense of humor, he declared, "it's always open season on me," and then compared his situation to "Mao's long march, Fidel in the hills, Lenny Bruce on stage (smile)."[47]

Still, there is no doubt that what made him distinctive — and trouble — was his uncompromising spirit. In a postscript to one of his letters to Clark he offered a kind of coda for his life.

> During our rap I mentioned people thinking me nuts. Yes, that's always pissed me off. One day, I'll explain that in detail, or try. Simply put, "all black men who speak out against the system are labeled madmen." Hey, I'm just a dude who has been a rebel all his life. A rebel who would be a little extreme at times, and a pain in the ass most of the time! (Smile) Wait till these people see my children.[48]

The making (and remaking) of that rebel sitting in Walpole state prison in winter 1977 is a story that demands telling.

The Birth of a Panther

Frank Grace Jr. was born on 6 April 1944 to children of Cape Verdean immigrants in the principal population center of American Cape Verdeans, New Bedford's South End.[49] Because of their complex lineage and the world into which they entered, first as whalers and merchant seamen in the early Republic, then as cranberry pickers and textile workers in the late nineteenth century and early twentieth, the Cape Verdeans in New Bedford were typically shunned as "colored" by the so-called white Portuguese. In turn, they sought to distinguish themselves from what they called "Americans de couer" — that is, the African Americans, West Indians, and Afro-Indians located primarily in the city's West End.[50] Though the Cape Verdeans were involved in labor and leftist struggles as early as the late 1920s (there was even a reported cranberry bog riot in 1900), they were deeply ambivalent about color, race, and ethnicity during Parky's formative years in the 1950s and early 1960s. The issue intensified with the black consciousness movement of the mid-to-late sixties, especially as a growing minority began to identify with Amilcar Cabral's African Party for the Independence of Guinea Bissau and Cape Verde (PAIGC).⁵¹ Indeed, even today locals of all ages, at the beginning of any conversation about the city in the 1960s, remark on the peculiarities of the Cape Verdeans. Parky—a born storyteller who offers a prime example of Alessandro Portelli's maxim that "oral sources tell us not just what people did, but what they wanted to do, what they believed they were doing, and what they now think they did"—began a narrative of his life this way.

> The South End was where I was born and brought up [was] basically made up of Cape Verdeans, Portuguese, and Puerto Ricans. And the West End . . . to me an' others of the Cape Verdeans . . . that's where the *colores* live, Americans of color, the Negroes. . . . The West End and the South End used to fight one another. And Cape Verdeans, they referred to the West Enders as niggers. . . . Cape Verdeans thought they were, I can't say all, they were white, they were different.⁵²

Then, during Parky's early teens in the late 1950s, his family moved to the West End, and he came to identify with a section of the city that, though racially and ethnically mixed, was seen as the Negro section of town. By the 1960s Parky's identity was not fixed, as he continued to move back and forth across County Street (young people then called it the Mason-Dixon Line), which divided the West End from downtown, and thus the South End as well. At the end of his life Parky tried, in sometimes apparently contradictory ways, to explain the complexities of identity in New Bedford when he was coming of age.

> We were just like African Americans. People considered themselves *Negroes*. . . . If someone called somebody "black," you'd be in a beef—say, "I ain't *black*, I'm a Negro!" And then, you know, it's a process. "Oh, yeah, I'm black now." And then, ah, "I'm African"; and, "I ain't no African; I'm Indian!" Even in Africa, people there, "I ain't African" (laughs). "I'm Indian, Chinese," or somethin.' . . . There's such a way where you be anything.⁵³

Often in trouble at school, he never completed the ninth grade after being suspended for a year—"I forget [for] what."⁵⁴ In the early 1960s, then in his late teens, he searched for employment:

> I caddied, worked in the bowlin' alley . . . I finally got a job . . . in Eastern Sportswear . . . my mother worked there. . . . And, then they were closing a lot of factories down; they were movin' down South. . . . It was pretty decent, but, then,

y'know, we had like these speedups.... Say you have a shirt, and ... one side of this shirt would be stitched together, you'd have to cut that thread and put it in piles of fifty, and at first I had four people to cut, but I was just fast. And, then they made it six, and then eight, and then ten. That's one whole line. And I was just keepin' up; and then they, another line, right? And I mean, like, I'm doin' the work of four to six people. And, it would just pile up, pile up. And, ah, the boss they had there, Joe, he was steady fuckin' with me, right? And I said, "Man, leave me alone, just leave me alone!" And, ah, one day he came and I just went in my jacket, took out a knife, and I started chasin' him all over that place.[55]

His next job was as a spray painter, where, he says, he was the only black, "The rest was all Portuguese guys." As he tells it, he had the same kind of altercation with his new boss as he had had with the old one. And so he left — "that was the beginning of summer" — and started "just hangin' out down at the beach, and down by Montes Playground [in the South End], where we all hung out in the West End, like that." In 1962, at the age of eighteen, he spent an increasing amount of time in an unpaved area in the West End called the Lane, and the group he ran with called themselves the Lane Gang (which sometimes morphed into "Lang" Gang, in order to rhyme). He had become, as he would claim later, a "volunteer lumpen."[56] By mid-1962 he was in the court system, and by early 1963, when he was still eighteen years old, the police arrested him for assault and battery with a dangerous weapon during a gang fight.[57] There is no indication that he was in any way political at this time, though later in life he would tell a different story.

He claimed that his family — particularly his mother and grandmother — had engendered a fierce sense of justice in him. "My father was one of the founders of the Cape Verdean Veterans' Association ... [He was] a World War II veteran. My mother and them, they were active, right, in various ways." And, he tells a story, likely apocryphal, about his grandmother.

When I was, I imagine, three years old, my grandmother on my mother's side ... we were in the house ... an' she used to always have the doors open and curtains open. And, one day, she just closed them. And, she had an American flag and a Portuguese flag crossin' over each other; and over the top of it, there was a picture of Franklin Delano Roosevelt. So, she took the Portuguese flag and she kissed it, and she touched her heart to it; then, she took that American flag and she spit on it, rubbed it on her behind ... threw it on the floor, and then stomped on it. You know, so you're three years old, y'know ... I never forgot that, you know? And it left a deep impression on me.[58]

He also insisted that his gang activity was in fact political.

> My mind was already on revolution, but I didn't know, I couldn't articulate it. I said, "We want to start a club." . . . Something that could help the people, y'know? And I was always headin' towards the Party, y'know? And, ah, there we found a club called "Club 100." And, what it was was dudes from different sections of the city—South End, West End, Upper West, North, Puerto Rican, white, Cape Verdean, African American, right? And, these were like, these guys that, these were like gangs. But, we managed to bring them all together. We didn't realize how significant that was. Y'know? At that time, I became the President of that Club 100. We had a hundred members.[59]

By late 1965, though, he had decided to join a different army. In 1984, serving the eleventh year of his life sentence for murder, he told a local reporter that he had joined the military because "I wanted to become a man."[60] In other interviews, he did mention wanting to make his "parents proud" ("military persons were always respected in our community"), as well as noting the "lack of jobs" in New Bedford, but other evidence suggests that there was something more to it. In fact, he gave a variety of reasons for enlisting just as the war in Vietnam was escalating—reasons ranging from generally "bein' hounded by the police"[61] to a very bloody incident with his lifelong friend and later political comrade Charlie Perry, for which he was arrested on charges of assault with a deadly weapon and faced jailed time. Moreover, a Cape Verdean New Bedford police detective who had known Parky all his life, and who would intersect with him at key moments of his career, claims that he brokered a deal with the courts: in exchange for enlisting he would receive no jail time.[62] Grace's sister, Clo, verifies this story in its essence, remembering the judge, "a little short white man," pronouncing in court, "Service or time!"

Parky's troubles continued in the army, especially in Vietnam where he served as a combat engineer. He was, he said, "just a soldier," though he added, "I was still a rebel, you know." Later in life, he told lots of stories about "beefs" with other soldiers and especially with commanding officers, sometimes of a petty nature (typically a refusal to acknowledge arbitrary authority) and other times concerning issues of perceived racial discrimination, particularly the different way that white and black soldiers were treated for minor infractions. But, too, he remembered vividly the insensitivity, even hostility, of whites after King's assassination. As a result of his response—"In those days my solution to everything was lock and load," he told a reporter in 1985 — he was subject to frequent disciplining, including repeated stretches in the stockade.[63] In the middle of telling one such story, he digressed to explain his sometimes exaggerated responses to everyday situations — "My temper, you know?"[64]

But his politics, not just his militancy, developed while he was in Vietnam, at least as he told it. His first day there in 1967, he claimed, he knew something was wrong. Elderly Vietnamese in rice paddies, he said, seemed no worse off than his own relatives, like his grandmother who had worked in the cranberry bogs of southeastern Massachusetts.[65] When the Vietnamese near his base asked him why he was there, he remembered that he would say it was to fight for their freedom. But, when they asked about freedom in the United States, it "started me asking lots of questions."[66] Indeed, though there is no documentary evidence of it, Parky claimed he was being tracked by the U.S. government in Vietnam, "'cause they were askin' me there if I was a communist. And I hated communists! Are you crazy? I'm over here fightin' communists, right?"[67] This formed a persistent theme of Grace's story of his Vietnam years: he was there fighting communism and defending the Constitution, which in his view was both an illusion and the root of his sense of fairness and justice that he carried over into his leftist politics after he came home. Most important, perhaps, was his exposure in Vietnam to the movements going on stateside. He told stories later, for example, of hearing about demonstrators on the radio — especially one story about demonstrators laying across railroad tracks in order to stop trains carrying munitions (most likely this refers to the Stop the Draft Week action in Oakland in October 1967): "They must have *somethin'* there . . . 'cause *I* wouldn't lay out in front of no goddamn train." He was also impressed by the guys in California who talked about LSD. "Just start question[ing]" Grace remembered. "*Something* ain't right."[68]

Grace returned from Vietnam in late 1968, sporting an Afro. He states that he "was beginning to become political," though for the first eight months back in New Bedford he seems to have returned to his old habits of hanging out on the streets in the West End. Predictably, he ended up in trouble with the police — for disorderly conduct, assault, threatening bodily harm, and carrying a switchblade.[69] The streets had changed, however, as a result of the sixties coming to New Bedford. There had been the long and sometimes bloody and racially charged battle over an interracial experiment,

A Rebel All His Life 117

the Fort Rodman Job Corps, which was part of the War on Poverty. In 1965, the same year that Rodman opened, the NAACP established a Youth Council that rejuvenated a venerable but previously very traditional local branch. Three years later, just as Rodman closed, a Black United Front emerged, which was modeled on an organization of the same name established by Stokely Carmichael in Boston. All of these events, albeit in different ways, had raised the consciousness of the area's Cape Verdean youth in particular.[70] In Parky's absence, the New Bedford Cape Verdeans had become "black."

In fall 1969 Grace's life took a momentous turn when he enrolled in the New Careers Program at a community college in nearby Fall River. It was this experience that led him, in short order, to the Black Panther Party.

> I'd been interested in the Panthers from the time I was in Vietnam [he recalled], but I didn't know much about 'em. [I] read about 'em in *Jet* magazine; and, then, when I got home . . . [and] was going to BCC [Bristol Community College] . . . on my very first day there, I ran into a [anti]war demonstration. Which really educated me. It put everything into place—like the Vietnam War, what was happenin' in the black ghetto, communities, whatever, and I was seein' things clearly. Met up with them people, and got a leaflet from one, newspaper, sat down and talked with them, and I started to become politicized.[71]

Aiding in this process was his relationship with one of his teachers, Gloria Clark, his prison correspondent of later years. As a graduate of the teacher preparation program at Boston's Wheelock College in 1963, Clark had taught elementary school for a year in the New Bedford area when she answered the call for volunteers to teach in a "freedom school" in Mississippi during the Freedom Summer of 1964. She stayed on into winter 1965, and then returned to New Bedford where, among other things, she worked at the local antipoverty agency, taught at Rodman, spearheaded the NAACP Youth Council, worked with the Black United Front, organized an antiwar coalition, and participated in the Harvard Strike of 1969 as a graduate student at the School of Education. In fall 1969, she joined a group of area radicals (mostly former members of SDS) in a group called the Regional Action Group (RAG).[72] By then, she was an instructor in the New Careers Program at BCC, and Parky was her student.

According to Clark, Parky was then "inquisitive, curious, vocal" but not political, though she quickly adds, "He was against the war . . . he was a returning vet against the war. Which immediately made you political, I think

—in some ways."[73] The first activity conducted by RAG was an antiwar demonstration in New Bedford—the first the city had witnessed—and Parky participated in it. More important, though, was his attendance at the massive November antiwar mobilization in Washington a week later, to which he traveled with Gloria on a bus she and others at BCC had chartered. Thirteen years later, writing from the federal penitentiary in Memphis, he would exhort Clark to work with others in New Bedford who had formed a defense coalition for him, reminding her of their roots in antiwar activity: "Seeing you the one who got me in all this trouble in the first place."[74] About Grace at the Washington demonstration, Clark remembered,

> Parky was great. That's when I got to see Parky in action. And, um, that was at the Pentagon[75] . . . and the Pentagon was surrounded by troops. . . . They had gas masks on, and gas guns and things like that. And they were standing all around it. So, the demonstrators came up and approached them. Some demonstrators just crashed through them and created violent scenes. But we went there, Parky came and me and a bunch of other people from BCC. And Parky just started doing a number on 'em (laughs). He went to the guy, right in his face, right to the gas mask—the kid was eighteen—and he said, "Man, you know, I used to be like you; I used to have to have a gun on this side, and," he said, "aim at people, you know; and you're just one o' us and we're just one of you, you know, and it's just the Man that's making you do this, just the way he made me do it." You know. And, he ran in on this guy to the point where we saw the tears coming down outside the gas mask, and the kid was just crying, and he was not moving, but his tears were coming down. Very moving moment, you know? And, see that was Parky.[76]

There was a mix-up on the way back and Parky got on the wrong bus. He ended up in Boston, where he visited the headquarters of the Black Panther Party on Blue Hill Avenue in Roxbury. "Just goin' in there, enterin' the door," he said thirty years later, "there was Big Bob [Heard] teaching a PE class. . . . And I knew right then . . . *This is what I want.*[77] Throughout that fall and in the following winter and spring of 1970, "just about every week," according to Parky, he—sometimes with Clark—would hitchhike to Boston to attend Panther classes. In addition to bringing back papers, buttons, and posters, they would set up informal sessions with Boston Panthers for West End residents at the old African Church and, especially, at an abandoned building on Kempton Street known only as "the Club."[78]

At about the same time, Parky and other veterans formed a group called the Black Brothers, which would meet in homes, on street corners, and often in the West End Social Club just off Kempton Street (across the street from "the Club"). Sometimes referred to by the media as a community organization, a political organization, or even a political party, the group's relationship to the Panthers is instructive here.[79] As Parky later described the radical ferment in New Bedford at the time:

> When I used to leave Boston, I used to leave with newspapers, buttons and posters, leaflets, y'know different information—stimulate the community, educate the community. So, people would say that there was Panthers in New Bedford; they sold posters of Huey and Bobby on the streets.... And clothes, people wearing buttons, "Off the pigs!" buttons.... And then, people wearing Panther gear—leather jackets and berets, in peoples' minds were the Panther Party.
>
> Q: Now, would this be *before* the Black Brothers were established?
> Parky: It was just, y'know, I came from Boston with newspapers, and would pass 'em out, and all the clubs and bars, and on the streets people would have discussions.... We were all together... and we'd sit there and we'd talk... So, sittin' there, and one night talking, and so... I don't know exactly how it went, but I'm sure we're discussing things previously, same thing, about organizing. Then, one night, we just came up with the name. What we were gonna do. And got there started, an' I was still goin' to Boston, comin' up to Boston to Political Education class and various other things dealing with the Panther Party.
>
> Q: And what did the Black Brothers do?
> Oh, what we were tryin' to do was educate ourselves and other people in the community. We were trying to form a group; it would be a more military group. Consider that just about everybody in the Brothers were all Vietnam vets; our view of revolutions was *fighting*.
>
> Q: But, why not just form a chapter of the Black Panther Party?
> There are a lot of reasons. I don't know. "We don't need him to come in here and tell us what to do," and, y'know, I guess a lotta old guys and people that had mistrust for organizations, and different people [whose] lives [were] abused by various groups.[80]

And none of the Black Brothers ever did join the Panthers as Parky did, even though Grace did put up Panther posters at the West End Social Club. By July 1970, however, Panthers and Brothers would be together in the streets, when New Bedford, which had simmered for the better part of a decade, finally exploded in a "major civil disturbance," according to the criteria used by the Kerner Commission of 1968.[81] And these events would draw in the Boston Panthers, not just as occasional speakers but as what might be called "colonizers"—just what the Brothers had feared but exactly what Parky Grace had been working toward for the better part of a year.

The event that some locals often call "the riots," and radicals like Grace always call "the Rebellion," began on Wednesday, 8 July, during a routine traffic stop in the city's West End—routine in the sense that a kind of low-level combat between police and young people had long been a regular feature of summer life and yet had increased in the late 1960s and intensified in May and June 1970. The first night witnessed clashes with police and firemen, chants of "Off the Pig," street barricades, scattered fires, sniper fire, and arrests. Although Parky was in the thick of the fighting that night he was not arrested, yet some of his friends were: the local militant Warren Houtmann; Black Brother Jimmy Magnett; and future Panther and lifelong friend Charlie Perry. Parky claimed that throughout the event he played a defensive role: manning barricades, shooting out streetlights, organizing the collection of weapons and ammunition, but restraining a younger, less-disciplined generation of angry teens from engaging in indiscriminate arson and looting. Violence escalated on the second night and then spread to the South End, where it even drew in several members of RAG who tried to draw police away from the center of the action on Kempton Street by firebombing nearby abandoned buildings.[82] One rookie cop, also recently returned from Vietnam, said later, "It reminded me of the war."[83] By Friday, the crew of the black-produced public television show *Say, Brother!* had arrived from Boston to take the pulse of the New Bedford streets. The anger captured on the film is palpable, much of it racial, as is evident in the interview with Jimmy Magnett.[84] Again Parky stood out; and in retrospect he can be identified as someone who was already a Panther. For example, he is the only one on camera who speaks of "capitalists" and explicitly rejects the notion that the issue was white versus black.[85]

The *Say Brother!* crew was still in the city on Saturday, 11 July, when three white kids from neighboring towns breached the barricades that Parky and others had erected to block off much of the West End, drove down Kempton Street, and stopped in front of "the Club" where thirty to forty blacks, Cape Verdeans, and Latinos were gathered in a kind of informal celebration of their newly won "liberated territory."[86] Parky, who had been on the streets almost continuously since the evening of 8 July, went to the beach that afternoon and evening, and so was not present for what was about to happen — the most horrific event of New Bedford's July Days. The driver of the car, a twenty-year-old New Bedford High graduate named Ralph Brown, stepped out of the car, placed a shotgun over its hood, and fired into the crowd. Killed by the gunfire was a seventeen-year-old Cape Verdean, Lester Lima, whom the press identified as "a black youth." In addition, three others were injured: a local teen who had been with Parky at Boston Panther headquarters the previous fall and who was identified as a Panther and two others who were sympathetic to the Panther cause.[87] New Bedford exploded in response to the shooting, leading to the intervention of state political leaders, including Ed Brooke, who at the time was the first black Republican U.S. Senator since the nineteenth century. In the wake of all this, too, came the Boston Panthers, who sought a permanent presence in the strife-torn city.[88]

With Parky Grace and other New Bedford residents — mostly young Cape Verdean males living in the West End — who would become Panthers, along with a range of community people of all ages, the Panthers established a makeshift headquarters of a National Committee to Combat Fascism (NCCF) branch in the partially burned and looted remains of a local store called Pieraccini's Variety.[89] Throughout the month, as attempts to resolve long-standing issues that helped spark the violence occupied local and state officials in negotiations with a complex array of community activists (some of whom had already identified with the Panthers), and as violence ebbed and flowed on the streets, Pieraccini's became a focal point of community hostility and energy. For Grace, it was a cross-generational community center, a liberation school, a distribution center for Panther literature; it was also a fortress of sorts (complete with sandbags, gun slots, and a cache of weapons and ammunition).[90] Cleaning up the space, painting and decorating it with Panther posters, and welcoming to it neighborhood grandmothers and children — this was Parky in his element, and his days and nights were consumed by the activity.[91]

By the end of the month, those with the most guns had had enough, and a predawn raid on Pieraccini's netted twenty-one "Panthers" — hence, for a time, the celebrated case of the "New Bedford 21" — most of whom were promptly charged with, among lesser crimes, conspiracy to commit murder, anarchy, and inciting riots.[92] Though police reports detailed how each of the twenty-one were arrested either coming out of the front or back of the building, in fact most were netted by a sweep of the area not in Pieraccini's but around it.[93] Grace's participation in the event was, as usual, distinctive. He had gone home to sleep—the first time in days—in the evening of 30 July, and he heard about the raid on the radio. Marching up to Kempton and brushing off friends' arguments to stay away, he banged on the police wagon and demanded to be taken, too. As one of those already in the wagon remembered it, "Here comes my boy, Parky! Coming out of the crowd. 'Take me!'"[94] And so they did.

Grace and several of the others, including four associated with the Boston Panthers, would have charges hanging over them for nearly a year. In the meantime, a local Panther movement developed, initially under the aegis of the local NCCF. It was relocated to Ernie's Drugstore, another storefront on Kempton down the block from Pieraccini's.[95] Infused with members and leadership from Boston—a source of continuing tension, according to several local Panthers—the group established a breakfast program, free food and clothing programs, free sickle cell anemia screening, and a liberation school.[96] For some in New Bedford it was a real community institution, yet others barely remember it.[97] A principal activity, of course, was the propaganda work around the upcoming Panther trial. In spring 1971, all of the major charges were dropped by the then new district attorney, Phillip A. Rollins. Further, only two of the indicted were prosecuted, and only one served a short sentence. Many at the time believed—as do some to this day—that these actions were part of a deal to avoid a replay of the previous summer pending the outcome of the murder trial of the three whites charged in the death of Lester Lima. In that trial, the shooter admitted to the crime in court, though during a hearing on the suppression of evidence (with the jury absent). The jury, all whites, deliberated for forty-five minutes and voted to acquit on all charges.[98]

There was much grumbling after the acquittal, but other than some arson and rock throwing; an attempt to get the U.S. attorney in Boston to take up the matter as a civil rights case; and talk of exacting vengeance on the acquitted, New Bedford did not erupt as it had the previous summer.[99] Meanwhile, Parky drifted in and out of Panther activities. Like his old running partner Charlie Perry, he frequented the headquarters, sold newspapers, showed up at picket lines and some public events, and worked in what the Panthers were now calling "survival programs pending revolution."[100] At the same time, Parky's troubles with the law continued, including arrests for shoplifting, disturbing the peace, illegal possession of a firearm, assault, bar fighting, and accusations of taunting police as "pigs."[101] Parky (and even some reporters later) would see this as harassment by the police, and there is a measure of truth to this assertion.[102] Indeed, sometime in 1970 the FBI began tracking him in their Administrative Index.[103] For example, in October 1971 the FBI, reporting to the U.S. Secret Service in Boston, described Parky's recent political activities as follows: "During late 1970 and early 1971, the subject was very active in the Black Panther Party (BPP), attending rallies, soliciting funds and clothing for BPP programs, selling newspapers, distributing posters, and performing other BPP tasks. He was allegedly out of the party in early 1971, but according to informants, subject is now back in the BPP, New Bedford branch. ARMED AND DANGEROUS.[104]

The Commonwealth of Massachusetts vs. Frank Grace

By summer 1972, the national Panther organization was feeling the effects of the previous year's violent split, and Huey Newton was consolidating his power base in Oakland. As a result, most of the nation's Panther chapters were closing, and the New Bedford branch of the BPP had ceased to exist.[105] But with increasing frequency throughout the summer, Grace was in trouble with the New Bedford police. By then, the heroin trade had made a significant mark locally; by virtually all accounts it was a new phenomenon in the area.[106] Though Grace's run-ins were not specifically drug related, and most of his friends and family — indeed, even some local police — adamantly deny that he was ever engaged in dealing heroin (save for the claim that he stole from drug dealers to redistribute wealth in the community), he did consort with known dealers, and some of his arrests involved alleged violent conflict with dealers. Moreover, two key witnesses — his sister and his close friend, Vern Rudolf, who later served five years for dealing heroin — verify Parky's involvement in the trade.[107] And although today he deflects questions about his involvement, Parky's brother Ross had his own run-ins with drug dealers, most notably from nearby Providence, Rhode Island.[108] Ross's kidnapping and robbery by several Providence men in June 1972 — which he now claims was about money and not drugs — led directly to the shooting death of Marvin Morgan on 8 August, the crime for which Parky Grace would spend eleven years in prison. Meanwhile, during all the events of that summer of 1972 Parky was being tracked by the FBI.

Though the story of the Morgan shooting is the subject of thousands of pages of legal documents—police reports, the 1974 trial transcript, numerous appeals, and the Superior Court decision in early 1985 to grant Parky a new trial—the basic outline of what happened that hot Tuesday night in August can be gleaned from a series of written confessions, sworn affidavits, and recantations. First, Ross Grace confessed in 1982 (which was made public in the local press in 1983) to having fired the shot that killed Morgan, a claim that all of his lawyers would later swear he had told them from the time of his arrest. Second, numerous eyewitnesses eventually came forward and told essentially the same story. Third, one of the prosecution's original two key witnesses also corroborated Ross's account. The story told by these sources supports Parky's contention from the moment of his arrest that he was not in the area at the time of the shooting. Morgan, his cousin Eric "Ricky" Baker, and a friend, Jasper Lassiter, all heroin users, and, at least in the case of Baker and Morgan, dealers as well, came to New Bedford to buy drugs. Unable to purchase from their supplier at the appointed time, they waited at a nearby club, the West End Social Club, located on Cedar Street a few doors north of Kempton, about a half block from Pieraccini's and, in the other direction, about a half block from where Lester Lima was killed and another half block from Ernie's Drugstore. Ross, who stopped in sometime before midnight for some cigarettes, spotted the trio, and thinking that he recognized Morgan as one of those who had kidnapped him six weeks earlier, left and returned with friends who were at a house party nearby.[109] They confronted Morgan as he exited the Club, and, berating him with gun in hand—as one of those present would put it later, "using the gun like he was pointing his finger at the guy"—Ross shot him in the chest, apparently by accident.[110] According to the report of the first officers on the scene, Kenny Gifford and Matthew Lihares, Baker told them that he and his friends had been accosted outside the Club by three men unknown to them, along with "Rossy Delionit," and "a man with a funny nickname." Ross and the "man with the nickname" had guns, and, Baker said, he would recognize both if he saw them again.[111] As the officers named people who frequented the area, they reported that Baker "immediately responded to the name 'Parky,' stating, 'That's it, that's it!'"[112]

Parky, according to numerous eyewitnesses, was below the Mason-Dixon Line at the time of the shooting.[113] Out on the town with Vern Rudolph that evening after he had watched the first airing of the TV show *Kung Fu*, according to his trial testimony, he was seen by numerous witnesses at the

Cape Verdean Band Club, the Tropicana Café, and finally, when he heard about the shooting from his girlfriend, Eileen "Peachy" Sylvia, at the Cozy Lounge. All of these venues were located in the southern part of the city. Speeding to the West End in Rudolph's car, Parky and Rudolph, were told by people still milling about outside the West End Social Club that police were at Parky's house—a few blocks north—where he had left his young son, Che, with a babysitter.[114] Then, as Parky jogged *toward* the policemen who were looking for him at his home, he was arrested by his longtime police antagonist, Harry Albino. Later, he claimed that he was beaten in the stationhouse by Albino and others the following morning.[115] Meanwhile, neither Baker nor Lassiter were asked to identify either of the Grace brothers in a lineup. Instead, Baker left the station early Wednesday morning, 9 August, after which he went directly to his dealer's house and purchased his heroin. He then returned to the station and signed a statement accusing Parky of the shooting and Ross of having been on the scene with a gun in hand as well.

Former mayor Edward F. Harrington—who had a relationship with the Grace family; who had represented Parky in the past; and who, according to both Parky and Ross, had illicit dealings with them—was appointed as a public defender to represent Parky, Ross, and a third defendant, Donald "Dolomite" Arum. Ross told Harrington that he had been the shooter, and that Parky had been nowhere near the scene at the time of the shooting, but the lawyer advised Ross against coming forward with this evidence.[116] Then, a year later, and four-and-a-half months before trial, Harrington suddenly decided to represent only Arum, who, along with a fourth defendant, would be acquitted at trial of the lesser charge of assault with a dangerous weapon.[117] Harrington recommended that Ross retain Donald Zeman, a divorce lawyer with virtually no criminal experience, though Harrington insisted Zeman was "a very experienced criminal attorney."[118] Parky was assigned Kenneth Sullivan, the former assistant district attorney who had prosecuted two of the New Bedford 21 in spring 1971. According to Parky, he met with Sullivan on just one occasion for "about a half hour" before trial.[119] Moreover, Parky claimed later in a sworn affidavit, although he had asked Sullivan to contact witnesses "who could account for my whereabouts on the night of the shooting, as well as the names of several people in the neighborhood whom I believed had witnessed the shooting and thus could testify that I had not been involved, . . . to my knowledge, Sullivan never contacted any of the witnesses to the crime."[120] Finally, again according to Parky—a claim supported by Ross, who says he was witness to the event, as were all of the defendants' lawyers—the assistant district attorney offered him three to five years for a lesser plea, telling him, "we know you're innocent; we just want you off the streets for a while."[121]

Meanwhile, after the Morgan shooting but before the trial, the FBI apparently dropped Parky Grace from its security index. A communication from Boston to the director early in 1973 described Parky's activities retroactively, and now, having followed him for over two years, it suggested dropping him.

> Informants describe him as being in and out of the BPP on several occasions. He was reportedly out of the Party in early 1971 because of policy differences but was reported to be back in July 1971 and in late 1971 was active in the New Bedford Branch of the BPP Clothing Program. He was out of the party again in January, 1972, and was heavily involved in crime, particularly drug related. Through 1972, the subject's only BPP activity was attendance at a public meeting of the New Bedford School Board on Februrary 3, 1972, to support the BPP Breakfast Program. In March, 1972, all informants consistently described the subject as out of the BPP.
>
> Although the subject has numerous arrests for crimes of violence and he is currently on bail on murder charges, these arrests are strictly drug related and have no connection with BPP philosophies. . . .
>
> Since the subject has initiated no consistent extremist philosophy throughout his sporadic association with the BPP and since his involvement as a self serving criminal and drug oriented rather than Black Extremist and since he does not meet current criteria his removal from ADEX is recommended.[122]

One of Parky's champions would later conclude that "once the FBI realized that Parky would be convicted of 'murder' it would be safe for the FBI to drop their investigations into Parky's political activities. In other words, the FBI had Parky nailed even before the conviction and thus they would end his political activities, meaning that further investigations were really no longer necessary. The FBI had him."[123]

Whatever the FBI's intentions, the trial itself was a travesty of justice. Both witnesses for the prosecution were high on heroin when they testified, according to the 1984 recanted testimony of one of them. That witness, Jasper Lassiter, would also claim that he needed police to identify the Grace brothers for him in court—indeed, that it was Baker who had told him on the night of the shooting that Parky had been the shooter.[124] Baker, according to Parky's then-fiancée, Lynette Bingham, mistook ex-Panther and close friend Charlie Perry for Ross in the hall outside the courtroom.[125] The arresting officer, Harry Albino, testified that he had received a radio report of Grace's clothing, though Baker later testified he never told police what Parky was wearing.[126] But, there were two witnesses who identified both Parky and Ross as having brandished guns that night, and both identified Parky as the one who had shot Morgan. Most critically for the defense, Ross took the stand, and—out of sibling rivalry, the inexperience of his lawyer, bullying by the more dominant attorney Harrington, or a combination thereof—denied any motive for killing Morgan (i.e., the earlier abduction, which he had reported to the police).[127] Once the prosecution produced the police report on the June abduction, Ross was undone and the case was lost. As Parky's fifth and last lawyer in the case—Hale and Dorr's Bob Thuotte—told the *Phoenix* in 1985, "In the context of a joint trial, the jury tended to assume that both brothers were either innocent or guilty. When Ross's alibi collapsed, it took Frank down too."[128]

The all-white jury, which was not sequestered during the trial, deliberated for four-and-a-half hours and returned not-guilty verdicts on assault charges for Arum and Glover and guilty verdicts for the Grace brothers in the murder of Marvin Morgan. The courtroom erupted when the verdicts were read, with the family crying out in disbelief and Parky cursing the court as he was led away. Further, according to Parky's sister Clo, one of the principal police witnesses, Richard Nobre, rushed to the pay telephone and yelled into the receiver, "We got him! We got him!"[129] Ross was sentenced to "natural life," which provided for parole after fifteen years; Parky was sentenced to life without provision for parole, and the two men were taken away to Walpole. As Parky put it later, "They didn't waste no time. We were there. And we were gone."[130]

In the ensuing years, as the Grace brothers served their respective sentences, a new attorney, the "Movement lawyer" Daniel Featherston, sought several times, in several venues, and without success, to get them a new trial.[131] Featherston, like Harrington and the other lawyers before him, knew Ross was the shooter, and, advising silence, acted as counsel to both him and Parky. Yet another attorney, Stephen J. Rappaport, appointed by the judge to handle a habeas corpus motion that Parky filed in 1982, also seemed unable to move the case forward. By early 1984, Parky was deeply frustrated with Rappaport's apparent lack of interest in the case, especially after Ross had given an interview to a newspaper in which he admitted to the shooting and, in the same article, Harrington and Featherston had made statements indicating a conflict of interest. What's more, members of the Justice for Parky Coalition had found Jasper Lassiter, who was now willing to recant his trial testimony. Parky thus wrote to Bob Thuotte, who had worked on the ARV suit at Hale and Dorr, asking for representation by his firm.[132] Characteristically, he ended his letter with an appeal for justice that maintained the political stance he had taken from the start, apparently evincing faith in the system for which he had contempt, but simultaneously reiterating his unwavering faith in "the people." "You have all served as an inspiration to me," he wrote, "confirming the belief within me that with dedication and hard/thorough work the judicial system will indeed function for the people."[133] The following month, Daniel Mitchell of the Justice for Parky Coalition wrote Thuotte another letter, praising his recent presentation on behalf of the ARV and declaring, "we feel we need an attorney who can be as aggressive as we are."[134]

They had indeed found their man in this young lawyer who had begun working at Hale and Dorr as a summer intern in the early 1980s and achieved full-time status by fall 1982. If Gloria Clark was "the one who got me in all this trouble in the first place," Thuotte was instrumental in getting Parky out of it. The path that led Thuotte to Parky is a sixties story in itself. As a descendant of Italian and French-Canadian shoe workers in Brockton and Haverhill, Massachusetts, where "radicalism went with the smell of leather," Thuotte imbibed a sense of social justice early on.[135] His grandfather, who had participated in the "Bread and Roses" textile strike of 1912, had taught him as a young boy of "the great injustice of the Sacco and Vanzetti trial." His parents were teachers, and they had engendered in him a spirit that emerged by the mid-1960s as self-generated advocacy for civil rights. As a high school student in the late sixties he became an antiwar activist, helping to lead a student strike in the wake of Kent State, which led to his "exclusion" from school for the remainder of his senior year and thus nearly prevented him from going to the prestigious college to which he had already been accepted. He was even, in that spring of 1970 as New Bedford was boiling over, falsely identified by his teachers as a Black Panther.[136]

A first-rate student who remained politically radical in college during the early 1970s — the years of Parky's Panther activity — Thuotte was singularly unsuccessful once out in the world. He graduated from Vassar College in three years, with a self-designed major in Education and Urban Studies that he titled "The Psychological Effects of Poverty on Children." Though he wanted to become a teacher — deeply influenced by the radical educator Jonathan Kozol, he taught in a prisoner education program at a nearby maximum security prison and, briefly, worked at a school in the Bedford-Stuyvesant section of New York City — he did not complete a teaching practicum at Vassar and thus did not receive certification. Instead, amid the investigative frenzy of the Watergate scandal of 1973–1974, he decided to go into journalism and sought a position at the *Poughkeepsie Journal*. The only position available, however, was driving the delivery truck. After a period making deliveries he was accepted to the School of Journalism at Boston University — just as Parky Grace, serving a life sentence in nearby Walpole, was switching lawyers and mounting a series of unsuccessful appeals. But the Vassar graduate found he could not land a journalism job even with a degree in the field. After reading an article on progressive investment funds in *Liberation* magazine, he decided to switch to banking: "I came to have this strong belief that the reason that people in America are poor . . . is that they don't have access to capital. And that's because capital, I came to believe, is extracted from cities and sent to other places. And the corollary for that was that if you could find a way to attract capital into poor, urban, Black communities primarily, you could give those communities the opportunity to become economically self-sustaining."

Thuotte went to work for the Norfolk County Trust Company in Brookline, with the view that, "I'll work in a bank, get some experience, and then I'll go work in a progressive bank in a poor community." After a year or so, he contacted the author of the *Liberation* magazine article, Robert Zevin at the US Trust Company in Boston, and worked there for a year and a half. But, he says now, "I wasn't qualified to work in the investment area; and, basically, after three years in commercial banking and having been unsuccessful in trying to teach and to work in journalism and to work in banking in a meaningful way, I decided to apply to law school." By the time Thuotte entered Boston University Law School in fall 1979, Parky Grace, at war with prison authorities for nearly six years, was just months away from an illegal, middle-of-the-night transfer out of the state. Thuotte, meanwhile, had finally found something he was willing to commit to: "I worked *very* hard — it was the first time." And, also for the first time, his hard work and planning paid off. After finishing in the top 5 percent of his class at the end of his first year, he found he had his pick of firms to work for. He chose Hale and Dorr, notoriously antiunion but with a national reputation — and thus perhaps in part *because* of its work on behalf of corporations — for its pro bono work:

> I do all different kinds of stuff, but almost exclusively in litigation [he says of his work there from the beginning]. And I know I definitely want to do it, and I'd met a bunch of people who were doing pro bono work, and I think, 'This is the place; I'd like to come work here.' And I . . . understand that this has got to be one of the best law firms anywhere in terms of the capability of the people who were there. And so I decided I want to go work there, and I'm gonna do a ton of pro bono work.

Thuotte always expressed a strong interest in working with prisoners, so in December 1982 one of the associates approached him to work on the ARV case, particularly on the issue of the 1980 transfer by the Department of Corrections of the group's two leaders, Albert Blake and Frank Grace. After spending, by his count, some eighty-five hours between 21 December and New Year's Eve reviewing "three boxes of files containing documents [piled to a height of] about five to six feet," Thuotte states that it "quickly became obvious to me . . . that [Frank Grace] had been shipped out for being a charismatic, effective political leader, who had brought together white and black prisoners."[137] In 1983, the federal judge in the case ruled against the firm, and, in early 1984, Thuotte assisted a senior partner in oral argument on the matter before the U.S. Court of Appeals. It was at that hearing that Thuotte first met members of the Justice for Parky Coalition, most notably the New Bedford activist and onetime Grace paramour, Robin "Carlene" Cordwell, who later raised with the young lawyer the prospect of his "looking into Mr. Grace's conviction."[138]

Two weeks later Parky called from the federal prison in Memphis, to which he had been transferred three years earlier. The following week, Thuotte sought and received approval from his firm's public service committee to expand their representation of the prisoner. Immediately impressed by what he would later call "the incredible pettiness" of the Massachusetts Department of Corrections, Thuotte recalled experiencing "a combination of anger, a sense of urgency, and great energy" — akin to what he had felt as an antiwar high school student fifteen years earlier. Once he had met

Grace—first at the Massachusetts Correctional Institution at Concord—Thuotte was hooked. He was struck by this "bright, articulate, extraordinarily principled individual" who seemed to have a charismatic hold on the population at Walpole, though he had been gone for years.[139] On a visit with Cordwell later that month, he learned of Lassiter's willingness to recant. He also learned of the charges pending against Baker during the 1974 trial and of the apparent special treatment that Baker had received in the aftermath. He discovered that Harrington had represented three defendants at arraignment, but only Arum at trial. And, he met prisoners like ex-Panther Dickie Duarte, director of the Walpole law library, who, while acknowledging that most people in the prison were guilty, stated "everyone here knows Parky didn't do it."[140]

In March, Thuotte submitted a sixty-page proposal to Hale and Dorr's Public Service Committee requesting permission to represent Grace on a new trial motion. The following month the committee agreed, assigning senior partner Richard Innis to supervise. Given how political Parky was, how political his case had become, and how Thuotte was so clearly drawing connections between the issues before him and the politics of his youth and heritage, it is notable that he insists today that he was at the same time deeply impressed by Innis's warning to him as they began: "Remember: a case, not a cause."[141] Still, there is no question that Thuotte was, for the first time in his adult life, involved in something bigger than a mere "case."

According to Thuotte, Innis masterminded the court presentation for a new trial before the Middlesex Superior Court judge Elizabeth Dolan. But the driving force was Thuotte himself, who would later remark that he thought of himself "as having been disaffected and ineffectual, until I decided to use the tools of the system to try to change it."[142] The two attorneys presented their argument for retrial in two separate hearings in July and September 1984, offering Lassiter's recantation, Ross's admission (along with attorney testimony that he had claimed to be the shooter from the very beginning), and witnesses not heard at trial who testified Parky was not present at the shooting.[143] This last element of the case, in a surprising way, exposed something significant about Parky and his reputation in at least a portion of the New Bedford community. On cross-examination during the 1984 hearing, the state tried to impeach Bruce Ribeiro's testimony that "Parky wasn't there," given that he had earlier testified that he did not know everyone else who was there.

A. I would have known if Parky was there.

Q. Why would you have known if Parky was there?
A. He's that kind of guy.

Q. What kind of guy?
A. He would have been right out there defending his brother. He wouldn't have been in the background. He would have been out there. It wouldn't have went as far as it did if Parky was there.[144]

In the end, really, only the testimony of Eric Baker, a heroin addict whose "fix" had been delayed by his supplier, remained.[145] In their "Post-Hearing Memorandum," attorneys Innis and Thuotte reviewed the inconsistencies in Baker's account over a period of a decade, concluding that he had "told a different story on the crucial factual issues of this case every time he [had] testified or talked to the police."[146] Moreover, in late 1972, he was arrested while on bail on narcotics and burglary charges, sentenced the following year, and paroled after five months in protective custody. Immediately upon release he became the assistant director of a halfway house for parolees, a position from which he was fired after the Grace trial. Most curiously—and raising the question of whether, and for how long, Baker was a government informant—beginning on 31 May 1973 his Rhode Island probation record was sealed and was thus unavailable to Grace's attorneys. Also suggestive of Baker's possible state connections is that upon his release from prison in the late 1970s after serving time for armed robbery, he immediately secured more government positions, first with the National Center for Attitude Change and then with the Department of Youth Services.[147]

Though Dolan rejected the claim that "Eric Baker was a totally unreliable witness [or] incompetent to testify," she did find Lassiter's recantation "material" and several of the new eyewitness testimonies "corroborative." Further, she found the affidavits of Harrington and Featherston "admitting that Ross stated from the begining (*sic*) that he shot Marvin Morgan and that his brother was not there" a "buttress" for Ross's confession. At the same time, the judge rejected the Commonwealth's contention that even if "credible evidence" now placed the gun in Ross's hand, "that evidence does not show that Frank Grace was not present"—that is, a theory of joint venture, only now with the roles reversed from the 1974 case. Dolan concluded that she could not "point to one witness or area of testimony . . . and say that it was sufficient to carry the defendant's burden"; rather, she found "a survey of the whole case in its totality" to warrant granting relief.[148] She issued her decision on 11 January 1985; three weeks later, Parky Grace was released on bail.[149] The Commonwealth had until January 1986 to retry him. Without earlier notification to Grace's lawyers, all the while indicating in the press that he was seriously considering their options, the Bristol County district attorney allowed the time to lapse. Thus Parky was free of the Marvin Morgan case for the first time in over fourteen years.[150]

"I Go Down Panther, Y'know"

Out of prison in the late 1980s and 1990s, and now into his forties, Parky worked with the Cambridge Friends community and then the Freedom House in Roxbury, counseling gang members.[151] But, as in the old days, his "work record" was erratic and his trouble with the law continued—for example, he was arrested on a marijuana possession charge in Boston in 1991 and was back in court during the last year of his life for threatening a woman with a knife in a New Bedford barroom.[152] Meanwhile, he traveled back and forth between Boston and New Bedford—he claimed he could not live in New Bedford because of constant police harassment—and, in the Boston area, he spent time in Mattapan, Jamaica Plain, Medford, and Charlestown. Most notably, during these last years he simultaneously maintained both the appearance and the rhetoric of his hard-won radicalism and militancy. He spoke until the end about "the people's struggle," about "revolutionary intercommunalism," and even about starting a new movement. He was proudly Cape Verdean and black, maintaining close friendships with a rainbow of ex-colleagues, ranging from the street to the college campus, while he always sought connection to the next generation.[153] He was also keen to have the Panther story—his story—told by those who were willing to tell it straight.[154]

Grace's story raises a host of questions that remain largely unaddressed in the historiography of the Panthers—for example, the complex interplay of ethnicity, race, family, and region in the emergence and development of the Party in a particular locale; or the twin influences on certain key Panthers of military service in Vietnam and college attendance during the most radical period of sixties ferment. Marbled throughout Parky's story, too, though, is evidence of a porous boundary between his criminal and political activity. This is a fact about the Panthers that scholars have often remarked on but have rarely examined at the local level in an exhaustive manner—which returns us to Parky's persistent rebellious character.[155] The persistence might be explained, as some have suggested, by his experience in Vietnam. After all, in later years he was diagnosed at the Veterans Administration in Boston as suffering from post-traumatic stress disorder, and he himself more than once traced his radicalization to his opposition to the war.[156] We also cannot discount his years in prison, which, his letters to Gloria Clark make clear, entailed significant deprivation and punishment over a long period of time, during which he maintained, for perhaps personal as well as political reasons, the stance of a "revolutionary soldier." Indeed, many today insist that Parky changed dramatically, becoming more volatile, as a result of both experiences. His cousin, Rhoda Livramento, acknowledges that he was "more guarded, more suspicious, more angry" after his stint in Vietnam, while most of his friends and family note, rather, his politicization by that experience. Prison, Livramento says, actually made him "more philosophical," more able to use his mind than his physicality.[157] Not always, though. Indeed, his friend Vern Rudolph tells a postprison story that is shocking in its details. Rudolph, the godfather to Grace's oldest daughter, was with him in the New Careers Program at Bristol Community College in fall 1969, as well as on the morning of the raid on Pieraccini's, on the night of the Marvin Morgan shooting, and "for a minute" in Walpole. The year after Parky was released from prison, Rudolph remembers, Grace shot up a man's house in Boston with a sawed-off shotgun (because the man had refused him a regular ride from Boston to New Bedford) and, that same night, carried a kilo of cocaine in his backpack. "He was out of jail a year!" Rudolph says now in amazement. "That was just Parky."[158]

Perhaps from this vantage point, beyond the all-too-frequent recourse in the literature to romanticization or demonization, that was in fact the Panthers in all their contradictions: seemingly forever skirting the border — particularly permeable during the late sixties especially — between radical politics and illegal activity. For Parky Grace, his primary identification as a Black Panther, from the age of twenty-five until his death at fifty-seven — for all that that entailed — gave political expression to what he had told Gloria Clark in 1977: he was "a rebel all his life." At the same time, the Panther story, in light of Parky's story, is both larger and smaller than that typically told: larger, because the Panthers encompassed so many tendencies at the local level; smaller, because Parky Grace, the life-long rebel, transcended the single moment that the Panthers inhabited in the late 1960s.

Notes

I would like to thank Ellen Fitzpatrick, Irene Scharf, Bob Thuotte, Yohuru Williams, and Duke's anonymous readers for their insightful commentary; and to Thuotte and Gloria Clark for giving me access to a wealth of documentary evidence. Thanks also to June Harner, my interview transcriber, who made it possible for me, and my readers, to hear "voices" from the past.

1. Jack Olsen, *Last Man Standing: The Tragedy and Triumph of Geronimo Pratt* (New York: Doubleday, 2000), 19, 34. See also Akinyele Umoja, "Repression Breeds Resistance: The Black Liberation Army and the Radical Legacy of the Black Panther Party," and Ji Jaga, "Every Nation Struggling to Be Free Has a Right to Struggle, a Duty to Struggle," both in *Liberation, Imagination, and the Black Panther Party: A New Look at the Panthers and Their Legacy*, edited by Kathleen Cleaver and George Katsiaficas (New York: Routledge, 2001).

2. In a series of taped interviews with the author from 1999 to 2001, Grace—who from childhood was called "Parky," a corruption of "Frankie"—described both his natural rebelliousness and his Vietnam experience in virtually the same language as does ji Jaga. As for Grace's murder case, if his post-prison musings can be believed, the fact that virtually everyone in New Bedford knew he was innocent actually helped him in prison. "The whole city felt guilt, you know," he told Michael Matza of the *Boston Phoenix* ("A Man Out of Time: After 11 Years in Prison, A Black Panther Walks Free," 19 March 1985). "It was on them. That's what I used to say when I was in prison. I'm okay. They're the ones who are gonna suffer out there."

3. Steven F. Lawson, "Freedom Then, Freedom Now: The Historiography of the Civil Rights Movement," in *Civil Rights Crossroads: Nation, Community, and the Black Freedom Struggle* (Lexington: University of Kentucky Press, 2003); Charles W. Eagles, "Toward New Histories of the Civil Rights Era," *Journal of Southern History* 66 (November 2000): 815–48; Jeanne F. Theoharis and Komozi Woodard, eds., *Freedom North: Black Freedom Struggles Outside the South, 1940–1980* (New York: Palgrave Macmillan, 2003); Kevin Boyle, "The Times They Aren't a-Changing," review of Maurice Isserman and Michael Kazin, *America Divided: The Civil War of the 1960s* (New York: Oxford University Press, 2000), *Reviews in American History* 29 (June 2001): 308.

4. For a model, see George Lipsitz, *A Life in the Struggle: Ivory Perry and the Culture of Opposition* (Philadelphia: Temple University Press, 1988).

5. For recent demonology of the Panthers through biography, see Hugh Pearson, *The Shadow of the Panther: Huey Newton and the Price of Black Power in America* (Reading, Mass.: Additson-Wesley, 1994); for sixties-era hagiography, see Bobby Seale, *Seize the Time: The Story of the Black Panther Party and Huey P. Newton* (New York: Vintage Books, 1970).

6. Grace did tell Matza, "Legends, man, a whole lot of it is bullshit" ("Man Out of Time"). Perhaps he was thinking of a comment his brother Ross had made about him in an earlier interview: "Parky was a danger. People followed him. I wouldn't put him in the same class with a Malcolm X, but in New Bedford he was the same"

(Alan Levin, "Brother Is Political Scapegoat in '72 Slaying, Convict Says," *Standard Times* [New Bedford], 28 August 1983). On the other hand, ex-Panther "Dukie" Matthews says that Parky was a "legend in his own mind" (telephone interview with the author, March 2001). In any case, the staff writer for the local paper, John Doherty, announced in Grace's obituary that "death [had] brought the fiery and contradictory Mr. Grace full legend status" ("Radical 'Legend' Never Lost His Fire: 'Parky' Grace Left a Legacy to Learn From," *Standard Times*, 26 October 2001). Meanwhile, a new memoir by an ex-Panther of New Bedford, who employs a series of pseudonyms for local figures, refers to Grace simply as "Legend," even though the memoirist was fully aware of Grace's dark side (Gerald Ribeiro, "Don't Just Mourn — Organize!" edited by Robert French (unpublished manuscript in possession of author), chapter 6.

7. John Xifaras, interview by the author, New Bedford, 4 June 2002.
8. "Bobby" Pemberton, telephone interview by the author, 20 May 2002.
9. Margaret A. Charig, in her article "'Parky' Grace: A Story of Black Pride, Anger" (*Standard Times*, 7 October 1984), claimed that he had been arrested thirty-five times between 1970 and 1972.
10. The police characterization is attributed to the former mayor Edward F. Harrington, the court-appointed lawyer for Parky and Ross (who was also charged in the shooting), in Ross M. Grace to Advisory Board of Pardons and Commutations, West Concord, 1982. See n. 119.
11. Virtually everyone I interviewed remarked on this aspect of Parky's personality. As his cousin, Lavalle Livramento, said of Grace as a kid, "He was always one willing to fight," while also referring to him in his early years as a "renegade" and as an "agitator" (interview by the author, New Bedford, 28 July 2003).
12. The name and nature of Grace's gang is a matter of dispute. One of Parky's brothers — who at the time was perhaps too young to have known — claims that Frank hung in the "Lane" (a dirt path off Kempton Street, the main drag running through New Bedford's West End, the heart of the city's black community). He adds that the group was not a gang as such, insisting they "weren't bad" (Arnold Grace, telephone interview by the author, 17 March 2003).
13. Here, Grace linked the site of Khazan's legendary entry into the civil rights movement — a place and event Parky may not have heard of at the time — with his ethnic heritage as Cape Verdean, known familiarly as "green people."
14. Telephone interview by the author, 31 May 2000.
15. Interview by the author, Roxbury, 8 June 2002. Another version comes from Parky's sister: "Parky was Parky" (Clotilde [Clo] Grace Edwards, telephone interview by the author, 3 April 2003). See also the sentiments attributed to Robin "Carlene" Cordwell, Parky's close friend and ex-lover who was instrumental in the popular campaign to free him from prison, and who waxed poetic about his life and exploits to a local reporter after his death. "He was tough," she also said. "He was a horror show" (quoted in Doherty, "Radical 'Legend'").
16. Ross was likely never "officially" a Panther, though he was active in New Bedford

Panther circles and was arrested in the 1970 raid on a Panther storefront there (discussed below). The "enigma" label turned up in separate interviews with Ross and Parky's old friend and running partner, Vern Rudolph (New Bedford, 26 April 2003).

17. "He never changed," a member of the Suns of Panthers told Doherty after Grace's death. He was, Doherty offered, "one of the strongest links to a period of the city that in retrospect seems too weird, too intense to have really happened." Rudolph concurs: "[Parky] was stuck back in the 60s and 70s, man."

18. Perhaps, then, one of the few mentions of Parky Grace in the scholarly literature—Marilyn Halter's notation that he "maintained his militancy and Left politics during his years of incarceration"—understates the case (Halter, "Cape Verdean Americans," in *Encyclopedia of the American Left*, edited by Mari Jo Buhle et al. [Urbana: University of Illinois Press, 1990], 125). For his part, Grace told me, "To this day, y'know, I go down *Panther*" (interview by the author, Jamaica Plain, 29 March 2000).

19. The letters, from Grace to Clark only, cover the period 1976–1984, but are mostly from the late 1970s. Clark generously shared the documents with the author.

20. Interview by the author, Acushnet, 6 August 2002.

21. "When I got there," Rudolph remembered, "this guy . . . they had all kind o' trouble with 'm." But, too, "he left a bag for me—you know, with magazines and cookies, cigarettes 'n' stuff. . . . And, um, I didn't touch the bag. I didn't know who it was's bag; and all the guards would tell me was that they was probably some friends o' your, right? So, ah, when I did get to see 'im, he says . . . 'tonight, I'm gonna come by an . . . get you out o' your cell, an, uh, we'll go walkin' in the corridors, right?' I said, 'you got that kind o' clout, man?' He said, 'oh, yeah, yeah; they'll do it for me,' you know. . . . So, he came an, uh, you know, they let me out an' we walk up an' down" (interview by author, New Bedford, 26 April 2003).

22. Halter, "Cape Verdean Americans," 125. On the ARV, see Ronald A Witmer and Robert W. Thuotte, "Brief of the Plaintiffs/Appellants, Association for Reduction of Violence, et al.," United States Court of Appeal for the First Circuit, *Association for the Reduction of Violence, et al. v. Frank A. Hall, et al.*, No. 83–1515, October 1983 (note that unlesss otherwise indicated, all such documents were provided to the author by Bob Thuotte); Grace to Thuotte, Walpole, 24 February 1984; Daniel Mitchell (for the Justice for Parky Coalition) to Thuotte, New Bedford, 5 March 1984; Innis and Thuotte, "Appendix of the Defendant-Appellee Frank Grace, On Appeal from an Order of the Superior Court of Bristol County," *Commonwealth of Massachusetts v. Frank Grace*, No. 3881, 1985. According to the Witmer-Thuotte "Brief" ("Statement of Facts," 11–14), as racial tensions increased at Walpole in 1976, the ARV developed out of the "Self-Awareness Workshop," an inmate-run group seeking to alleviate "frustration, violence and, ultimately, recidivism" "through a combination of outside volunteers and inmate operated programs" (11). Moreover, the ARV plaintiff Albert Blake claimed he had been told by more than one Walpole official that the "main reason behind the lengthy lockup was to eliminate ARV and its programs" (13).

23. Grace to Clark, 27 February 1977; 10 November 1977; 27 December 1976.
24. Ibid., 26 December 1976.
25. Ibid., 10 February 1978.
26. Ibid., 24 October 1977.
27. Ibid., 7 October 1978.
28. Ibid., 9 July 1977.
29. Ibid., 10 February 1978.
30. Ibid., 26 December 1976.
31. Ibid., 13 September 1978.
32. Ibid., 22 August 1978.
33. Ibid., 27 February 1977.
34. Ibid., 24 October 1977.
35. Ibid., 24 January 1982.
36. Matza, "Man Out of Time."
37. The card is undated, but various references in it suggest that it was written in 1982.
38. On the purge of the original Boston Panther leadership for "racism," see the *Black Panther*, 19 July 1969.
39. Grace to Clark, 10 November 1977.
40. Ibid., 10 February 1978.
41. Ibid., 9 July 1978.
42. Ibid., 24 July 1978.
43. Ibid., 13 September 1978.
44. Ibid., 24 July 1978.
45. Ibid., August 1980.
46. Ibid., 22 August 1978.
47. Ibid., 10 November 1977. In his "Frank Grace Motion Hearing: Chronology of the Case" (Confidential), 12 September 1985, 16, Thuotte notes, parenthetically, that "despite the extremely serious matters Frank and I often had to discuss when I went to see him at Walpole, almost inevitably, it seems we ended up laughing about something, Frank often regaled me with stories about the foibles of the guards (he had a keen insight into their psyches, and discussed them sometimes as 'children'; Frank also described his response to the idiocy and insanity of the prison environment thusly: 'Beam me up, Scotty—there's no intelligent life down here')."
48. Grace to Clark, 10 February 1978.
49. Sometimes the Cape Verdean area where the Graces lived during Parky's early years is called South Central (parts of which are Puerto Rican as well), with the South End label reserved for New Bedford's farthest southern reaches, near Clark's Point, a very different, overwhelmingly white, neighborhood. Typically, though, locals use the more general designation South End to distinguish that area from the West End. On the subject of Cape Verdeans in general and southeastern Massachusetts Cape Verdeans in particular, see Halter, "Cape Verdean Americans"; Marilyn Halter, *Between Race and Ethnicity: Cape Verdean Immigrants, 1860–1965* (Urbana: University of Illinois Press, 1993); Marian Aguiar, "Cape Verde," in *Africana: The Encyclopedia of the African and African American Experience*, edited by

Kwame Anthony Appiah and Henry Louis Gates Jr. (New York: Basic Books, 1999), 368–71; Raymond Anthony Almeida, ed., *Cape Verdeans in America: Our Story* (Boston: American Committee for Cape Verde, 1978); Barry Glassner, "Cape Verdeans: The People without a Race," *Sepia* (November 1975): 65–71; Africa Information Service, ed., *Return to the Source: Selected Speeches by Amilcar Cabral* (New York: Monthly Review Press, 1973); Laura J. Pires-Hester, "A Study of Cape Verdean-American Ethnic Development: The Emergence of Bilateral Diaspora Ethnicity and Its Impact in a Southeastern New England Locality" (Ph.D. diss., Columbia University, 1994); Kingston William Heath, *The Patina of Place: The Cultural Weathering of a New England Industrial Landscape* (Knoxville: University of Tennessee Press, 2001), 166; Waltrand Berger Coli and Richard A. Lobban, *The Cape Verdeans in Rhode Island* (Providence: Rhode Island Heritage Commission and the Rhode Island Publication Society, 1990); Michael E. Whatley and Shirley C. Sabin, *From Cape to Cape: The Story of the Cape Verdean People of Cape Cod, Southeastern Massachusetts and Rhode Island* (n.p.: Eastern National, 2002); John C. Reardon, interviewer, "Black, White or Portuguese," in *Spinner: People and Culture in Southeastern Massachusetts*, vol. 1 (New Bedford: Reynolds-DeWalt Printing, 1981); Carmen Maiocio, *The Avenue: Memories of Acushnet Avenue* (n.p.; n.d), 59–64.

50. Sometimes, in slang, "mecan de cor" (Livramento, interview by the author, New Bedford, 28 July 2003).

51. The nature and status of the New Bedford Cape Verdeans remained problematic after the sixties revolution in color consciousness, even after Cape Verde and Guinea Bissau won independence in 1975 and "Cape Verdean" became an ethnic option in the 1980 U.S. Census. For a post-sixties meditation of the problem, see Paul Ramos, "Cape Verdeans Wrestle with Issue of Racial Discrimination," *Standard Times*, 28 July 1983.

52. Portelli, "What Makes Oral History Different?" in *The Death of Luigi Trastulli and Other Stories: Form and Meaning in Oral History* (Albany: State University of New York Press, 1991), reprinted in Robert Perks and Alistair Thomson, eds., *The Oral History Reader* (London: Routledge, 1998), 67; Grace, interview by the author, 18 March 2000.

53. Grace, interview by the author, 18 March 2000. Note the complex identity issues in the following exchange I had with Ross Grace in New Bedford on 26 April 2003.

> JL What about the whole Cape Verdean-Portuguese-white-black, all that sort of thing?
> RG That was never an issue. Matter 'v fact, I never knew — I remember thinkin,' "Wow! If I grew up, say, back with the Indians, what would I be? Because, my mother, right? Portuguese, I mean . . . and you have to — not white, but we weren't black. We weren't black; I mean . . .
> JL But, not white.
> RG See, I didn't know what I was.
> JL Uh-huh.

RG I didn't know *what* I was. My . . . grandfather — right? — and I remember my grandmother tellin' me, "Your father, your grandfather was Portuguese, he was a professor," an' all this here, right? So, I was thinkin' to myself, I said, "*well, if I was, I'm not Indian, I'm not black* — this, this is what they told us.
JL Mm-hmm.
RG "Oh, you're not black." So, I never knew what I was. Or we didn't, as a people."

On the other hand, Parky's cousin, Lavalle, claims Parky became "one of the brothers of the West End" once his family moved there, and "then he became *black*" (interview by the author, New Bedford, 28 July 2003).

For a fuller treatment of the Cape Verdean dimension in New Bedford, and especially its imprint on Panther politics there, see my forthcoming volume *The Awakening of a Sleeping Giant: New Bedford, the Black Panthers, and the 1960s*.

54. His siblings cannot remember, either. Arnold and Ross were too young; Clo, states flatly, "He didn't like it" (telephone interview by the author, 3 April 2003). His cousin, Lavalle, said the same thing: "He just said that he didn't want to go to school any more" (interview by the author, New Bedford, 28 July 2003).
55. Interview by the author, Jamaica Plain, 29 March 2000.
56. Interview by the author, Charlestown, 14 July 1999. "I chose to be a lumpen," he wrote Clark (13 September 1978). Though Grace grew up in Bay Village, a housing project in the South End, his father worked in construction and the family owned their own home by the time Parky was a teen.
57. Frank Grace FBI File, redacted copy in possession of author (obtained through a Freedom of Information Act request by the Committee to Free Parky); "Seven Youths Held on Bail in Aftermath of Fight," *Standard Times*, 8 January 1963.
58. Interview by the author, 29 March 2000. Parky's cousin (the daughter of his mother's twin sister), Rhoda Livramento, verifies the female-dominated character of the family, along with the older women's tough sense of justice, but she doubts the flag story. She remembers her grandmother Maya's conspicuously displayed American flag and that she was "proud she could say the pledge of allegiance" (interview by the author, North Dartmouth, 26 April 2003). Moreover, Grace's story is inconsistent with his claim that he went to Vietnam a patriot and returned an antiwar radical.
59. Interview by the author, 29 March 2000.
60. Charig, "'Parky' Grace" (which misidentifies the date of his entry into the army as late 1964). Matza, using the date 1966, says Grace "saw it as a job, and a way to shape himself up" ("Man Out of Time").
61. Interview by the author, 29 March 2000.
62. Guy Oliveira, interview by the author, New Bedford, 21 May 2002.
63. He told me (interview, 29 March 2000) and Matza ("Man Out of Time") that he had received a court martial and spent time in Long Binh jail, which the prisoners called "the LBJ." On the weeks-long race riot there in late summer 1968 (when Parky was still "in country"), see Robert Stokes, "The War in Vietnam: Riot at

Long Binh," *Newsweek*, 30 September 1968, p. 35. Although I have petitioned for Grace's military records, they have not yet been released.
64. Interview by the author, 29 March 2000.
65. Charig, "'Parky' Grace."
66. Interview by the author, 29 March 2000. Matza quotes him as saying, "I actually thought we were in Vietnam to bring freedom to the people," but his explanation for his epiphany in that interview was his encounter with Vietnamese kids who threw rocks at American convoys and "gave them the finger" ("Man Out of Time").
67. Interview by the author, 29 March 2000. (Grace's FBI file covers only the early 1970s.)
68. Ibid.
69. Grace's police record through 1972 is in the FBI file; probation file, copy provided to the author by Bob Thuotte; police reports (redacted, but with Parky's records easily identifiable by address), provided to the author by the New Bedford Police Department.
70. For this crucial background to the emergence of the New Bedford Panthers, see my *The Awakening of a Sleeping Giant*.
71. Interview by the author, Jamaica Plain, 18 March 2000.
72. She remembers it as the Radical Action Group (telephone interview by the author, 13 June 2000).
73. Ibid.
74. Grace to Clark, 5 December 1982.
75. Clark here confuses the Pentagon with the Justice Department.
76. Interview by the author, 27 June 2000.
77. Interview by the author, 18 March 2000 (PE is Panther shorthand for political education).
78. Ibid. Also, Gordon Rebeiro, interview by the author, New Bedford, 26 May 2000 and 16 May 2002; Kim Holland, telephone interview by the author, 8 June 2000; and Guy Oliveira, telephone interview by the author, 15 June 2000. According to Grace, the advertising was done by word of mouth and people of all ages came: "The whole West End, fifty.... There were a lot of people."
79. E.g., *Standard Times*, 11 March 1970; *Say Brother!* 17 July 2000, WGBH, Boston.
80. Interview by the author, 18 March 2000.
81. With exception of the use of the National Guard—on alert, but never deployed—the New Bedford eruption fulfilled all the criteria used by the commission to denote a "major" disturbance (*Report of the National Advisory Commission on Civil Disorders* [New York: Bantam Books, 1968], 113).
82. According to one of those "mother country radicals," as Grace and other Panthers called them, the idea was that of Kim Holland, a local high school student who was born in New York and later lived in the West End. She was with Parky on that first visit to the Boston Panther headquarters after the November 1969 demonstration, and she would became one of the principal New Bedford Panthers in the aftermath

of the July Days (Mark Dworkin, telephone interview by the author, 12 June 2002; Kim Holland, telephone interview by the author, 6 August 2001, 11 February 2001).

83. That policeman, Kenny Gifford, would be the first patrolman at the scene of the Morgan shooting.
84. The footage also contains some fiery rhetoric by Black Brother and future Walpole guard, Ernie Santos.
85. The fact that he was obviously high during the interview — probably on beer and marijuana, his drugs of choice — did not prevent him from cogently making what had become the distinctive Panther Party line.
86. Ronnie Cruz, who was on the scene, describes the mood as festive, with the police and mayor having agreed not to come inside the barriers (interview by the author, 29 May 2002).
87. One of the injured, Randy Robinson, who was witness to the Morgan incident, would die many years later from causes related to the shooting. The Panther was Kim Holland. The third victim, Gordon Rebeiro, whose older sister dated Parky, had years earlier formed a young gang called the "Junior Panthers."
88. Precisely when, how, and why the Panthers arrived is difficult to sort out, in part because of the variations in people's memories of the event (Parky himself told different stories) and because key figures like Audrea Jones, the Area Captain in Boston, and Robert "Big Bob" Heard, one of the Panthers sent down to establish a headquarters in town, refused to be interviewed. Interviews by the author: "Cappy" Pinderhughes, Brookline, 17 August 1999, 9 December 1999 (telephone), 1 June 2000 (telephone), and 13 June 2000 (telephone); Johnny "Butch" Viera, 22 October 2000 (telephone); Parky Grace, 14 July 1999–8 June 2000.
89. Among the Panthers involved that month, the community worker Johnny "Butch" Viera (a New Bedford Cape Verdean living with the Boston Panthers at the time), Kim Holland, and Grace all claim significant community participation at the "headquarters."
90. Grace tells the story of Heard holding political education classes, just as he had the first time Parky visited the Boston Panther office. Meanwhile, the district attorney called the building a "bunker" ("Atkins Blasts Panther Bail Ruling," *Boston Globe*, 19 August 1970), as did local leaders then and in recent interviews.
91. The Clark letters reveal the same burst of energy when organizing and cleaning up prison "space."
92. Grace was charged with unlawful assembly, inciting a riot, conspiracy to commit murder, conspiracy to commit anarchy, possession of narcotic drugs (marijuana found in Pieraccini's), and receiving stolen property (electronic equipment, also found in Pieraccini's, from the recently looted Burns Electric, apparently used for organizing the "Rebellion"). "Dickie" Duarte, interview by the author, New Bedford, 6 May 2000.
93. New Bedford Police Department, Criminal Offense Report (COR), H-8918, July 1, 1970 (redacted copy in possession of author; unredacted copy viewed courtesy of Officer Octavio Pragana, New Bedford, 1 June 2002). I have interviewed four-

teen of the twenty-one involved, and they tell identical stories about who was in the building at the time of the raid, as well as who was arrested, where, and how. Moreover, FBI reports of the raid, which often relied on police sources, refer to arrests of those "in or around" the building. In light of the apparent police falsification of this event, their reports on the Morgan case must be read with skepticism.

94. Interviews by the author: Parky Grace, 29 March 2000; Johnny "Butch" Viera, telephone, 22 October 2000; "Dickie" Duarte, 6 May 2000; Guy Oliveira, 21 May 2002. Grace was connected in another way to the raid. The occasion, or perhaps pretext, for the police action was the wounding of a local resident named Stephen Botelho who claimed he was shot in the right ankle as he passed by Pieraccini's on his way home from work. Botelho, who had relatives in the New Bedford Police Department, reported a second shooting that summer. In late August, while riding past the Tropicana Café in the South End, he told police, he had been shot in the left forearm, for which he was treated at the local hospital. He had asked a rowdy crowd to stop swearing because he had his wife and sister in the car; they refused, and when he tried to leave he heard two shots, one of which hit him. A police report identified Grace as the shooter ("South End Man Shot in Arm Near City Café," *Standard Times*, 30 August 1970; Grace FBI file).

95. Ernie, a local bookie, moved his operations across the street, and the Panthers, led by Parky Grace, opened the new headquarters in mid-September 1970. See Grace FBI file; see also the FBI Freedom of Information release to author on the New Bedford NCCF. The following spring, the group officially reconstituted itself as a branch of the Black Panther Party under the leadership of Boston's Tony Marshall.

96. On the tension, see Gerald Ribiero, interviews by the author, New Bedford, 16 May 2002 and 13 June 2002; Marshall, telephone interviews by the author, 24 May 2002 and 2 July 2002. Ribiero, like his brother Bruce—both involved in the Marvin Morgan incident—were cousins of Gordon (wounded in the Lima shooting) and his brother, Russell (arrested in the raid on Pieraccini's).

97. The newspaper noted the group's existence periodically for the roughly two years of its existence: David Branco, "Panthers Tell Center Merchants of New Policy, *Standard Times*, 27 May 1971; David Branco, "Black Panthers Sponsor Free City Disease Clinic," *Standard Times*, 17 September 1971; Marilee Hartley, "Panther Breakfast Hits Snag: Kitchen Facilities Questioned," *Standard Times*, 31 December 1971; "Hot Breakfasts Cease: Access to Building Is Problem," *Standard Times*, 22 January 1972; Joe Murphy, "School Board Acts: Breakfasts, Lunch Service Voted," *Standard Times*, 4 February 1972. See also interviews by the author, as follows: Grace, 14 July 1999–8 June 2000; Holland, telephone, 11 February 2001; Donna Howell, telephone, 11 June 2000; Michael Fultz, telephone, 5 June 2001; and *NAACP News*. Documents from the FBI files indicate an organized Panther presence in New Bedford until at least spring 1972, with membership numbers roughly comparable to those of Boston. Moreover, contrary to what was occurring in most other parts of the country, it appears that here the organization was growing in late 1971. Finally,

the documents reveal significant numbers of FBI informants throughout the period, apparently in response to the takeover of Pieraccini's.

98. "Brown Admits Firing Shotgun Blast that Killed Lima," *Standard Times*, 13 May 1971; "Three Defendants Acquitted in Lima Shooting," *Standard Times*, 19 May 1971. Buffalo Rebeiro states: "We always got the inkling, but never any concrete proof, that a deal was made with the so-called black leaders" (interview by author, telephone, 28 December 2000).

99. "Three Defendants Acquitted in Lima Slaying," *Standard Times*, 19 May 1971; "Fire Chief's Car Stoned in West End: Two Fires Set," *Standard Times*, 19 May 1971; (Mrs.) Claudette Blake, chair, West End Neighborhood Associations, to U.S. Attorney, Boston, 19 May 1971 (copy provided to author by Blake); "US Doubts Jurisdiction in Lima Trial," *Standard Times*, 21 May 1971; COR (Sgt. Detective Guy Oliveira), H-7978, 21 May 1971; Taylor, "New Bedford Feels Acquittal Effects," *Boston Globe*, 22 May 1971. On plans for vengeance, see interviews by the author: Robert Stevens, Cambridge, 13 December 2000; Gordon Rebeiro, 16 May 2002. See also, Bob Hall, "No Further West End Trials Planned," *Standard Times*, 10 June 1971; Roger Martin, "Federal Probe of Lima Slaying Again Asked," *Standard Times*, 17 December 1971; Roger Martin, "Rights Panel Stymied, Calls Lima Probe Bid 'Protest,'" *Standard Times*, 18 December 1971; Roger Martin, "For the Record: SMU Professor's Report on Civil Rights Cases Assessed," *Standard Times*, 26 March 1972; T. Noel Stern, "Author of Friends Service Committee Report Replies," *Standard Times*, 14 April 1972; T. Noel Stern "Due Process Is 'Guarantee of Liberty,'" letter to the editor, *Standard Times*, 20 April 1972.

100. Interview by the author, 28 March 2000; Grace to Clark, 10 November 1977. Steady work was never Grace's strong suit. In a sense, his work ethic was more akin to preindustrial than industrial rhythms (see E. P. Thompson, "Time, Work-Discipline, and Industrial Capitalism," *Past and Present*, no. 38 [1967]). Stories of bouts of intense labor—especially associated with cleaning and organization—recur in his biography, whether in establishing the NCCF headquarters in Pieraccini's during summer 1970 or getting new inmates "squared away" in the Walpole "garbage can" in the late 1970s.

101. New Bedford Police Department, Incident and Misdemeanor Report (IMP), J-11, 399, 7 April 1971; IMP, J-16, 120, 18 December 1971; "Third District Court Action," *Standard Times*, 29 December 1971; IMP, K-4676, 15 April 1972; COR, K-5317, 29 April 1972.

102. See Charig, "'Parky' Grace"; Jack Shepardson and Carol Lee Costa-Crowell, "Summer of Discontent Changed a City and Its People Forever," *Standard Times*, 30 July 1995.

103. Oliveira claims tracking before the July Days (telephone interview by the author, 15 June 2000); Grace's FBI file indicates the surveillance began some time in fall 1970. All of the principals arrested in the 31 July raid claim to have been questioned, and later followed, by the FBI; recently released documents verify at least the government's intention to do so. An air-tel from Washington dated July 27–31,

1970 (105–165706), directs the Special Agent in Charge (SAC) in Boston to "initiate investigations of the individuals arrested," and to "consider interviews . . . so as to determine whether they have informant potential or whether they present a threat to internal security."

104. Boston SAC Report, 14 October 1971, Grace FBI files. A 17 February 1972 report from the Boston SAC to the Director identified Grace as a "rank-and-file member" of the BPP. The reference to Parky being "out of the Party in early 1971" is verified by Viera, who claims he expelled his old friend at about that time for being unreliable. But here the timing—at the moment of the Newton-Cleaver "split"—is key. According to at least two ex-Boston Panthers, in early 1971 the Boston chapter became a key recruiting ground for assassins by the Newton (or Oakland) Panthers, primarily because its reputation as an intellectual group would make it an unlikely source of such activity (anonymous interviews by the author, 2000–2001). Moreover, Viera says another reason he purged his friend was to protect him from being drafted into such activity. As for Viera himself, he would leave shortly after Parky's expulsion because he did not like the direction that Newton was taking the Party. It appears Parky remained loyal to the Newton faction, with which the New Bedford chapter remained allied, and Viera himself was considered persona non grata for a time by local Panthers (Paul Almeida, interview by the author, New Bedford, 17 May 2002). There is a further mention in the files of Parky's falling out—without explanation, however.

105. The Panther who closed the office, Dukie Matthews, estimates the time as late spring 1972 (interview by the author, Cape Cod, Massachusetts, 1 April 2001). Documents from the FBI indicate the New Bedford Panther headquarters was abandoned in late March, though that may not have been the end of Panther activity in the area. Gerald Ribeiro, who worked with the local Party in late 1970 and 1971, remembers it disappearing at about the same time (i.e., spring 1972). By then, however, he had joined with Parky—and unnamed others—in underground activities involving plans to steal weapons and "make revolution" on their own, which bore some resemblance to the often amorphous entity called the Black Liberation Army. On the latter, see Umoja, "Repression Breeds Resistance."

106. Indeed, several local activists—Holland, Ribeiro, and Stevens, for example—believe the influx was a deliberate attempt to dampen political activity in the area. Charig, "'Parky' Grace," notes the same phenomenon in 1971–1972. The notion that "the authorities" deliberately flooded the black community with drugs "to destroy the Panther power base" is advanced in Melvin Van Peebles's novel *Panther* (New York: Thunder's Mouth Press, 1995), 228, and, most famously, in the movie of the same name (Polygram Filmed Entertainment and Gramercy Pictures, 1995).

107. His sister, Clo, claiming little knowledge of drugs, says she knew only that he was involved in selling illegal substances in the form of "white powder" that she assumes was heroin (telephone interview by the author, 3 April 2003). Rudolph insists, "we were all involved," and he laughed at the notion that Parky was in-

volved in getting *rid* of drugs—a claim Grace made to me in many interviews—although Rudolph did acknowledge that Grace was not involved in selling heroin until he got involved with the Panthers, which, according the Rudolph, "was financed by drugs."

108. Ross admitted to Matza that he had been a dealer in "smoke and smack," with a twist: he would shake down dealers, for cash and drugs, and sell the drugs back for a profit ("Man Out of Time").

109. The party was at the apartment of brothers Gerald and Bruce Ribeiro.

110. "Affidavit of Bruce W. Ribeiro," 12 June 1984, in Innis and Thuotte, "Appendix of the Defendant-Appellee Frank Grace." Donald "Dolomite" Arum, one of Ross's friends at the scene (and charged in the case), told Thuotte in 1984 that Ross had been high on quaaludes that night (copy of Thuotte's handwritten notes, provided to author). Arum was a member of the Lane Gang—as were most of the others there that night—who claimed to have sold Panther papers with Parky Grace and is identified as a victim of police harassment in a Panther leaflet of September 1971 ("Political Harassment of Youth Intensifies," in FBI release). Whether Morgan had been one of the four who had robbed Ross Grace in June 1972 is unclear. In any case, Ross did two portentous things in the aftermath of the incident: he reported it to the police (COR [and Supplementary Reports] K-7642, copy in possession of author) and he bought a "Saturday night special" for protection.

111. The primary officers and detectives involved in the arrests, interrogation, and investigation in this case—Gifford, Albino, Oliveira, Rainville, and Gauthier—were important players in the tumultuous political events of the late 1960s and early 1970s in New Bedford (all were arresting officers in the raid on Pieraccini's), and they all had had many interactions with Parky Grace. Parky later claimed to have been threatened and beaten by Gifford on more than one occasion. See "Affidavit of Frank Grace" (6 June 1984), in Innis and Thuotte, "Appendix of the Defendant-Appellee Frank Grace," 7–8.

112. "Affidavit of Frank Grace" (6 June 1984), in Innis and Thuotte, "Appendix of the Defendant-Appellee Frank Grace," 7–8.

113. Arum told Thuotte in 1984 that he had told the police on the night of the shooting that Parky was not there, and they had responded, "You and Ross gullible—we know Parky militant radical fanatic—cops knew Parky didn't do it." In Arum's view, they were out to get his friend. "Rainville pulled up next to Dolo and FG on street—Parky said why are you a pig type—your M.F.—you know Parky when I get off force—I'll buy house up on hill—I'll get a 50mm machine gun—and if I see your black ass—I'll gun you down" (quoted from copy of Thuotte's handwritten notes, provided to author). At trial, over a half-dozen witnesses testified to Parky's version of the events. However, no one said what probably a dozen people or more knew—namely, that Ross had shot Morgan. That would take another decade. For an example of how eyewitnesses sought to exonerate Parky while protecting Ross and themselves during the initial appeal process, see, e.g., "Affidavit

of Donald Arum," December 1974, *Commonwealth vs. Grace, Supplemental Summary of the Record (SSR)*, Superior Court, Bristol County, No. 42285, 1974, 4, in Innis and Thuotte, "Appendix of the Defendant-Appellee Frank Grace." "Marvin Morgan, Erik (*sic*) Baker, and Jasper Lassiter came out of the Club," Arum said, "and some guys came across the street and came up to them, saying something. . . . I saw that one of the guys had a gun pointed at Marvin Morgan. Erik (*sic*) Baker was trying to stop the guy with the gun, so I grabbed Baker and threw him to the ground out of the way. Turning back I saw the guy shoot Morgan, and although I didn't know the gunman's name, I had seem him around before. As for Frank Grace . . . I knew him then, and not only do I know he did not shoot Morgan, I know he was not even on the corner there when it took place." Arum was at the house party nearby with Ross and accompanied him and others to the Social Club when Ross returned to report that "the guys from Providence who had ripped him off" were there (quote from "Affidavit of Ronald H. Rose"; see also affidavits of Gerald and Bruce Ribeiro, all in Innis and Thuotte, "Appendix of the Defendant-Appellee Frank Grace"). More explicit was Ronnie Cruz, who witnessed the event from his bedroom window across from the Social Club: "On August 9, 1972, I remember seeing and reading in the newspaper that Frank Grace had been arrested. I was in a terrible quandary. I knew that if I came forward to exonerate Frank Grace I would by that act be incriminating Ross Grace" ("Affidavit of Ronald Cruz," 7 November 1983, *Commonwealth vs. Grace*, Exhibit 8, Rappaport Files, copy in possession of author). Perhaps most significant, the FBI had an informant on the scene—inside the West End Social Club—who claims to have repeatedly told both his FBI handler and those to whom he reported in the New Bedford Police Department that "Parky wasn't there." He was so disappointed in the response he received—"they wouldn't take my word for it. . . . But they would take my word on other things"—that he promptly ended what he says was four years of informing on narcotics and radical activities in the New Bedford and Boston area (anonymous, interview by the author 2003).

114. Among the many curiosities in the case—explicable if one assumes that the goal was to "get" Parky Grace—is that Rudolph, who had pulled up to the scene of the crime with Grace minutes after the shooting, was never charged as an accessory after the fact (Thuotte, "Frank Grace Motion Hearing: Chronology of the Case," 8).

115. Affidavit of Frank Grace," 9. "Peachy," Che's mother, swore in September 1974, "We were riding to the West End and came on a bunch of people on the corner and someone yelled to Parky, 'The pigs are at your house.' Rudy started to drive off, but Parky told him to stop, and said, 'My son's in that house.' Parky then got out of the car and started running up the street, but he was stopped by the cops" (*Commonwealth vs. Grace, SSR*, 15–16, in Innis and Thuotte, "Appendix of the Defendant-Appellee Frank Grace"). In his affidavit, Grace claimed to have had several run-ins with Albino. Russell Glitman, who produced a partial, never-published manuscript about Grace in the mid-1980s ("The Rights of Grace" [1996], copy in

possession of author, 43–48), has a graphic description of the beating—in his telling, it was more like an unfair fight in which Parky inflicts both physical and psychological damage on his tormentors. The story could only have come from Grace himself, and, perhaps, Glitman's imagination. Arum claimed later "he could hear Parky being beaten up—head swollen blood on *face*" (Thuotte notes, 1984), and Parky's mother testified at trial that he "had lumps on his face and head" at the arraignment the following morning (Herb Arral, "Frank, Ross Grace Deny Roles in Morgan Murder," *Standard Times*, 25 January 1974).

116. Though after more than a decade in prison, Parky would imply in a sworn affidavit that Harrington had suppressed this crucial information, in fact the older Grace had favored the strategy. As there were many people who could testify that he had been elsewhere that night—people he claimed later Harrington had failed to find—and as he was alleged to be the shooter, he believed the jury would acquit both him and his brother. Besides, he (apparently) told Glitman, "you never rat, not even on yourself" ("Rights of Grace," 20). Out of prison, Parky told Matza he would do the same again: "I had a shared responsibility for what happened, you know? Like I'm a leader up there, you know? If my brother went in there, it would be like squealing on himself. We can't have that. No way in the world was I gonna let him go it alone" ("Man Out of Time"). In his request for commutation, Ross claimed, "My brother . . . told me to stay quiet. He didn't want me to admit to anything. His reason was that since he was being charged with the crime, I shouldn't worry, since he wasn't there, and could prove it." For his part, Ross swore in a 6 June 1984 affidavit that he met with Harrington alone after the arraignment hearing and told him he had shot Morgan by accident. But, "Harrington told me that the police were calling the killing an 'execution,' and that if I admitted that I had shot Morgan, I would be convicted of first-degree murder. Harrington then told me to lie and say that I wasn't there when Morgan was shot" (Innis and Thuotte, "Appendix of the Defendant-Appellee Frank Grace," 2–3). Moreover, Ross claimed, Harrington directed him to testify, for which he was not prepared by counsel. In a sworn affidavit in July 1984, Harrington acknowledged that Ross had admitted shooting Morgan and that Parky had not been present. The appeal lawyer for the Grace brothers in the late 1970s, Daniel F. Featherston Jr., also swore later (24 July 1984) that, from the moment he agreed to represent them, Ross told him "that he had shot Marvin Morgan, and that his brother Frank 'Parky' Grace had not been present and had no involvement in the shooting" (Innis and Thuotte, "Appendix of the Defendant-Appellee Frank Grace," 2–3).

117. Harrington claimed a conflict of clients' interest ("Defense Lawyers in Trial of Grace Case Change," *Standard Times*, 1 September 1973). The fourth defendant, Phillip "Juggy" Glover, was represented by John A. Tierney, the lawyer for one of the three whites accused of murdering Lester Lima (Arral, "Defense Opens in Morgan Case," *Standard Times*, 18 January 1974).

118. As Ross swore in his 1984 affidavit, "When Zeman first came to see me in the fall of 1972 he said that he was surprised that I had requested him to be my attorney, and

couldn't figure out why I had requested him" (Innis and Thuotte, "Appendix of the Defendant-Appellee Frank Grace," 2–3). A handwritten addition reads, "During the trial he told me he had no experience in criminal matters" (3). Ross claimed to have met with Zeman only twice before trial, both for short meetings.

119. Innis and Thuotte, "Appendix of the Defendant-Appellee Frank Grace," 2–3. Grace, "Affidavit," 6 June 1984. Thuotte found Sullivan's bill in the clerk's records in Taunton, the county seat; it showed six hours of preparation for trial. "I was appalled," Thuotte wrote ("Frank Grace Motion Hearing: Chronology of the Case" 9).

120. Innis and Thuotte, "Appendix of the Defendant-Appellee Frank Grace," 2–3. Grace, "Affadavit," 6 June 1984, 10.

121. Innis and Thuotte, "Appendix of the Defendant-Appellee Frank Grace," 2–3. See also Ross Grace, interview by the author, 26 April 2003. "[Assistant District Attorney] Perry offered me a three to five year sentence if I would plead guilty to a charge of manslaughter," Parky wrote. "He also said that if I agreed to plead guilty, he would let my brother Ross plead guilty to second degree murder. I told him that what Ross had done was not murder, because a man who wants to murder someone does not shoot him once in the lower part of the body. I told Perry that I was rejecting his offer because I was innocent." There is some corroboration of a proffered plea deal, though the evidence is not direct eyewitness testimony. In 1985, Grace's attorneys provided a sworn affidavit of one Benjamin Rose Jr., a recreation officer at the Bristol County House of Correction, just before Parky's trial for the murder of Marvin Morgan. Rose recalled Grace telling him that Perry "had offered him a reduced sentence if he would agree to plead guilty to manslaughter" (affidavit, 5 June 1984, in Innis and Thuotte, "Appendix of the Defendant-Appellee Frank Grace"). Meanwhile, the trial judge, Superior Court Justice Vincent Brogna, had been censured two years earlier for allowing the appearance of impropriety in his contacts with the principal in an influence-peddling case. *Matter of DeSaulnier, Jr., et al.* (No. 1) 360 Mass. 757 (1971), pp. 811, 813, 814.

122. Boston SAC to FBI Director, 17 July 1974, 2. ADEX is the FBI acronym for Administrative Index.

123. Notes at the end of the FBI file, in author's possession, signed by Jim Bordern.

124. This testimony conflicts with the story that Baker's supplier, Michael Tuitt, told later (affidavit, 12 July 1984, in Innis and Thuotte, "Appendix of the Defendant-Appellee Frank Grace") about the conversation he had had with Baker the morning after the shooting: when "asked . . . if he knew who had done it . . . he said [before five witnesses], '*No*' that it was a bunch of guys who thought Marvin was his brother, who had been doing drug stickups in New Bedford." But, whether Baker did or did not know who the shooter was, on 21 April 1984 Lassiter swore that "the first time I ever saw Frank Grace was at his murder trial." "The reason I testified that Frank had shot Morgan was because Eric 'Ricky' Baker . . . told me to say that Ross and Frank Grace had committed the crime," he continued. "Baker told me to do this while we were at St. Luke's hospital after Morgan died." And,

further, "prior to my testimony, police officers rehearsed my testimony with me and told me that Frank Grace would be sitting next to Ross in the courtroom, so that I would be able to identify Frank." And, finally, "Eric Baker provided me with heroin before I testified at the trial."

125. Lynette Bingham, affidavit, described in *Commonwealth vs. Grace* 370 Mass 746 (1974), 753, in Innis and Thuotte, "Appendix of the Defendant-Appellee Frank Grace. "Bingham, initially on the defense witness list and thus "sequestered," swore she was sitting in the courthouse hallway on the fourth day of the trial and overheard a conversation between Baker and Detective Gauthier. "Gauthier told Baker he would be the next witness called to the stand, and I heard him say to Baker, 'Frank Grace is wearing dark green pants, a green print shirt and glasses. Ross is wearing a dark green shirt and green plaid pants. . . . At this point Charlie Perry . . . entered the building and came over to speak to me, and we heard Baker ask Gauthier who he was." When Gauthier left, Bingham claimed, Perry went over to Baker and asked why his name had been mentioned. "Baker told him he thought he was Ross," she swore. Perry verified the story in an affidavit on 10 October 1974 (13–14). In his statement to the police, Baker claimed to have seen Parky around and identified him as having been in the West End Social Club before the incident; at trial, he testified that he had purchased drugs from Parky (Arral, "Witness Ties Morgan Murder to Heroin Trafficking," *Standard Times*, 24 January 1974). But, on cross-examination, Gifford "recalled . . . that Baker did not know Frank Grace" (Arral, "Jury Picked for Morgan Murder Trial," *Standard Times*, 18 January 1974).

126. Among the many curiosities of that night is the fact that Albino's report recorded the call for assistance as 11:35, while Gifford's report has a frantic Eric Baker flagging down his police cruiser at Kempton and Cedar at "approximately 11:45." More important, though, while there is nothing in Gifford's report describing "the man with the funny nickname," Albino's report claims to have had a radio description, from Gifford's car, of a black man, five feet seven or eight inches, 140 pounds, wearing a brown shirt with white flowers, dungarees and boots (i.e., Parky Grace). At trial, Gifford said only that he had sent out a message alerting police to "be on the lookout for Frank and Ross Grace." Baker testified that he could not remember how Parky had been dressed, and at a 1984 hearing said he had told police only that "one was short, one was tall" (Innis and Thuotte, "Defendant's Post-Hearing Memorandum," *Commonweatlh vs. Grace*, Superior Court, Bristol County, 19 October 1984, 42, n.24). Moreover, under cross-examination, Albino admitted that the first radio message he heard gave only the description "two black males" (Arral, "Witness Describes Morgan Killing: Says He saw Grace Pull Trigger," *Standard Times*, n.d.). Still, Brogna, in his "Findings and Order Re Motions for New Trial," 26 February 1975, clearly relying on Albino's Incident and Criminal Offense Report, K-9717, 8 August 1972. noted that "the police . . . got within minutes a description of the shirt that 'Parky' Grace was wearing, and when the police 6 or 7 minutes later saw Frank ('Parky') Grace running on Cedar Street,

he was wearing a shirt that conformed exactly to the description that had been given" (*Commonwealth vs. Grace, SSR*, 19, in Innis and Thuotte, "Appendix of the Defendant-Appellee Frank Grace").

127. Ross also claimed he had been somewhere else that night, testifying that he, too, had watched the premier of *Kung Fu* (indeed, so many witnesses talked about having watched the program that police talked derisively of the "Kung Fu defense") but the key to his demise, as well as that of Parky, was telling the demonstrable lie that he had had no previous dealings with Morgan (Trial Transcript, 1216–1219, 1254, cited in Innis and Thuotte, "Defendant's Post-Hearing Memorandum," 7, n.5). In his 1984 affidavit (12), Parky claimed that, against his advice, and without input from Ross's lawyer, Harrington decided Ross would testify. Ross claimed likewise in his affidavit, and thus was the brothers' lifelong claim that there had been a conspiracy to insure Parky's conviction. On the other hand, Parky also told Matza that "when you look at the psychology of the thing . . . [Ross is] still trying to live up to my reputation, right? Trying to take that stand, right? Trying to outdo me" ("Man Out of Time").

128. Quoted in Matza, "Man Out of Time."

129. Clo Grace, telephone interview by the author, 3 April 2003. Nobre, a Cape Verdean, was well known for his rough tactics; his reputation was verified by a fellow police officer who claims Nobre carved notches on his nightstick for each beating he administered (Richard Nobrega, interview by the author New Bedford, 28 May 2002; Nobre declined my request for an interview). Other details appeared in the local press: "When the foreman of the jury announced the guilty finding, Frank Grace leaped to his feet, cursing the court and yelled that he had been 'railroaded' by police and the court. 'I didn't kill a damned person!' he shouted. The mother of Frank and Ross, screamed, 'He didn't do it! He didn't do it!'" And then: "Frank leaped over the rail of the defendant's booth and had to be restrained by police and court officers who removed him from the courtroom, but not before he knocked over a blackboard on which a sketch of the area of the murder scene had been drawn by witnesses." As he was being led away, "he looked up at Judge Brogna and shouted, 'You're the one who should be in jail'" (Arral, "Grace Brothers Found Guilty of Murder: Near Pandemonium Erupts in City Court," *Standard Times*, 30 January 1974). "Getting" Parky was not just about politics — at least not the radical politics associated with the Black Panthers — despite what some (e.g., Glitman, "Rights of Grace") have suggested. First, as noted, there was no organized Panther presence in New Bedford by summer 1972. More important, Parky's very presence rattled local police. As Rudolph put it, "they were afraid of him. You know? Because of the reputation that he had, man. . . . They wanted 'm off the streets" (interview by the author, New Bedford, 26 April 2003). Khazan, with a very different vantage than Rudolph's, told me the same thing.

130. Quoted in Matza, "Man Out of Time."

131. The plan was to present new alibi witnesses as "newly discovered evidence"; Parky, with Featherston's apparent support, continued to resist Ross telling the truth. No

less than five appeals were filed in the late 1970s, two in federal court and one to the U.S. Supreme Court, which refused to hear the case. In every ruling, which often seemed at odds with those in similar contemporary cases, the attorney told Matza later, there was the not-so-subtle message, "Let this fucking Panther stay in the cage. We hear ya, Featherston. But don't worry about it." However, what Featherston did not do was to suggest separating the cases and getting Parky his own counsel.

132. The documentary record suggests why Parky was frustrated, and it supports his contention to Thuotte that "since Mr. Rappaport has been assigned to the case almost nothing has happened," and that he had told him in December 1983 that whenever he started work on his case, "someone would show up with five or ten thousand dollars" for another case. Indeed, in Rappaport's "Bill for Services and Affidavit" for the fiscal year ending 30 June 1983 (he had been appointed by the court on 16 September 1982), he had logged just 13.5 hours, which included 1.5 hours on the phone with Parky, whom he had never met (copy of bill, provided to author). Moreover, Grace had expressed serious reservations about Featherston in his letters to Clark in the 1970s, even at one point suggesting he might be part of the "conspiracy." The Lassiter find was a product, apparently, of the dogged detective work of Carlene Cordwell.

133. Grace to Thuotte, Walpole, 24 February 1984, copy provided to author.

134. Mitchell to Thuotte, New Bedford, 5 March 1984, copy provided to author. Mitchell, for the committee, explained that the group had been doing investigative work since 1980, identifying themselves as "people [who] grew up with Parky and were active with him in the Black Panther Party . . . or are family and friends."

135. Thomas Wentworth Higginson, *Cheerful Yesterdays* (Boston: Houghton Mifflin, 1898).

136. Thuotte, interview by the author Boston, 16 August 2002 (unless otherwise noted, all subsequent quotations about Thuotte are from this interview).

137. Thuotte, "Frank Grace Motion Hearing: Chronology of the Case." The Department of Corrections claimed, in contrast, that Grace and Blake were involved in illegal activities, specifically "strong-arming of inmates, assaults, drug-related activities, illicit sex, homicides." In their pleading on behalf of the ARV before the Court of Appeals, Witmer and Thuotte note that "none of these allegations have (*sic*) been supported by a single document or disciplinary report" ("Brief of the Plaintiffs/Appellants," 4–5).

138. Thuotte, "Frank Grace Motion Hearing: Chronology of the Case," 2.

139. Ibid., 2–5. Thuotte found a strong contrast between Parky—"intensely political, committed, and principled"—and Ross, whom he found "a 'savvy' guy in the street sense" (though he acknowledged Ross would have been "a 'babe in the woods' of the court system in 1972" [9]).

140. Ibid., 6.

141. Thuotte to author, 24 May 2003. In his "Frank Grace Motion Hearing: Chronology of the Case" (10), Thuotte wrote simply that Innis had warned him "to be

careful never to let my zeal cloud my judgment as a lawyer." During the week before officially approving Thuotte's representation of Grace, the attorney had to deal with what appeared to be an attempt by prison authorities to frame Parky for the stabbing of a guard, an episode that would only deepen Thuotte's commitment to the case. In early April 1984, Parky was placed back in Walpole's notorious Block 10 for the crime, but on the 13 April Thuotte received a letter from a prisoner, Brian McKay, who admitted to the stabbing. As Thuotte writes: "McKay stated that Frank had had nothing to do with the incident and that he (McKay) wanted me to come visit him so he could tell me the truth about what had happened. I was extremely impressed that this individual, who had by accounts I had heard been badly beaten after this incident, who was no doubt going to be kept in prison for most of the rest of his life for this attack, and whom I understood to be a white man from South Boston, would risk sending a letter out to someone he had never met to state that Frank had not been involved. McKay's letter to me was, I thought, a powerful example of the loyalty of prisoners to each other and to Frank in particular, and brought home to me once again why prison officials considered him such a 'dangerous,' i.e. charismatic and politically effective individual" ("Frank Grace Motion Hearing: Chronology of the Case," 13–14). McKay noted that Parky had been "put into segregation, and charged with something he did not do or have not put in," and concluded his letter with the charge that "what they have to Frank . . . is '*CRIMINAL*'" (McKay to Thuotte, copy provided to author). In his "Frank Grace Motion Hearing: Chronology of the Case" Thuotte confuses the home of the prison guard (South Boston) with that of the prisoner (Gloucester). Jerry Taylor, "Prison Stabbing Case in Hands of Jurors," *Boston Globe*, 14 October 1985; "Inmate Convicted in Stabbing of Guard," *Boston Globe*, 16 October 1985. McKay, already serving 18 to 30 years for armed robbery, was sentenced to an additional 21 to 25 more years ("21–25 Years Added for Attack on Guard," *Boston Globe*, 24 October 1985); Grace had been exonerated of the crime the previous May (Thuotte, "Frank Grace Motion Hearing: Chronology of the Case," 15–16).

142. Glitman, "The Rights of Grace," 12 (handwritten notes).
143. The lawyers' "Second Amended Motion for Post-Conviction Relief" (Rappaport filed the original and amended motions in 1982–1983) argued four grounds for a new trial but presented evidence only of "false testimony." The other grounds were "ineffective assistance of counsel," "conflict of interest by defendant's counsel," and "the Commonwealth's failure to disclose evidence of promise, rewards or inducements to its witnesses" (Dolan, "Findings, Rulings and Decision on Defendant's Second Amended Motion for Post-Conviction Relief," 11 January 1985, 2). Lassiter's recantation devastated the state's case. In an interview with Thuotte in South Providence on 26 February 1984, Lassiter explained why he had come forward: "Now I seen that what happened with Ricky, it all do look like some kind of conspiracy or something." Thuotte noted, "He believes he told cops Ross fired gun." Among others newly testifying was Gerald Ribeiro, the ex-Panther who had

participated in Parky's nascent underground, but who was increasingly drawn into the heroin trade by late summer 1972. At the 1984 hearing, Ribeiro testified that he had been afraid to come forward in 1972 because "the police were bugging out . . . , kicking people's doors in and just grabbing people off the streets" — an apt description, too, of what happened during the Pieraccini raid and its aftermath. Though Ribeiro had been overseas during that raid, he surely knew the details of it once he returned the following fall and immediately joined area Panthers. Ribeiro also suggested a motive for his brother, Bruce, who may have been the other gunman that night: he testified that he knew "the Providence guys" to be "the guys that had ripped off him [Ross] and my brother" (Innis and Thuotte, "Defendant's Post-Hearing Memorandum," 13–15; Ribeiro, interview by the author, New Bedford, 6 June 2002). Bruce is not mentioned in Ross's police statement on the kidnapping incident. It is possible that there was more than one "rip off" that summer or, more likely, that the money Ross was holding belonged to Bruce as well.

144. Quoted in Innis and Thuotte, "Defendant's Post-Hearing Memorandum," 16–17.
145. At the 1972 trial, Baker testified that he had a two-bag-a-day habit; after Lassiter testified at the 1984 hearing that Baker had had a six-bag-a-day habit, Baker admitted to having used that much over a two-day period. As for the extent of his impairment without the proper dosage of the drug, he admitted, "I had been using heroin for a little while, and I get to feel normal because if I didn't, then it would alter my state of mind" (quoted in Innis and Thuotte, "Defendant's Post-Hearing Memorandum," 31–32). Moreover, as Innis and Thuotte point out in a footnote, "by his own admission, Baker — who had just seen his cousin shot and killed — went directly to the house of his supplier to pick up his package of heroin" (33, n.17).
146. Dolan rejected this argument (quotation in Innis and Thuotte, "Post-Hearing Memorandum," 37; inconsistencies, 37–44, including the matter of the police suspect description).
147. Ibid., 44–46. The record suggests that Baker was some kind of informant, though it does not state when he became one. It seems unlikely, given the circumstances of the Morgan shooting, that Parky was the target of a COINTELPRO operation in this particular instance. More plausibly, 8 August was a fortuitous event that fell into the laps of the New Bedford Police Department and their FBI confederates. Thuotte, however, suggests the intriguing possibility that Ross's kidnapping may have exacerbated an ongoing tension between rival Providence and New Bedford gangs, offering authorities an opportunity to take advantage — precisely the way COINTELPRO often worked (Thuotte to author, 27 May 2003). Ross remains adamant that the Morgan prosecution was a conspiracy to "get Parky" that included not only the police, prosecutors, and the judge, but the two principal defense lawyers, Harrington and Sullivan (interview by the author, 26 April 2003). He also insists that the jury foreman, whom he claims he and Parky sought to challenge but were overruled in the event by Harrington, was a police plant

(telephone interview by the author, 8 May 2003). As for the New Bedford police, the record is replete with accusations of police pressure on witnesses and suspects to implicate Parky in the Morgan death. See, e.g., "Affidavit of Paul Bowen," 19 December 1974, 3; "Affidavit of Jo Ann Metts," September 1974, 9, both in Innis and Thuotte, "Appendix of the Defendant-Appellee Frank Grace." On COINTELPRO and the Panthers, see, e.g., Ward Churchill, "'To Disrupt, Discredit and Destroy': The FBI's Secret War Against the Black Panther Party," in Cleaver and Katsiaficas, eds., *Liberation, Imagination, and the Black Panther Party*.

148. Dolan, "Findings, Rulings and Decisions," 10, 4, 5, 7, 12–13, 14.
149. In the interim, Parky's old lawyer, Daniel Featherston, offered his services again, claiming that his involvement would dissuade the state from seeking another trial. "I would very much doubt that Pina [the district attorney] will want to hazard a new trial. . . . It might help dissuade him from retrying you if he knew now that I would be representing you at any such trial, rather than those kids from Hale & Dorr" (Featherston to Grace, Boston, 1 February 1985).
150. A week after Dolan's decision, the Commonwealth filed a notice of appeal. Then, Pina told Matza "[that] he wants to talk to Lassiter before making any decisions, that state police are looking for Lassiter, and that he has an assistant researching the statute of limitations with respect to possible perjury in a capital case." Admitting to no miscarriage of justice in the case, Pina said he had been "reading the trial transcript, and he says he has been asking himself three questions: 'Are they still playing games with the system? Are we being had in the process? Or did they just try to outsmart everybody and end up outsmarting themselves?'" (Marza, *Man Out of Time*). But, there was more. Just after Dolan's decision, the Commonwealth offered the defense the option of letting Parky "plead out," with "time served," so that, in Thuotte's words, "he would still be labeled 'guilty' but would get out of prison." Hale and Dorr declined, and Thuotte argued the case before the Supreme Judicial Court the following December. In April 1986, the Court vacated Dolan's decision, "remanding the case for further consideration" regarding the status of two defense witnesses. The effect, Thuotte notes, "was to deprive Parky of a published appellate decision by our highest court admitting that this man had been wrongly convicted of murder, and that the wrongful conviction had been repeatedly affirmed." Dolan ruled in Grace's favor, delivering her decision on 20 May 1986. Again, as Thuotte remembers it, "[I feared] what could happen in terms of the worst case scenario. If Parky went to the hearing, and the judge ruled adverse to him, he would be returned to Walpole and might never be released" (Thuotte to author, e-mail, 8 June, 2003).
151. Thuotte to Presiding Judge, Boston Municipal Court, 6 February 1991.
152. Walter Conward (senior probation officer for the Third District Court), interview by the author, New Bedford, 4 July 2004.
153. Most of my interviews with him were, by his request, outdoors in locations around Boston or New Bedford, and in every instance he struck up conversations with young black men hanging out on street corners, in bars, or on basketball courts.

154. Strikingly different from many ex-Panthers, Grace was especially eager to not only talk at great length about his experiences, but also he repeatedly sought to provide me access to others — policemen as well as Panthers.
155. For the view that the Panthers used politics as a "cover" for their criminal intent from the beginning and throughout, see Pearson, *Shadow of the Panther*.
156. See "Affidavit of Frank Grace" (6 June 1984), in Innis and Thuotte, "Appendix of the Defendant-Appellee Frank Grace," 2.
157. Interview by the author, North Dartmouth, 26 April 2002. According to Rudolph, "they ended up puttin' 'im in isolation, man, oh! 'Cause he, he, he went mad up there, lost's mind up there."
158. As Rudolph remembers from summer 1986: "Well, I go pick 'im up an' . . . he says, 'I gotta go by this guy's house.' An,' um, he goes, tell me where the guy lives at, we pull up in front of the house . . . he jumps out o' the car, and pulls a sawed-off shotgun outta the . . . knapsack, an' starts shootin' at the guy's house, man. . . . An, uh, I said, 'whose house is this?' He says, 'oh, the guy that brought me down here with the black limousine.' I says, 'you're supposed to be friends.' He said, 'well, he didn't wanna give me a ride, okay? So, that's, uh, how I repay my friends who treat me like that, you know.' So . . . we come back down here and he says, 'hey, anybody at your house?' Well, at this time, my, uh, everybody should be sleepin' so, says, 'can I stop here for a couple of . . . ?' 'Sure.' Goes upstairs, dumps the bag on the table, he's got a kilo o' cocaine in the bag. So, I, you know, *this guy's crazy*." I asked whether Parky would have done that before he went to prison, "or was that just Parky?" Rudolph responded, without hesitation, "that was just Parky. You know, that was just him" (interview by the author, 26 April 2003). If Rudolph is correct about the date, Parky had been free of the Morgan case only weeks before the alleged incident took place.

WACing Off: Gossip, Sex, Race, and Politics in the World of FBI Special Case Agent William A. Cohendet

ROZ PAYNE

> Just the minute the FBI begins making recommendations on what should be done with its information, it becomes a Gestapo.
>
> — J. Edgar Hoover, *Look* magazine, 14 June 1956

The oft-repeated cliché that "one man's terrorist is another man's freedom fighter" might seem out of place in a discussion of law enforcement and the civil rights movement. But for many in the United States, the campaign to suppress black dissent was conceived as a struggle to preserve peace and good order — and, in the process, American freedom. The law enforcement community was hailed by some as the best defense against the menace of violence, and yet despite the voluminous number of studies on the FBI's role in dismantling the civil rights and Black Power movements — what one historian has called a "secret war" — the role of the field agent has been largely ignored. With very few exceptions, scholars have focused on the FBI director J. Edgar Hoover and on others in the FBI high command like Cartha Deloach and William Sullivan.[1] To be sure, Agent Roy Mitchell, who directed the operation that resulted in the deaths of the Black Panthers Fred Hampton and Mark Clark, and special agent David Price, who was implicated in the death and cover up of American Indian Movement member, Anna Mae Aquash, have been the focus of intensive studies. In both cases, however, the agents are portrayed as one-dimensional government functionaries, and little about them is revealed. FBI agents in general appear as "jack boot thugs" or simply as frontline soldiers in a war against terrorists — especially regarding the Black Panthers, where the literature stresses either state repression or Panther criminality. The human dimension is entirely lost.[2] Among the many unfinished tasks of Panther history, then, is the attempt to explain just who were these agents who were tasked with combating what Hoover famously called "the greatest threat to the internal security" of America. Not surprisingly, close examination reveals them to be just as complex as were their adversaries. In the process, the view from the field sheds important light on a range of issues about the Panthers that have bedeviled the chroniclers of that group since their inception.

Such an inquiry is itself problematic, of course, given the nature of the sources accessible to scholars. First, the FBI operated in total secrecy; even today, all FBI documents from that period containing the names of FBI staff are sanitized for the "protection" of its agents and confidential informants, and thus, in part, the stories that scholars tell are typically top-down. For example, because the director of the FBI clearly harbored racist sentiments, there is often a presumption that the same racism animated the agency itself. And yet, the evidence in some studies suggests alternative interpretations. Kenneth O'Reilly, for example—in his groundbreaking study of the Bureau's covert actions against black leaders in general in the 1960s and 1970s— acknowledges that a whole division of the FBI's Panther squad in the crucial city of San Francisco expressed opposition to their superiors' call for action against the Panthers' breakfast for children program.[3] Though our specific knowledge of such lapses in discipline is sparse, can we assume that they were not more common? Again, the standard sources are problematic: the official FBI correspondence between agents would not reveal much about their thoughts concerning the Bureau's program. A more accurate chronicle of the FBI-Panther story in the sixties would have to seek out and use the kind of oral testimony that is so often relied on by those interested in the Panther Party.

Hoover himself, of course, had been the nation's chief cop for decades by the time the Panthers arrived on the scene.[4] His meteoric rise to power grew out of an uncanny ability to personally designate the enemies of American freedom and democracy. In the 1920s, it was the Bolsheviks and Marcus Garvey's Universal Negro Improvement Association. In the 1930s, it was the bootleggers, bank robbers, and bookies of the criminal underworld. After World War II, the Communists again took center stage, with Hoover leading the charge against alleged subversives in Hollywood, the schools, and the government. By the late 1950s, though, he increasingly focused on a newly invigorated civil rights movement. Then, with the rash of "long hot summers" and the rise of the Black Power movement in the mid-to-late 1960s, Hoover rallied his agents and the rest of the law enforcement community to root out what he now insisted was America's main internal adversary, the Black Panther Party (BPP). His principal tool was the program COINTELPRO (short for Counter-Intelligence Program), which was established in 1956 to combat the Communist Party of the United States.

For decades the FBI had been celebrated for its work. But the civil rights era would complicate matters, as Hoover's targets and their allies fought back. The rumblings about civil liberties violations that had barely raised an eyebrow during the FBI's vigorous prosecution of "godless" Bolsheviks and dangerous criminals now found sympathetic ears when applied to the nonviolent civil rights struggle. Indeed, the application of the same kind of offensive action to black militant groups might have passed without notice if not for those who had experience in that earlier phase of the struggle. For by 1970, even moderates like Roy Wilkins of the oldest and most staid of America's civil rights organizations, the National Association for the Advancement of Colored People, would condemn the systematic repression of the Black Panthers. Then, in a series of investigations in the wake of the Watergate scandal of the early 1970s (the most famous of which became known as the Church Committee), Congress confirmed that the FBI had been engaged in a long war against, among many others, black activists. Unlike in the case of some political scandals involving bureaucracies, there was no call for a mass firing of the agents who had taken part in the abuses, but rather for the accountability of those in command. For, with the death of Hoover in 1973, Congress could safely lay the blame at his feet, thereby conveniently preserving within the Bureau itself the very framework that put the director's game plan into action.[5]

Finding WAC

But the sixties had changed America. Shortly after Congress finished its work, lawsuits filed across the country for the first time exposed the names and faces of FBI agents who had spearheaded the day-to-day persecution of supposed "enemies of the state." In some cases, such as those involving events in New Haven and in Chicago, lawsuits revealed a highly complex, if not always efficient, intelligence web that linked all elements of the law enforcement community in a common effort to destroy the Black Panthers. It was in this context that I first learned of an agent named William Cohendet and his role in the surveillance of the group. Here, it turned out, was a source that had the potential to move the discussion beyond the narrow predilections of the Left and the Right — and from the top-down to the bottom-up.

My search for FBI Agent WAC, as Cohendet was always called in Bureau documents, began in the 1980s when I discovered him during my efforts to go through boxes of FBI and counterintelligence files on the Black Panthers and black extremists while working in the law offices of the attorneys for Dhoruba Bin Wahad (né Richand Moore). The New York police had apprehended Bin Wahad, a member of the famed Panther 21 defendants, outside an "after hours" club in the Bronx in June 1971, and he was charged with the attempted murder of two police officers, Thomas Curry and Nicholas Binetti, in Manhattan two months earlier. After three trials in the case of *The People v. Dhoruba Bin Wahad*, a jury convicted him in July 1973 and sentenced him to twenty-five years to life. In 1975, he and his attorneys filed a civil suit against the FBI for withholding information during his criminal trial. That year, the Church Committee hearings brought COINTELPRO in particular under semipublic scrutiny, and Bin Wahad's lawyers subsequently requested all documents pertaining to him and the New York BPP.

Years of litigation followed, but when the case was turned over to Judge Mary Johnson Lowe in the Southern District Court of New York the attorneys for Bin Wahad — Elizabeth Fink, Robert Boyle, and Bob Bloom — showed that material had indeed been withheld during Bin Wahad's trial. Lowe, a black judge, ordered the agent testifying for the FBI to release all of the Panther files, but the Bureau refused to comply. Retired FBI agent Wesley Swearingen, however, who would later write about his role in illegal activities against the Panthers, presented a sworn affidavit that revealed where the files could be found, as he had filed some of them himself.[6] Lowe instructed the FBI's representative that he would be held in contempt of court if the defense lawyers did not receive the material in question within two weeks. Soon, boxes of files began arriving at the law office.[7] But the documents, even though in excess of some 300,000 pages, were marked up, excised, and often unreadable. Still, they did reveal forged letters, phone calls, and anonymous articles aimed at defaming the reputation, alliances, and unity of the Black Panther Party. During my work in the office, we found voluminous evidence that the FBI had willfully engaged in a campaign of repression against the Panthers. And yet because of the excessive deletions we were unable to snare the devil in the details.

Twice, Bin Wahad's lawyers objected to the redactions, and even though by the mid-1980s the FBI still obscured much of the detail in the documents (despite repeated rulings by the court in Bin Wahad's favor on the point), these "discovery" materials were enormously revealing. Unlike many of the releases through the Freedom of Information Act, and unlike the previous releases in the Bin Wahad case, these documents were often surprisingly free of redactions. Although much of the information in the files had presumably been collected with the intent to "destroy" the Party, the FBI had unwittingly become an invaluable archivist of the times. The boxes contained FBI memos, air-tels (or air-telegram reports written to other FBI offices), leaflets, word-for-word Panther speeches, transcriptions of tapped phone conversations, interviews, drawings, surveillance reports, and information from the Panther newspaper, all of which helped document Party activities across the country. But in going through the boxes I realized that within the files was the story of the Black Panther Party from the perspective of the FBI brass and, most crucially, the agents in the field. And, from that position emerged a startling point, one that has only fleetingly appeared in the scholarly literature: there was a significant disconnect between Washington and its resident agencies on the subject of the Panthers. Indeed, I discovered, COINTELPRO duty was not always popular among agents in the field. While typically playing along, some agents questioned not only the legality of certain government activity but also its very necessity, given the "domestic enemy" in question.

While sorting and reading these documents, I became acquainted with the work of Cohendet, whose initials WAC often appeared in FBI air-tels. Of course, in the files there were also many reports from other agents, but the writings of Agent WAC, as he became known to us, developed into something of an office event. His reports from the San Francisco office were always extremely well documented and written with a literary flair for the dramatic that set them apart from the rest. In spite of the venomous content of many of Cohendet's reports, we began to look forward to them. A bright moment during the many slow and tedious days going through files came when someone would shout out, "Another WAC report!" Everyone would then gather around while the report was read aloud, and sounds and shrieks of "unbelievable," "my god," "listen to this," and "he actually wrote that" would fill the room.

One day we found among the documents we had requested a list of the names, addresses, and phone numbers of San Francisco FBI agents. Having learned from the list that Agent WAC was William A. Cohendet, I asked a friend in the Bay Area to contact him, who in so doing told him she had gotten his phone number from an admirer of his, a person who had included his FBI reports in the syllabus of her history class at Burlington College in Vermont and who would very much like to talk to him. In 1989, I received a letter from WAC that read in part: "Let me say that I am happy that someone is finding use for five years work keeping track of the BPP. I guess that you can tell from my air-tels what I actually thought of the alleged danger from Huey P. Newton, et al. Unfortunately, my views were not identical with those of the chaps in Washington who were bedeviled by the strident threats duly reported by an overly zealous news media. It was clear the BPP was 'all bark and no bite.'" I wrote back, "I don't agree with your belief that nothing came out of COINTELPRO. I feel after reading the documents it was very effective." Despite my position, we continued to correspond, and two years later I had dinner with Agent Cohendet and his wife in Vermont. The tall, well-dressed, and graying man before me was not at all hesitant to talk about his Bureau work on the Panthers. "You did a good job in destroying the Black Panther Party," I commented wryly, to which he responded with a smile, "Thank you." His wife patted me on my shoulder and said, "you appreciate him more than his own children."

Having earned his trust through my expressions of admiration for his work, in 1992 I was invited to his home in California. I brought a camera crew with me, and we spent the day recording his stories. I had hoped the interview with Agent WAC would help me make sense of government repression of the Party by allowing me to penetrate the bureaucratic mist surrounding the men who had actually headed the effort at the local level. Cohendet did not disappoint me. Over the next several hours, he talked at length of his experience with the Panthers and his other work with the Bureau. His reminiscences in fact provided unique insight into the world of the government agent whom FBI director Hoover commanded "to expose, disrupt, misdirect, discredit, or otherwise neutralize" black militant organizations, most especially the BPP. Cohendet's answers to my questions shattered some myths about the FBI and the Panthers while reinforcing others. But perhaps more than anything else I came to see that his story tells a great deal about his own view of himself as a "cog in the wheel" of the government crackdown on radical racial dissent in the 1960s — a standpoint that historians rarely see, much less seek.

Another Man's Freedom Fighter: Agent WAC

Despite the soiled image of the FBI that grew out of the 1960s, decades earlier various law enforcement agencies and, most particularly, the nation's youth held the Bureau in high esteem. Millions of children growing up in 1930s and 1940s fantasized about becoming the "G-men" featured in movie theater newsreels who captured dangerous desperadoes like John Dillinger, Ma Barker, and Pretty Boy Floyd, all of whom gained international notoriety partly because of their exploits and partly because of the FBI. At the same time, the FBI's Ten Most Wanted list constituted Bureau propaganda as much as did its routine warnings to the public about the dangers of communism. Unlike the sly and dishonorable criminals they sought, the G-men were consistently portrayed as smart, dedicated, and honorable in their pursuit of justice. And what was perhaps more seductive to young people at the time, FBI agents were also portrayed as crack shots like the heroes of the popular westerns who fearlessly hunted down evildoers in the name of the law. The Bureau's well-oiled propaganda machine further encouraged the production of Bureau-friendly books, films, and, later, television programs to advertise its work and, ostensibly, to recruit other agents—who joined as super patriots with the same set of convictions attributed to the organization itself: namely, Fidelity, Bravery and Integrity.[8]

While this supposed organizational jingoism would later on fuel criticism of perceived lock-step actions of Bureau agents, it hardly was a case of "one size fits all." Cohendet, for example, did not join the Bureau because of a childhood fantasy or a sense of personal duty. His motivation, he explained, was purely financial. His father had passed away, and, as a recent graduate of Williams College, he inherited the task of caring for his aging mother. A friend alerted him that the Bureau was hiring and that they were seeking to diversify their fields of specialization. At the time, Cohendet earned $2,000 a year as a representative for the Travelers Insurance Company. The Bureau, on the other hand, paid $3,200. So he filled out an application and was accepted into the very next class for new agents.[9]

Born in 1914 in New Jersey, nothing notable in Cohendet's youth explained the direction of his future work, except perhaps that he had very little experience with African Americans. As the product of the lily-white environment of an all-boys' preparatory school and an elite liberal arts college, he felt at home in a Bureau that, he remembered, had no black agents when he joined in the late 1930s. After graduating from the FBI academy, Agent WAC worked in Los Angeles for a short period and then went to San Francisco. As a new agent, he worked on a variety of cases before settling on a specialty. During World War II, he became an expert at hunting down draft dodgers, a skill that would serve him well in his later work tracking the movements of black militants. He also was assigned to tracking projects in Yugoslavia, which he enjoyed because it involved important and substantive analysis that was far different from the mind-numbing work of running down draft board no-shows. But such work was scarce. Despite the legendary exploits of agents portrayed in Bureau-approved novels and on the silver screen, his experiences confirm that FBI agents did more with a calculator and tape recorder than with their revolvers. Agent WAC confessed that he spent the majority of his thirty-plus-year career in the Bureau behind a desk preparing reports for Washington.

By the time the Black Panthers came on the scene in the late 1960s, Cohendet was a senior agent at the end of his career. It was not his seniority, however, that garnered him the key role he came to play as Panther "archivist"; rather, it was a matter proximity. His home office of San Francisco was given the task to take the lead on the Panthers because it was the first to open a file on the organization. Situated across the bay from Oakland, where Huey Newton and Bobby Seale had founded the Black Panther Party for Self-Defense in late 1966, Agent WAC's office was the closest resident agency of the Bureau with a staff large enough to accommodate the director's growing interest in the beret-wearing, gun-toting black militants. Division Five of San Francisco's resident agency thus became the intelligence hub for the Bureau on the Panthers.[10]

Agent WAC's seniority aside, he was not particularly well suited for the task at hand. His minimal exposure to blacks, coupled with his scant interest in cases on civil rights or racial matters before being assigned to the Panther detail, made him an unlikely choice to head up this initiative. As he recalled, such FBI efforts were typically concentrated in the South. Yet now WAC was being asked to monitor an organization that Hoover would later call the number one threat to the nation's internal security. Indeed, in the heyday of the Panther Party's existence (1967–1972), WAC wrote biweekly intelligence summaries to be relayed as air-tels directly to Hoover. Still, as he told it, he simply sat at a desk in a little room with his filing cabinets, in which he collated his Black Panther material. He insisted he never saw COINTELPRO material—reflecting the most explosive aspect of the government-

Panthers story. He simply pulled together field agent reports and transformed them into biweekly briefings. Agent WAC rarely witnessed anything he wrote about, nor did he suggest any counterintelligence ploys — such matters, he insisted, were handled by another agent who dealt directly with Washington.

In fact, WAC flatly denied that the program was as extensive or sinister as it had been made out to be by the media and by professional historians. "We never did 'black bag jobs,'" he insisted. "We had no mail or trash covers. No one would want to get into the Panther trash [laughs]. We already had all the information sources we needed. We had names, phone taps, microphones, lots of information from the Panther newspaper, and field agent reports." And, referring to Kenneth O'Reilly's *"Racial Matters,"* WAC proclaimed, "O'Reilly was grossly wrong when he said we had sixty-seven effective informers. We had none."[11] Instead, Cohendet claimed, the Bureau culled its information on the BPP from "a handful of ineffective informers like low-level kids in cribs."

Agent WAC's observations about FBI informants are intriguing in light of most accounts of government repression of the Party. His designation of informants as "low-level kids in cribs" is equally compelling as it suggests something about the people who were drawn to the Panthers' programs, the so-called street people whom men like Cohendet had very little respect for but whom the Panthers sought to organize. Nevertheless, Cohendet claimed that his best sources of information were in fact newspapers and technological coverage of Party headquarters. In this case, human intelligence was simply too unreliable, he maintained. "You get down into some of those cribs and you get a bunch of teenagers, some of them, you know, kids just living together and not doing much." Asked if he recruited them to be informants, he responded, "they were too low-level, and what would they tell you? They go to class and tell you about their readings of Mao Tse-Tung. You see them the next month and say, 'what did you do?' And they'd say, 'we are still on the first chapter.'" As for rumors to this day about high-level informants among the Panthers, WAC again downplayed the Bureau's reach. "We couldn't get to the top. We didn't have Huey, Elaine, Bobby, or David.[12] We had an interview program, but the Panthers wouldn't talk to us. We just collected and collated information." Then, expressing his bottom-line explanation about the Panthers' demise, he declared flatly, "the Panthers destroyed themselves."

In fact, to hear WAC tell it, the Panthers—unlike the Yugoslavs, for example—"never did much" anyway. In responding to the critical question of whether Hoover really felt that the Panthers were dangerous, Cohendet gave more blame to the media than the aging director for propping up the Party. "Sure, he felt that way about a lot of things," but "you have to begin with the press; they raised this big specter of danger." WAC also blamed the Panthers. "Sure, they were going to burn Oakland and they were going to send troops to Vietnam—a lot of talk, see, but you had to know the difference between talk and action. You have to know the difference between big on rhetoric and short on action." Such denials, however, clearly do not square with the massive amount of evidence to the contrary. The Bureau placed high-level informants in chapters across the country, many of whom secured sensitive positions within the Party, such as the Chicago Panther informant William O'Neal, who became that chapter's head of security. But, WAC's complex defense of his position is revealing. Confronted with documents showing evidence of COINTELPRO, he at first seemed taken aback. After poring over a few of them, however, he settled back in his chair and sighed. He then explained that he had not been aware of the activities of his fellow agents in COINTELPRO. In his telling, his job had been basically to collate reports, intimating that the work was so secretive that the right hand may not have known what the left hand was doing. Then he declared matter-of-factly that any such activity would have been for naught, in any case, because "the Panthers weren't doing anything anyway."

Indeed, he explained, "our work showed that the Panthers were not dangerous." "We should have left them alone. Lots of crimes were committed by criminals, but the Panthers or the Party didn't make them do it. The Panthers weren't criminals, although some Panther members were." Asked why the Bureau maintained its surveillance despite the minimal threat, WAC pled bureaucratic inertia. "Mr. Hoover had said they're dangerous," he recalled, noting (again) that they had threatened to "send a legion to Vietnam." But the field agents were well aware that the Panthers "didn't have one soldier they could send over."[13] They decided to "keep it up," however, hoping that reports of such a ridiculous nature might ultimately dissuade the Bureau from continuing the program. Again, in a manner strikingly like that of certain Panther scholars, Cohendet blamed the media, noting, "the press . . . the fact that we predicted [the Panthers'] demise was . . . more important." "[But] that's the press . . . we can't stop them from writing books but a lot of it's not true."[14] Still, he recognized the role that the Bureau had played in the process. "Once Hoover declared the Panthers as the most dangerous thing going, we [i.e., agents in the field] had to do something." And, he noted further, "I did what I was told in the best way I could. . . . I opposed some of the policies. Some of the assistant directors agreed with me, but they wouldn't let Hoover know that we disagreed with him."[15] On the other hand, Cohendet did not allow his reservations about the Bureau's program to keep him from throwing himself into his work. The members of Bin Wahad's legal team were not the only ones captivated by WAC's insensitive, if amusing, commentary on the Panthers. "Clerks and assistant directors enjoyed reading my reports," Cohendet proudly recalled, "and said to keep them coming." "I was really writing for my friends," he continued, noting that "Hoover never or seldom saw or read FBI agents' reports. I didn't care." He seemed genuinely surprised when shown a copy of a report he wrote suggesting a letter-writing campaign, with Hoover's handwriting on it urging, "Why Wait?"

Cohendet's mix of pride and bitterness about the campaign against the BPP was not simply predicated on what it did to the Panthers but also to his fellow FBI agents in the field. "The FBI should not have had COINTELPRO against the BPP," he stated at one point. "They should not have caused harm and told lies." "I didn't like COINTELPRO," he insisted. "It was like hazing, it demeans a person. If you had a smart guy in the FBI you don't need to go so far." Cohendet also chided the Bureau higher-ups for wasting resources on arresting so-called nefarious activities like some of the Panther community programs, which he perceived as having had positive benefits. "I thought breakfast for children was a good program," he said. But "FBI Headquarters wanted to stop [it]. The San Francisco Office let it go on and we were inspected by Washington and told to stop it." As he conceptualized the problem, "We wanted to do better things than try to stop a breakfast program," but they were pressured by headquarters to do otherwise.

Fortunately, in WAC's case there is also the written record—and that record is voluminous. In it, we catch glimpses of WAC the senior agent. In each of the biweekly air-tels he sent to Hoover's office was a section titled "The Voice of the Panther," which was reserved for tidbits on sex, race, gossip, and politics. Compiled largely from secondhand information, WAC constructed in his writing a portrait of the Panthers as social deviants warranting the type of surveillance and harassment he would later condemn.

The World That WAC Made

With his pen, Agent WAC had the power to shape the Panther's image, which he did with great relish. Accustomed to writing about alien political and social systems in his work on the Yugoslavs, perhaps his view of blacks in general and the Panthers in particular fueled his analysis and biting humor. His most common musings were on the social and sexual habits of Party members. Sometimes his humor took the form of a mere play on words, such as in an article titled "No Right Guard?" in which he poked fun at a proposed restructuring of the BPP to include a politburo that David Hilliard said "would be composed of the old guard" and the "rear guard." In an equally humorous article devoted to Huey Newton, titled "High Liver," WAC charged that "Newton's impecunious state does not preclude him from eating, at least not as long as the party still has the kitchen at the Lamp Post. One recent afternoon Newton decided that he was hungry and ordered a dinner of chicken or oysters. The Post that day was featuring roast beef and baked ham and had neither chicken nor oysters. They did not even have chicken livers, Newton's next choice. He finally settled for beef liver and onions and ordered it to be delivered to the penthouse by taxicab. Based on the above evidence, Newton may well be termed a 'high liver.'" Not all of WAC's musings, however, were harmless observations on the Panthers' eating and drinking habits or their lack of formal training in political science. The vast majority of his writings were rife with racial prejudice that touched on every prevailing black stereotype, ranging from laziness to loose moral character. When Newton accepted a position to teach a course at Merritt College, WAC decried his efforts in an article titled, "Huey, the Professor." "Newton was reportedly disappointed in the results of his teaching efforts," WAC contended, "and indicated that he would not try it again." "Newton considered 'teaching' an unpleasant experience," he continued, "For one thing, it was too much work." "[He] asserted that 'life was easier in prison.'"

Agent WAC seemed to take his greatest pleasures in discussing the sex lives of the Panthers, thereby raising serious question about his repeated claims that his writings were essentially harmless. In "Gestation Period Lengthening," for instance, WAC noted that "[the] wives of Charles Bursey, Landon Williams, and Bobby Seale are about to give birth. All husbands have been in jail almost two years, thus indicating that the gestation period for male Panthers has increased to at least twice the normal time required. It should be noted that the African elephant requires only 21 months." In another article titled, "Baby News," WAC announced, "Karen Williams had a baby, the father being unannounced, Phyllis Jackson was pregnant, the father being unannounced. Shelley Bursey (the wife of Charles Bursey in jail) is pregnant by John Seale. Ora Williams, the wife of Landon Williams is pregnant by Michael Hill. Artie Seale, the wife of Bobby Seale, is pregnant by the deceased Fred Bennett." Seale would later be implicated in Bennett's murder, which police theorized he had ordered as retaliation. The Panthers were not WAC's only targets; their supporters also rarely escaped his poison pen. In "Sounds Like Blackmail," WAC reported that "Bert Schneider, Hollywood personality, has been a large financial benefactor to the Panthers. Recently he ceased his aid and Elaine Brown, his one time bedmate, was told to try to bring him around. Huey Newton became angry with Schneider's attitude and finally agreed to see him only under the following condition: 'Tell him to bring his wife and his checkbook.'"

At times, WAC's analysis did broach larger issues in the Party, which may provide scholars with some insights into Party organization and other issues. Although obviously intended to embarrass the Panthers, WAC's article "Free Kathleen," for example, raised the issue of a double standard in the sexual politics of the Party. There, WAC reported on what he described as "the brutality visited on Kathleen by Eldridge, who allegedly refused her freedom to have sexual relations with others, while he, himself, openly lived with an Algerian woman named Malika." "The most serious charge," WAC continued, "was that Cleaver had killed Clinton 'Rahim' Smith, the aircraft hijacker who attempted a love affair with Kathleen Cleaver in Algiers." "As an accompanying interesting charge," WAC concluded, "Elaine Brown alleged the President of Algeria had endorsed this action of Cleaver's and like the chauvinist and opportunist he was, had given Cleaver a plot of ground to bury Rahim in, and then kept the whole episode quiet." The article further alleged that Kathleen's life was in danger, and that she was being held a "prisoner in Algeria by her 'personal mad oppressor.'"

Agent WAC also provided interesting commentary on BPP finances. Again, while his intent was clearly to malign the Panthers, his article, "The Money-Changer in the Temple," chronicles some of the excesses that later helped destroy the Party. As he wrote, "David Lubell is the 'money-changer' in the temple. He keeps Newton in a style fit for a king, paying and buying him luxurious apartments. The BPP is still Huey P. Newton. He lives in style, being apparently willingly served by the lower echelon, who seem, as primitive peoples have always done, to take pride in the Temple where their spiritual leader resides. The people themselves live on mattresses thrown on floors in condemned houses in the worst parts of the ghetto, not knowing where their next meal may be coming from."

Reconciling Irreconcilable Memories

Reconciling what Agent WAC claimed in light of what he did is a tall order. Special Agent William Cohendet was perhaps one of the most important cogs in the FBI intelligence web dedicated to the Black Panthers. His analysis, reports, and suggestions found their way directly to Hoover's desk. Although Cohendet did not read — or even know about — Hoover's responses, scholars from Kenneth O'Reilly to Ward Churchill and Jim Vander Wall suggest that higher-ups did take careful note of WAC's writings. While Cohendet denied that his reports had any real influence, his reaction to the documents detailing informant provocation initiatives and other questionable tactics tells a different story. Indeed, what is most striking is Cohendet's dismissal of the Party, which seems to have been predicated on his view of blacks in general — a kind of flip side to Hoover's racially tinged assessment. Agent WAC's commentary on Party membership, which simultaneously enthralled and alarmed the defenders of Bin Wahad, indicates at least a degree of racism, perhaps invisible to WAC but apparent in his work. For despite the mountain of COINTELPRO documents readily available to him that suggested otherwise, Cohendet persisted in his insistence that the Bureau exercise restraint in its pursuit of the Party. "You had to be careful [about] what you should do," he explained, "Was any harm going to come to anybody or any misstatements?" When asked, however, about the egregious case of actress Jean Seberg, whose career and life were destroyed by an FBI-inspired poison pen campaign, the agent could hardly contain a chuckle as he delighted in the details of her alleged affair with Black Panther leader Masai Hewitt and her miscarriage, all of which was brought to light by a Bureau missive to a Hollywood gossip columnist.[16]

There was this horror, and there was also the humor. Cohendet's attitude toward the work of the Party might thus best be summed up by this exchange in our interview.

Payne: Who was the Panther that you liked the most?
WAC: June Bug Hilliard. He was funny. He could be a comic with Amos and Andy. He was really good. David's younger brother. Not a factor of any kind, but he was

> in the office all the time. I got a lot of stuff from the Party from June Bug. . . .
>
> Payne: From the wiretaps you mean. . . .
>
> WAC: Sure, he used to get on there and talk forever funny; no harm done. He was a good guy . . . I don't know [laughs] . . . he never got in any fighting.

Cohendet denied any ill will toward Hilliard, or that any ill will was implied in similar statements he had made in the past. "It's a pity they [black people] resent when you say they're funny," he noted at one point, "because, really, they are. I go back to Amos and Andy when I was growing up because they were funny."

Further, Cohendet argued that he wrote his reports in a tongue-in-cheek fashion so as to downplay the Party's significance — perhaps he felt the need to make it so. This critical element of his work was missed by many of those reading it. Though he maintained in 1992 that his aim was to downscale the reports "so somebody would read them and say, well, you can't worry about these people," clearly elements of his writings resonated with agents all over the country, including assistant director Sullivan and director Hoover. Swearingen has written that a "culture of racism" permeated the Bureau and at times was evident in activities undertaken by its agents and directors. On the Seberg case, for example, Swearingen recalled that agents were particularly obsessed with — even seethed with — anger toward white women who associated with Black Panthers. "The giving of her white body to a black man," he explained, "was an unbearable thought for many of the white agents." "In the view of the Bureau . . . Jean was giving aid and comfort to the enemy, the BPP."[17] It thus seems certain that Agent WAC's reports tapped into the latent racism of the agency that clearly undergirded some of its more egregious assaults on the Panthers and other black organizations — regardless of Cohendet's intentions. At the same time, the Bureau's fascination with the sex lives and living habits of the Panthers — reflected in the WAC documents — supports David Garrow's description of the agency as a group of "Puritans and Voyeurs" who satiated their infantile desires in the name of preserving law and order.[18]

At least in part, WAC may have been doing just that. The Panthers, in his estimation, were simply big talkers who managed to garner the attention of the media through their fiery rhetoric. Their prognostication was little more than elaborate performances undeserving of the attention the Bureau paid to them. Nothing drove this point home to him more, he claimed, than the Panthers' actions, or, rather, their lack of action after Newton was convicted of murdering a police officer in 1968. The Panthers, he noted, had proclaimed that if Newton were convicted they were going to "burn Oakland." Their failure to make good on this threat left Cohendet with the impression that they were not serious about fomenting any type of revolution. Newton was "convicted, went to jail and they didn't do a damn thing." "They disbanded their legions around the courthouse and went home." For WAC, again at least the way he told it in the 1990s, the Panthers' lack of action convinced him they were little more than a nuisance. Asked what the Panthers might have done to prove themselves, Cohendet replied, "They could have run around the neighborhood and started fires, sure, but they were afraid to do that . . . they could have gone to jail."

Of course, this reality does not square with the "Big Bad Panthers" of the mainstream media, or of the FBI brass for that matter.[19] In fact, it is hard to believe that the group soon to be designated by Hoover as the number one threat to the nation's internal security is the same group that WAC states "never really did much." Asked why agents who shared his belief did not then pursue an end to the Bureau's program, Cohendet claimed institutional inertia. "Everybody had to show an interest in doing this thing because that was Bureau policy and down the line you don't question it openly." "We all had different opinions. We had some that go by the book, everything they were told to do they do; and we had others who were more independent." "When they set a policy in Washington," he explained, "that's it." "There is nothing the lower field can do," he continued, "It just goes on and on. And so once the Bureau declared that this was the most dangerous thing going then it had to be most dangerous. You had to do something about it. And it happens all the time. You accommodate yourself to it."

In addressing the most touted justification for the surveillance and infiltration of the BPP—their alleged propensity for violence—Agent WAC was even more conciliatory (or, alternatively, contemptuous) toward the Panthers. Denying the Party's propensity toward violence, Cohendet nonetheless argued that it tended to attract a criminal element. The Panthers' celebration of the lumpen proletariat, he charged, was a weakness. "A lot of the crimes that were committed," he observed, "were done by fellows who were criminals before. The Panthers did not make them do it. It happened that they were aligned with the Panthers at one time or another. The party did not urge them to do that." Notably here, in stark contrast to what some have argued about the Panthers and their criminality, WAC made an explicit distinction between criminals on the one hand and Panthers on the other.

About this matter WAC was consistent. When in 1975 he was called to testify before the Church Committee, he declared, "It is true that the BPP could be described as a product of the black ghetto conditions, and as such is entitled to the sympathy of all conscientious citizens. In any analysis, the BPP represented very few blacks anywhere. Their strident tones raised in well-attended press conferences made the Party seem more important than they were."[20] He then offered the same conclusion that he gave later when he was interviewed in 1992 by stating that the BPP ultimately destroyed itself by its pathological behavior—a perspective potentially at odds with his notion that Panther leaders were *not* inclined toward violence. As he explained in 1975,

> When Newton came out of prison he installed himself in a luxurious tower apartment, attired himself in tailor-made garments, had his food sent in to him, along with daily fresh flowers. He isolated himself from the common troops. Perhaps he feared for his life. . . . Hilliard, DC,[21] and Cleaver were involved with an ambush and shoot-out with the Oakland Police Department, during the course of which Li'l Bobby Hutton, a black teenager, was killed. Cleaver fled the country, had a falling out with Huey and was expelled from the party. David Hilliard was sent to prison notwithstanding his assertion on the witness stand that the shoot-out had been Cleaver's idea, and he [Hilliard] had spent the time of the shooting ingloriously hiding under the bed of a girl friend. . . . Bobby Seale turned alcoholic and was expelled from the party. Finally Newton himself, about to be arrested on murder charges, disappeared and like Cleaver, remains a fugitive. . . . The BPP backed the Palestinian guerrilla activities against Israel [thus] losing themselves some early support from certain Jewish elements in so doing. . . . Members of the BPP hijacked airplanes in flights to Cuba and books were published allegedly written by Newton but ghostwritten by a black professor with more literary skill as well as industry than Newton could command.[22]

"Thus," Agent WAC concluded, "the BPP gradually faded away, no longer able to command the attention of the press, and it can be said to have been reduced to impotencies." "Now all the old leadership is gone. In all the above the counterintelligence program of the FBI played no part."[23]

Cohendet's words matter for our historical understanding of the Panthers, because both his and the FBI's assessment of the national Party clearly have influenced popular remembrances of the time. Journalistic accounts like those penned by Kate Coleman and Hugh Pearson follow the gossipy tales of the FBI in the national press with little regard to their actual truth. From this, the Panthers emerge as gun-totting thugs elevated to national significance by the press. But as Agent WAC's own recollections indicate, the FBI helped to fuel the media's fascination with the Panthers, even when WAC himself sought to blame that same media for the damage done. More important, many of the Panther programs, like the political education classes and the breakfasts for children, actually had an impact in the community, even if not in the way the FBI anticipated. The WAC documents — indeed, thousands of FBI documents — reveal a rank-and-file FBI view that the Party was a failure because it did not succeed in fomenting the black revolution that Hoover so desperately feared. But they failed to measure the Party's impact in the communities where it took hold.

Historians must make agents like William Cohendet as much a part of the Panthers' story for the role he played in "recording their deeds" — in creating their legacy and mythology — as they do for the efforts of his office to derail the party. The enlightened position of Division Five in San Francisco did not stop them from doing their job, as gossip filled their missives and as they worked on other malicious campaigns. But in their work lies another perspective on the Panthers that has only cursorily been explored — that is, that their *assessment* of the Party was fueled by the mandate to "expose, misdirect and otherwise neutralize it" that came from their superiors in Washington. Political education classes that did not result in armed revolution; breakfast for children that did not include political indoctrination; and other social programs that ultimately did not result in blood in the streets were failures from the Bureau's perspective. And, from the retrospective assessment of certain agents like WAC, this was reason enough to abandon the campaign against the Panthers. Agent WAC's own words demonstrate the nature of the problem. "Our few black agents couldn't get into the inner circle. The Oakland Police Department had a black racial squad, but we never got much from them. They were only interested in crimes like bank robberies or shootouts." By focusing on such issues the local police, like the media, helped to enhance the image of the Party as a violent criminal clique, even when the bank robberies and shootouts did not happen or were perpetrated by nominal Panthers.

Coda

After Hoover's death the Bureau remained conscious of creating good public relations. In the 1970s, for example, Efrem Zimbalist Jr. starred in a short-lived televison program aimed at rehabilitating the image of the nation's law enforcement agency. Replacing the special agent in charge of the scandal-plagued Winston-Salem, North Carolina, office of the FBI, Louis A. Giovantti commented, "Zimbalist . . . has done a lot for us. He portrayed what we like to think of as the image of FBI agents—attractive, professional and never a hint of any prejudice."[24] In the 1980s, *Today's FBI* took a stab at introducing a generation of youth to the exploits of America's version of the Canadian Royal Mounties, who always "got their man." As with other such shows, in *Today's FBI* the mundane routine of most agents in the field were jettisoned for a more action-oriented view of the Bureau chasing down the "bad guys" in jet planes and powerboats. However, the show's lukewarm reception and low ratings relegated it to the trash heap of television after just one season. It would not be until the 1990's release of the movie *The Silence of the Lambs*, and the Fox TV series *The X-Files*, that the FBI enjoyed a brief return to glory on the screen. Ironically, *The X-Files* featured a rogue agent who regularly violated Bureau policy in search of supernatural and extraterrestrial phenomena. He was aided by his skeptical, by-the-book partner as well as a sympathetic assistant director who consistently sought to reign him in but also occasionally was drawn into the world of "Agent Spooky." The motto of the show and that of its main character was "The truth is out there."

The same motto could be applied to the complex relationship between the media, the FBI, and the Panthers. "The truth"—or, more appropriately, some amount of analytical objectivity—is out there, if scholars choose to pursue it. As Yohuru Williams has explained, "In the final analysis, the importance of memory in writing history is critical. But, whose memories can one trust? In popular culture, the selective memory of the past—the proverbial, 'lie agreed upon'—has relegated the Panthers to gun-toting thugs, even when the memories of those who pursued them deny the dominance of this element in the group." "Thus," he concludes, "the Panthers and the FBI emerge as cookie cutter actors in the contrived morality play of good-versus-evil that passes for history in popular culture. All nuance is lost. What remains barely reflects the historical record."[25]

Part of that record—in an area of scholarship still relatively spare of "archives"—is buried in the work of those most self-interested of archivists, the FBI agents in the field. Though highly problematic, these sources have much to tell us about the sixties, and thus about one of that era's least understood groups. As historian and activist Howard Zinn observed in a 1995 article in *Covert Action Quarterly*, "If I found that the FBI did not have any dossier on me, it would have been tremendously embarrassing and I wouldn't have been able to face my friends." Why? Because so much of the period was defined by the Bureau's attention to the era's social and political dissent. And, no matter how seemingly irrelevant or "harmless" the FBI may have seemed to those in the organization, it had a tremendous impact on those it victimized. Zinn notes how fortunate he felt when he discovered that his dossier contained only "several hundred pages of absolutely inconsequential material." At the same time, however, he recognized how consequential some of such material had been for certain individuals and groups.[26]

People like William Cohendet as Agent WAC thus offer a way to help with the complex reconstruction of a historical record too long taken for granted. On the one hand, he offers a view from the field that cannot be seen as a simple reflection of the Bureau's face (J. Edgar Hoover). On the other hand, despite WAC's often-eloquent defense of his own actions, and his conclusion that "the Panthers were going to destroy themselves, counterintelligence or whatever," in the end he did the job his directors asked him to do. Or, as he put it, "I did what I was told in the best way I could." As insignificant as it may have seemed to some at the time, or even since, what he and others like him wrote to Washington about the Panthers — call it rhetorical masturbation — ultimately bore fruit on the streets of Seattle, Chicago, Houston, and New Haven in the blood of both Panthers and police.

Notes

1. An exception is Ward Churchill and Jim Vander Wall, *Agents of Repression: The FBI's Secret Wars against the Black Panther Party and the American Indian Movement* (Boston: South End Press, 1988). For a sampling of the standard fare, see Nelson Blackstock, COINTELPRO: *The FBI's Secret War on Political Freedom* (New York: Pathfinder, 1975); Athan Theoharis, *Spying on Americans: Political Surveillance from Hoover to the Huston Plan* (Philadelphia: Temple University Press, 1978); Athan Theoharis, ed., *From the Secret Files of J. Edgar Hoover* (Chicago: Ivan R. Dee, 1991); William C. Sullivan, *The Bureau: My Thirty Years in Hoover's FBI* (New York: Norton, 1979); Kenneth O'Reilly, *Hoover and the Un-Americans: The FBI, HUAC, and the Red Menace* (Philadelphia: Temple University Press, 1983); Curt Gentry, *J. Edgar Hoover: The Man and the Secrets* (New York: Norton, 1991); Frank Donner, *The Age of Surveillance: The Aims and Methods of America's Political Intelligence System* (New York: Knopf, 1985); Frank M. Sorrentino, *Ideological Warfare: The FBI's Path toward Power* (Port Washington, N.Y.: Associated Faculty Press, 1985); Richard Gid Powers, *Secrecy and Power: The Life of J. Edgar Hoover* (New York: Free Press, 1987); Athan Theoharis and John Stuart Cox, *The Boss: J. Edgar Hoover and the Great American Inquisition* (Philadelphia: Temple University Press, 1988); Kenneth

O'Reilly, *"Racial Matters": The FBI's Secret War on Black America, 1960–1972* (New York: Free Press, 1989); Ward Churchill and Jim Vander Wall, *The COINTELPRO Papers: Documents from the FBI's Secret Wars Against Dissent in the United States* (Boston: South End Press, 1990); Alexander Charns, *Cloak and Gavel: FBI Wiretaps, Bugs, Informers, and the Supreme Court* (Urbana: University of Illinois Press, 1992); M. Wesley Swearingen, *FBI Secrets: An Agent's Expose* (Boston: South End Press, 1995).

2. For the latter, see, e.g., Kate Coleman and Paul Avery, "The Party's Over," *New Times*, 10 July 1978; David Horowitz, "Black Murder Inc.," *Heterodoxy* 1.10 (March 1993): 1, 11–15; Hugh Pearson, *The Shadow of the Panther: Huey Newton and the Price of Black Power in America* (Reading, Mass.: Addison-Wesley, 1994).

3. O'Reilly, *"Racial Matters,"* 300. See also, Yohuru Williams, *Black Politics/White Power: Civil Rights, Black Power, and the Black Panthers in New Haven* (St. James, N.Y.: Brandywine Press, 2000), 134.

4. In 1919, Hoover was named head of the new General Intelligence Division of the Justice Department. In 1921, he joined the Bureau of Investigation (BI) as deputy head, and in 1924 the attorney general named him director of the organization. When Hoover took over, the BI had approximately 650 employees, including 441 special agents. The organization was renamed the Federal Bureau of Investigation in 1935, and by 1939 it was preeminent in the field of domestic intelligence.

5. U.S. Senate, 94th Congress, 2nd Session, *Final Report of the Select Committee to Study Governmental Operations with Respect to Intelligence Activities, Book III (Supplementary Detailed Staff Reports on Intelligence Activities and the Rights of America)* (Washington, D.C.: U.S. Government Printing Office, 1976).

6. Swearingen, *FBI Secrets*, 81–83.

7. These documents contained over two hundred previously undisclosed pages of three FBI reports pertaining to the case, including an anonymous call to the police in which the prosecution's key witness, Pauline Joseph, exonerated Bin Wahad. The defense received the final set of documents in 1987, twelve years after the initial civil rights action to procure the evidence. Citing the inconsistency and possible perjury of Joseph in the 1973 trial, Bin Wahad and his lawyers filed for a retrial. With key material showing important evidence had been withheld in his original trial, he was released in 1990. On 19 January 1995, the district attorney's office dismissed his case, formally ending Bin Wahad's twenty-six-year court struggle that began with the New York Panther 21 case. Meanwhile, by the time the case was over, we had read more than 350,000 pages of documents, the computerized index of which is in my possession. On reading declassified FBI files, see Gerald K. Haines and David A. Langbart, *Unlocking the Files of the FBI: A Guide to Its Records and Classification System* (New York: Scholarly Resources, Inc., 1993).

8. On the FBI's massive propaganda machine and its influence on mass culture, see Richard Powers, *G-Men: Hoover's FBI in America's Popular Culture* (Carbondale: Southern Illinois University Press, 1983); Claire B. Potter, *War on Crime: Bandits, G-Men, and the Politics of Mass Culture* (New Brunswick: Rutgers University Press,

1998); and Tom Wicker, "What Have They Done since They Shot Dillinger?" *New York Times Magazine*, 28 December 1969. See also J. Edgar Hoover, *Masters of Deceit* (New York: Pocket Books, 1959); Don Whitehead, *The FBI Story: A Report to the People* (New York: Random House, 1956); and Max Lowenthal, *The Federal Bureau of Investigation* (New York: William Sloane, 1950).

9. William A. Cohendet, video interview with the author, Hillsborough, California, 1992. Unless otherwise noted, all biographical information on Agent WAC and all direct quotes of him come from this four-hour interview.

10. O'Reilly, *"Racial Matters,"* 299.

11. Ibid., 310.

12. Huey Newton, Party cofounder and Minister of Defense; Elaine Brown, chair (1974–1977); Bobby Seale, cofounder and chair; David Hilliard, chief of staff.

13. In August 1970 Newton stated that "in the spirit of international revolutionary solidarity," the Party would send "an undetermined number of troops" to assist the Vietnamese in their "fight against American imperialism" (Newton, "To the National Liberation Front of South Vietnam: August 29, 1970," in *To Die for the People: The Writings of Huey P. Newton* (New York: Vintage Books, 1972), 178.

14. E.g., Pearson, *Shadow of the Panther*.

15. Muddying the waters further, Cohendet added: "Hoover ran a good organization in the early days. Mothers in Iowa loved him. His only problem was that he lived too long. He just wouldn't retire."

16. In April 1970, a "neutralization" plot was mounted against Seberg, who had provided financial support to the Panthers. Ignoring information that she was in a fragile emotional state because of her pregnancy, the Los Angeles FBI sent an erroneous missive to a gossip columnist suggesting that Seberg was carrying a Panther child. Such a union was still taboo in Hollywood, and the FBI anticipated that Seberg would be ostracized for it. The fraudulent news was widely reported in the national press. Faced with the prospect of the breakup of her marriage and the end of her career, Seberg tried desperately to clear her name, but ultimately she succumbed to the public humiliation and attempted suicide. Although she was unsuccessful, the attempt induced premature labor, which claimed the life of her unborn child. She never recovered from this event, and for the next nine years she attempted suicide repeatedly on or around the anniversary of her baby's death. In 1979, she finally succeeded. See Churchill and Vander Wall, *COINTELPRO Papers*, 215; and David Richards, *Played Out: The Jean Seberg Story* (New York: Playboy Press, 1991), 237–38.

17. Quoted in Churchill and Vander Wall, *COINTELPRO Papers*, 215.

18. Garrow, The *FBI and Martin Luther King* (New York: Penguin, 1983).

19. For the complex historical "construction" of the Panthers by media outlets, then and now, along with how that process influenced politics and history, see Ted Morgan's essay in this volume.

20. Cohendet testimony before the Senate Select Committee to Study Governmental Operations with Respect to Intelligence Activities (Church Committee) in Bin Wahad "discovery" materials, in possession of the author.

21. Field Marshal Don Cox ("DC") was not involved in the events Cohendet describes here.
22. Cohendet Church Committee testimony. In an e-mail to me on 28 May 2003, J. Herman Blake, Newton's dissertation adviser at the University of California, Santa Cruz, stated, "I did write all of *Revolutionary Suicide*. As well, I wrote many of the articles Huey published in the BPP newspaper, and most of those published in the book, 'To Die for the People.' During Huey's incarceration at San Luis Obispo, I visited him every Friday and spent the entire day with him."
23. Cohendet Church Committee testimony.
24. "Hoover Would Have Been Proud," *Winston-Salem Journal and Sentinel*, 16 February 1975, in SAC to Director, FBI, Charlotte Subject: Black Panther Party. FBI Freedom of Information Act Reading Room, Washington, D.C.
25. Yohuru Williams, "In Defense of Self-Defense: The Black Panther Party in History and Memory," unpublished lecture, Stetson University, Deland, Florida, 2001 (cited by permission of the author).
26. Howard Zinn, "Federal Bureau of Intimidation," *Covert Action Quarterly* (1995): http://mediafilter.org/MFF/FBI.html.

PART FOUR Coalition Politics: The Panthers as a "Revolutionary Vanguard"

Introductory Comment

White Tigers, Brown Berets, Black Panthers, Oh My!

YOHURU WILLIAMS

Black men. Black people, colored persons of America, revolt everywhere! Arm yourselves. The only culture worth keeping is a revolutionary culture.
 — George Mason Murray, Black Panther Party minister of education, 1968

Our program is Cultural Revolution through a total assault on the culture, which makes us use every tool, every energy and any media we can get our collective hands on. We take our program with us everywhere we go and use any means necessary to expose people to it.
 — John Sinclair, White Panther Party minister of information, 1968

When mandatory retirement laws compelled sixty-five-year-old Maggie Kuhn to give up her position as the administrator of the Presbyterian Church's Council on Church and Race in Philadelphia in 1970, her coworkers threw her a party. As a token of their appreciation for her years of service, they presented her with a brand-new sewing machine. They thought it projected all that retirement was supposed to represent — peace, tranquility, leisure. But Kuhn saw retirement as an artificially enforced exile: banishment to the realm of the non–wage-earners; social segregation in the restricted space of the retiree; political alienation in the camp of the irrelevant. Comparing the plight of the elderly with someone seeking to purchase a car, she complained, "Only the newest model is desirable. The old are condemned to obsolescence; left to rot like wrinkled babies in glorified playpens — forced to succumb to a trivial, purposeless waste of their years and their time." So, instead of opening her new sewing machine and embracing her new life, Maggie Kuhn resolved to resist. Joining with a small band of four other retirees she knew, she emerged as a leader for the rights of the elderly. The confrontational protest style and tactics of the organization she formed, including its penchant for leading marches and staging guerrilla theater to protest discrimination against the elderly, earned them the nickname the Gray Panthers.[1] In aiming to radicalize older Americans to fight the image of the old as useless, infirm, and withdrawn, they followed in the footsteps of their namesake, the Black Panthers.

At first blush, Maggie Kuhn would seem a world away from one of the most controversial movements of the twentieth century, the gun-toting revolutionary cadre founded by Huey Newton and Bobby Seale in Oakland, California, in 1966. As the Panthers emulated revolutionaries from Africa to Asia to Latin America, groups all over the world — from England to Israel to India — emulated the Panthers. But the Panthers inspired all sorts of groups in the United States itself, many of them well beyond the boundaries of urban politics and black radicalism, who adopted the Party's action-oriented style, its language, and sometimes even its politics. These organizations fall into three broad, sometimes overlapping, categories: Panther mimics, Panther supporters, and Panther allies.

The Panther mimics were organizations built on the Panther model while not necessarily embracing Panthers politics. They borrowed the boisterousness and the bravado of the Party, for example, but not its socialist agenda. True, the Gray Panthers did sometimes exhibit a kind of radical analysis that echoed Panther radicalism. As the Panthers said of racism, for example, Kuhn's group said of its issue, "ageism is a condition of society that will not be cured by concentrating on the needs of the elderly alone." "We're not hung up on old folks' issues," Kuhn intoned, "and we're not delivering services like meals on wheels. We're trying to find the root causes of the alienation that brings about the need for those services."[2] And, the Gray Panthers did adopt an agenda modeled to some extent on the 1966 Panther Ten-Point Platform and Program. Among other demands, they called for a clean and safe environment, nuclear disarmament, affordable housing, low utilities, and free health care — precisely the points of intersection that the Panthers had hoped would provide fertile ground for alliances and community organizing.

Still, it was mostly a politics of style that tied the Gray Panthers to the Black Panthers. Indeed, it was precisely that mimicry that showed how the

Panthers, through language, art, and culture, had transformed modes of political communication in America. A far cry from the street-corner orators of a previous generation of radicals, the Panthers demonstrated how a carefully crafted militant image could win both recognition and support. It was a lesson that Maggie Kuhn learned early on. Her small band of "wrinkled radicals" was fading in 1970, until she was invited to deliver a speech before the 181st General Assembly of the United Presbyterian Church in Denver. Her fiery oratory in support of senior rights that day helped propel her fledging organization into the national spotlight and win converts nationwide. But avoiding the kind of revolutionary politics advanced by the BPP surely explains the Gray Panthers' peak membership of some sixty thousand, which was larger than that of the Black Panthers by a factor of thirty.

By "revolutionary politics" I mean both the culture and politics of the Panther movement and the people they sought to rally. So, for example, while the Black Panthers experimented with communal living as a means of building revolutionary camaraderie, the Gray Panthers embraced it as a means of economic survival, and they consciously distinguished themselves from their youthful progenitors, even when they lived among them. In commenting on her decision to share a pair of three-story stucco houses with six other significantly younger rent-paying tenants, Kuhn referred to having "'created an alternative family here,'" and yet, clearly concerned to counter any preconceptions about "hippie" communes, she insisted, "'I like to think we can replicate it.'"[3] Like a host of other such organizations, the Gray Panthers cast themselves in the Panther mold but always reflected the politics and culture of their own constituency.

Some Panther mimics went further, of course, imagining their group as an important, if separate, corollary to the Black Panthers themselves. Among the most colorful were the White Panthers, founded in Ann Arbor, Michigan, in 1968 by John Sinclair and Lawrence Pun Plamondon. This group felt so akin to the Black Panther Party that in 1969 it even sought—unsuccessfully—to join the BPP ranks. That rejection did not stop their efforts on behalf of the Panther movement, however, nor did it diminish their revolutionary élan. Investigated by a Senate subcommittee in 1971, for example, the group was accused of drafting a plan to create a rock group as a front to distribute Party literature to the nation's youth. They were also accused of plotting to kidnap key government officials in an effort to emulate the Tupamaros guerrillas in Uruguay.[4] These White Panthers dressed the part, adopting Panther rhetoric and symbols. That they attached their own cultural meanings to those symbols reflected the social problems and cultural divides that could get in the way of the kind of larger movement that the Panthers had envisioned from their founding. So, while the Gray Panthers might make a conscious effort to reach out to the youth culture in their first incarnation in 1970 as the Consultation of Older and Younger Adults for Social Change, John Sinclair's White Panther Manifesto of 1968 instructed white mother country revolutionaries to "BE FREE, goddammit and fuck them old dudes."[5]

The White Panthers could shock in the fashion of the early Black Panthers. They played on mainstream fears about youth culture to convey a sense of their revolutionary agenda. They claimed among their long-range goals the legalization of marijuana and the release of all political prisoners, including especially jailed Black Panthers.[6] And there was more: "We don't have guns yet — not all of us anyway — because we have more powerful weapons — direct access to millions of teenagers is one of our most potent, and their belief in us is another. But we will use guns if we have to — we will do anything — if we have to." Despite these and other threats — like the one to infect nation's youth with the powerful narcotic of SDRR (sex, drugs, and rock 'n' roll) — the White Panthers paled next to their mentors in their ability to attract members. By 1970, the organization claimed to have seventy chapters nationwide, but to conceal its ranks, female and male members adopted the same name. More important, there were significant cultural differences between the White and Black Panthers. The indulgence of drugs and alcoholic beverages — not to mention the talk of "sex in the streets" — flew in the face of Black Panther Party rules, if not its actual practice. The White Panthers' founding manifesto made clear their emulation of the Panthers, but through their own cultural lens: "Our culture, our art, the music, newspapers, books, posters, our clothing, our homes, the way we walk and talk, the way our hair grows, the way we smoke dope and fuck and eat and sleep — it is all one message, and the message is FREEDOM!"[7]

Any group in this era that talked loud and advocated armed resistance was likely to be compared with the Black Panthers. Still, few of these imitators possessed the Panthers' social revolutionary dedication to improving conditions in their own communities, which the BPP made its hallmark from 1968. The Panthers did not discriminate in offering their services, but they did encourage individuals to organize around problems in their own particular community. Black people must organize black people, white people must organize white people, brown people must organize brown people on the road to a "rainbow coalition" that could represent the disparate needs of all those so allied.[8]

Perhaps the most bizarre of the Panther mimics was the infamous White Tigers, a militant band of New York City police officers who were united in their opposition to the Black Panthers. Although the group was purported to have used the name only once, the attention they received was enormous. Mocking the Panthers' use of violent rhetoric, the Tigers used violence, intimidation, and their badges to bring down a veritable reign of terror on the Party and other black militant groups whom they denounced as antipolice and traitors to the United States. Beyond showing support for fellow officers, however, the White Tigers were devoid of any social program at all.[9] Indeed, their most notable action was a violent attack on several Black Panthers in the hallway of a Brooklyn courthouse in late 1968. The Tigers, according to several who participated in the mobbing that day, were actually members of a hard-line police organization called the Law Enforcement Group or LEG. Denying reports that the group had affiliations with white supremacist organizations, New York police commissioner Howard R. Leary blamed the violence on police culture. What happened in Brooklyn, he explained, reflected "the community atmosphere." "They are responsive to what they say the community wants," he told reporters inquiring into the incident. He added that the desire for more rigid law enforcement was far-reaching, especially among younger officers who were upset over the way the courts coddled criminals like the Black Panthers.[10]

Apparently the beating that the Panthers took from the police on that day was no worse than the flogging they received from some of their staunchest supporters—white leftists, for example, who were eager to exploit the breadth of support that the Panthers had generated in late-sixties America. Culture made it impossible for everyone to join the Panthers, both literally and figuratively. But that did not prevent white radicals from emulating the Panthers; from drawing revolutionary inspiration from the Panthers; or from standing alongside the Panthers—all, apparently, in support of the Panthers. In the case of the Students for a Democratic Society (SDS), however, David Barber shows that figurative support was not the same as literal support. He makes the argument here that a racist undercurrent in the SDS leadership sought continually to recast the Panther movement to meet its own ends in the crucial years 1968–1971. While consistently claiming to follow Panther leadership — an SDS National Council meeting even voted the Panthers the "vanguard of the revolution" — SDS leaders just as consistently acted otherwise, in effect seeking to lead the Panthers themselves.

While both mimics and supporters could claim to be allies with the Panthers in maintaining a cordial working relationship with them, only a much smaller number of groups actually shared with the Panthers enough of the same social, economic, and cultural terrain to really be counted as such. One of these organizations was the group of Puerto Rican nationalists called the Young Lords. Their experience, as discussed by Jeffrey Ogbar in this section was analogous in some striking ways to that of the Cape Verdeans discussed by Jama Lazerow in his essay on Frank "Parky" Grace. Though these Panther allies were typically not black — or, at least had been raised in a culture not primarily identified as black — they often experienced the kind of alienation that produced a unique solidarity with other people of color. To be sure, the prevailing power of their culture operated on Puerto Ricans as divisively as on blacks and whites, but their unique situation produced more areas of common ground with the former than with the latter. Especially among the young, the stigma of being "gangsters," "thugs," and "troublemakers" living by the violent code of streets controlled by brutal police — all led to their identifying with much of what constituted the Panthers. The same was true, even earlier, of radical Latinos in the West who adopted the name Brown Berets. It is difficult to argue with Ogbar's assertion here that "Latino radicals in general had always been the obvious allies for the Panthers from the moment the Party expanded its operations south from Oakland in 1967." Moreover, as the Panthers moved increasingly toward the condemnation of sexism — and public support for the women's liberation and gay liberation movements — the Young Lords, after much struggle, adopted a *thirteen*-point program that rejected part of American culture and the culture of their own community: machismo.

Like the BPP, the Young Lords and the Brown Berets sought to organize the lumpen masses. Rarely could white radical organizations make such claims, except in abstract terms meant to frighten the so-called Establishment. Rejecting "honkie culture," as the White Panthers called it, would be impossible without engaging it and everything it stood for. Joel Wilson, in his essay here on the Peace and Freedom Party (PFP), takes the Panthers to task for crafting a racial ideology in early 1968 — but at least it was an ideology crafted from the reality of the experience of black Americans in politics.

From this perspective, we must distinguish movements among poor whites — like the Panther-allied Chicago group the Young Patriots — from countercultural organizations like the White Panthers, the SDS, or the PFP.

In the PFP, for example, divisions over culture as well as politics (reformist or revolutionary?) strained relations with the Black Panthers, with whom some elements of the PFP sought to ally. Those Wilson calls "pragmatists," for a host of reasons, could not embrace the Panthers' rhetoric of violence; they also rejected the BPP Ten-Point Platform and Program as their own political objectives. Other elements in the PFP, led by those Wilson calls "visionaries," envisaged the inauguration of a new era of radical politics in their alliance with the Black Panther Party. The Panthers, for their own reasons, thought for a moment that alliance might advance their vision of revolution. The union would prove to be troubled and short-lived, however, in great measure because of the inability of both sides to bridge both cultural and political divides. At the same time, the very attempt is a measure of the appeal of the Black Panther Party even as it was just starting out.

By 1990, Maggie Kuhn rearticulated the vision of the Gray Panthers, which she maintained had sustained them for twenty years. In her words, the Gray Panthers "envision a future when the rigid life-span boxes of youth, adulthood and old age with their corresponding functions of education, work, and leisure will be broken open so all ages will go to school, participate in productive life and enjoy periodic leisure. There will be a new structure to the workplace starting with alternatives like job sharing, the four-day workweek, flextime, sabbaticals and work-retirement scheduling. Opportunities for education will be life long. Health care will be available to all and preventive care and health education will be top priorities."[11] In the dim light of the present such sentiments among sixties radicals — young and old — seem visionary, or perhaps simply naive, but in the sixties they were more common than might now be imagined. In reality, of course, the means by which many of these radicals hoped to obtain certain ends mired them in conflict and left in shambles what many assumed was the potential for a great social revolution. The right to affordable medicine and the legalization of marijuana (even if limited to medical purposes) do not an alliance or a revolution make. Still, for a brief moment, the Black Panther Party seemed to be on the cusp of unifying a number of groups into a movement so capacious that even revolution appeared possible. In the end, their influence would be felt in far more subtle ways, among which were the militant and uncompromising demands of dozens of groups who found inspiration in the shadow of the Panther.

Notes

1. "Maggie Growls: Maggie Kuhn and the Grey Panthers" (Goldwater, Attie Productions, 2000). The Gray Panther papers are currently housed at the Temple University Library in Philadelphia, see http://library.temple.edu/collections/urbana/gray-924.htm. The group's achievements are many, including the repeal of the mandatory retirement law in the United States.
2. Maggie Kuhn, quoted in "Still Prowling, Still Growling," *New Internationalist* (June 1982).
3. Ibid.
4. "Allege White Panthers Seek 'Tupamaros' Status," *Holland (Michigan) Evening Sentinel*, 16 March 1971, 8; Marsha Low, "'60s Radical Takes Long Trip Back to His Roots," *Detroit Free Press*, 27 October 2004, sec. B.; see also Plamondon's newly self-published autobiography, *Lost from the Ottawa: The Story of the Journey Back* (Cloverdale, Mich.: Plamondon, 2004).
5. "White Panther Manifesto," http://www.signal66.com/music/lostindc/00_03246.html.
6. "Milwaukee White Panthers Plan Fund-Raising Affair," *Daily Northwestern*, 20 January 1970, 21.
7. "White Panther Manifesto," 3.
8. On 7 June 1969, the Black Panther newspaper announced an alliance called the Rainbow Coalition (no relation to the later organization of that name associated with Jesse Jackson). In addition to the Black Panthers, and what was then the Young Lords Organization, the alliance also included the Young Patriots Organization, a street gang of white youths that had turned political. The Coalition sent representatives to the annual convention of Students for a Democratic Society (SDS) that year.
9. At least the White Panthers had talked about social programs. Though mostly advocating the revolutionary potential of rock music, John Sinclair did call for "a total revolutionary program of self-reliance and serving the people any way you can." Of course, the fact that he promised in return, "you will have a good time forever," marked his cultural and political distance from the Black Panthers (Sinclair quoted in "Rock and Roll Is a Weapon of Cultural Revolution," excerpt reprinted in Alexander Bloom and Wini Breines, eds., *"Takin' It to the Streets: A Sixties Reader*, 2nd ed. [New York: Oxford University Press, 2003], 244).
10. On the White Tigers, see "Off Duty Police Attack Negroes," *Coshocton Tribune*, 5 September 1968, 22; "White Tigers v Black Panthers: Score: Trouble," *Coshocton Tribune*, 19 September 1968, 22; "Why Police and Black Panthers Battled," *Bucks County Courier*, 17 September 1968, 7.
11. Quoted in "Background: Ageism Hurts Us All; Aging Is Shared by All," Temple University Urban Archives, Gray Panthers Accession 835 Records, 1950s-mid 1990s, http://library.temple.edu/collections/urbana/gray-01.htm.

Invisible Cages: Racialized Politics and the Alliance between the Panthers and the Peace and Freedom Party

JOEL WILSON

On 31 August 1967 the National Conference for New Politics (NCNP) convened at the Palmer House in Chicago. In the ebullient words of an NCNP press release for the event, there was "nothing less than the nation's rebirth on the agenda" and *Ramparts* later called the convention "the biggest and most representative gathering of America's Left opposition in over two decades."[1] The NCNP organizers hoped their conference, which came two years after the Students for a Democratic Society's seminal demonstration in April 1965 against the war in Vietnam and one year after Stokely Carmichael's June 1966 call for Black Power, could reunite leftists of different races and ideological persuasions around an agenda for change that included the "common goals of ending poverty, racism, and the war in Vietnam."[2] The Left was sorely in need of a rebirth of unity at summer's end in 1967: massive outbreaks of violence in Detroit and Newark; the continuing escalation of the American commitment in Vietnam; and growing protest against the war all raised questions of strategy and tactics that accentuated the divisions among activists. That night in August, NCNP executive director William Pepper addressed convention delegates who represented roughly two hundred anti-war, anti-racist, and New Left organizations of varying degrees of solidity. "It may well be," Pepper optimistically declared, "that what you begin here may ultimately result in a new social, economic, and political system in the United States."[3] The first step toward realizing that vision, as stated in the convention's call, would be to "end the reign of Lyndon Baines Johnson."[4] However, as events would demonstrate, the hope that electoral opposition to Johnson could provide fertile ground for a rebirth of unity among whites and blacks of liberal and radical persuasions proved ill-founded.

It was the racial gulf between white and black delegates rather than the creation of a movement unified around achieving goals of social justice and peace that became the central story of NCNP. Roughly four hundred African American delegates, initially angered that so few blacks had been involved in convention planning, formed a black caucus soon after the NCNP commenced. Shortly thereafter, they submitted a list of thirteen nonnegotiable demands.[5] Though blacks represented 15 to 20 percent of the convention delegates, the whites in attendance acceded to the list of demands—which included a call for equal representation for African Americans on convention committees as well as a subsequent insistence that blacks be given 50 percent of the convention votes. Many white delegates who supported the black caucus demands did so "because they felt that a wider and more important issue was at stake—the issue of black-white unity."[6] Some celebrated the concessions as laying the foundation for "the first major political bond between blacks and whites in the 20th century U.S."; alternatively, Arthur Waskow perceived the vote in support of the black caucus demands as "an act of self-castration by good liberals trying to be good radicals."[7] Bob Avakian, of Berkeley's Community for New Politics (CNP), denounced the conference's decision, calling support for the black caucus humiliating to whites, patronizing to blacks, and inimical to real interracial cooperation.[8] Simon Hall has perceptively argued that the acrimony that took place at the convention at the Palmer House stemmed from the fact that "there were two movements in Chicago—one white and one black." Further, he noted, "The white branch was obsessed with Vietnam, American imperialism, and student affairs . . . the black branch was concerned with destroying a culture of oppression and creating a new kind of identity for African Americans."[9] The NCNP thus witnessed the forging of a superficial unity between blacks and whites. However, that unity proved in the months to come to be short-lived as the black and white branches of the Left continued to evolve in different directions.[10]

Close on the heels of the NCNP, activists in California who favored the sort of electoral action rejected in Chicago announced the creation of the Peace and Freedom Party (PFP), the platform of which would include the basic commitments to oppose the war in Vietnam and to support the black liberation movement. When PFP's first statewide meeting produced a walkout by black delegates who were angered by whites' unwillingness to follow precedents created in Chicago, a white delegate pointedly inquired, "If this is going to be a peace and freedom party, whose freedom — the white people in the room?"[11] Another delegate took an entirely different tack, but in an equally confrontational manner. The PFP, he said, could not "go out to white people and ask them to join an organization already committed to being the white tail on a black dog."[12] It appeared that in summer and fall 1967 there were two movements on the Left, and it was very much an open question whether or not activists of different races could find enough common ground to work in concert.

The Origins of the Alliance

In early May 1967, armed members of the Black Panther Party for Self-Defense (BPP) entered the California State Assembly to protest the imminent passage of a bill that would limit the Panthers' right to carry firearms in public. The protest resulted in significant media attention for the BPP, including what have become iconic images of armed Panthers boldly striding down the halls of the capitol.[13] Furthermore, the protest introduced a broader audience to Panther ideology after chairman Bobby Seale read for reporters Panther founder Huey Newton's incendiary "Executive Mandate No. 1," which denounced "the racist power structure of America" and its policies of "repression, genocide, terror, and the big stick."[14]

Unfortunately for the BPP, the protest also led to the arrest of cofounder Seale and many other demonstration participants. While the Sacramento protest dramatically raised the group's public profile, its legal aftermath so taxed the young organization's resources that the BPP went into a period of significant, though momentary, decline.[15] To raise bail money for its jailed compatriots, BPP members increased contact with white leftist organizations in the San Francisco Bay Area, such as the Communist Party and the Socialist Workers' Party. But that experience so antagonized Party Minister of Information Eldridge Cleaver that he penned for the July 1967 issue of the *Black Panther* a rhetorical broadside leveled against white leftists in the Bay Area.[16] In a polemic titled "White 'Mother Country' Radicals," Cleaver called white leftists "so infected with racism ... that they do not really see the community of interest between revolutionaries everywhere."[17] That harsh evaluation of white leftists would, however, change dramatically in the wake of subsequent events.

In the early morning hours of 28 October 1967, a gunfight erupted between two white Oakland police officers and Huey Newton, which left one police officer dead.[18] Following Newton's arrest, the Panthers found themselves in need of new sources of support as the organization sought to publicize Newton's cause and raise money for his defense. The matter was particularly urgent because, in this case, the founder and leading light of the Party was to be tried for the murder of a policeman. In December 1967, therefore, the BPP formed a working coalition with the PFP, which was then engaged in a feverish effort to register enough members to qualify for the November 1968 ballot. In January, following a successful PFP registration drive, Cleaver reflected positively on the fledgling association between the Panthers and white progressives. "We felt . . . it was time to establish some meaningful coalitions," Cleaver explained, coalitions that could deflate what he called the "dangerous tensions" that had made it difficult for "people who share a community of interests" to work together.[19] By April 1968, in fact, Panther leaders were downplaying earlier statements about "the prevailing idiocy of white radicals," and Huey Newton, Bobby Seale, and Eldridge Cleaver's wife, Kathleen, the Party's communications secretary, soon became Peace and Freedom candidates for state and local offices.[20]

The alliance between the Black Panthers and the Peace and Freedom Party briefly revived hopes quashed by the NCNP that the Left, fractured along lines of race by the growth of the antiwar movement and the emergence of Black Power, could reunite around an anti-racist, anti-imperialist agenda that could challenge racial inequality and curb American militarism. However, the short-lived coalition between the BPP and the diverse array of primarily white activists in the PFP was not to deliver on such hopes. In fact, divergent views about race and its impact on American society prevented the development of a healthy, interracial movement that might have breathed new life into the late-sixties Left; indeed, the troubled relationship between the BPP and PFP represented in microcosm the same tensions and lack of effective communication that plagued efforts to unite the black liberation movement and the New Left nationwide. An examination of the early stages of the relationship between these organizations, from the initiation of their alliance in December 1967 to April 1968, reveals much about how deeply held beliefs about race shaped the thoughts and actions of black and white activists ostensibly committed to undercutting race as a category of privilege and subordination in the United States.

In its early years, the Black Panther Party advocated the empowerment of all African Americans as well as the end of racial oppression in the United States, to be achieved by an African American mass movement led by blacks from the same social stratum as the Panthers themselves. The precise nature of how the BPP envisioned that movement shifted noticeably between 1967 and 1968, though. In 1967, the Panthers' public rhetoric drew upon their Ten-Point Platform and Program to articulate a complete indictment of what they believed was the white supremacist status quo, while simultaneously stressing the importance of armed confrontation with the white power structure.[21] In the wake of Newton's imprisonment, Party members in the Bay Area poured their energies into advocating for his plight in hopes that doing so would earn the Panthers new recruits, challenge the power structure, and save Newton's life.[22] What remained constant in these months of shifting priorities and emphases was the Panthers' uncompromising insistence that only a movement conceived and led by African Americans could hope to challenge the racism ingrained in American culture.[23] While Panther advocates of the alliance with the PFP characterized it in different manners between December 1967 and April 1968, they invariably insisted that the BPP remain the senior partner in any joint activity with whites, an assurance that did not still the lasting disquiet within the Party over such cooperation.

At the same time, two broad factions vied for power within the Peace and Freedom Party. What primarily divided them was their contrasting approach to political organizing, which might best be seen as "pragmatist" and "visionary." That same division was already visible in Chicago the previous August at the National Conference for New Politics, where advocates of third-party electoral activity clashed with those who stressed instead the importance of community organizing. To be sure, both pragmatists and visionaries in the PFP believed that racial inequality could be surmounted through their organization's stirring of a popular movement that would expose racism and militarism in American life and also increase the state's commitment to ending racial inequality. However, adherents to these differing positions advanced contrasting conceptions of how such a popular movement would occur. The pragmatists stressed the importance of democracy at all levels of the PFP; believed change would come quickest through direct appeals to middle-class whites that downplayed sympathy for black liberation while extolling racial equality; emphasized opposition to the war in Vietnam; and sought some degree of electoral success. Alternatively, the visionaries favored a more centralized organization that downplayed the importance of electoral politics in favor of intensive efforts at community organizing; instead, they worked toward an interracial alliance that would fuse poor and working-class Americans with organized labor and the antiwar movement.

This matrix of conflicting beliefs about race and its role in creating social change fundamentally shaped the development of the alliance between the Black Panthers and Peace and Freedom in early 1968. A brief examination of how each side in this dispute represented the alliance in print and in public discussion demonstrates how members of the BPP and pragmatists and visionaries in the PFP articulated mutually exclusive understandings of the role of race and racial identity in their common struggle against inequality in America. Between December 1967 and April 1968, each faction in this process of ideological contention found their assumptions called into question by those with alternative viewpoints, as Black Panthers, pragmatists, and visionaries all sought to mold the contours of an alliance that appeared to hold high stakes for the future of interracial cooperation. A consideration of how each group advocated its position illuminates how beliefs about race influenced each group's politics and also demonstrates how each group utilized race as a powerful tool to advance particular political agendas and with which to undermine political adversaries. In the process, though committed to the goals of human rights and anti-racism, black and white activists in the BPP and the PFP alike fell prey to patterns of belief about race that they believed would provide the key to creating social change but that instead ultimately eroded the possibility of interracial cooperation.

Race, Class, and the Black Panther Party

Throughout their alliance with Peace and Freedom, BPP spokespeople insisted that racial oppression represented the fundamental form of inequality in America; the tendency of mainstream white society to ignore, minimize, or dismiss the racial violence and economic subordination experienced by African Americans only increased the urgency of the Panthers' mission and their boiling, righteous anger. The Panthers' sense of crisis flowed from the belief that inaction against the manifestations of racism would be to stand idle in the face of what Newton called "the progression of a trend that leads inevitably to [our] own destruction."[24] Leaders in the BPP expressed the belief that the physical threat to African Americans posed by the violent racism of white Americans, along with blacks' historical experience of racism, made blacks the uniquely qualified vanguard of any antiracist social movement.

In their efforts to analyze American society, the Black Panthers drew heavily on the work of Frantz Fanon, a psychiatrist from Martinique whose seminal work, *The Wretched of the Earth*, described the ideological evolution of the Algerian revolt against French colonialism and the conflicts between different classes involved in nationalist struggles.[25] Fanon emphasized the essentially violent nature of successful anticolonial struggles with statements like, "Between oppressors and oppressed everything can be solved by force."[26] Moreover, he insisted that the most disempowered elements in colonized society were best qualified to lead a thoroughgoing struggle against colonial domination, because the colonial bourgeoisie were essentially "violent in their words and reformist in their attitudes."[27] Black Panther spokespeople refined that position by insisting that unemployed, disenfranchised blacks—members of what would be called in Marxist parlance the lumpen proletariat—held legitimate title to leadership of any domestic decolonizing effort.[28]

The Panthers' inversion of race-based and class-based hierarchies, then, was both strategic and tactical in that it served the BPP's ideological goals of undercutting racism and capitalism as two of the organizing principles of American society. Strategically, the Panthers argued that ending insidious forms of racial oppression required, as Newton later stated, placing in black people's hands "the ability to . . . define phenomena and . . . to make these phenomena act in a desired manner."[29] The advocacy of this goal sufficed to make the Panthers thoroughgoing revolutionaries in American society, with or without the Fanon-inspired rhetoric and the trappings of armed rebellion against colonialism that quickly made the BPP notorious in the mainstream media. The Panthers' insistence that American society incorporated two separate nations, one black and one white, defined by different histories and value systems, conferred upon the BPP an incisive ability to articulate profound grievances against a status quo that had long relegated African Americans to subordinate status.[30] The group's positing of racialized, class-based qualifications for leadership of any anti-racist movement was also tactical: it allowed the Panthers to legitimately cast themselves as the American embodiment of the colonized masses. This stance empowered the Panther Party in alliances with the predominantly white, middle-class PFP or any African American organization with middle-class roots such as the Student Nonviolent Coordinating Committee (SNCC). In the climate of the late 1960s, no radical group would directly challenge the argument that the oppressed best understood their own oppression.[31]

However, the Panthers' arguments on behalf of blackness as the most legitimate claim to membership in a revolutionary community constituted a double-edged sword. Dean Robinson has noted the tendency of Black Nationalist organizations to "inadvertently . . . reproduce some of the thinking and practices that created black disadvantage in the first place" by arguing that blacks and whites represent separate "organic" units.[32] That is, if the Panthers opposed the racism inherent in American society, did it not represent a fundamental contradiction for them to appeal to race as a source of identity and strength? Moreover, the Panthers' insistence that their first priority was to lead African Americans in the construction of an imagined community of blackness and in the resistance to economic dispossession left unanswered other pressing questions in the opening months of 1968. For instance, would the Panthers' attainment of their goal mean the expansion or the lessening of the gap between whites and blacks? Would the BPP lend its energies to the task that few on the Left had shown the inclination to tackle—namely, conceiving new forms of identity rooted on different terrain than race?

What wrought the turnaround in the Black Panthers' interest in working with a predominantly white organization such as Peace and Freedom was the need to mount a vigorous defense campaign for Huey Newton.[33] As part of its broader defense strategy, the BPP strove to replace the conception in the public mind of their organization as violence-prone by reimagining itself as a legitimate political party that sought to inject radicalizing content into mainstream politics. The coalition with the PFP was essential to this BPP project, for the former provided the Panthers with entrée into electoral politics, an arena they had been disinclined to enter independently in the months before Newton's imprisonment. And, in fact, participation in electoral politics in 1968 did dramatically increase the BPP's stature by providing Black Panther candidates a public platform from which to cast themselves as the leaders of a movement of African Americans committed to reshaping American society and ending the depredations of the capitalist economy among poor blacks.

On 31 January 1968, the Peace and Freedom Party of Alameda County held a candidates forum for Party members to get acquainted with individuals seeking nominations for the local congressional district. The county-level leadership of the PFP, a body dominated by visionaries, initially felt the Party should "meet only with the Black Panthers regarding who to run for Congress in this district," but they relented when it was noted that the more democratic course would be for PFP membership to make that decision.[34] That led to a speech by Kathleen Cleaver at the candidates' forum in front of a white audience, a key moment in the Black Panthers' evolution as a political organization. Over the previous span of their organizational existence, they had condemned "controlled outlets" such as electoral politics as unlikely to "interfere with the process of exploitation." Newton himself had referred to African American politicians as "nothing more than apologizing parrots" who "[turned] a deaf ear to the cries of the suffering and the downtrodden, the unemployed and welfare recipients who hunger for liberation by any means necessary."[35] Reflecting the Panthers' early emphasis on building their Party as a prefigurative base of liberation from the status quo, his expressed distaste for the compromises made by black politicians and for the political process as a whole was principled. But with Newton now facing the death penalty in a capital murder case, the BPP needed to engage more fully in the effort to shape opinion in the public sphere, not just in the minds of recruits and sympathizers.

In her speech of 31 January, Kathleen Cleaver articulated the Panthers' new conception of themselves as an electoral political party, an identity they felt compelled to embrace, she said, out of concern for the plight of African Americans. The Panthers were drawn to the electoral process, because they were "a political party dedicated to resisting all forms of exploitation and aggression imposed upon the black community." Far from being a means of cooptation of black struggle, electoral action comprised "one tool that can be used for the benefit of the black community—if it is not tied to the aims of the power structure."[36] The Black Panthers would practice new forms of politics, Cleaver assured her audience, dissimilar from those of the "bootlickers, Uncle Toms, and black Anglo-Saxons who are willing to rise to prominence on the backs of the oppressed masses." Casting black politicians as puppets of white colonial masters, Cleaver insisted that only by embracing "revolutionary black power" could African Americans free themselves from racist brutality. "The task before black politicians of any integrity," she charged, "is to lead black people away from the Democratic machine"; any other course would be "but one more move to exploit the struggle of the black masses for the advantage of the power structure."[37] Cleaver thus indicted the traditional hierarchies that anointed members of the middle- or upper- classes with political power. In fact, the Panthers' political legitimacy in the black community flowed, she said, from their subordinate economic status: BPP members were distant from the compromise and cooptation to which the black middle class had succumbed, for the Panthers had direct experience with the disfranchisement and economic exploitation suffered by poor African Americans. Articulated in front of an almost entirely white audience, Cleaver's speech positioned the Panthers as leaders of the black community and, at the same time, stated unalloyed support for the cause dearest to some PFP activists' hearts: to destabilize the two-party system in the service of revolutionary goals.

However, Cleaver also aimed to establish a balance of power between the PFP and the BPP that favored the Panthers. To accomplish that end, she turned to race as the ultimate means of gaining advantage for the Panthers' political agenda. In Alameda County, which includes Oakland and Berkeley, PFP chapters debated in winter 1968 whether their Party should endorse Newton as their candidate for a congressional primary, a heated dispute discussed below. For her part, Cleaver insisted that the BPP spoke for the African American community, which, she said, wanted Newton as its candidate. Indeed, failure to support him, she warned, would be taken as "an admission of the inability of whites to change their pattern of oppression and exploitation and an invitation to certain destruction."[38] The Peace and Freedom Party now faced a choice: it could accept the direction offered by the Black Panthers and become relevant to the black liberation movement, or it could "fall into the same pit of cynicism, hypocrisy, and decadence of the Democratic and Republican parties." The Black Panthers could not exert influence on opinion within the PFP based solely on their numbers or through control of a large bloc of votes, of course. However, Cleaver's speech shrewdly played upon the desire of PFP members to participate in the fight against racial oppression and the wishes of some in the group to earn the approval of a black organization such as the Black Panthers as a means to begin construction of an interracial social movement. Though the PFP had a far larger mass base in Alameda County, the Panthers deftly used race to maneuver their new prospective allies into a corner: whites could accede to the BPP's wishes or be labeled irrelevant to the struggle against racism, tantamount to "an invitation to certain destruction" on the Left.[39] The clear threat of the withdrawal of the Panthers' support loomed menacingly in the air until Cleaver's speech concluded, when the crowd rose to its feet and defused any potential discord with a standing ovation.[40]

A few weeks later, the BPP announced that they had entered into another alliance, this time with one of the most storied organizations in the history of the civil rights movement—SNCC, now in its "Black Power" phase. The association would prove short-lived, however, at least in part over the issue of alliances with whites. According to SNCC Executive Secretary James Forman, the relationship between SNCC and the BPP stretched back to 1966, mostly involving statements of support by SNCC for Panther demonstrations like the May 1967 action at Sacramento.[41] In June 1967, Newton had drafted former SNCC chairman Stokely Carmichael into the BPP as a "field marshal" with the high-flying charge to "establish revolutionary law, order and justice" from the Continental Divide to the Atlantic Ocean.[42] However, it was not until January 1968 that the BPP established a more direct, personal relationship with Carmichael and Forman. During that month, Eldridge Cleaver and Bobby Seale traveled to Washington, D.C., to invite Carmichael to speak at a fund-raising rally in Newton's honor.[43] Carmichael agreed, but not before registering his discontent regarding the Panthers' alliance with the PFP; its choice of a white lawyer to defend Newton; and the fact that Carmichael was to share the stage at the rally with a white PFP representative.[44] In February, Cleaver also invited Forman to address the rally, setting off what Carmichael later characterized as a struggle between himself and Forman to control the BPP, an organization Carmichael called "sorely in need of ideological leadership."[45] The revelation that the BPP and SNCC were uniting produced great excitement in activist circles across the country, but the relationship never proved to be anything but symbolic.[46] The break between the BPP and SNCC came quickly in July 1968, ostensibly over an attempted protest at the United Nations. Poor planning and mutual suspicion between SNCC representatives and the BPP kept the protest from attaining the hoped-for publicity; a plan to enter the United Nations to speak with delegates about Huey Newton's case never came off.[47]

In the immediate foreground of these events, during winter 1968, Eldridge Cleaver, along with Bobby Seale, insisted on the right of poor blacks to direct any anti-racist mass movement and to determine the proper relationship between black and white activists—under the leadership of the Black Panther Party. The stance did not bode well for relations with either SNCC or the PFP. In analyzing American race relations and their significance for black Americans, for example, Cleaver planted his feet squarely on Fanon's shoulders. To an audience at the PFP's founding convention, he proclaimed, "We start with the basic definition: that black people in America are a colonized people in every sense of the term . . . white America is an organized Imperialist force holding black people in colonial bondage."[48] In characterizing American society as inherently racist and responding with a program that posited black unity as the starting point of effective resistance, the Panthers sought "to unify the black population in this country within a national structure . . . inclusive enough to pull in all black people." Blacks experienced a "dual status," Cleaver said, that combined a "mythical right of citizenship" with "the concrete reality of our situation." The contradiction between American nationalist myths and blacks' lived experience created "the national consciousness of an oppressed and colonized people"; this consciousness dictated that African Americans turn their focus "inward—into the black heart of the colony." The Panthers considered themselves qualified to lead the unified mass of African Americans because of their ability to "relate to the brother on the block in a political fashion." Here, Cleaver contrasted the BPP with SNCC, whose organizing work he derided as the efforts of "black hippies . . . black college students who have dropped out of the middle class."[49] Leaders of SNCC like H. Rap Brown learned their most confrontational rhetoric, Cleaver crowed, "precisely because they had come to the West Coast and spent a little time with the Black Panthers out here."[50]

In addition to challenging the hierarchies of class within the black community in the effort to legitimate their assertion of primacy in the black liberation struggle, Black Panther leaders also insisted that the gulf between the races necessitated that African Americans assume the leading role in any interracial coalition. They charged that whites' ignorance of conditions in black communities and their inability to appeal to the black masses necessitated two separate but interconnected movements in which whites constituted junior partners. Those skeptics in the African American community who questioned the BPP's insistence that racial domination precluded the possibility of interracial organizations were dismissed as "misguided political freaks" making "a political mistake of the first order."[51] Questioning Peace and Freedom's knowledge of life in the black community, Seale observed, "The abstract term 'freedom' is empty without specific demands and methods of attaining freedom." In contrast, he said, the concrete nature of the Black Panther Party's Ten-Point Platform and Program authentically voiced the aspirations and needs of African Americans.[52] BPP leaders also found proof for their contention that race divided Americans more than nationality united them in the antiwar movement: whites' elevation of opposition to the war over fighting racial inequality raised suspicions that racism and self-interest blinded whites to the contradictions between the values they espoused and life in the ghettos. In clearly expressing his frustrations with such hypocrisy, Seale told a crowd of PFP supporters in February 1968 that "you white people . . . can get 65,000 people to march against the war in Vietnam. Well, you better get 65,000 to march against the war against black people in your own backyard. We're not going to march, we're going to be defending ourselves."[53]

Though there is scant documentation of Panther leaders' misgivings about the coalition during its lifespan, subsequent evidence indicates that BPP leadership retained lasting doubts about the firmness of the PFP's commitment to black liberation. As Seale commented retrospectively: "Some members of the Peace and Freedom Party weren't really concerned with brother Huey P. Newton as a political prisoner . . . some of them just weren't interested."[54] While Seale saw an insufficient commitment to Newton's cause, Hilliard felt cooperation with the BPP gave Peace and Freedom "a focus and urgency the organization would [have] otherwise [lacked]," an observation that somehow overlooked the PFP's obvious and intense opposition to the war in Vietnam.[55] Differences of style also exacerbated a cultural gap between the two organizations that complementary political outlooks could only partially bridge. Hilliard, for example, found white leftists as a group "uptight — even when trying to be loose. They [were] always trying to figure out how to live their lives as revolutionaries, never doing it."[56] He later recalled a long-haired PFP member arriving at the Panthers' Grove Street office driving a bus outfitted with a public address system to help spread the word about Huey Newton's plight. Witnessing the bus painted in psychedelic colors and its driver's shaggy appearance, Hilliard and another Panther on the scene were disgusted. "Clothes and looks reflect who you are: with their stringy arms and pasty faces these long-haired, bell-bottomed, tie-dyed flakes stoned on acid or weed seem to have no self-respect."[57]

These reservations on the part of Panther leaders about working with the PFP hint at a broader discontent among African Americans sympathetic to the BPP in cooperating with whites, regardless of the mutual benefits that flowed from the association. On 22 December 1967, the same day that the

Berkeley Barb announced the BPP-PFP alliance, the two groups held a joint rally at Hunter's Point in San Francisco. The cool response to the speeches by Bobby Seale and PFP organizer (and close Panther friend) Bob Avakian extolling the alliance "marked the end of our honeymoon in the black community in general, and the black liberation movement, in particular," recalled Earl Anthony. Indeed, sharp criticism expressed in public and private, Anthony said, "[came] from many quarters."[58] Some African Americans, the sympathetic *Ramparts* reporter Gene Marine observed, "feared that once again they were being used by whites for the whites' own purposes."[59] "By aligning with white radicals, even on a limited basis," wrote Reginald Major later, "the Panthers caused quite a few revolutionary blacks to dismiss the Party as being run by white people."[60] The sentiment could be found as well in the Panther rank and file. Regina Jennings, for example, because of her past experience with whites, simply refused to work with PFP members. Even after witnessing the efforts of white radicals on behalf of Huey Newton, Jennings "wondered and openly asked why [white members of PFP] were not working as aggressively to solve the racism that existed within their own communities."[61] Eldridge Cleaver himself admitted in an editorial in the *Black Panther* in March 1968 that the coalition with the PFP "has freaked out a lot of people," though he did not identify anyone specifically. Cleaver optimistically attributed that discomfort to "the history of isolation of the last few years." The BPP could never get sidetracked, he proclaimed, by "getting into a futile, racist bag."[62] The current lack of documentary evidence makes it difficult to assess the depth of resistance to the coalition within the BPP. Nevertheless, it is likely that Jennings was not alone in questioning how cooperation with whites would serve to unify the black community or make the Black Panther Party a stronger organization.

To mitigate such discontent, Cleaver reiterated throughout winter and spring 1968 that collaboration between radical whites and blacks was "absolutely and unequivocally desirable and necessary," though blacks would "supply the form of . . . cooperation" between the races that best served efforts to liberate the colonized minority.[63] The alliance, then, was mutually beneficial. "The movement in the black community," he asserted, "feeds the movement in the white community."[64] Whites who challenged blacks' direction of the liberation struggle would, he warned on another occasion, "destroy what you are trying to build for yourself."[65] Meanwhile, the Panthers' insistence on primacy in their relationship with the PFP, justified with references to blacks' subordinated status in American society, provided important political cover for the BPP. For the Panthers' claims to leadership camouflaged the fact that the BPP edged toward compromising what was perhaps the central aim of the black liberation movement: freedom from white input. The alliance between the Panthers and the PFP brought the BPP tangible benefits in the form of augmented political stature and invaluable publicity for Huey Newton, but the coalition represented a tacit admission that the BPP could not effectively wage its struggle alone, at least at that particular juncture. At the same time, the Panthers had masterfully articulated a race-based and class-based identity that not only placed them—if precariously—in the vanguard of the black liberation movement, but used race as a means to leverage themselves into a position of influence with the Peace and Freedom Party without appearing—at least to most—indebted or obligated to white activists.

Pragmatists, Visionaries, and Race in the Peace and Freedom Party

One former member of the Peace and Freedom Party has observed that the organization itself was a coalition of diverse groups whose political inclinations ran in contradictory directions. Unlike the BPP, that is, the PFP did not speak with a unified voice about how best to combat racial oppression in America.[66] The pragmatist and visionary factions emerged early in Peace and Freedom's organizational life; each group diagnosed American social problems and their remedies differently. The pragmatists insisted that the path to power for their organization lay in rehabilitating democratic participation in the political affairs of the nation, a process they believed they could catalyze by cultivating white middle-class voters' opposition to the war in Vietnam. Once encouraged to defect from mainstream politics by distaste for the war, the pragmatists argued, disaffected middle-class whites' expanded sense of political agency would lead them to push for new initiatives such as increased social programs that would then ameliorate racial inequality. Implicit in this argument was the belief that social change was unlikely to stem from a movement of the disempowered, but instead from an activist, concerned majority. The pragmatists voiced support for black liberation but also indirectly questioned the BPP's confrontational tactics and even the Panthers' ability to effect social change. Furthermore, the pragmatists doubted that a close alliance with the BPP would benefit Peace and Freedom, arguing that any association with the Panthers would undermine the PFP's efforts to fashion a political image that would make the Party politically relevant to white voters focused on opposition to the Vietnam war.[67] Rather than voicing these criticisms directly, though, the pragmatists instead took issue with the *nature* of the alliance between the two groups.

Peace and Freedom visionaries, on the other hand, wanted their Party to "deal with what are the real issues"—namely, the intertwined patterns of imperialism abroad and economic inequality imbricated with structural racism at home. They rejected the liberals' watered-down calls for withdrawal from Vietnam and for greater commitment to racial integration.[68] Echoing the community organizing position expressed at the National Conference for New Politics, the visionaries believed that the PFP could best create change by organizing the dispossessed rather than by turning to a political process dominated by established interests. The Black Panthers would organize African Americans, while the PFP would fashion disadvantaged whites into a political force that could then coalesce with blacks in an anti-racist, anti-imperialist movement.[69] In this view, cooperation with the Black Panther Party was a critical prefigurative step toward a just society in which race became a matter of personal identity rather than a means of subordination, making possible the peaceful coexistence between blacks and whites. The visionaries took seriously the Fanonian injunction that as citizens of the "mother country" it was their place to aid the primary revolutionary struggle —the black uprising. They internalized the belief central to black liberation that the oppressed could best define their own oppression. However, they believed that the BPP would see the wisdom of cooperating with whites in order to attain shared goals. At bottom, then, the visionaries held to the conviction that race was not a fundamental category of human difference.

As the events of the NCNP demonstrated, many elements of the white radical Left had by the late sixties discarded electoral politics as a viable avenue for change, and white leftists increasingly accepted the arguments advanced by organizations such as the BPP that meaningful social change could only emanate from the bottom rungs of American society. The pragmatists in the PFP questioned both of these assumptions, and in so doing opened themselves up to charges of political irrelevance, naïveté, or "worst of all" being tarred as "those horrid beasts, Liberals" by their more radical brethren.[70] Nevertheless, the pragmatists made the case that Peace and Freedom should convince middle-class white Americans to vote for an electoral party with an antiwar message and opt out of the undemocratic two-party status quo. In an article written for the *Los Angeles Free Press*, Farrel Broslawsky, a college professor from the area, articulated the identity that pragmatists believed the PFP should embrace: "The groups that are directly oppressed by American society need no reminder that they are powerless," he wrote, "but middle class people, who are indirectly victimized, must be made aware of the fact that they . . . are powerless to transform a society that perpetuates racism and poverty while promoting wars."[71] Not only was a strategy of organizing the dispossessed into an electoral party wrong-headed, Broslawsky argued, it was also doomed to failure, for blacks and Mexican Americans, he said, tended not to vote. Peace and Freedom should instead politicize those Americans — implicitly white — whose political involvement was typically "traditional," or confined to voting. This was the group that wielded real power in American society, a group Broslawsky and other pragmatists believed could catalyze a mass movement that could bring peace and justice to all Americans.

This vision of social change contrasted markedly with that supported by radical sectors of the Left; indeed, it can be characterized as verging on liberalism, for it implied that the middle class, not the dispossessed, would understand the alterations necessary in American society. Broslawsky presumed that once middle-class whites were sufficiently politicized to realize racism's impact on African Americans, they would take action to re-create American society in a more egalitarian mode. An antiwar message pitched to the ear of the white middle-class could put in train a process that would eventually result in black liberation. However, Broslawsky's flat assertions that people of color did not vote and that the oppressed needed no reminder of their lack of power stated rather clearly that middle-class whites, not African Americans, would play the primary role in determining the pace and content of change. Broslawsky and other pragmatists believed that the attainment of the greater good of swaying what he called the powerless, victimized middle class required downplaying Peace and Freedom's commitment to Black Power, because the middle class, once dislodged from its inertia, could transform American society. The subordination of the black freedom struggle to the goal of bringing middle-class whites into an oppositional third party advocated by PFP pragmatists, of course, ran counter to the Panthers' view that the fight against racism was the most important issue in American politics. Broslawsky's argument for a liberal, top-down process of radicalization contrasted painfully with the Panthers' conceptualization of social change, as the BPP argued explicitly that only through the empowerment of those oppressed by racism could American society redeem the democratic promise of its founding documents. In fact, Broslawsky's position could be construed as a reconceptualization of how a process of integration might take place, with the white middle class actively reaching out to African Americans after its political awakening. Perhaps Broslawsky's belief in the middle class as a potential force for social change stemmed from the fact that the majority of PFP members were themselves middle class. In any case, his abiding faith in the ability of bourgeois whites to reinvent their society contrasted markedly with the BPP's vision of America as a colonized society —just as it contrasted with the vision of the more radical members of his own organization.[72]

At Peace and Freedom's founding convention, following speeches by Bobby Seale and Eldridge Cleaver that brought convention delegates to life "as explosively as if [they] had started throwing hand grenades into the audience," Robert Scheer, a popular favorite for the PFP nomination for the U.S. Senate, spoke against a close identification between the organization and the BPP.[73] Echoing pragmatist sentiments, Scheer insisted that efficacy trumped moral outrage in politics. In his view, Peace and Freedom members had to choose between making an impact and counteractive venting. Criticizing the passage of resolutions endorsing the PFP alliance with the BPP and declaring support for Huey Newton, Scheer warned of the difficulties inherent in going out "to the person in the white community and [convincing] him that Black Power is in his own self-interest."[74] The painfully evident inequalities that concerned the politicized members of the PFP remained imperceptible to the typical white middle-class American, Scheer observed, and "until that becomes visible to that person, you can't organize around that issue. You may know it very clearly, but until he does it's not a live issue." The question, Scheer said, was "not how do you feel about what you're doing, but how effective is it in raising the issues that have to be raised in this society, and changing that society"; people who desired change in the here and now had to choose issues relevant to middle-class whites.[75] Despite his close friendships with Black Panther leaders like Eldridge Cleaver (he would edit Cleaver's second book), and despite his own sympathy for the black liberation movement, Scheer distinguished his own convictions from what he believed would be politically palatable to mainstream Americans.

In Scheer's eyes, that meant publicizing militarism's negative effects on the United States, not aligning the PFP with the BPP. He recommended that Peace and Freedom's message to the average American should be, "Look, buddy, you ought not to be working in a defense industry. You ought not to require that bloody money to make it . . . this society ought to provide you with a job that would allow you to work in peacetime."[76] Efficacy for the PFP meant stoking the *sub rosa* opposition to war among middle-class whites that Scheer, Broslawsky, and other pragmatists insisted lay waiting to be activated. An effort focused on sensitizing members of the middle class to their own white-skin privilege might feel good, in Scheer's words, but it would not create social change. Racism could only be confronted after antiwar sentiment pulled middle-class whites leftward.

The pragmatists' discontent with the Black Panther alliance surfaced openly in winter and spring 1968 during local debates about various aspects of the relationship between the two organizations. The pragmatists tended to take the Panthers' rhetoric and their open display of weapons at face value and then dismiss the BPP out of hand as an organization whose stated commitment to armed struggle ran counter to the desire for nonviolent social change common in the PFP.[77] For instance, in December 1967, PFP representative Michael Schon declared in a radio debate with the Communist Party organizer Dorothy Healey that he opposed Black Power just as he rejected white supremacy in the South, a statement that communicated a noteworthy misperception of the general principles and goals of the black liberation movement.[78] Members of a local group in San Francisco opposed the coalition because the PFP had begun to "[lean] toward violence" in support of the BPP's violent rhetoric, thereby effectively delegitimating Peace and Freedom's primary goal of providing "an alternative at the polls." A PFP member in Los Angeles, Howard Ballinger, decried what he saw as one of the major results of the alliance on the PFP: "The confusion of personal self-defense as a right, with violent revolt as a political tactic."[79] Finally, the minutes of a meeting of a local PFP group in Berkeley noted that "although the general consensus of the body supported the right of self-defense," it was feared that a vote of endorsement of the Panthers' right to self-defense "might work against those ends we hope to achieve in the PandF Movement"—namely, appealing to as broad a cross-section of the population as possible."[80] Partly for these reasons, the pragmatists urged support for the slogan "Fair Trial for Huey Newton" over the more militant "Free Huey," which some feared could be interpreted as a call to take extralegal means on Newton's behalf. They also echoed arguments by Broslawsky and Scheer that support for Newton, who might have murdered a police officer, posed "the danger of alienating an unknowledgeable public."[81] Finally, the pragmatists also pointed out that the identification of Peace and Freedom with Newton and the Panthers could drive away those initially drawn to PandF by its opposition to the Vietnam War.[82]

The potential threat to Peace and Freedom's ability to appeal to whites represented by the alliance with the BPP was a theme reiterated in a position paper by Mario Savio, one of the best-known organizers of the Free Speech Movement, which was coauthored by Barbara Israel and presented by both at a local debate.[83] In addition to pointing out how the alliance compromised the PFP's commitment to democratic procedures, Savio and Israel urged the organization to recognize that "right now our job is to build an independent, white organization, based on exploited whites," a position closely akin to Black Power arguments. Savio and Israel disagreed with the middle-class thrust advocated by the pragmatists, but they also believed that too close an identification between the PFP and the BPP would hinder organizing work among poor whites. Dispossessed whites, said Savio and Israel, could create the basis for "a permanent radical movement." "The coalition with the Panthers might undercut" that long-sought-after achievement, presumably because of racism among poor whites.[84] Speaking to a more militant slice of PFP membership in Berkeley, Savio and Israel differed from other pragmatists in emphasizing the need to work with dispossessed whites, but their opposition to the BPP alliance shared common ground with others who favored reaching out to the middle class. Overall, the pragmatists' desire to downplay the relationship between the two organizations stemmed from their belief that social change would originate among established whites because of their greater engagement and stake in the existing political process.

In all this, too, there was palpable resentment by some of their leadership's vigorous pursuit of a relationship with the BPP without consulting the rank and file, thereby impeaching Peace and Freedom's commitment to grassroots democracy — ironically, given the visionaries' emphasis on grassroots organizing. One San Francisco member wrote that many felt "infuriated by the fact that what was being publicized as official Peace and Freedom Party policy had not yet been voted upon [by] the San Francisco neighborhood group."[85] Moreover, Howard Ballinger wondered pointedly, was it not antidemocratic to "back one particular Black Liberation organization to the exclusion of others? What does this mean to the Black community in general?"[86] This question of broader participation by people of color was something that the PFP somehow never got around to confronting as an organization, an omission that continued to bother organizers such as James Vann. As he recalled, "Peace and Freedom never really did anything to try to utilize the Panthers as a conduit to build a kind of support. It was basically . . . a one-way relationship."[87] Another PFP member, Julio Ramirez, argued that the decision to work exclusively with the Panthers stemmed from the fact that "many of the white [PFP] registrars were afraid to go into the ghettos." Cooperation with the BPP provided a ready-made solution to that problem.[88]

For their part, the visionaries expressed contempt for the pragmatists' concerns with ending the war in Vietnam and practicing a politics built on grassroots democracy, calling those "essentially middle class issues" of interest only to "economically secure" individuals.[89] The visionaries dismissed the idea that middle-class whites could become a vanguard for social change. Instead, Peace and Freedom needed to branch out from the campuses to work with whites "who are also suffering from bad housing, bad education . . . police brutality" in the same way as many African Americans.[90] The visionaries believed that economic dislocations experienced by poor whites, combined with police violence suffered by white activists, could help whites of different social strata identify more closely with the segment of the black community represented by the Black Panther Party. Black Nationalism and militant antiwar protest were two arms of the same movement, the visionaries insisted. "The growing militancy of the anti-war movement, coupled with the legitimate struggle of the black people for self-determination in their communities, has the power structure scared," proclaimed one PFP flier.[91] However, instead of merely seeking votes, the visionaries urged the group to focus on the work of community organizing—that is, educating individuals about how their communities fit into a larger matrix of imperialist domination whose worst manifestations were economic stratification and racial inequality. Through painstaking education and organization, the visionaries argued, dispossessed whites and blacks could craft new solutions to social problems that would render the old political system irrelevant; in comparison, the pragmatists' search for votes on the basis of an antiwar platform seemed superficial indeed.

The visionaries in the Peace and Freedom Party conceived of themselves as a force that could positively interpret the black liberation movement to the pragmatists in their own Party while working indirectly to restrain the racial separatist tendencies in the black liberation movement. Their ultimate goal was to replicate in some form the sort of interracial movement exemplified by early SNCC. Throughout winter 1968, visionaries consistently defended the coalition in PFP circles as something that could spark a transformative new social movement in the United States—a vision that the pragmatists responded to lukewarmly at best. As Mike Parker, who had negotiated the coalition, commented caustically at one point, "It's not very easy to defend the Black Panther Party for Self-Defense to your liberal friends, it's not very easy at all";[92] though he did assay the task when he proclaimed: "White liberals, if they're serious about changing this society, need to face the fact that they have no right to ask oppressed people to be the ones to put down their guns when they can't even control their own police forces."[93] In fact, the visionaries regularly brushed aside the pragmatists' qualms about supporting Newton as a PFP candidate. As one ardent Newton supporter asserted, "the notions of evidence, impartial judgment, innocence and guilt are transcended by the reality of Newton's role as a black political leader" who would project a new kind of political leadership in the black community independent of white control and beholden only to the interests of average African Americans.[94] In debates at the local level, the visionaries defined coalition with the BPP as "extremely important" for the future of the PFP: the BPP was the "healthiest" extant militant black organization, because "it is not racist and it has a program for social change." Moreover, the coalition conferred the ability to relate in a "healthy" way to African Americans through an organization "whose perspective is most like ours," as well as the capacity to "raise issues in the white community about black liberation."[95] In short, joining with the BPP was the *sine qua non* for Peace and Freedom's efforts to forge an anti-racist movement among black and white Americans.

In addition to rebutting the pragmatists' misgivings by arguing for the alliance as the best means to advance the cause of social change, PFP visionaries also argued against the racial separatist sentiment that was present in the black radical community, even among some members of the Black Panther Party.[96] Indeed, they pointed out, the failure to support the BPP, whose leadership opposed that tendency, could lead to the increased prominence of "other black militant groups . . . whose position is survival—black against white. This is a position which, when taken to its logical ends, results in a race war."[97] But, in order to buttress the BPP's position within the black radical community as a check against racial separatism, the PFP visionaries continually downplayed their own desire to create an interracial movement. Throughout winter 1968, they described the coalition between the two organizations as a limited one of "specific issues for specific situations" in which "each organization maintains its own identity and serves the interests of its own constituency, but where these interests coincide, there is a basis for cooperation on a truly equal basis."[98] When SNCC leaders Stokely Carmichael, H. Rap Brown, and James Forman, at a February 1968 rally to honor Huey Newton, voiced explicitly separatist sentiments, proponents of the alliance spoke out directly. One alternative newspaper ridiculed Carmichael's call for "all-inclusive [black] unity and disinterest in the struggles of exploited white Americans" as "in the long and short run, disastrous for any struggle for black survival."[99] For their pains, the visionaries earned a stinging rejoinder from Eldridge Cleaver in the *Black Panther*. "What would [you] have us do, put Stokely down and place our faith in white America?" Cleaver retorted. "We cannot and will not place ourselves in a position where the survival of black people depends upon white progressives who like to call themselves radicals."[100] Thus, while the Black Panthers remained publicly committed to interracial cooperation, they also never retreated from their commitment to a black-led social movement. The Panthers did not embrace racial separatism, but they also made the visionaries aware that they held few cards to play in their relationship with the BPP.

The visionaries' support for the self-determination of oppressed peoples placed them in the vanguard of the New Left in 1968; as demonstrated by their struggle with the pragmatists, many were reluctant to champion a movement that assigned whites a secondary role. As noted above, the visionaries believed oppressed African Americans could create more authentic and thoroughgoing responses to the oppression they suffered than could whites, but the visionaries also entirely opposed the idea that racial inequality was anything other than a socially constructed fact. However, the visionaries' firm stand in favor of the BPP and black liberation placed them in a dilemma, for the Panthers' insistence on black leadership of an anti-racist social movement reinforced a form of racial hierarchy that ran counter to the desire to destabilize race by pointing out its socially constructed nature. Forced to choose between arguing for a course that articulated how black liberation could become part of an interracial movement and a shaky but potentially far-reaching alliance with a black radical organization "whose perspective is most like ours," the Peace and Freedom visionaries understandably chose the latter. In the process, they became beholden to the BPP as the only black radical organization that would cooperate with white leftists, and the visionaries' ability to advocate on behalf of their own racial project decreased concomitantly. Though the Panthers' racial project was undeniably oppositional, and their organizing for their vision of Black Nationalism destabilized existing racial hierarchies, the BPP's conceptualization of an anti-racist mass movement was also racialized in the same way as was the racial project of the Peace and Freedom pragmatists. The visionaries in the PFP could have articulated a competing vision, but they chose not to in the interest of preserving their relationship with the BPP and perhaps being able to participate in a process of equal dialogue at some point in the future. Unfortunately for opponents of racism and American imperialism, that interchange of ideas never came to pass, and a tantalizing opportunity to synthesize the black liberation movement with the antiwar movement evaporated like the raindrops left behind by a sunshower.

The Peace and Freedom Party held its founding convention on 16–18 March 1968 in Richmond, California. Over one thousand delegates and alternates attended, and what many believed was the high point of the convention came when the delegates voted unanimous support for the slogan "Free Huey Newton." However, an angry controversy ensued when radical delegate Bob Avakian urged the convention to adopt the slogan "Free Huey Newton by any means necessary." After Avakian's motion was voted down by a narrow margin, Bobby Seale stormed off the convention floor, chiding delegates, "'I asked you, did you support black people in the black community.... We didn't come into your community and brutalize you. If you don't want to support us, it's no sweat, baby, no sweat." "Get him out of here!" shouted someone in reply.[101] The visionaries won the convention's validation of the coalition with the BPP, but as indicated by the anger expressed over the alliance, the pragmatists continued to resist a relationship they believed would weaken the PFP's appeal. In the months that followed, as registrants deserted in droves, the pragmatists pointed to the alliance with the BPP as a primary factor, and the visionaries argued that Democrats felt drawn back to their party after Robert Kennedy entered the presidential race in March 1968 and Lyndon Johnson withdrew his candidacy at the end of the same month. By June 1968, almost thirty thousand registrants had left the PFP, a downward trend that continued throughout summer and fall 1968.

At the same time, the Black Panther Party expanded its membership and its national profile. Panther leaders criss-crossed the country throughout spring and summer 1968, giving speeches and organizing new chapters. Eldridge Cleaver's candidacy as the Peace and Freedom nominee for president played no small part in helping the BPP spread its message. Huey Newton's trial in summer 1968 also attracted national attention to the BPP and its message, producing what quickly became iconic images of Black Panthers waving flags emblazoned with the words "Free Huey" as well as riveting courtroom testimony about the black liberation movement by Newton and by other witnesses. By fall 1968, the BPP had grown substantially, and its increased profile attracted the attention of national security agencies such as the FBI; it was in September 1968 that J. Edgar Hoover called the Panthers "the greatest threat to the internal security of the country."

In winter 1968, activists in the Black Panther Party and the Peace and Freedom Party did their best to craft directions for their respective organizations that they believed would best serve the cause of social justice. They faced a changing political climate in which opposition to the war was on the rise following the Tet Offensive of January-February 1968, but the desire for social stability had begun to trump support for social reform. Concerned about expressing what they thought were the beliefs of their core constituencies, Black Panthers, pragmatists, and visionaries advanced visions of social change that sought to subvert dominant understandings of race but ended up also being shaped by them. As James Baldwin observed in *Notes of a Native Son*, "We take our shape . . . within and against that cage of reality that is bequeathed us at our birth; yet it is precisely through our dependence on this reality that we are most endlessly betrayed." "Escape is not effected through a bitter railing at this trap," Baldwin continued, but only through an act of creation that could bring a new world into existence.[102] The pragmatists, visionaries, and members of the BPP believed they possessed the blueprint for this act of creation; however, their ideas for combating the impact of race on American life ended up being shaped by the same racialized world they sought to subvert.

Notes

I would like to thank David Brundage, Jama Lazerow, Alice Yang Murray, and Yohuru Williams for their support, guidance, and insightful commentary.

1. Simon Hall, "On the Tail of the Panther: Black Power and the 1967 Convention of the National Conference for New Politics," *Journal of American Studies* 37 (2003): 64; "Symposium: Chicago's 'Black Caucus,'" *Ramparts* (November 1967): 99.
2. Hall, "On the Tail of the Panther," 61. The NCNP's executive committee included the

Students for a Democratic Society's Paul Booth, Simon Casady of the California Democratic Caucus, Benjamin Spock, and Arthur Waskow of the Center for the Study of Democratic Institutions. Julian Bond of the Student Nonviolent Coordinating Committee was its one African American member.

3. Hall, "On the Tail of the Panther," 59.
4. Ibid., 63.
5. Ibid., 70.
6. Ibid., 67.
7. William A. Price, "New Politics of Black and White," *National Guardian* 19 (9 September 1967); "The Whites: A Clown Show II," *Berkeley Barb*, 22 September 1967. For disapproving coverage of NCNP, see Hall, "On the Tail of the Panther," 70.
8. "The Whites: A Clown Show," *Berkeley Barb*, 15 September 1967.
9. Hall, "On the Tail of the Panther," 72. When the question of creating a third party was put to a vote, it lost by a razor-thin margin. "We believe," the resolution read, "[electoral action] would at this point in our history be top-heavy and would be mostly empty shells with little local content." Electoral action "would tend to cut off many Americans who are on the verge of breaking with the old politics but need to be organized before making the leap" (NCNP Perspectives Resolution, quoted in "The Whites: A Clown Show II." See also Hall, "On the Tail of the Panther," 76).
10. In fact, the NCNP did very little to accomplish its goal of reordering the political landscape in the United States; the organization announced its dissolution in April 1968 (Hall, "On the Tail of the Panther," 73–74).
11. *People's World*, 23 September 1967. The PFP's first statewide conference took place in San Luis Obispo on 16–17 September 1967. Controversy erupted at the conference when white delegates countered an ad hoc black caucus's demand for 50 percent voting rights with a bicameral structure. In contrast to the NCNP, though, the bicameral structure proposed at San Luis Obispo would permit white and black caucuses to pursue different courses if they could not agree on a mutual course of action. Part of the reason PFP and the Black Panther Party could later form an alliance lay in the fact that the two organizations intended to remain independent of each other while cooperating on projects of mutual interest, thus obviating the need to come up with a vote-weighting formula that would help equalize black and white control of a joint organization.
12. *People's World*, 23 September 1967.
13. As Eldridge Cleaver commented, "The news media . . . gave the Panthers a million dollars worth of publicity" ("Affidavit No. 1: I Am 33 Years Old," in *Eldridge Cleaver: Post-Prison Writings and Speeches* [New York: Vintage, 1969], 6).
14. Reprinted in Newton, *To Die for the People* (New York: Writers and Readers Publishing, 1995 [1972]), 7–8.
15. According to David Hilliard, later party chief of staff, the BPP consisted of "twelve to fifteen guys with no office, money, media outlets, or program" before an October 1967 shootout between Newton and Oakland police led to the national "Free Huey" campaign, and a new lease on life for the group (Hilliard and Lewis Cole,

This Side of Glory: The Autobiography of David Hilliard and the Story of the Black Panther Party [Boston: Little, Brown, 1993], 139). Seale presented a more optimistic picture in a 1970 account, claiming that the BPP had "about seventy-five Black Panther Party members and two chapters, Los Angeles and Oakland" in October 1967 (*Seize the Time: The Story of the Black Panther Party and Huey P. Newton* [Baltimore: Black Classic Press, 1991 (1970)], ii). According to Earl Anthony, an early Party member, there were fifteen "hardcore" members in the organization as of late October 1967 (*Picking up the Gun: A Report on the Black Panthers* [New York: Dial Press, 1970], 39).

16. Cleaver, an ex-convict turned journalist for *Ramparts* magazine, would soon achieve national fame for his abilities as an author with the publication of his first book, *Soul on Ice,* in February 1968. Newton actively recruited Cleaver to join the nascent BPP because of his skills as a writer and his confidence as a public speaker (Seale, *Seize the Time,* 132–34).

17. "White 'Mother Country' Radicals," *Black Panther,* 20 July 1967. While Cleaver couched his attack as a response to both groups' patronizing treatment of the BPP, it appears that the source of Cleaver's ire against the Communist Party (CP) and the Socialist Workers' Party (SWP) stemmed from their potential threat to the BPP's membership and fundraising base. The CP represented a group with a multiracial membership, which meant that they could compete with the Panthers for potential recruits among African Americans. Cleaver's primary complaint with the SWP stemmed from its sale of literature about Malcolm X and other African American leaders, which presumably reduced the BPP's ability to do the same. At the same time, the matter of Cleaver's relationship to Bay Area Communists — among them his attorney and erstwhile lover, Beverly Axlerod — is clearly complex and worthy of further study. See also n. 58.

18. The dead officer's name was John Frey. He died at the scene of the shootout, having received several gunshot wounds at close range. The shootout also resulted in grave wounds being inflicted on Newton and the other police officer, Herbert Heanes.

19. "Explains Why Blacks Joined PFP," *Berkeley Barb,* 5 January 1968.

20. "White 'Mother Country' Radicals."

21. E.g., Newton, "The Correct Handling of a Revolution," *The Black Panther,* 20 July 1967.

22. Newton made clear from the start his desire to make his trial a tool for political education. See his retrospective account in *Revolutionary Suicide* (New York: Harcourt Brace, 1973), 184–85.

23. For more on the evolving public identity of the BPP in 1967 and 1968, see my "'Free Huey': The Black Panther Party, the Peace and Freedom Party, and the Politics of Race in 1968" (Ph.D. diss., University of California, Santa Cruz, 2002), 34–80.

24. Newton," Executive Mandate No.1," in *To Die for the People,* 8.

25. First published in an English translation in 1965, the influence of Fanon's *The Wretched of the Earth* (New York: Grove Press) on the ideological development of the black liberation movement in general and the Black Panther Party in particular

cannot be overstated; for example, Seale, *Seize the Time*, 25–26, 34. Fanon based his observations in *The Wretched of the Earth* and his other highly influential work, *Black Skin, White Masks,* on his participation in the Algerian resistance and his psychiatric treatment of Algerian victims of French colonialism. For more on Fanon's life and intellectual genesis, see David Macey's excellent *Frantz Fanon: A Biography* (New York: Picador, 2000).

26. Fanon, *Wretched of the Earth*, 72.
27. Ibid., 59.
28. Charles E. Jones and Judson Jeffries, "'Don't Believe the Hype': Debunking the Panther Mythology," in *The Black Panther Party [Reconsidered]*, edited by Charles E. Jones (Baltimore: Black Classic Press, 1998), 44–47.
29. Newton, "Black Capitalism Re-Analyzed I: 5 June 1971," in *To Die for the People*, 101. Newton's words succinctly stated the Panthers' raison d'etre in their revolutionary nationalist phase and later. His insistence on the need for blacks to define the nature of a society that had for so long sought to control definitions of African Americans, and his call for the power necessary to put new definitions in place, represented core principles for the Panthers throughout the arc of their existence.
30. Newton would argue during his murder trial in summer 1968 that the differences between whites and blacks lay in their divergent historical experiences in the United States, not in characteristics intrinsic to members of either racial group. For more on his views about race, see Wilson, "Free Huey," 313–15.
31. For a fascinating discussion of the gulf between what (white) radicals said on this question and what they did in this period, see David Barber's essay in this section.
32. *Black Nationalism in American Politics and Thought* (New York: Cambridge University Press, 2001), 1–2 (italics in original).
33. Chris Booker, "Lumpenization: A Critical Error of the Black Panther Party," in Jones, ed., *The Black Panther Party,* 343.
34. "Minutes of County Steering Committee," Carton 12, Folder 15, Social Protest Collection, University of California, Berkeley.
35. "In Defense of Self-Defense," *Black Panther*, 20 July 1967; 3 July 1967.
36. "Position of the Black Panther Party for Self-Defense on the Seventh Congressional District Election in Alameda County and the Candidacy of John George in the Democratic Party," Box 18, Folder 5a, Social Protest Collection, University of California, Berkeley.
37. This distinction between revolutionary and reactionary forms of Black Power is echoed in James Forman's November 1967 speech in Los Angeles "Liberation Will Come from a Black Thing." See Foreman, *The Making of Black Revolutionaries* (Seattle: Open Hand Publishing, 1985 [1972]), 512–18.
38. "Position of the Black Panther Party."
39. Ibid. As of 2 January 1968, Peace and Freedom had 20,284 registrants in Alameda County ("Registration Breakdown," *Peace and Freedom News,* 4 March 1968, 4).
40. "Huey May Be PFP Candidate," *Berkeley Barb*, 2 February 1968; "Peace and Freedom Talks Candidates—John George or Huey Newton for Congress?" *San Fran-*

cisco Express-Times, 8 February 1968. The PFP subsequently printed ten thousand copies of the Cleaver speech and mailed them to it members (Tom Condit, interview with author, 7 November 2000).

41. *The Making of Black Revolutionaries,* 523.
42. Newton, "Executive Mandate No. 2: June 29, 1967," in *To Die for the People,* 10.
43. Seale's description of cadging the money for plane tickets and expenses from Mike Parker at the PFP office is instructive about the state of BPP finances as well as of how the relationship between the two groups functioned—namely, mostly as a relationship between leaders. When Parker tried to beg off, Seale writes, he and Cleaver used white guilt to accomplish their ends, calling Parker a "racist" before he came up with the money. The power dynamics in Seale's reconstruction (*Seize the Time,* 213–14) exclusively favor the Panthers.
44. Seale, *Seize the Time,* 217–19.
45. Forman, *Making of Black Revolutionaries,* 529; Clayborne Carson, *In Struggle:* SNCC and the Black Awakening of the 1960s (Cambridge, Mass.: Harvard University Press, 1996 [1982]), 280. Neither Forman nor Carmichael had a great deal of success gaining any control over the BPP. They lacked a popular base in the organization, they lived on the East Coast, and they had significant ideological differences with the Party leadership (Seale, *Seize the Time,* 254), though note that he is discussing Carmichael in the aftermath of his split from the Panthers.
46. Julius Lester, *Revolutionary Notes* (New York: Grove Press, 1969), 146.
47. For different accounts of events in New York and the deterioration of relations between SNCC and the BPP, see Hilliard, *This Side of Glory,* 202–4; Cleveland Sellers and Robert Terrell, *River of No Return: The Autobiography of a Black Militant and the Life and Death of SNCC* (Jackson: University of Mississippi Press, 1990), 247–49; Forman, *Making of Black Revolutionaries,* 534–41; and, relying heavily on FBI accounts leaked to the press and some questionable oral testimony, Hugh Pearson's *The Shadow of the Panther: Huey Newton and the Price of Black Power in America* (Reading, Mass.: Addison-Wesley, 1994), 159–63.
48. "Revolution in the White Mother Country and National Liberation in the Black Colony," Box 12, Folder 7, Social Protest Collection, University of California, Berkeley.
49. All cleaver quotations are from his speech of 11 February 1968, "Political Struggle in America: 1968," Peace and Freedom Collection, Box 2, Folder 4, Social Protest Collection, University of California, Berkeley.
50. Quoted in Gene Marine, *The Black Panthers* (New York: Signet, 1969), 123.
51. "Transcript of Student Communications Telex Coverage of Founding Convention of Peace and Freedom, Richmond, California" and "Revolution in the White Mother Country and National Liberation in the Black Colony" in Box 12, Folder 7, Social Protest Collection, University of California, Berkeley.
52. "Alameda County Council Meeting, Stiles Hall, 8 PM, 3 March 1967 (*sic*)," Carton 12, Folder 18, Social Protest Collection, University of California, Berkeley.
53. "Panthers Flay Cops in False Murder Raps," *People's World,* 2 March 1968.

54. Seale, *Seize the Time,* 209.
55. Hilliard, *This Side of Glory,* 141.
56. Ibid., 145.
57. Ibid., 147.
58. Anthony, *Picking up the Gun,* 65–66. Anthony, a problematic source because of his association with the FBI during his time as a Panther—as an informant and agent provocateur—traced his own disaffection with the Panthers to Cleaver's close ties to Communists and to a corresponding decline of Black Nationalist sentiment in the Party in *Spitting in the Wind: The True Story Behind the Violent Legacy of the Black Panther Party* (Malibu, Calif.: Roundtable, 1990), 31, 41–42, 61.
59. Marine, *The Black Panthers,* 111.
60. *A Panther Is a Black Cat* (New York: William Morrow, 1971), 95.
61. "Why I Joined the Party: An Africana Womanist Reflection," in Jones, ed., *Black Panther Party,* 261.
62. "Editorial: BPP and PFP," *Black Panther,* 16 March 1968.
63. "Revolution in the White Mother Country and National Liberation in the Black Colony."
64. "Minutes of state steering committee meeting—May 11, 1968," Peace and Freedom Collection, Box 7, Folder 6, Social Protest Collection, University of California, Berkeley.
65. "Political Struggle in America: 1968," *Black Panther,* 16 March 1968.
66. Charles Weber, "Peace and Freedom Party of California: Early Organizational Growth—Public Policy Impacts" (MA thesis, California State University, Long Beach, 1980), 56.
67. Marine, *The Black Panthers,* 111–13.
68. "Are the Black Panthers Violent?" Pacifica Radio Archive, Los Angeles, 1968.
69. In February 1968, at a forum held to defend the coalition, Bob Avakian dismissed concerns with antiwar organizing and grassroots democracy as "essentially middle class issues." Peace and Freedom, in his view, should instead focus on meeting "the needs of the oppressed whites and blacks, many of whom have not yet registered in PandF" (quoted in "Dialogue for PandF and Black Panthers," *People's World,* 17 February 1968).
70. "The True and Accurate Account of the Post Natal History of the Puff Party," Carton 12, Folder 10, Social Protest Collection, University of California, Berkeley.
71. "'Legitimate' Protest Sustain Institutions," *Los Angeles Free Press,* 17 November 1967, 5–6.
72. In their study of Peace and Freedom in the Los Angeles area, James M. Elden and David R. Schweitzer found that "the most salient social characteristic of PFP radicals is that they are essentially 'middle class.'" The majority of members in Los Angeles were white-collar workers of one kind or another (Elden and Schweitzer, "New Third Party Radicalism: The Case of the California Peace and Freedom Party," *Western Political Quarterly* 24.4 [1971]: 763–65).
73. "Peace, Freedom, and Dissent," *West,* 5 May 1968. Scheer had almost unseated Rep.

Jeffrey Cohelan in a Democratic primary in 1966 in which Scheer ran on an antiwar platform; individuals from his campaign were instrumental in founding Peace and Freedom. The organization founded by Scheer and his supporters in the East Bay, the Community for New Politics, became one of the seedbeds from which the PFP grew.

74. Scheer did not criticize the BPP by name, but instead spoke of "Black Power," a shorthand reference that ignored the substantial ideological daylight between the Black Panthers and other Black Power groups. As Scheer complained during the convention, "My basic unhappiness with this party, and the reason I'd rather be a rank-and-filer than a candidate, is that I think this party's not going to be healthy until we seize control of this party and bring in as many people as possible," a goal he believed was being stymied by the radical rhetoric increasingly favored by visionaries ("Peace and Freedom Nominates Jacobs," *Los Angeles Free Press,* 22 March 1968, 3).

75. "Peace and Freedom Nominates Jacobs," *Los Angeles Free Press,* 22 March 1968, 3.

76. Ibid.

77. "Are the Black Panthers Violent?" The PFP organizer Mike Parker declared during this radio forum that "white radicals and white liberals, if they're serious about changing this society, need to face the fact that they have no right to ask oppressed people to be the ones to put down their guns when they can't even control their own police forces." Parker spoke for those in Peace and Freedom who believed that whites could not condemn the BPP's advocacy of self-defense, because the overwhelming majority of whites lacked an understanding of the reality of police brutality in the lives of African Americans.

78. "What Direction the Left?" Pacifica Radio Archive, Los Angeles, 1967.

79. "Caucus for a Relevant Party," Box 161, Folder 21, Library of Social History, University of California, Berkeley.

80. Area 1 minutes, 29 February 1968, Carton 12, Folder 14, Social Protest Collection, University of California, Berkeley.

81. Area 1 minutes, 15 February 1968, in ibid.

82. Marine, *The Black Panthers,* 113.

83. Savio ran as a Peace and Freedom candidate for the California State Senate in 1968.

84. "Arguments against Passing the Motion that 'We Endorse the Panther's 10-point Program,'" Carton 12, Folder 14, Social Protest Collection, University of California, Berkeley.

85. Weber, "Peace and Freedom Party of California," 57.

86. "Caucus for a Relevant Party."

87. Vann, interview with author, 15 February 2001. Vann also observed that "seldom discussed even at statewide . . . meetings [was] the relative absence of [people of color in the PFP]. . . . There were African Americans and maybe a few Asians involved in those steering committees, but there was not a major thrust to try to organize in the minority communities at the time."

88. "Black Liberation May Join Anti-War Group," *Daily Californian,* 1 March 1968.

89. "Dialogue for PandF and Black Panthers."
90. "Are the Black Panthers Violent?"
91. Flier describing Rusk demonstration, Box 18, Folder 17A, Social Protest Collection, University of California, Berkeley. Demonstrators at Stop the Draft Week (STDW) in October 1967 and in San Francisco in January 1968 were set upon by police using batons and tear gas to disperse crowds. The experience of having police violence directed at them resulted in some empathy with African Americans. Tom Wells has written that STDW planners modeled their plans "after a black street rebellion" and that organizers sought to appeal to working-class white and black youth by creating violent confrontations with the police "that would demonstrate the 'strength' and 'seriousness' of the middle class anti-draft movement" (Wells, *The War Within: America's Battle over Vietnam* [Berkeley: University of California Press, 1994], 173).
92. "Panther Still Cagey on White Radicals Here," *Berkeley Barb*, 16–22 February 1968.
93. "Are the Black Panthers Violent?"
94. Ibid.; "PFP Says 'Free Huey,'" *Communiqué for New Politics and Left-Out News*, 15 January 1968, 2.
95. "Position Paper on Coalitions," Carton 12, Folder 14, Social Protest Collection, University of California, Berkeley.
96. Jennings, as already noted, was one. See n. 61.
97. "Position Paper on Coalitions."
98. It should be added that portrayals of the coalition as limited were also intended to tamp down resistance to the alliance with the PFP ranks. See, e.g., "Black Panthers and PFM," *Peace and Freedom News*, 4 March 1968, 1–3.
99. "Carmichael and 'Black Unity,'" *Independent Socialist*, April 1968.
100. "Checking Honky Marvin Garson," *Black Panther*, 16 March 1968. A year later, Cleaver would attack Carmichael on virtually the same grounds, in his "An Open Letter to Stokely Carmichael," in *The Black Panthers Speak*, edited by Philip S. Foner (New York: Da Capo Press, 1995 [1970]), 104–8.
101. "Convention in Expert Hands," *Berkeley Barb*, 22 March 1968.
102. James Baldwin, *Notes of a Native Son* (New York: Bantam, 1968), 15.

Leading the Vanguard: White New Leftists School the Panthers on Black Revolution

DAVID BARBER

Some of the most prominent historians of the New Left link its downfall to the rise of the Black Power movement and of the Black Panthers specifically. In a variety of forms, these historians argue that the Panthers, with their emphasis on violence and macho posturing, led the New Left astray with a romanticized vision of revolution. As the New Left's principal organization, Students for a Democratic Society (SDS), increasingly emulated Panther militant rhetoric, violence, and style, it alienated itself from its base and rapidly fell to pieces. The Weathermen, the SDS faction most closely aligned with the Panthers, adopted the most violent tactics and alienated the overwhelming majority of SDS's one hundred thousand members. Thus, the New Left disintegrated because it adopted the black movement's "politics of rage" and the Panthers' macho style and stilted "revolutionary" rhetoric.[1]

In March 1969, SDS's National Council did pass a resolution proclaiming that the Black Panther Party (BPP) was the vanguard of the black revolution. Moreover, according to the theory of social change that SDS was at the time developing, leading the black revolution placed the Panthers in the role of leadership in the worldwide struggle against U.S. imperialism. But the BPP that SDS designated as vanguard was a Party that did not exist in the social reality of black people; rather, SDS conferred leadership status on Panthers that existed in the minds of young white activists and nowhere else. In short, the vanguard Party that SDS was willing to follow was a Party that SDS itself invented. Those in SDS found this kind of "black leadership" particularly easy to follow. However, whenever the *real* Black Panthers departed from SDS's image of them and sought SDS's concrete programmatic support, SDS rejected BPP leadership.

Contrary to the generally accepted narrative of the New Left's decline that links SDS's demise to its alleged uncritical support for the Panthers; to the Panthers' "violent" influence; or to the problem of black "rage" more generally, the national organization SDS never systematically or seriously supported the BPP. In fact, the relationship between the two organizations was characterized, on SDS's side, by five factors. First, SDS continually emphasized its support for the Panthers' "military program" while downplaying or outright rejecting their "survival programs" and electoral strategy. Second, SDS repeatedly rejected Panther projects that sought to push SDS into organizing in white communities on behalf of black self-determination and against racism. Third, SDS repeatedly rejected Panther critiques of its tactics and of its white mind-set, and it ultimately betrayed the Party at the height of government repression against the black movement. Fourth, SDS's lack of real support for the Panthers, on terms the Panthers themselves set for that support, did not stop SDS from proclaiming that the Panthers were the vanguard of the revolution. Neither did it stop SDS from repeatedly prefacing its rejections of Panther programs with affirmations of fealty to "black leadership." Indeed, SDS, and the Weathermen in particular, rested their legitimacy on this verbal support and used that support as a bludgeon against the women's movement and against recalcitrant SDS factions and members. And, finally, SDS repeatedly sought to school the Panthers in the meaning, strategy, and tactics of black liberation and revolution, and in the battle against white supremacy.

These factors can be glimpsed in four key moments over the year-and-a-half period from mid-1968 to early 1970 that defined the relationship between SDS and the Panthers. First, in early summer 1968 SDS rejected Party leader Eldridge Cleaver's proposal that SDS leader Carl Oglesby serve as Cleaver's 1968 Peace and Freedom Party vice-presidential running mate. In this initial encounter between the two organizations, SDS clearly articulated the white mind-set that would characterize its entire history with the Panthers. Second, in March 1969 SDS set a tone of apparent white radical fealty to the BPP by passing its Panthers-as-vanguard resolution. But this resolution was marked by a number of significant contradictions that signaled SDS's continued reticence in taking a back seat to the Panthers and to the black freedom movement. Third, three months after SDS had proclaimed the

Panthers the vanguard of the revolution in the United States, it refused to support the Panthers' attempt at creating the United Front Against Fascism, and thus definitively broke with its "vanguard." Finally, in the months following SDS's effective dissolution, both wings of SDS — the Weathermen, and its rival, Revolutionary Youth Movement II (RYM II) — began the search for new black revolutionary vanguards that would fit the needs of white radicals more comfortably than the extant Black Panther Party.

SDS, Peace and Freedom, and the Black Panther Party

The relation of SDS to the Panthers followed closely on the heels of SDS's relation to the Student Nonviolent Coordinating Committee (SNCC), particularly after SNCC's Black Power turn in 1966. Although SDS was the first white organization to welcome SNCC chairman Stokely Carmichael's call for Black Power, members of SDS had great difficulty with SNCC's developing Black Nationalism. Black Power — and the Black Nationalist ideology that underlay it — presented two challenges to SDS. First, SNCC insisted that black people would define the terms, strategy, and organization of their own liberation. Concretely, this meant that white activists were no longer wanted in the black community, except as allies on terms established by black activists. Second, SNCC demanded that white activists organize in their own white communities against racism. Both of these challenges presented problems for SDS's white activists — young whites who, in common with the society from which they came, simply assumed that they had a superior vision of social change and that they would take the lead in bringing about that change. It followed, then, that they would be the people who would define the role of others in the effort.[2]

Consequently, SDS consistently interpreted Black Power in a self-serving fashion. As Staughton Lynd, a senior New Left leader, explained it: "What SNCC is saying is: 'Blacks should be organized by blacks, and what white organizers do is something for white organizers to decide.'" In short, SDS saw Black Power not as a demand to intensify its work against racism, nor to increase its accountability to the black struggle. Rather, SDS'ers saw Black Power as an opportunity to avoid dealing with questions of race (seen as a black issue) and move on to other issues of its own choosing.[3]

In their early interactions with white New Leftists, from their founding in October 1966 to mid-1968, the Panthers did not explicitly challenge white radicals in the ways that SNCC had challenged them: while the Panthers insisted on their exclusive right to organize in the black community, they made no demand on white radicals to organize white communities against racism. However, the Panthers did demand two things of white activists. First, the BPP insisted that white New Leftists seeking to act in concert with the black liberation movement needed to give complete support to the Panther program. But the BPP program itself said nothing about the role of whites in the revolution, and Panther leaders left undefined the meaning of complete support for their program. Second, Panther leader Huey P. Newton insisted that white radicals attack the police in the white community when black radicals were attacked in the black community. As Newton explained: "When something happens in the black colony—when we're attacked and ambushed in the black colony—then the white revolutionary students and intellectuals and all the other whites who support the colony should respond by defending us, by attacking the enemy in their community. Every time that we're attacked in our community there should be a reaction by the white revolutionaries, they should respond by defending us, by attacking part of the security force." Again, Newton did not define what he meant by "attacking the enemy" in the white community. These two demands thus left white activists a far larger scope of activity than had SNCC's definition of the white New Left's role. Moreover, Newton's vision was far more in line with the New Left's understanding of itself as "revolutionary" than was SNCC's demand on SDS.[4] Members of SDS could avoid the seemingly tedious—and at times truly dangerous—work of seriously organizing white communities against racism, so long as they were willing to periodically shout the Panther slogan, "Off the Pig." What New Leftists did with the rest of their time, apparently, remained up to them.

At the same time, however, the Panthers did make more concrete demands on SDS than did SNCC. And these specific demands had an implicit content that pushed white radicals to organize against racism in their own white communities—just what SNCC had asked of them. In their first national contact with SDS, for example, the Panthers sought a national alliance around Cleaver's 1968 Peace and Freedom Party (PFP) presidential campaign. The PFP had developed as a joint project of white liberals and radicals in late 1967 and sought, through an electoral strategy, to tie together the main social movements of the day, the black movement and the antiwar movement. Peace and Freedom's radical wing correctly understood that such an alliance could only be achieved by accepting the lead of a militant black organization like the Panthers. Consequently, the PFP endorsed the Panthers'

Ten-Point Platform and Program and nominated Panther minister of information Eldridge Cleaver as its 1968 standard-bearer.[5] Perhaps to push the PFP to the Left, or simply to take advantage of SDS's national structure, Cleaver proposed that former SDS resident Carl Oglesby run as his vice-presidential candidate. Oglesby had been SDS president in 1965–1966, leading the group in its growing understanding of imperialism—a topic on which he had recently published an important book, *Containment and Change*.[6] Out of deference to SDS's process, Oglesby refused to accept Cleaver's offer and referred the Panthers to SDS's executive committee, the National Interim Committee (NIC). In its first formal discussion of a national relationship with the Panthers, SDS rejected the Panthers' proposal.[7] Crucially, the rejection itself took characteristic form—SDS had repeatedly dismissed the black movement in the past—but it also foreshadowed the development of a significant new tendency in the white radical organization, the Weathermen.

The newly elected SDS interorganizational secretary, Bernardine Dohrn, publicly reported SDS's decision to the organization's membership in its weekly membership publication *New Left Notes*. She titled her report, "White Mother Country Radicals"—a term Newton had coined and popularized in a widely circulated prison interview—and opened by quoting the Panther minister of defense: white radicals had to choose their friends and enemies and, having made that decision, put it into practice "by attacking the protectors of the institutions"—that is, the police.[8] Having thus established her affinity with the Panthers, Dohrn continued by acknowledging that the Panthers' "existence and growth . . . has posed the question of black/white revolutionary movements in clear, immediate, and real form." For those not familiar with the Panthers, Dohrn sketched a favorable summary of Panther politics. The Panthers self-consciously saw themselves as organizing the "field niggers," Malcolm X's term for the most downtrodden working-class and unemployed blacks. They were inveterate opponents of both black capitalism and nonrevolutionary cultural nationalism. They were willing to ally with white radicals in pursuit of "tactical necessities." And, they were seeking to use Cleaver's Peace and Freedom candidacy as a means of promoting Panther "politics and organization." Nevertheless, declared Dohrn, SDS rejected Cleaver's proposal of Oglesby's candidacy, insisting that while SDS respected the Panthers' alliance with the PFP, "alliances made by us must be evaluated on our own terms."

Dohrn further noted that the white and the black movement had "different levels of consciousness" and these different levels dictated different strategies. Oglesby's candidacy would commit SDS to an alliance not only with the Panthers but also with the white Left liberals in the Peace and Freedom Party and would involve the "vehicle of electoral politics." And, she maintained, since SDS had numerous differences with the PFP, Oglesby's candidacy ran the risk of misrepresenting SDS. Thus, SDS leaders rejected the alliance because of the PFP's associations and because SDS leaders felt electoral politics were inappropriate for the level of consciousness in SDS's white constituency.

How then would SDS continue to develop a relationship with the Panthers? Dohrn argued that SDS was seeking "to develop not exclusive or opportunistic alliances, but solid political relationships based on common experiences and goals." Moreover, SDS sought to build alliances "not on least common denominator politics" but on clear recognition of differences as well as similarities. Thus, insisted Dohrn, SDS felt there were stronger means available for promoting a Panther-SDS alliance than the means Cleaver had proposed. These included the national promotion of the Panthers by SDS in SDS's chapters; joint speaking tours by Panther and SDS leaders; and "the development of Defense and Self-Defense organizations." In any case, Dohrn recognized the Panthers' growing influence nationally, and she suggested that SDS needed to be in close communication with the Panthers by linking up with their programs and issues "when—and as long as—our political perspectives are similar."

Dohrn closed her report in a telling fashion by rejecting the Panthers' concrete leadership but doing so by one-upping the Panthers' revolutionary rhetoric: "The main point is: the best thing that we can be doing for ourselves, as well as for the Panthers and the revolutionary black liberation struggle, is to build a fucking white revolutionary mass movement, not a national paper alliance. Building a white Left movement from the ground up means we need the Panthers and black radicals there—at the ground level." In fact, Dohrn's entire piece was infused with an inflated sense of self-importance: SDS knew what was best for the movement as a whole. And, apparently, the Panthers and black radicals generally had to know their place in this greater scheme of things.

As Cleaver understood, there was no necessary contradiction between SDS's building of a mass revolutionary movement and his presidential campaign. On the contrary, the campaign's value lay in its ability to reach out to millions of people with a radical program and analysis of American society. Apparently, though, this was not militant enough for SDS. If very few members of SDS were ready to take up weapons, still, talking tough was far more in keeping with the SDS leaders' developing self-image than was working in an election campaign. This would not be the last time that SDS would reject the Panthers' leadership using the same "more revolutionary than thou" posturing. In rejecting the Panther proposal, however, SDS was doing more than simply rejecting the Panthers' leadership; it was rejecting in practical form SNCC's demand that white activists go into their own communities and organize against racism there.

Following SDS's rejection of the proposal, Cleaver appealed to SDS twice more on the matter, and twice more SDS publicly rejected the proposal.[9] One new concern articulated in these subsequent rejections centered on divisions within the Black Nationalist movement itself: the two most prominent Black Nationalist organizations of the day, SNCC and the Black Panthers, after a brief attempt at unity in early 1968, were at odds with each other. Members of NIC pointed out that some SDS chapters had a relationship with SNCC, while other chapters had a relationship with the Panthers. The NIC thus expressed the fear that allowing Oglesby to run with Cleaver would cast SDS nationally with the Panthers in this struggle internal to the black movement.

To be sure, this was a serious consideration that demanded serious thought. But whatever the real problems that might have arisen from SDS's electoral cooperation with the Panthers at a time when black liberation forces were divided, the NIC also made it clear that Dohrn had already articulated the main basis for rejecting Oglesby's candidacy: electoral work was not militant enough for SDS. The militant and widely publicized demonstrations at Chicago's August 1968 Democratic National Convention—just weeks before—had demonstrated "that young people in this country are not necessarily caught up in the bullshit that is the American electoral process, that young people are willing and able to 'vote with their feet' in the streets of America. This is where the potential for a real functional relationship will be built. This is where the makings of an insurgent cross-strata youth movement lie. This is the one place where both black and white radicals are being forced to take their case."[10]

Here was SDS's white-centeredness asserting itself once again. On almost every level, the New Left's history had been one of following the black movement's practical lead: SDS had followed the civil rights movement into activism in the early 1960s; into community organizing following SNCC practice from 1963 to 1965; and from "protest to resistance" following the tumultuous summer rebellions of 1967. Now SDS was following the black movement, and the Panthers specifically, from resistance to "revolution." Yet SDS, while following this practical leadership, had never appreciated the black movement's intellectual leadership, always jealously guarding its own white vision and, ultimately, the resources accruing to it out of its white privilege.

In *Soul on Ice,* the immediately celebrated collection of essays and letters published in early 1968, Cleaver had developed an interesting psychological characterization of blacks and whites: from slavery times, it had been necessary for the slave owner to characterize the slave as mindless, as all brawn and no brains — the "supermasculine menial," in Cleaver's words. On the other hand, the slave owner, who did no physical work, had to characterize himself as having an intellect that suited him to the job of running the plantation and running the lives of those on it — the "omnipotent administrator." According to Cleaver, those same basic psychological traits held in the present, even in movements for social change. On a psychological level, these roles defined what was revolutionary for blacks and for whites. For blacks, the task was to recover the mind. And, argued Cleaver, the Panthers embodied that recovery. Black people would lead their own struggle for liberation. On the other hand, whites had to recover their bodies, and, by implication, respect black people's minds.[11] In choosing the Panthers' militancy over their electoral strategy, SDS chose the black body over the black mind, or — in what was the same thing — they chose the white mind over the black mind. It was what the white Left in the United States had always done.[12]

Leading the Vanguard

In the months after SDS rejected Cleaver's proposal for the final time, the Progressive Labor Party (PL), an Old Left formation working at the time within SDS, began its most concerted bid for leadership over the student organization. PL had left the Communist Party USA (CPUSA) after the Sino-Soviet split in 1956, following the Maoist lead and denouncing the Soviet Union and the CPUSA as "revisionist." In 1964, PL founded a youth organization, the May 2nd Movement, which had been involved in the first demonstrations in the United States against the Vietnam War. But in February 1966, PL opted to dismantle the May 2nd Movement and work within the larger and more rapidly growing SDS.[13] Whether PL's initial impetus in entering SDS was to take over the youth organization is unclear. What is clear is that PL's undoubted determination to take over the organization in 1968 was not a chance development but rather was wholly related to the rising stature of the Panthers in particular and the Black Power movement in general. Like most of the Old Left, PL subordinated race to class. In this Old Left vision, black people could attain their liberation only as part of the united working class under the leadership of that class's Marxist vanguard organization. Black Power, in positing black self-determination and black leadership over the whole of the American revolutionary process, thus threatened PL's most central tenet and claim to leadership. Therefore, PL had to fight Black Power ideology and the organization that now stood as its foremost exponent. Thus, at SDS's December 1968 National Council meeting PL mobilized its forces and narrowly won passage for its centerpiece proposal, "Fight Racism; Build a Worker-Student Alliance; Smash Imperialism." The resolution's heart lay in PL's discovery that all nationalism, including Black Nationalism, was reactionary:[14] PL had thrown down the gauntlet. It would contend for leadership over SDS under the banner of opposition to Black Nationalism.

However equivocal SDS had been in its relations with the Panthers — however much SDS had discounted Black Nationalism or sought to interpret that ideology in ways most comfortable to white people — SDS had never so systematically and unambiguously opposed the Black Nationalist current as PL now did. Indeed, a good part of SDS's legitimacy and self-identification came from its verbal support for SNCC and the Panthers and from its attempts at real support for the dozens of local black-led campus struggles of the day. Opposing the Panthers and opposing Black Nationalism would transform SDS from a mass student movement into a sect.

The SDS national office leaders and the most active SDS chapters sought to defend the organization from this fate. Necessarily, that defense, behind a politics dubbed "Revolutionary Youth Movement" (RYM) politics, involved a systematic defense of Black Nationalism, and of the Panthers specifically. At SDS's National Council meeting in Austin in March 1969, RYM partisans presented four proposals attacking white supremacy, defending Black Nationalism, and repudiating PL's line. The most important — and curious — of the RYM proposals was the Panther support proposal titled "The Black Panther Party: Toward the Liberation of the Colony." It began by affirming that "the sharpest struggles in the world today" were the struggles of the oppressed "against imperialism and for national liberation." Within the United States, "the sharpest struggle is that of the black colony for its liberation." But then RYM went beyond anything SDS had argued in the past and asserted that the Panthers constituted the "vanguard" of the black liberation movement in the United States. As the vanguard, the Panthers had brought down on themselves "the most vicious repression" from the government. With the number of Panthers falling to such repression mounting daily, the resolution insisted that it would be a "mockery" for SDS to do less than offer total support for the BPP. Moreover, that support required SDS to engage in the strongest possible struggle against white supremacy, both outside and inside the movement.

This call to challenge white supremacy would be the closest SDS would ever come to answering SNCC's original demand that white radicals organize white communities against racism. Nevertheless, the Panther vanguard resolution had two significant shortcomings. First, while the resolution praised the Panthers' entire program as "essentially correct," it insisted that "An especially important part of the Panther program is the Black People's Army — a military force to be used not only in the defense of the black community but also for its liberation."[15] This was a typical SDS determination. It emphasized the Panthers' military program just as the Panthers themselves were deemphasizing that program — in self-defense against the repression they faced — and strengthening their community-organizing programs. Evidently, SDS was attempting to provide some leadership for the vanguard.

Given SDS's emphasis on Panther militancy, one older SDS member wondered pointedly whether "we really mean to follow them, or just let them get mowed down?"[16] It was a good question, one that would have increasing weight over the next several months. For SDS had not simply affirmed support for the Panther program in the face of concerted government attacks. Rather, it had declared that the Panthers were the vanguard of the black revolution. Six months earlier, recall, SDS had rejected Cleaver's proposed electoral alliance on the grounds, in part, that that alliance would involve an unwarranted intervention in the internal affairs of the black liberation movement. Whether entering into that electoral alliance actually intervened in the black movement was debatable; however, designating the Panthers the vanguard of the black struggle very clearly intervened in the black movement's internal process. The former black SNCC worker Julius Lester took SDS to task for precisely this intervention. He acknowledged that the Panthers were under significant government attack, and he insisted that SDS was within its rights to support the Panthers against this attack. However, by asserting that the Panthers were the vanguard of the black liberation movement, SDS had gone beyond simply defending the beleaguered group and instead had intruded on the internal business of the black movement and, according to Lester, had revealed its white supremacy in the process. The real business of SDS, Lester contended, was organizing *whites*. At that, it had fallen far short of defining the parameters of a "revolutionary ideology, program and strategy." Yet SDS presumed to determine for the black community "categorically who the black vanguard is, what the correct ideology is, what the correct military strategy is and what the correct program is." On the one hand, SDS was in no position to know what was correct for the black community's struggle; on the other, if it presumed to determine that the Panther program was correct, it needed to discuss why the programs of other black organizations, SNCC included, were incorrect. To have done so, of course, would have made it clearer still that SDS was intervening in a debate within the black community.[17]

Kathleen Cleaver, representing the Panthers, defended SDS against Lester's critique, but in a manner that really evaded the heart of Lester's criticism. Her argument boiled down to two items: first, the Panthers really were the vanguard — the repression against the organization proved that status — and SDS had simply recognized the reality; and second, Cleaver argued, in any case SDS could not influence the black community's internal political struggles. Perhaps the latter point was true, perhaps not. But the real question was the propriety of SDS entering into that debate and having its membership line up behind the Panthers as the vanguard of the revolution. Cleaver herself also recognized the curious nature of the resolution, noting that it affirmed an "essentially correct" BPP program — implying that SDS had discerned parts of the program that were incorrect.[18]

At Austin, then, at the high tide of the black liberation movement, and at a time when the New Left was most seriously trying to understand and defend Black Nationalism, those in SDS found it difficult to break with their traditional views on race. Designating the Panthers as vanguard of the black revolution reinscribed the organization's whiteness at a new and higher level. SDS had, over the life of the organization, continually played catch up with the black movement. But it had tried to deny that it was playing catch up by defining the black movement's work as particular work, or by taking advanced black social thought and rewriting it into white language, and in so doing forgetting its origins. Determining that the Panther organization was the black revolutionary vanguard put SDS in the driver's seat, if only in the organization's collective imagination.

A United Front against Fascism?

The Austin National Council occurred at the very outset of the government's all-out assault on the Panthers. Two months earlier, in January 1969, an FBI counterintelligence operation in Los Angeles helped lay the foundations for the shooting deaths of Los Angeles Panther leaders Alprentice Bunchy Carter and John Huggins, which in turn led to the subsequent arrest of most of the Los Angeles Panther leadership. Shortly after the Austin National Council, on April 2, 1969, New York City police rounded up the New York Panther leadership in the first of a series of conspiracy arrests that affected virtually every Panther chapter in the United States. From January 1969 to December 1969, Panthers were arrested or killed in San Francisco, Chicago, Salt Lake City, Indianapolis, Denver, San Diego, Sacramento, and Los Angeles, including four separate raids in Chicago, two in San Diego, and two in Los Angeles. In September 1969 alone, police across the nation arrested Panthers in forty-six separate incidents, destroying and ransacking offices, shutting down breakfast programs, and so on.[19] This repression had a contradictory effect on RYM forces. On the one hand, it pushed SDS to defend the Panthers and to understand the significance of the attack being waged upon them. But the repression decisively weakened the BPP and undermined the organization's ability to work in its own communities. Consequently, it also undermined the Panthers' ability to guide the New Left. In the past, the black movement had had the ability to check SDS's vanguardist tendencies — that is, to bring SDS back down to earth. The black movement — expressing itself through organizations like SNCC and the Panthers and through massive social struggles — had had the gravitational pull to continually reorient SDS's perspective on developing social conditions, and to direct the evolution of the New Left activists' own identities as young white people. Now, however, the government's assault on the Panthers was dissipating the black movement's gravity and creating the conditions for SDS to spin off into its own white vanguardist fantasies. Moreover, SDS's phenomenal growth — the organization had more than doubled in size from April 1968 to November 1968 — added further fuel to these fantasies and made the black movement's ability to check the New Left all the more difficult.[20] As one white radical Panther supporter, Arlene Eisen Bergman, summarized the problem in late 1969: "A lot of movement people have resigned themselves to being witnesses of the destruction of the Black Panther Party. We chant 'off the pig,' but don't mean it. We affirm support for the BPP, but give none in practice. Some would like to provide support, but don't know how. Others find all sorts of excuses for not supporting the Panthers, 'they're taking a bad line,' etc. Some are even honest enough to use the rats-leaving-a-sinking-ship metaphor. The Panthers have many fair weather ideological friends."[21]

One further factor, ironically, encouraged the rejection of BPP leadership: the expulsion of PL at SDS's June 1969 national convention. The expulsion was warranted, on grounds of racism alone. However, the danger in expelling PL was simply that having dramatically rid itself of a racist force, SDS, unchecked by the strength of the black movement, could foist off onto PL all of its own white supremacy. In other words, PL could serve as the white supremacist "other" to SDS's purity and antiwhite supremacism.

These forces—the government repression of the Panthers, the dramatic growth of SDS, and the expulsion of PL—came together in July 1969 at the Panthers' conference to build a United Front Against Fascism (UFAF). In seeking to cope with the government's mounting attacks, the Panthers called on all of their potential allies to unite behind a single program of political self-defense: namely, a petition campaign for community control of the police. The petition demanded black community control of the police in black communities and white community control of the police in white communities. The BPP hoped to create hundreds of committees involving thousands of people and, in so doing, create a buffer between themselves and the repressive forces stalking them.[22]

In effect, the Panthers once again were asking SDS to take the notion of black self-determination into racist white communities—giving practical substance to the demand that SNCC had made back in 1966. As 80 percent of the three thousand people who showed up at the UFAF conference were white, it was not a wholly unrealistic strategy. Yet, at a time when the government assault against the Panthers was at its height, SDS—divided at the time of PL's expulsion into two RYM factions, the Weathermen and RYM II—rejected the Panther program, once again.

The rejection took characteristic form. The organization's National Interim Committee members—four Weatherman members and three from RYM II—jointly declared that: "SDS participation in the UFAF conference was based on our complete support of the black liberation struggle and of the leadership of that struggle, especially the Black Panther Party. At a time when the black and brown peoples and the Panthers and other organizations are facing increasingly brutal fascist attacks by the ruling class and their agents, the police, all revolutionaries must defend those who are leading the anti-imperialist struggle." Having established their fealty to the black revolution's leadership (which no longer, apparently, was the BPP by itself as had been the case three months earlier in Austin), SDS's tone began to shift. As the NIC members explained in the very next sentence: "Strategically, this defense, this attack on fascism is accomplished by continuing to build the anti-imperialist movement; our part of the task is to involve the white working class in the struggle against imperialism. This can only be done by winning whites to support and fight on the side of black and brown people within this country, and on the side of all oppressed and colonized peoples abroad."

The SDS then lectured the Panthers on the significance of combating white supremacy and the importance of class politics. Unless SDS attacked white supremacy, it could not build a real working-class solidarity. Of course, SDS wholly supported community control of the police in black and brown communities. But white community control of the police deflected the issues of fascism, racism, and self-determination by creating a "parity" between communities that, because of white supremacy, were not equal. Moreover, the authors maintained, class divided white communities, and SDS stood only for the working class.

Finally, the two RYM factions also worried over the use of the legal tactic of petitioning. While not raising "principled opposition" to legal forms of struggle, SDS patiently explained to the Panthers the significance of using militant tactics: "We should understand that at this time smashing the illusion of reform through voting and other capitalist channels is a priority in the building of a revolutionary anti-imperialist movement. The level of struggle is being raised and should continue to be raised among white youth. This is a necessity in building the 'fighting force' which will eventually defeat imperialism."[23] In short, RYM's "complete support of the black liberation struggle and of the leadership of that struggle, especially the Black Panther Party" meant RYM's rejection of the UFAF proposal.[24]

Here was the denouement of an era. From 1966 to 1969, the black movement had repeatedly urged SDS to take on racism in the white community. Now, despite continual resistance to that charge, SDS, in a variety of RYM proposals, slowly came to define its role in just such terms. Still, the Panthers, whom SDS three months earlier had designated as the vanguard of the revolution, had posed the question to SDS point-blank: Will you support us on the terms that we are asking for your support? Will you organize in your own white communities for black self-determination on the terms that we set for your organizing? And SDS—both its principal factions—answered in unqualified fashion, "No. What you have asked of us does not accord with our conception of ourselves as revolutionaries."

Other white radicals, like Arlene Eisen Bergman, understood that the problem with UFAF was neither the Panthers nor the UFAF program but rather SDS's inability to do the real work of organizing whites against racism. Columbia SDS member Lew Cole understood that the Panthers saw UFAF as creating a "first real attempt to reach the white working-class in a mass way, and begin to organize it into a consciously anti-racist force within society." If, Cole argued, the Panthers had erroneously structured this attempt at organizing white workers against racism in the "lowest common denominator" terms—black community control in black communities and white community control in white communities—"the fault lay not with the Panthers but with SDS, which had done nothing to demonstrate that whites could be organized on any other basis."[25] Cole was the exception, however, in taking this view. Boston's underground paper, the *Old Mole*, reported the more typical white left response: "Many of the delegates left the conference confused and disappointed. The radical movement feared that the Panthers' UF tactic was attempting to enlist liberal support at the expense of revolutionary militancy."[26]

The Weathermen's Susan Stern was one of the disappointed delegates. In recalling the UFAF conference in her memoir, Stern complained that the Panthers seemed to be "stepping back from armed struggle and militancy" at the very moment the Weathermen were "gearing to become urban guerrillas." When the Panthers, following SDS's rejection of UFAF, denounced the Weathermen as "adventurists" and refused to work with any SDS faction, the Weathermen were shocked. "It was hard to follow a vanguard who despised you," Stern remembered concluding.[27] In this way, she neatly summarized the united RYM position: it would willingly follow a black vanguard whose requests coincided with its inclinations. But if that vanguard requested something that RYM rejected, that was clearly a problem for the vanguard and not for RYM. And the Panthers and the Black Nationalist movement it represented, reeling from government attacks, no longer had the strength to call RYM to task for their desertion of "the vanguard."

Following this rejection of the UFAF, the Panthers unsurprisingly denounced SDS, correctly concluding that these white activists were attempting to politically educate — to lead — the Panthers. In a devastating attack, BPP chairman Bobby Seale lumped SDS together with its hated foe, PL. He assured both organizations that "we have a mind of our own . . . that we make our decisions and we support who we want to support, and that we're here to make revolution."[28]

The Search for a New Vanguard

The contradiction between the Panthers as real representatives of the black community, seriously attempting to organize a popular struggle for black liberation, and the Panthers as vanguard representatives in the imagination of young white leftists, had become too great. Something would have to give. Quietly, both RYM factions — the Weathermen and RYM II — would drop the real Panthers and cast about for new black vanguards that more closely conformed to white radical needs.

The Weathermen's retreat from Panther leadership corresponded with its organizing for a national action in Chicago called the "Days of Rage." A July 1969 Detroit flyer titled "Break On through to the Other Side" was typical of how the Weathermen promoted the Panthers and "black leadership" in its national action work. Oriented to the Weathermen's conception of white working-class youth, the flyer began by asserting that "cats are being fucked over *everywhere*," in the schools, on the job, and being shipped off to Vietnam to fight and die for rich people. "Like, what is there to do?" asked the Weathermen. People were fighting all over the world against these same rich folks. "And dig it, man," Vietnam, "that little country is *winning*." And blacks in the United States, who had been fighting for four hundred years, were "*leading* the fight against the ruling class and the pigs. That means that if we're gonna fight the pigs, we have to follow their leadership . . . black people are leading the fight for *everyone's* freedom." Thus, at the very moment that it was rejecting the Panthers' UFAF program, the Weathermen were telling white youth that they needed to follow black leadership.

> And just dig what's happening in Chicago. A lot of the gangs stopped fighting each other and got together to stop the Man. The Black Panthers, the Young Lords (a Spanish gang), the Young Patriots (a southern white gang) and SDS are all fighting side by side. . . .
>
> The thing is this: *the Man can't fight everywhere*. He can't even beat the Viet-

namese. And when other Vietnams start, man, he's just gonna fall apart. SDS is recruiting an army right now, man, a people's army, under black leadership, that's gonna fight against the pigs and *win*!!![29]

On its face, the Weathermen certainly seemed to advocate following black leadership. But, what did this "black leadership" mean in a concrete sense? Did it mean supporting the Panthers? Did it mean supporting *any* black liberation groups in Detroit, which at the time was the burgeoning center of a number of Black Nationalist groups within the auto industry? Or even organizing Detroit's segregated white communities against racism? No. White working-class youth could follow black leadership by "fighting the pigs" — under the Weathermen's direction, of course. The Weathermen, in short, had invented their own black leadership and was asking white youth to follow *that* black leadership.[30]

On the other hand, however strongly the Weathermen touted black leadership, the black organization that SDS had proclaimed as the vanguard of the black revolution only a few months earlier was not cooperating with the Weathermen. In preparing for the organization's October 1969 national action in Chicago, the young radicals themselves admitted that local Panthers and the militant Puerto Rican nationalist group, the Young Lords organization, had "raised strong reservations about the action." The Panthers feared that the Weathermen action would leave behind an increased police presence in the black community. Indeed, Chicago Panther head Fred Hampton repeatedly denounced the Weathermen's action as adventuristic and "Custeristic." This did not faze the Weathermen, however. Resorting to an argument that they had used when they rejected the Panther request for Carl Oglesby's vice presidential candidacy the year before, the Weathermen insisted that while the black and brown movements did not need the kind of action that the Weathermen were projecting, whites — "riddled by timidity" and lacking experience in the struggle — did.[31]

Still, despite the Panthers' condemnation, the Weathermen's leaders were supremely confident of their course. Susan Stern, who was working in a Seattle Weatherman project at the time, recalled later that all of the Weathermen's "big wheels" — Dohrn, Rudd, John Jacobs — "had promised us . . . that at least 25,000 people were coming to the Days of Rage." The Weathermen projected that these twenty-five thousand youths would partake in four days of action — tearing up "Pig City," Chicago.

The Weathermen kicked off their "Days of Rage" two days early by dynamiting a monument to Chicago policemen at Haymarket Square on Monday. But however uplifting this surprise attack may have been for the Weatherman cadre, it must have been dispiriting for at least a few of them when they arrived at Lincoln Park on the night of 8 October. Instead of the promised twenty-five thousand white youths ready to tear up "Pig City," between seven hundred and eight hundred people gathered. Half of these, it would turn out, were simply spectators. Still, it was an unprecedented action. A round of inspirational speeches addressed the disappointments and fears of the assembled. Stern remembered the basic theme of the speeches: the need for courage, the realization that "we were the only white people in the country who realized what it . . . took to make the revolution," that "we were the revolutionary vanguard in America." Somewhat sardonically, she summarized the Weatherman leadership rap: "Only five hundred people in this country were good, strong, and brilliant enough to come to Chicago." After an hour of speeches, Stern and several hundred others were ready for action, although several years later she herself did not understand why she and the others went ahead with it. "Maybe," she thought, "it was mass hypnosis. Maybe it was just that the notion of us being the only non-racists, and the only americong in the country appealed to our egos, and spurred on our revolutionary lust."[32]

Over the next several days, the Weathermen went on two sprees of destruction through Chicago's downtown area, smashing hundreds of store, apartment, and automobile windows and charging directly into police lines. Over the four Days of Rage, the Weathermen incurred 290 arrests and over a million dollars in bail bonds, and police shot and wounded seven members of the group. On the flip side, the Weathermen managed to send fifty-seven police to the hospital, along with the city's corporation counsel, Richard Elrod. Elrod, in his enthusiasm for pursuing the Weathermen, had attempted a diving tackle and had broken his neck when he smacked into a wall, paralyzing himself from the waist down. The Weathermen also caused a million dollars in damages to a "ruling class neighborhood." The several hundred Weathermen members involved also claimed to have preoccupied for several days the "same amount of imperialist pig power that a VC [Viet Cong] regiment would attract." Moreover, they claimed that some of the police that were occupied with Days of Rage had been withdrawn from the city's black communities. This was what the Weathermen termed "material support" to the Vietnamese and to the black liberation movement.[33]

Of course, this was not the kind of support that either the black movement or the Vietnamese had been asking for. Black radicals had been asking for several years now that groups like SDS take up the task of winning white Americans to an anti-racist solidarity.[34] In its organizing for Chicago, the Weathermen had claimed that it was answering this call; that it was seeking, by its militancy, to win whites to the black and Vietnamese struggles. When white "kids" did not respond, however, when they did not rise to the challenge of "fighting pigs," the fault lay with these young white people and not with the Weathermen. The revolution would happen anyway, only now in *opposition* to white people. The Weathermen, in short, had renounced the job of building an anti-racist and antiwar solidarity in the name of the backwardness of white Americans.[35]

But if white Americans would not en masse join the anti-imperialist revolution, this left blacks and other minorities in the United States to make the revolution. The revolution itself, which would topple imperialism, would unfold in as race war. *The Weatherman*'s responsibility, it determined, was to help blacks make *this* revolution. Unfortunately, black people needed a vanguard for the task, and the Panthers, following Chicago, continued to denounce the group.[36] Internally, then, the Weathermen began to build its case against the Panthers: the Panthers had been smashed by government repression; they were leaning on the revisionist Communist Party for support; they themselves had become revisionist.[37]

Many years later, a Bay Area activist recalled having heard this line when the Weathermen attempted to recruit him during a meeting he attended out of interest. A Weatherman member in a "short mini-skirt and knee-high boots," he remembered, insisted that "we were living in historic times; the anti-war movement was intensifying. Unfortunately, because of the recent police attacks against the black community (particularly against Fred Hampton and the Chicago Panther office) the black community was suffering from great demoralization. What could we do about this?" In answer to her own question, the woman "suggested this scenario": the Weatherman cadre would don burnt-cork "black face" and assassinate a prominent oppressor of black people. The potential recruit recalled being stunned at the suggestion. "Shaken from the lethargy induced from the long meeting, I began to ask some questions. Wouldn't this action, I asked, only bring down more heat on a beleaguered black community? On the contrary, was the reply: the black community, suffering from demoralization, would be revived by this action, especially because it would appear to have been done by 'their own.'"[38]

Four former Weatherman activists who left the organization during this period publicly denounced these same politics. "Since black and third world revolutionary groups such as the Black Panther Party, the League of Revolutionary Black Workers and the Young Lords Organization disagreed with" the Weathermen's call for black armed struggle and race war against the United States right now, "Weathermen labeled them 'revisionist.' The Weathermen then argued that whites would 'fight on the side of blacks' only if there was 'non-revisionist' black leadership. Therefore, *it was necessary for white revolutionaries to carry out actions in black communities in order to develop new black leadership* which believed in race war, armed struggle now, and other Weathermen positions. This was the height of their [the Weathermen's] racism" (my emphasis).[39] In short, the Weathermen determined that it would carry out militant, armed actions whose authorship was racially ambiguous or even deliberately designed to appear as black. By doing so, the Weathermen would inspire the emergence of a new black revolutionary vanguard, committed to the kind of armed struggle the Weathermen deemed essential for the revolution.

To be sure, following the Days of Rage, the Weathermen did receive some reassurance in its quest for a new black vanguard. Shortly after Fred Hampton's criticism of the Weathermen appeared in the *Black Panther* newspaper, Eldridge Cleaver, then in exile, responded. In a clear reference to the Weathermen's Chicago action, Cleaver affirmed that he preferred "a paralyzed pig to well-criticized pig." Moreover, he insisted, while a "dead pig" was "desirable, a paralyzed pig is preferable to a mobile pig. And a determined revolutionary doesn't require an authorization from a Central Committee before offing a pig. As a matter of fact, when the need arises a true revolutionary will off the Central Committee."[40] Cleaver's reassurance to the Weathermen thus presaged the coming split in the Black Panther Party itself, which occurred in February 1971. Moreover, the BPP's evident position on the Weathermen was signaled by the fact that Cleaver's essay first appeared not in the *Black Panther*, but in the white radical underground paper, the *Berkeley Tribe*.

But whether or not Cleaver and a fraction of the Panthers supported the Weathermen, the fact remains that these white radicals—like their predecessors—had already repeatedly dismissed BPP leadership. And now they were casting about for a new black revolutionary vanguard that simply did not exist in the black community. The Weathermen, in short, were looking to school the black movement in the meaning of revolutionary politics. Moreover, they were even willing to carry out actions that might be attributed to black people in order to inspire the emergence of this black vanguard. So much for the politics of nonintervention in the black community's politics.

In New York City, a small Weathermen cell began to implement this political strategy. In the early morning hours of 21 February 1970 — the fifth anniversary of Malcolm X's assassination — a Weatherman cell fire-bombed the home of John Murtagh, the judge presiding over the trial of the New York Panther 21. On the same night, the cell apparently also fire-bombed a navy recruiting station in Brooklyn, a police patrol car in Greenwich Village, and the International Law Library at Columbia University.[41] Two weeks later, as the cell was constructing antipersonnel bombs for an attack on a noncommissioned officers' dance at Fort Dix, New Jersey, a member of the group accidentally crossed a wire and detonated a cache of dynamite. Three members died in the explosion, and the entire Weathermen organization went underground.[42]

Meanwhile, on the other side of the RYM split, RYM II also sought to tutor the Panthers. As noted, the tendency was already evident when the Weathermen and RYM II united to reject the Panthers' UFAF. RYM II's leaders had been more steeped in Old Left Marxism, with its emphasis on the vanguard role of the *united* proletariat, black *and* white, than had the Weathermen leaders. The upsurge of national liberation movements in general and of Black Nationalism in particular put its imprint on RYM II's Marxism, however. Thus, while RYM II proclaimed the vanguard role of the oppressed nations against imperialism and acknowledged black liberation's vanguard role in the United States, it also — though uneasily at first — retained a vanguard role for the industrial proletariat.

In its first position paper, RYM II balanced these two vanguards — black people and the industrial proletariat — by defining the parameters of a black nation in the United States. In doing so, these white radicals had dredged up the deliberations of the Communist International in 1928 and recovered from those arcane debates the existence of a black nation in the "black belt" region of the South. White workers, RYM II insisted, had to support the self-determination of *this* black-belt nation.[43] The line temporarily resolved the problem of contending vanguards. Black Nationalists would lead the struggle for the "black belt" nation. In the rest of the country, the united industrial proletariat would lead the revolution and support "black belt" self-determination and black democratic rights outside the South. But of course, the Panthers, whom RYM II partisans had designated as the vanguard of the black struggle just two months prior to their discovery of a "black belt" nation, had not asked for such a nation, much less defined the parameters of it. Neither for that matter had SNCC, the other leading Black Nationalist organization with whom SDS members worked. On the contrary, both the Panthers and SNCC insisted on the vanguard character of the black struggle, not only in black communities but in the United States as a whole. Indeed, SNCC's Stokely Carmichael had years before argued that black people would define the terms of their own liberation, and that it was inappropriate for the oppressor to tell the oppressed how that liberation would be achieved. Yet RYM II, like the Weathermen, knew differently.

Over time, RYM II increasingly stressed the leading role of the industrial proletariat. The difference between the Weathermen's attempts at instructing the Panthers and RYM II's attempts was simply this: the Weathermen sought to create a black vanguard that would lead the revolution in the absence of *sold-old* white workers. Thus RYM II sought a black vanguard that would better appreciate the necessity for allying with these same — but now, *revolutionary* — white workers, as part of a united working-class revolution.

Conclusion

During the latter part of the 1960s, SDS chapters often debated the meaning of solidarity with the black and Vietnamese struggles for self-determination. Positions ranged from PL's condemnation of both the Panthers and Vietnam's National Liberation Front — the former for its nationalism, reactionary by definition, and the latter for its revisionism — to moderate positions of "critical support" for these national liberation struggles, to the more radical RYM positions of "unconditional solidarity" with them. Particularly in late 1968 and 1969, as the RYM forces came to dominate the SDS National Office and the organization's more active chapters, SDS leaders increasingly touted this more radical position. Unfortunately, historians have taken SDS at its word on this "unconditional solidarity"; have translated the phrase as "uncritical support" (read: unthinking, knee-jerk support); and have seen that uncritical support as one of the causal factors in the New Left's demise. The problem with this "declensionist" narrative is that it overlooks the actual relations SDS had with groups like the Black Panthers.[44]

As a national organization, SDS never offered "unconditional solidarity" with the Panthers, although the RYM factions often proclaimed it. To the contrary, SDS consistently sought to guide the Panthers, to create a black militant group that met the needs of the organization's young white activists. Consequently, SDS, and particularly its Weatherman faction, always emphasized support for the Panthers' "military program," while downplaying or outright rejecting its "survival programs" and electoral programs. Moreover, SDS repeatedly rejected BPP requests that young white activists take responsibility for organizing white communities against racism, in solidarity with black liberation. Those requests came in concrete fashion, like support for Cleaver's presidential campaign or the proposed United Front Against Fascism. Further, SDS rejected all criticisms by the Panthers concerning SDS tactics or concerning SDS's failures to take up Panther programs. Fred Hampton criticized the Weathermen in no uncertain terms concerning the Days of Rage and insisted that the Weathermen's real job was to organize whites into solidarity with the black struggle. Bobby Seale, following the rejection of the UFAF by both RYM factions, took SDS to task for its racist arrogance. Finally, when the Black Panther Party made it absolutely clear to SDS's factions that it would not be the kind of black liberation organization that served the fantasies of young white activists, the search began for a black liberation vanguard that fit their needs, not those of the Panthers.

In short, SDS never established a principled relation to the Black Panthers. The Weathermen's violence and RYM II's ideological rigidity did not result from SDS's uncritical support for the Panthers. Rather, SDS violence and sectarianism arose in opposition to the real will of the Black Panther Party as the Party existed during the last year and a half of the life of SDS.

Notes

1. This white-centered history is the quintessential version of the so-called declension narrative, which posits "the good (early) sixties" and "the bad (late) sixties" (Wini Breines, "Whose New Left?" *Journal of American History* 75.2 [September 1988]: 528–45). During "the good sixties," according to this view, well-meaning young white people — variously influenced by demography, affluence, and cultural trends uniquely shaped in the early Cold War atomic era, and, of course, by the civil rights movement — sought to change the world for the better. Most of what was positive in this era was the product of young white minds: the concept of "participatory democracy," for example, derived from the thinking of people like Tom Hayden, not the actual leadership of people like Ella Baker, or the practice of black Student Nonviolent Coordinating Committee (SNCC) activists in the South. Thus "the good sixties" had far more to do with young whites than with the initiative of young black people. On the other hand, as the sixties wore on, and as frustrations

over the war in Vietnam intensified, young whites increasingly romanticized and sought to emulate violent Third World and black revolutionaries. That is, if the declension narrative gives young black people less credit than they deserve for the rise of the sixties, it compensates by giving them more responsibility for the sixties' demise. Todd Gitlin's *The Sixties: Years of Hope, Days of Rage* (New York: Bantam Books, 1987), the preeminent representative of this school of thought, repeatedly dismisses Black Nationalism as "angry," "reckless nationalism," "bombast," and "rage" while never allowing the Black Nationalist voice itself to be heard. Moreover, he characterizes the New Left's support for Black Nationalism as "an orgy of white guilt": "black militancy held the New Left in thrall" (168, 245, 246). Historians of the New Left, like Maurice Isserman, echo Gitlin. The civil rights movement produced some "genuine 'convict heroes'" who were "justly celebrated in the Bay Area Left and elsewhere for their courage," he writes, but violent Black Panther prison inmates like Eldridge Cleaver and George Jackson, who "inherited some of the prestige and moral authority of the civil rights prisoners," "enjoyed the uncritical adulation of white New Leftists." The Panthers' advent in particular thus constituted an "unmitigated disaster" for the African American Left in the late 1960s and, perhaps more crucially for Isserman, their "glamorous machismo . . . helped derail the white New Left in the Bay Area" (Isserman, "Where Have All the Convicts Gone, Long Time Passing," *Radical History Review* [winter 1996]: 113–15; see also Isserman and Michael Kazin, *America Divided: The Civil War of the 1960s* [New York: Oxford University Press, 2000], 176–78). Tom Hayden, in his 1988 memoir, also weighs in against Black Nationalism, although somewhat apologetically: "The combined experience of racism, brutality, and official expediency had rusted SNCC's idealism until it gave way to the volcanic hatred and aggression that swells in the lower depths of the human personality. The politics of separatism and violent rhetoric were neither realistic nor humanistic" (Hayden, *Reunion: A Memoir* [New York: Collier Books, 1988], 161). This drumbeat of declension causality naturally enters the thinking of more thoughtful historians, like that of Ellen DuBois who offhandedly remarks in a book review that the "black/white split in the civil rights movement . . . set . . . the stage for the collapse of the left," as though it were well known that the turn to Black Power marked the turning point in a narrative of declension (DuBois, "Dare to Struggle, Dare to Win," *Radical History Review* [winter 1991]: 134).

2. For elaboration, see my "'A Fucking White Revolutionary Mass Movement' and Other Fables of Whiteness," *Race Traitor* 12 (2001): 10–37.

3. "On White People," *New Left Notes*, 24 August 1966, 18. "'A Fucking White Revolutionary Mass Movement'" contains a detailed account of SDS's difficulties with Black Power from SNCC's articulation of it to the Panthers' emergence on the national scene.

4. "A Prison Interview," in *The New Left Reader*, edited by Carl Oglesby (New York: Grove Press, 1969), 227–28, 229, 240. Typically, Gitlin interprets Newton's proclamations here as a product of the white imagination: "In a series of prison inter-

views widely circulated in the movement press, Huey Newton—*primed with reading matter by white leftists*—discoursed fluidly about socialism, anti-colonialism, anti-imperialism, and world revolution" (Gitlin, *The Sixties*, 349 [my emphasis]). Apparently, twenty years after the fact, Gitlin could not conceive of Newton's having had a powerful enough mind to have arrived at his understandings of revolution independently of white leftists. In fact, the Panthers "primed" the New Left and shaped the New Left's rhetoric. But, even when Gitlin sees evil, whites must be more central to his account than blacks.

5. For a discussion of the PFP's radical and "moderate" wings, see Joel Wilson's essay in this volume.
6. Carl Oglesby and Richard Schaull, *Containment and Change* (New York: Macmillan, 1967).
7. Local SDS chapters had already been cooperating with local Panther groups. But SDS's relationship with the Panthers on a national level had never been discussed at national conferences, conventions, or by the NIC until Cleaver's proposal forced the issue.
8. "White Mother Country Radicals," *New Left Notes*, 29 July 1968, 1, 5. The title was deceptive, as the article rejected the Panther proposal. Ron Jacobs, in *The Way the Wind Blew: A History of the Weather Underground* [New York: Verso, 1997], 13), takes SDS at its word—that its goal was to support the Panthers—and fails to see that SDS was professing its support as it rejected the Panther proposal.
9. NIC, "Fifth Party Ticket: Cleaver and Oglesby," *New Left Notes*, 9 September 1968, 3; NIC "Why Oglesby Won't Run," NIC, "Fifth Party Ticket: Cleaver and Oglesby," *New Left Notes*, 9 September 1968, 8.
10. Ibid.
11. *Soul on Ice* (Berkeley: Ramparts, 1968), 78. Newton explained the concept more completely in his "Prison Interview," 231–33.
12. Of course, this white proclivity to choose the white mind over the black had a long historical pedigree, even among abolitionists. For Frederick Douglass's understanding that his white abolitionist partners wanted him to provide testimony of slavery's brutality while allowing his white comrades to provide the analysis, see *My Bondage and My Freedom* (New York: Arno Press, 1968), 358–61. W. E. B. Du Bois similarly faced the arrogance of his white NAACP partners, one of whom decried the fact that Du Bois had never been "house-broken" (David Levering Lewis, *W. E. B. Du Bois: Biography of a Race, 1868–1919* [New York: Holt, 1993], 481–82).
13. Kirkpatrick Sale, *SDS* (New York: Vintage Books, 1973), 121–22, 263.
14. *New Left Notes*, 8 January 1969, 4.
15. Ed Jennings and Chicago Circle Campus SDS, "The Black Panther Party: Toward the Liberation of the Colony," *New Left Notes*, 5 April 1969, 3.
16. Clayton Van Lydegraf, "Reply to Mellen," *New Left Notes*, 6 June 1969, 8.
17. Originally in the *Guardian* (10 May 1969, 13) as Julius Lester, "From the Other Side of the Tracks."
18. "Kathleen Cleaver Replies to Julius Lester," *New Left Notes*, 1 May 1969, 5–6.

19. Philip S. Foner, ed., *The Black Panthers Speak* (New York: Lippincott, 1970), xxvi; Ward Churchill, and Jim Vander Wall, *The Cointelpro Papers: Documents from the FBI's Secret Wars against Dissent in the United States* (Boston: South End Press, 1989), 21. Certainly, the attack on the Panthers and on the Black Nationalist movement had begun earlier, the founding "Cointelpro—Black Nationalist Hate Groups" memo dating from August 1967, and surveillance and disruption of the black movement extending far back before this. But 1969 marked the intensification of this campaign against the black movement, sending numerous Panthers into jail, into exile, or into the grave.
20. Sale, SDS, 36.
21. Arlene Eisen Bergman, "Panther's Struggle Is the People's Struggle," *Movement*, October 1969, 3.
22. *Old Mole* staff, "UFAF Conference," *Old Mole*, 1–14 August 1969, 3; Lew Cole, "Volunteers," *Leviathan*, February 1970, 14.
23. NIC, "NIC Statement on UFAF," *New Left Notes*, 24 July 1969, 2–3.
24. Alice Echols's account of the UFAF is a good example of how historians have misinterpreted SDS's relation to the Panthers. While she gets the end product right—SDS rejected the UFAF proposal—she characterizes the Weathermen's relation to the Panthers as "obsequious," insisting that that conduct peaked at UFAF (Echols, *Daring to Be Bad: Radical Feminism in America, 1967–1975* [Minneapolis: University of Minnesota Press, 1989], 127–28).
25. Cole, "Volunteers," 14–17. At the time, Cole was part of a short-lived New York splinter within RYM, called RYM 1 1/2, or the "Mad Dogs." They sought to distance themselves from the Weathermen by renouncing their penchant for violence while at the same time distancing themselves from RYM II by maintaining a focus on race. Larry Bensky was another white radical who tried to appreciate the Panther position and saw the white Left being forced to contrast the image it had of the Panthers with their reality. At the UFAF conference, wrote Bensky, "The white left discovered the black revolution, and was amazed that it hated what it saw" (Bensky, "The Souls of White Folks," *Hard Times*, 18 July-4 August 1969, 3–4).
26. "UFAF Conference," 19.
27. Stern, *With the Weathermen: The Personal Journey of a Revolutionary Woman* (New York: Doubleday, 1975), 66–67. Stanley Aronowitz, writing in the *Guardian*, provided another typical white intellectual view on the UFAF proposal. Fascism, he argued, was a "special form of state power," and he explained at length the character of fascism in Germany and the U.S. history of violence against leftist movements, with nary a word on racism and the need to challenge racism in the white community (Aronowitz, "On the Line," *Guardian*, 28 June 1969, 13).
28. Quoted in Committee on Internal Security, House of Representatives, *The Black Panther Party: Its Origin and Development as Reflected in Its Official Weekly Newspaper, "The Black Panther Black Community News Service"* (Washington, D.C.: Government Printing Office, October 1970), 55; for the original, see the *Black Panther*, 9 August 1969.

29. Detroit Weatherman, "Break On Through to the Other Side," *Liberation News Service*, 28 August 1969, 6–7.
30. This advocacy of the Weathermen's own "black leadership" likely derived from at least two factors. First, the Weatherman needed black leadership for its own self-legitimization. Second, it needed black leadership to bludgeon its own cadre and other SDS tendencies into line: your opposition to the Weathermen (or the Weathermen's leadership) comes from your own racism, your own refusal to follow black leadership. It was this line, for example, that the Weathermen members Mark Rudd and Terry Robbins used to dismiss RYM II leader Mike Klonsky when he quit work on the Chicago National Action ("Days of Rage") (see Rudd and Robbins, "Goodbye, Mike," *New Left Notes*, 29 August 1969, 2). Earlier, SDS had used the necessity of supporting the black and Vietnamese struggles as a bludgeon against the burgeoning white women's liberation movement and in defense of the organization's own male supremacy (see Dohrn, "Toward a Revolutionary Women's Movement," *New Left Notes*, "International Women's Day" edition, March 1969, 1–4).
31. Kathy Boudin, Bernardine Dohrn, and Terry Robbins, "Bringing the War Back Home, Less Talk, More National Action," *New Left Notes*, 23 August 1969, 6; David Hilliard and Lewis Cole, *The Autobiography of David Hilliard and the Story of the Black Panther Party* (Boston: Little, Brown, 1993), 258; Gitlin, *The Sixties*, 393. Seattle's underground newspaper, *Helix*, also correctly noted that whites had never been reticent to engage in militant struggles. The problem was not "timidity" but politics. When the Weatherman spoke of timidity, it was revealing not a universal about the nature of white people, or of white youth, but a characteristic of white middle-class and upper-class youth.
32. Stern, *With the Weathermen*, 127–46. Also, *Old Mole* staff, "Weather Report," *Old Mole*, 14–24 October 1969, 14.
33. "Chicago: Weathereport," *Rat*, 29 October-12 November 1969. Tom Thomas, "The Second Battle of Chicago 1969," in *Weatherman*, edited by Harold Jacobs (Berkeley: Ramparts Press, 1970), 223; Shin'ya Ono, "You Do Need a Weatherman to Know Which Way the Wind Blows," in Jacobs, ed., *Weatherman*, 227–74; Weatherman, "Chicago 69," *Fire*, 21 October 1969, n.p.
34. "The 'Weathermen' should have spent their time organizing the White working and lumpen class instead of 'prematurely' engaging in combat with the trigger-happy pigs," insisted an Illinois Panther shortly after Days of Rage (Eugene Charles, "SDS: A Need for a Revolutionary Line," *Black Panther*, 18 October 1969, 3).
35. See, for example, Inessa, Victor Camilo, Lilina Jones, Norman Reed, "It's Only People's Games That You Got To Dodge," in Jacobs, ed., *Weatherman*, 425; Thomas, "The Second Battle of Chicago 1969," 196–226.
36. See, for example, Charles, "SDS: A Need for Revolutionary Line."
37. Cole, "Volunteers," 15. The foregoing is also based on the author's own recollections from the time, as a member of Columbia SDS and of an aboveground Weathermen collective in New York, and a discussion with an anonymous ex-Columbia SDS member, 28 April 2003.

38. Louis Segal to author, 23 November 2001.
39. Inessa et al., "It's Only People's Games," 436. In his *Revolution in the Air: Sixties Radicals Turn to Lenin, Mao, and Che* (London: Verso, 2002), 71; RYM II veteran Max Elbaum also refers to this Weatherman scheme to carry out actions in the black community in order to radicalize black people.
40. "On Weatherman," in Jacobs, ed., *Weatherman*, 295, reprinted from the *Berkeley Tribe*, 7 November 1969; *Black Panther*; 22 November 1969.
41. "Home of Justice Murtaugh (*sic*), Panther 21 Judge, Is Bombed," *Liberation News Service*, 25 February 1970, 16.
42. Sam Green and Bill Siegel, *The Weather Underground* (film documentary; Mark Rudd, "Truth or Consequences," unpublished memoir (c.1988–1989), 202, 260.
43. Mike Klonsky, Noel Ignatin, Sue Eanet, and Les Coleman, "Revolutionary Youth Movement II," *New Left Notes*, 5, 9. The COMINTERN's 1928 resolution on the "black belt" nation was a response to the rising tide of Black Nationalism in the United States during the 1920s and bore the same relationship to that nationalism as RYM II bore to the Black Nationalism of the 1960s. Both resolutions took the motion coming out of the black community and offered black people a nation they had not asked for, while sidestepping the questions that that community itself had raised.
44. Moreover, as Breines pointed out long ago, proponents of this kind of history are often themselves former leaders or partisans of the so-called good sixties. By falsely creating the category of uncritically supporting black and Third World struggles, the former leaders do two things. First, they cast aspersions on the very notion of unconditional solidarity. Second, and more important, they cover up the long-standing ambiguity that marked SDS's relation with the black movement, whether in the "good sixties" or the "bad sixties." The verbal professions by SDS of support for the black movement throughout the sixties were rarely matched by its deeds. On the contrary, SDS consistently dropped its interest in the black struggle whenever that struggle faded from view; and the group always had a hard time acknowledging the real leadership that came out of the black movement. Interestingly, in the last half dozen years or so, declensionist history has been rebuked from another quarter — some of the leading RYM characters and their intellectual defenders. They reject the good sixties/bad sixties dichotomy by insisting that they were motivated by a deep solidarity with the black and Vietnamese struggles, and that, breaking with race and empire, they were carrying on the best traditions of the early sixties. The Weathermen are the chief beneficiary of this new anti-declensionist history, with a half-dozen new works rehabilitating the group. Among these are Bill Ayers, *Fugitive Days* (Boston: Beacon, 2001); Jacobs, *The Way the Wind Blew*; Green and Siegel, *The Weather Underground* (documentary); Jeremy Varon, *Bringing the War Home: The Weather Underground, the Red Army Faction, and Revolutionary Violence in the Sixties and Seventies* (Berkeley: University of California Press, 2004); and Neil Gordon's fictional *The Company You Keep* (New York: Viking, 2003). All of these works give short shrift to the glaring discrepancy between the Weathermen's stated

aims — unconditional solidarity with black people and with Vietnam — and the faction's consistent disregard for the real leadership of black people (and the Vietnamese) as expressed by SNCC, the Panthers, and Vietnam's revolutionary movement. Although it has only one defender in the field, RYM II has also generated a defense on similar lines and with similar historical omissions. Elbaum champions the RYM II factions by insisting that from the beginning these Marxist-Leninist-Maoists saw the need for Third World leadership. But he overlooks the real rejection by RYM II of the Third World leadership that was offered it, in the form of the BPP. What both the declensionists and these new historians have in common is their mutual acceptance of the myth that RYM was guided by its devotion to black and Third World struggles, the former condemning it and the latter defending it. In fact, while SDS in its final years acted in the name of solidarity, it always retained its independence in opposition to the real demands made upon it by the black struggle.

Brown Power to Brown People:
Radical Ethnic Nationalism, the Black Panthers, and Latino Radicalism, 1967–1973

JEFFREY O. G. OGBAR

The activists of the late 1960s and early 1970s, though by no means reflecting the majority opinion of their generation, were the central agents of militant discourse of their time. They were raised in an era of new media with national and international dimensions, connecting them to the struggles of young people fighting against oppression from California and Mississippi to Mexico, Peru, and South Africa. Cold war rhetoric, coupled with a sophisticated technological and media apparatus, highlighted the black freedom movement in the United States for a global audience. At the same time, African Americans were inspired by anticolonial struggles throughout the Third World. Influenced by these events as well as by their unique circumstances in the United States, advocates of the Black Power movement in particular took black resistance to a new level, in turn altering the symbolism, rhetoric, and tactics of the New Left.[1] Nowhere was this process more dramatically felt than in the influence of the Black Panther Party (BPP) on the struggles of Latinos — particularly Mexican Americans and Puerto Ricans — which helped generate a new movement of radical ethnic nationalism in late-sixties America. Though the Party had alliances with radicals of various stripes, in many instances it was Latinos who proved to be the Panthers' most intimate allies. By 1967, for example, the Brown Berets had become the first major organization to model itself after the BPP, emerging as self-described "shock troops" for a burgeoning Chicano movement. About the same time, the primarily Puerto Rican Young Lords were evolving from a petty street gang into the newest and most salient expression yet of Puerto Rican nationalism.

Chicano Nationalism

The roots of Chicano nationalism can be found in the struggles of Indian and Mexican peoples in the American Southwest where indigenous people resisted Spanish and, later, Mexican encroachments in a long series of wars beginning in the sixteenth century. Mexicans faced the juggernaut of U.S. expansion from the early nineteenth century, culminating in the Mexican-American War of 1846–1848. The Treaty of Guadalupe Hidalgo, which ended the war, witnessed the cession by the losers of what is now California, Arizona, Utah, Nevada, New Mexico, and parts of Colorado, Wyoming, and Kansas — over a million square miles of territory, a total that is close in size to half of Mexico itself. Initially, the United States promised "full citizenship" for Mexicans who lived in the newly acquired land.[2] Instead, Anglos migrated into the new territories, usurping control from the landed, Spanish-descended Mexican elite, and continuing the long-standing discrimination against the mestizo Mexican majority. Because of the precarious notions of race in America at the time, rules and institutional practices that discriminated against Mexicans were rarely codified in federal or state law but rather were generally left to local authorities.[3] Throughout the region, however, communities with high concentrations of Mexican Americans passed laws barring Chicanos from attending schools with white children, obtaining municipal jobs, and even owning land.[4] Meanwhile, Anglos procured hundreds of thousands of acres of land from Mexicans between 1848 and 1960, and Chicanos became a source of cheap agricultural labor. In the mid-1960s, though, a convergence of forces gave birth to the Chicano civil rights movement.

One of those forces emerged from a massive Mexican farm workers' strike led by Cesar Chavez in California. The strike, against table-grape growers, evolved into one of the most successful boycotts in American labor history. Most crucially, it generated social activism in barrios across the state. East Los Angeles, home to one of the largest Spanish-speaking communities in the world, became a center of this activity.[5] Chicanos there suffered from police brutality and widespread discrimination in housing, education, and employment, as had their brethren throughout the Southwest. Although they were the second largest ethnic/racial group in California (after whites), Chicanos had elected only one state assembly member and no state senators.[6] In Los Angeles itself, there were no Chicano city council members or representatives on the county board of directors. By 1970, the school dropout rate among Mexican Americans was fully 80 percent, higher than any ethnic group in the city. And, though Chicanos in East Los Angeles had a lower unemployment rate than did blacks in South Central, Chicano men were much less likely to be professionally employed than were black men. Meanwhile, Chicanos suffered the highest tuberculosis and infant mortality rates in the county.[7] Thus, despite their occasional attempts to emphasize their European heritage, Chicanos experienced sharply the frustrations of being racialized as the "Other" in America.

The other key force in the emergence of a Chicano civil rights movement was the black freedom struggle. Scholars have long observed the power of the modern civil rights movement among African Americans — as it emerged in postwar America and especially in the early 1960s — in generating "spin-off" movements among other oppressed communities. As Ian F. Haney Lopez explains about the center of Chicano ferment in this era, "more than any [other factor] the African American campaign for social equality stands out as one of the most powerful forces leading to political mobilization in East Los Angeles."[8] What fired the imaginations of many young Chicanos, however, was not simply the black demand for equality but the way that demand was increasingly being raised by mid-decade. It was the rising tide of brash and bold black militancy exemplified by the fiery speeches of Malcolm X, for example, that ignited radical Chicano nationalism in this period.[9]

And then, the South Central Los Angeles neighborhood of Watts exploded in a graphic display of black rage.[10] Commissioned reports confirmed the anger among black youths — a consequence of joblessness or underemployment and especially of repeated violent encounters with police. Almost immediately, the city and the state initiated various community programs to mitigate future unrest. But the desperation — and daring — of the Watts Rebellion stemmed from the very same conditions that Chicano residents had long faced, and all groups recognized it. In April 1966, for example, the Los Angeles Human Rights Commission collaborated with the Wilshire Boulevard Temple's Camp Hess Kramer to form the Mexican-American Youth Leadership Conference. Out of the three-day meeting convened to launch that organization, which brought together high school students to discuss how constructive change might be brought to their communities, emerged an extraordinary group of young people. Among them were David Sanchez, Vickie Castro, Moctesuma Esparza, Ralph Ramires, John Ortiz, Rachel Ochoa, and George Licon, who organized the Young Citizens for Community Action (YCCA) in East Los Angeles. In attempting to meet the needs of the surrounding community, the YCCA surveyed the educational situation in the area and sought Chicano representation on the Los Angeles Board of Education. Initially a liberal, youth-oriented reformist organization, the YCCA caught the wave of radicalism then sweeping the country.

With the help of Father John Luce of the Episcopal Church of the Epiphany in Lincoln Heights, the group opened a coffee shop, La Piranya, in September 1967. The shop provided a meeting place for Chicano youth and for others to read poetry, hold meetings, and organize informal political discussion groups. There, young Chicanos were exposed to the tumultuous political and social climate that had given rise to Black Power, student radicalism, and a general mood of increasing militancy. The youths exchanged books and records by and about Malcolm X, and, like their black contemporaries, they gravitated toward a more salient affirmation of their racial and cultural identity unencumbered by dependence on whites. At the same time, La Piranya also served as a meeting place for many of the leaders of the Black Power movement, including local Black Nationalists such as Maulana Karenga, founder of the US Organization. Other visitors included H. Rap Brown (later, Jamil Al-Amin) and Stokely Carmichael (later, Kwame Ture) who were leaders of both the Student Nonviolent Coordinating Committee (SNCC) and the Black Panther Party.[11]

The Panthers, established in Oakland in October 1966 as the Black Panther Party for Self-Defense, were well known in Los Angeles by mid-1967. Their notoriety came in part from their daring armed protest in Sacramento, at the state capitol, in May. While protesting a gun control bill aimed directly at their armed patrols of the police, by accident they ended up on the Assembly floor, which made their demonstration appear more like an armed invasion than a simple citizens' protest. News, and especially pictures, of the event spread nationally, even internationally. By the summer, Panthers were organizing in Los Angeles, and that fall they stepped up their efforts to prevent police terror in black communities in the city. Young Chicanos especially took notice. The Panthers' Ten-Point Platform and Program marked them as Black Nationalists in their political orientation, at least initially, though they were open to interracial alliances, particularly with other people of color.[12] Here, especially in East Los Angeles, was an opportunity to unite with Chicanos, for their chief reason for organizing—as for the Panthers—was police abuse and corruption.

On 24 November 1967, police officers were called to a civil disturbance in

East Los Angeles. Upon their arrival, the police beat one man unconscious. According to eyewitnesses, his wife and daughter were also beaten, pulled by the hair to a squad car where they were arrested and taken to jail. Similar stories of police brutality had been long known in black and Chicano communities in Los Angeles. It was the new militant climate, however, that moved Sanchez and other members of YCCA (now called Young Chicanos for Community Action) to seek redress by elevating police brutality to the top of the Chicano activists' agenda.[13]

On 3 December YCCA's David Sanchez cofounded the first unit of the Brown Berets, which demonstrated in front of the East Los Angeles Sheriff Station and the Hollenbeck Division of the Los Angeles Police Department. In addition to creating a formal organization to protest police brutality and the general oppression of Chicanos, Sanchez and others developed a uniform for its membership, which included a military-styled khaki "bush jacket." Sanchez also purchased twelve brown berets, which each member wore as his new uniform, thereby demonstrating to spectators that the group operated as a military unit.[14] Many observers knew that the beret had been derived from the BPP uniform. Though some may have attributed it to European guerrillas of the 1930s and 1940s, the presence of Panthers in Los Angeles did not escape the notice of these young organizers.[15] Moreover, official alliances and public pronouncements clearly reflect the influence of the Panther Party on the development of the Berets.

The Panthers adopted the black beret as part of its uniform in 1966, along with the black leather jacket, black slacks, powder-blue shirt, and black shoes.[16] While black militants before the Party wore sunglasses and leather jackets, the beret was unique to the Panthers. Soon, it became an icon of militancy and radicalism throughout the country. For Sanchez, the beret symbolized "the dignity and pride in the color of my skin and my race."[17] But, crucially, it also signaled identification with the Panthers' revolutionary program, replacing their black beret with the brown color of Chicano people.

The Brown Berets, like other organizations and Latino leaders of the era, were influenced by the rhetoric of cultural nationalism as well as revolutionary discourse in black circles. They listened intensely as recordings of pre-1964 Malcolm X discussed "blue-eyed devils." But they also listened to the post-1964 Malcolm X, who articulated a deep sense of international solidarity that was not beholden to the ideological cul-de-sac of narrow Black Nationalism. His emphasis on multinational alliances and cooperation resonated with the Brown Berets and, within weeks of their founding, they established alliances with the Black Power movement. By early 1968, as a campaign sprang up around Newton's arrest for the killing of an Oakland police officer, the Berets assisted in Free Huey rallies throughout California.

The Berets and Panthers enjoyed such a close relationship that when Los Angeles Panther Tommy Lewis was killed in a gun battle with police in August 1968, Berets helped in the funeral procession, one of whom even served as a pallbearer. Pictures and articles in the *Black Panther*, the BPP newspaper, announced the Panther-Beret alliance to the larger national readership, thereby boosting both the revolutionary credibility and visibility of each organization outside of their respective black and Latino communities. Elaine Brown, of the Los Angeles Panther chapter, noted in her memoirs that the two organizations had close relations, though the alliance was not formalized until late 1968: "On New Year's Eve, we held our . . . formal coalition meeting with the Brown Berets. Mexicans, or Chicanos, had joined with other Latinos to form the group. Patterning their program after ours, they wore brown berets, à la the Panther black beret, to represent the unity of our common revolutionary commitment. Black Panthers and Brown Berets welcomed in the New Year: 1969."[18]

Under Sanchez's leadership, the Berets created titles for the offices in their organization that mirrored those in the Black Panther Party: minister of information, minister of defense, minister of education, prime minister. They also created a Central Committee. Eventually the Berets adopted "eight points of attention," which copied verbatim the Party's eight points:

(1) Speak politely to the people.
(2) Pay family for what you buy from the people.
(3) Return everything you borrow.
(4) Pay for anything you damage.
(5) Do not hit or swear at the people.
(6) Do not damage property or possessions of the people.
(7) Do not take liberties with women.
(8) When working for the people do not get loaded.[19]

In mid-1968, the Brown Berets developed their own "Ten-Point Program," which was later modified into the "Thirteen-Point Program." Modeled after the Panthers' Ten-Point Platform and Program, the Berets' program echoed eight of the ten demands of the Party, including "an end to the robbery of our community by the capitalist businessmen"; exemption for all Chicanos from military service; the release of all Chicanos from jails; and the immediate end to police brutality.[20] The Berets also embraced the Panthers' emphasis on organizing the lumpen proletariat, "the poorest of the poor." Party philosophy insisted that the "[brother] on the block was ten motherfuckers when politically educated and if you got him organized."[21] Panther Minister of Information Eldridge Cleaver, in a widely distributed pamphlet written in 1968, valorized the poorest of the poor who were ripe for revolution: "[They are] the so-called 'Criminal Element,' those who live by their wits, existing off that which they rip off, who stick guns in the faces of businessmen.... Those who don't even want a job, who hate to work and can't relate to punching some pig's time clock, who would rather punch a pig in the mouth and rob him than punch that same pig's time clock and work for him, those whom Huey P. Newton calls 'the illegitimate capitalists.' In short, all those who simply have been locked out of the economy and robbed of their rightful social heritage."[22]

For Berets, this lumpen element meant gang members and others known collectively as *vatos locos* (crazy street guys). Their systematic recruitment of these young people was explicitly designed to help neutralize the deadly gang violence in Chicano communities and to politicize those most likely to engage in revolutionary action. Meanwhile, the focus on vatos locos was matched by the Berets' distrust of college students, who were derisively referred to as disconnected "bureaucrats," much as the Panthers sometimes called some black college students "armchair revolutionaries."[23] Of course, Newton and Seale had themselves been in college when they met; moreover, they and the Berets attracted some college students and worked closely with college populations. But the valorization of the lumpen, originating with the Panthers and copied by the Berets, took its toll on both groups, for the result was a tendency to simplify complex class dynamics. Middle-class activists were thus reduced to the politically tepid and reformist, while simultaneously the poor were lionized as stronger and more principled. In the process, the Panthers and the Berets opened themselves up to infiltration and the fomenting of internal dissension by the state.

Though the influence of Black Power on Chicano nationalists was most evident in the case of the Brown Berets, Latino radicals in general had always been the obvious allies for the Panthers from the moment the Party expanded its operations south of Oakland in 1967. In February 1968, for example, when thousands met at the Los Angeles Sports Arena for a massive Free

Huey rally, there was a significant Latin presence. Bringing together major figures of the Black Power movement, including Rap Brown, Stokely Carmichael, Bobby Seale, and Maulana Karenga, the event also featured grassroots nationalist Reies Tijerina and the Denver writer-activist Corky Gonzalez. Tijerina had already signed a pact with the Panthers the previous year, in which they announced that "the two peoples agree, to take the same position as to the crimes and sins of the Government of the United States of America." Tijerina's general position was clear: "Black and Brown should be together."[24] For his part, Gonzalez was deeply influenced by Black Nationalism. As the historian Tony Castro notes, in this period Gonzalez "began preaching a Chicano nationalism theme that has familiar rings of the . . . Black Power and Black Nationalism that dominated the 1960s."[25] Gonzalez explained that he saw a model of militancy in the black struggle: "I learned from the Black movement. Look at Watts. The day after the riots the government was dumping millions of dollars to help the people."[26]

Not ones to ignore an opportunity to reach out to Latinos, the Panthers made significant efforts to express solidarity with the Chicano struggle. Several articles in the *Black Panther* were printed in Spanish as well as English, and reports of Latino activism appeared regularly in the newspaper. The Panthers also made certain Chicano legal cases causes celebre. For example, on 1 May 1969 a San Francisco police officer was shot and killed, and seven Latino men were charged with murder. Christened Los Siete de La Raza, the group galvanized a movement among Chicanos to publicize the incident as a case of self-defense against police terror. The Panthers declared unequivocal support for the defendants, calling them "revolutionary heroes" who will "always be welcome in our camp." Party leaders proclaimed, "the Black Panther Party stands in support of Los Siete de La Raza and in firm solidarity with the Latin community." Chairman Bobby Seale even met with the families of the seven men. The father of two of the men announced that he wished to "thank the Black Panther Party for giving us the opportunity . . . to explain the repression" experienced by "the brown people, the yellow people and the black people." A bilingual copy of the speech was published in the *Black Panther*.[27]

Chicano Cultural Nationalism

The centerpiece of the new Chicano nationalism was Atzlan, the mythic homeland of ancient Aztecs. It was this land in the American southwest that provided the livelihood for the ancestors of the Chicanos, long before there was a United States. As the Chicanos said frequently at the time, "We did not cross the border. The border crossed us."[28] This Mexican American brand of cultural nationalism, spearheaded by Corky Gonzales, also helped popularize the term Chicano, thereby supplanting Mexican American and Hispano, an older term used since the late nineteenth century.

People of Mexican descent in the United States, like other people of color, had sought to approximate the cultural standards of white Americans, despite the overt hostility they endured at the hands of those whites. From the European standard of beauty to the pride that people took in proclaiming European ancestry (or the denial of Indian or African ancestry), Mexican people experienced the psychological effects of racism, again as had black people. Thus, in a culture where Spanish ancestry and white skin had benefits, the Brown Berets nevertheless joined Chicano cultural nationalists in insisting that they were a "bronze" people, whose native ancestors built great monuments and civilizations. The Aztecs were revered for their cultural and material achievements. Some nationalists even dropped their Spanish names, which were considered symbols of European imperialism and its conquest of the Aztec empire. And, like the Black Nationalist adoration of ancient Egypt, the Swahili, or West African empires, the Berets and other Chicano nationalists conveniently overlooked the imperialistic nature of their ancestors who built massive empires on the backs of subjugated and exploited victims. But, in a political climate that witnessed Black Nationalists like the self-described revolutionary nationalist Panthers and the cultural nationalist US Organization bickering over the role of cultural and revolutionary nationalism, the Berets easily blended the two ideologies.[29] And, strikingly, there were no major ideological disputes within the Chicano movement over the issue.

The Berets were highly critical of Chicano pride that sought community development through capitalism ("the sign that says 'se habla espanol' [Spanish spoken here], really means, 'come in we'll speak in Spanish and I'll charge you 30% credit charge'").[30] Still, they celebrated cultural nationalism ("before we could move the system that oppressed us, we first had to realize our own identity").[31] Thus, for example, control of the public schools was central to the Berets' effort to realize the study of Chicano history and culture. Suffering from extremely high dropout rates and a school board that appeared indifferent, if not hostile, the Berets worked closely on the "Eastside Blowouts" of March 1968. During these events, nearly ten thousand

Chicano students in five East Los Angeles high schools walked out of classes, demanding better education and Chicano control of schools. The result was an upsurge in student and youth militancy in Chicano communities in the state and in the Southwest generally. Thousands of Chicano high school students walked out in cities in California, Texas, Arizona, and Colorado demanding similar reforms.[32]

With increased activism came new police attention. On 9 June 1968, three months after the initial blowouts, police raided the homes and offices of thirteen Chicano activists who were arrested on charges of "conspiracy to disrupt the schools." The district attorney for Los Angeles County, Evelle J. Younger, charged the activists with a felony with a maximum prison sentence of sixty-six years for each person convicted. Seven of the thirteen who were arrested were Brown Berets, including the organization's founder.[33] Although all were eventually acquitted after two years of appeals, police harassment continued as the Berets became more militant. In fact, despite the violent gang epidemic in East Los Angeles, police devoted more energy — including arrests, surveillance, and number of man-hours — in their efforts to disrupt the Berets than they expended on any gang in the city.[34]

Meanwhile, mirroring the free clinics established by the Black Panthers, in May 1969 the Berets opened the East Los Angeles Free Clinic on Whittier Boulevard to serve poor Chicanos in the area. They also worked with the antiwar Chicano Moratorium Committee on a rally in December that brought together two thousand people to protest the Vietnam War and the disproportionate death rate of Chicano soldiers. In fact, Latinos accounted for 19.9 percent of the deaths in Vietnam by soldiers coming from the Southwest (California, Texas, New Mexico, Colorado, Arizona, and Nevada), even though they comprised only 11.7 percent of the population of those states. The death rate was higher than that for whites or blacks from the region.[35] A Second Chicano Moratorium rally at Laguna Park produced some five thousand marchers.

But, it was the Third Chicano Moratorium — one of the largest Chicano rallies ever — that made history. On 29 August 1970, as between twenty thousand and thirty thousand people marched along Whittier Boulevard, two thousand members of the Los Angeles police and county sheriff departments were called to help arrest Chicano youths who had allegedly stolen drinks from a local store. Police entered the park where the antiwar rally was being held and clashed with marchers. Shoving began, and officers fired tear gas into the crowd and attacked protesters. Men, women, and children were struck by hundreds of nightstick-wielding police. Three Chicanos were killed, including Ruben Salazar, a popular journalist who was shot in the head by a tear gas projectile while sitting in a cafe.[36]

During this period, the Brown Berets endured the repeated arrest of their leader, the bombing of their headquarters, and rising internal factionalism, but the group remained viable for two more years until they disbanded in 1973. At a press conference in October 1972, Beret prime minister David Sanchez, who had been sanctioned by the Central Committee for autocratic behavior, announced that the organization of ninety chapters and five thousand members would dissolve shortly. Expelled by the Brown Berets' Central Committee and accused of committing various criminal activities, Sanchez argued that he had been a victim of police infiltration and that the imminent disbanding of the Berets was necessary in order to avoid further disruption of the Chicano Power movement by the state. Subsequent U.S. congressional hearings on the FBI and its COINTELPRO program confirmed that the Brown Berets were targeted for "neutralization" by federal and local law enforcement. As the hearings revealed, neutralization included, at times, extralegal activities such as break-ins, false correspondence, wiretaps, beatings, and even murder.[37]

Puerto Rican Nationalism

Though the earliest Panther alliances with brown people developed with Chicanos in California, none had more intimate ties with the Black Panther Party or the Black Power movement than the largely Puerto Rican Young Lords Organization. The roots of that relationship — in the history of Puerto Rican nationalism — can in part be traced to the late nineteenth century when Puerto Ricans joined with Cubans in the common fight against Spanish imperialism. The United States won Puerto Rico, which had been a colony of Spain for four hundred years, after the U.S. defeat of Spain in the Spanish-Cuban-Filipino-American war of 1898. Unlike the other possessions procured in the war, such as the Philippines, Puerto Rico (along with Guam) never received independence from the United States. Though Puerto Rican nationalism would ebb and flow among relatively small leftist circles between 1900 and the 1950s, the popular grassroots nationalism of the late 1960s developed simultaneously among Puerto Ricans in two different cities.

By the 1940s, large communities of Puerto Ricans were already established in New York City as well as in a few other cities. And although many European immigrants to New York experienced challenges as newcomers, most Puerto Rican immigrants encountered unique limitations. Not only were they an immigrant group, they were not generally perceived as white. By midcentury in the United States, white supremacy allowed economic mobility, social intercourse, and political opportunities for Jews, Irish, and other European groups — opportunities that Puerto Ricans could not easily access. As a mixture of European, African, and native Taino peoples, Puerto Ricans found discrimination pervasive. Like other economically marginalized groups, poor Puerto Ricans in particular soon experienced the problems that typically develop in circumstances of concentrated urban poverty, material deprivation, and oppression. High school dropout rates were higher than in any other ethnic group in the city. Unemployment and underemployment, police brutality, and gang interaction thus provided the common experience of young people Spanish Harlem by 1968, the year that students established the Puerto Rican Student Association at City College as a Puerto Rican independence organization. That same year, Eduardo "Pancho" Cruz founded the Puerto Rican Student Union (PRSU), which helped lead a City College strike on campus in 1969. That strike, which was almost identical to the better-known one mounted by the Third World Liberation Front in the Bay Area, began with activities initiated by black students working for a black studies department and for more black faculty and students. Here again was the key inspirational dynamic of Black Power rhetoric, as Puerto Rican students formed the PRSU and contributed significantly to the efforts of the student strike, which eventually broadened the movement's demands to include a general ethnic studies department.[38]

A different type of politicization was developing among Puerto Ricans in the country's second-largest city, Chicago. Like New York and other major U.S. cities, Chicago suffered from a pervasive gang problem. While gangs sometimes transcended ethnic lines, they were generally composed of different racial and ethnic groups, and they were more likely to engage in criminal behavior against people of the same ethnicity.[39] But, in the politically charged climate of the late 1960s, the ubiquitous influence of the Black Power movement and the nature of urban rebellions forced many black gang members to reconsider their activities. Many abandoned gang life and joined the Nation of Islam, the Panther Party, or any of the scores of largely local nationalists and Black Power organizations in cities across the country. For Puerto Ricans, the process of politicization was similar. But, unlike any major Black Power organization in the country, the leading Puerto Rican radical organization — the Young Lords — came out of gang culture.

Puerto Ricans migrated to Chicago in substantial numbers after World War II. Lured by the new Commonwealth Office in Puerto Rico and the Point Four Program, many first arrived in New York, but disaffected with conditions there, moved to Chicago to work in manufacturing jobs or to locations elsewhere to work as migrant farm laborers.[40] Initially, these groups were not racialized as a distinct and organic "Other" as African Americans had been. Even by 1960, there was no identifiable geographically contiguous Puerto Rican community in Chicago. For example, Puerto Ricans were commonly found in white areas such as Oldtown and Marquette Park. And, unlike Puerto Ricans in New York, Chicago migrants did not have a particularly close geographic relationship with area African Americans. Moreover, as the most residentially segregated city in the United States, Chicago provided not only significant social intercourse between whites and Puerto Ricans, it circumscribed contact with African Americans and helped extend the virulently anti-black sentiment common among white Chicagoans. Much to the dismay of many Puerto Ricans, however, they became nonwhite in the popular consciousness of white Americans as their numbers increased. Uptown, Humboldt Park, and Lincoln Park emerged as communities with high concentrations of Puerto Ricans on the city's white North Side. In these areas, clashes between white gangs and Puerto Rican youth gave rise to Puerto Rican gangs as well as an inchoate political and racial consciousness.

Not surprisingly, job and housing discrimination, as well as police brutality, laid the foundation for an explosion of racial violence on 12 June 1966. For four days, urban unrest among Puerto Ricans shook the city, including along Division Street in the areas of Uptown, Humbolt Park, and Lincoln Park. Though Puerto Rican leadership had long complained of discrimination, most were loathe to be lumped together with African Americans, who were largely seen as more marginalized and despised than they. In fact, when Martin Luther King Jr. offered to assist in negotiations between the aggrieved communities in the city, Puerto Rican leaders turned down his offer.[41] Despite the relatively tepid leadership of the Spanish Action Committee in the city, which embraced a variant of European (white) ethnicity, Puerto Rican street youth proved central to deconstructing traditional notions of community, racial, and ethnic identity as the Black Power movement took root. In this process no group was as important as the Young Lords.

The Young Lords

Formed in 1959 by seven Chicago Puerto Rican youths, the Young Lords engaged in battles with Italians, "Billigans" (Appalachian whites), and other Latinos—battles that increased in the early 1960s when Jose "Cha Cha" Jimenez was elected chairman of the organization. Then, the Division Street unrest, as well as the spread of Black Power, forced Young Lord leaders to reevaluate their organization by the late 1960s. In 1966, members of various Black Nationalist organizations fanned across the Southside and Westside to meet with various street gangs. The Deacons for Defense, the Revolutionary Action Movement, SNCC, the Nation of Islam, and others directed gangs to cease attacks on black people and instead prepare to be agents for black people's liberation. One gangster explained that "the militants came in and say why be a gangbanger and kill each other when you can kill the honkey[,] and we began to see that the enemy was not black." The hallmark of the new militancy was a renunciation of the fear of white power, and black youths were the first to do so. As Elzy, a twenty-year-old Vice Lord, stated, "We were scared of the honkies but this awareness thing has kicked all that bullshit aside."[42] By 1967, the three largest gangs, the Vice Lords, Blackstone Rangers, and the Gangster Disciples established the LSD (Lords, Stones, and Disciples) peace treaty and began investing in commercial endeavors, including cafés, pool halls, and even a bookstore. Owing to gang-related activities Cha Cha Jimenez had served a year in prison, and it was there where he was exposed to Black Nationalism. As a result, he now insisted that the Young Lords should similarly engage in constructive activities.[43]

The café opened by the Young Lords, Uptight #2, was a place for talk about the general political and cultural upheaval in the country as well as more mundane topics. Programs included a community summer picnic, drug education, and a Christmas giveaway of food and toys. The Lords even began a dialogue with the largest street gang in the country, the notorious Black Stone Rangers, and with them they cosponsored a program called a Month of Soul Dances.[44] While these efforts impressed many liberals, the Illinois deputy chairman Fred Hampton and the local Panthers hoped to make the Lords into revolutionaries. In December 1968 Hampton met with Cha Cha Jimenez.

In accordance with the Party's theories of class noted above, the Panthers viewed the politicization of street gangs as essential to the political transformation of the country's internal colonies. The urban rebellions that often included the poorest and most maligned elements in the community were the precursor to revolution, argued Party leaders. The lumpen had guns and were not afraid to use them. Unfortunately, the Panthers explained, that element was not yet politically sophisticated enough to target the "pig power structure" as frequently and in as organized a fashion as the circumstances dictated. The rebellions of the day, insisted Huey Newton, were "sporadic, short-lived, and costly in violence against the people." The task was clear: "The Vanguard Party must provide leadership for the people. It must teach correct strategic methods of prolonged resistance through literature and activities. If the activities of the Party are respected by the people, the people will follow the example."[45] In the Panthers' view, the efforts of the Lords and the Rangers had been indicative of the political transformation that would make agents of oppression into agents of liberation. But only if mobilized and directed politically. The Lords, Rangers, and other street gangs could be made into harbingers of freedom, justice, and power for the people, if they operated under the direction of the revolutionary vanguard.

As Hampton began his dialogue with Jimenez, he also met with Jeff Fort, the leader of the Blackstone Rangers. Fort, less warm to the idea of radical politics than Jimenez, was nevertheless impressed with the militancy that characterized the Panthers, and he began to envision a Puerto Rican revolutionary organization that could realize liberation for Puerto Ricans on the island as well as on the mainland. For their part, the Lords realized that they had been acting like social workers by only addressing the symptoms and not the cause of social illness. "Giving gifts wasn't going to help their people," Jimenez said of the Lords. "They had to deal with the system that was messing them over."[46] Like African American gangs, the Puerto Rican Lords became critical of their street violence. They initiated a peace treaty with virtually all of their former enemies, advising them to cease fighting with one other and to address their anger "against the capitalist institutions that are oppressing us." The Latin Kings, the city's largest Latino gang, began to organize politically as well, even opening a breakfast program for children. By May 1969, the Lords had officially made a pact with the Panthers and the Young Patriots, a gang of white Appalachian youths from the city's Uptown section on the North Side.[47]

In this new "Rainbow Coalition," the Lords and Patriots dutifully modeled themselves after the Panther Party, believing it to be the vanguard. Though the Panthers had been referring to themselves as a vanguard party from at least late 1968, it was not until early 1969 that the term was more widely adopted by other radical ethnic nationalists like the Chinese Red Guard, I Wor Kuen, and the Japanese Yellow Brotherhood.[48] The Lords Chairman explained that, "as we read and study other organizations . . . we see and we recognize the Black Panther Party as a revolutionary vanguard. And we feel that as revolutionaries we should follow the vanguard party."[49] In their respective communities, the Lords and Patriots held political education classes, organized free breakfast programs for poor children, and monitored police activities. They created an organizational structure that reflected Panther influence, which included ministers of information, defense, and education, and a Central Committee with field marshals. The Patriots developed an Eleven-Point Program and Platform that borrowed heavily from the Panthers, as did the Lords' Thirteen-Point Program and Platform.[50] All three organizations sponsored events together, with each providing speakers and security. The alliance sometimes produced a seemingly odd picture: Fred Hampton and Cha Cha Jimenez giving fiery speeches on revolutionary struggle, while white men wearing berets, sunglasses, and Confederate rebel flags sewn onto their jackets helped to provide security for them. Crucially, though, despite the conspicuous display of the battle flag of the notoriously racist Confederacy, the Patriots demonstrated the ability of a white group to allow a revolutionary black group to assume the lead role in a movement.[51] Most important, the Young Patriots and Young Lords became nationally known through this Rainbow Coalition, which was featured regularly in articles in the *Black Panther*, the *Guardian*, and elsewhere in the alternative press in early 1969. And, in March 1969, the Coalition sent representatives to the annual convention of the Students for a Democratic Society (SDS), where Joe Martinez, an SDS member from Florida, met with Young Lord founders and was granted permission to start a branch in New York.[52]

Amid militant protests early that year at New York's City College, students had formed the Sociedad de Albizu Campos (SAC) to bring together the militancy of college radicals with that of *El Barrio*. Named after the Puerto Rican nationalist Pedro Albizu Campos who, as "El Maestro," inspired Puerto Ricans with calls for independence and national pride, SAC reflected the spirit of the *indepentistas*. There were, however, other concerns about the plight of Puerto Ricans on the mainland. In a struggle to bridge the chasm between unorganized street militancy and that of the college campus, the community-based activists Pablo "Yoruba" Guzman and David Perez joined SAC and became the links to *El Barrio* that the organization sought. Yoruba, who took his name from a major ethnic group in Nigeria, had a strong affinity to Africa as well as Puerto Rico. Perez, who was born in Puerto Rico and raised in Chicago, had involved himself in radical politics before moving to New York. Simultaneously SAC members were regularly reading the *Black Panther* and had learned of the Rainbow Coalition established by Fred Hampton. After merging with other local Puerto Rican activist organizations SAC met with Martinez, and on 26 July 1969 a coalition was formed that became the New York State Chapter of the Young Lords Organization (YLO).[53]

The Young Lords from New York spread to several cities along the East Coast, including Philadelphia, Newark, and Bridgeport, Connecticut. Panthers in each city worked with the group in various ways, including protests and funerals. Panther paraphernalia was also available at the YLO's offices.[54] Within weeks, the Young Lords captured headlines. They organized against police brutality, poor city services, slum housing, and poor education, and in December 1969 they occupied a Methodist church at 111th and Lexington, declaring it the "People's Church." In this last action, they held off the police for ten days, as the church became a center for free breakfast, clothes, health care, political education, and cultural events. In an era of increasing public battles over the "law and order" conservatism of President Nixon's "silent majority," on the one hand, and the rising tide of baby boomer leftist activism, on the other, events like the occupation were sensational news. In turn, the media attention was crucial in popularizing the organization to millions. Several months later, on 17 July 1970, YLO activities had extended into Lincoln Hospital, where group members staged an occupation to protest neglect and inadequate health care for the poor by the city government. Though expelled by the police, the one hundred occupiers had brought public attention to insufficient medical care in poor communities. The mayor of New York, John Lindsay, promised community activists that the city would build a new hospital on East 149th Street to replace the dilapidated Lincoln Hospital. The new facility opened in 1976.[55]

As adherents of Puerto Rican independence, the Lords denounced the cardinal "three evils": capitalism, racism, and imperialism. The group was represented in significant numbers along the East Coast in every major Puerto Rican community, sponsoring free breakfasts, drug detoxification, and garbage clean-up programs in chapters in several states. They brought attention to police brutality, worked closely with students on college and high school campuses, and even found success organizing in prisons. Indeed, it came as no surprise to these activists that, during the Attica Prison uprising in September 1971, insurgents issued a list of over twenty demands to prison officials that included a request for the presence of the Young Lords and the Black Panther Party to serve as observers and advisors. In many cities, Lords worked in alliances with Black Power advocates and helped realize more community control of police, political reform, and political mobilization for poor and working-class people.

Interestingly, like the Brown Berets the Young Lords were able to work with organizations openly hostile to the Black Panthers, despite their official pact with the Party. The relationship between black and brown, that is, was not one-dimensional. In the early 1970s, for example, the Young Lords in Newark, New Jersey, established an alliance with the Committee for a Unified Newark, which was led by the cultural nationalist and ally of Maulana Karenga's, Amiri Baraka.[56] Ultimately, these alliances may suggest that those groups that the Panthers took to be their enemies may not necessarily have been so. More important, perhaps, the behavior of the Young Lords reflects the limits of Panther influence over the Lords, who were independent enough to determine which organizations were friendly to their particular concerns and needs. Indeed, there is no evidence that their alliance with Baraka disrupted their alliance with the Panthers, at least in part because Panther leaders had no desire to control or absorb the Lords.

Because of their alliances with black organizations, the politicization of Young Lords evoked a reevaluation of Puerto Rican notions of race. Many Puerto Ricans identified as white and simultaneously embraced negative views of black people, whether those people were fellow Puerto Ricans or not. The Lords, though, flatly rejected white supremacist color/racial hierarchies, and many, in fact, affirmed their affinity with Africa and grew Afro hairstyles — the first major example of Puerto Rican nationalism that simultaneously addressed the concerns of Puerto Ricans on the mainland and on the island, and inveighed against Puerto Ricans' own racial prejudice.[57] Further, revolutionary nationalist organizations like the Lords adopted an anticapitalist stance, picturing communities of color in the United States as cheap labor and resources for capitalists, with benefits for expanding the white middle and working classes. Since racism was real, the latter, out of ignorance and cultural tradition, rejected what they shared with working-class people of color, something the Young Patriots, Rising Up Angry, and the White Panthers sought to change by modeling themselves after the Black Panther Party. Meanwhile, for their own reasons, radicals of color gravitated toward the Party and the symbolism of Black Power.

The issue of class exploitation had long been a major concern for leftists in the Communist Party and the Socialist Workers Party, and more now for the Black Panther Party and even the Young Lords. However, the highly racialized climate in the United States made interracial political organization difficult, particularly with poor and working-class whites, who were considered by many to be a more overt and crude group of racists than the middle and upper classes. Moreover, the American tradition of class exploitation was significantly bolstered by white supremacy, which had profound psychological and cultural ramifications.[58] People of color who were involved in the leftist liberation movements of the late-sixties era, then, were committed to liberating themselves along class and cultural lines simultaneously. For Puerto Ricans in the East and Midwest, as for the Chicanos in the Southwest, the deep-rooted trappings of white supremacy were not always challenged, despite the myth of racial tolerance on the island. From folk songs, sayings such as *pelo malo* ("bad hair") for kinky hair, to the concept of *mejorar la raza* ("bettering the race") by whitening, white supremacy was ubiquitous, if different in its American variant. The Puerto Rican color hierarchy was fundamentally porous and allowed darker Puerto Ricans who were considered "Negroes" or "mulattoes" to "ascend" to whiteness with economic success. But, the aspersions of being dark were nonetheless insidious and widespread, on the island and in America.[59]

In the United States, however, some Puerto Rican baby boomers did begin to critically adjust their own notions of ethnicity, race, and identity. They increasingly challenged traditional notions of race, and explicitly addressed their own history of racism. These shifts were the result of the peculiar American racial landscape and its history of codified white supremacy, which chiefly rested on a white/black binary. Despite the special attention given to African Americans in their fight against white supremacy, Puerto Ricans could not deny their similar circumstances based on racism. Again, though, their exposure to the rhetoric of the Black Power movement, which stressed the need to resist the cultural and psychological entrapments of whiteness, had a significant impact. Black Power advocates not only celebrated black peoples' history and beauty, but many also openly vilified whites, calling them "honkies," "crackers," "ofays," and "devils." Some publicly joked about the way whites smelled, danced, and lacked hygiene or morality. Though not monolithic in their attitudes toward whites, Black Power proponents deconstructed whiteness in ways not seen in the civil rights movement. The generations of self-hate and internalization of white supremacy were being addressed in a profound moment of group catharsis. Young Puerto Ricans especially took notice; they, too, had to affirm themselves in ways not seen heretofore, while addressing the complicated racial politics of their time. Thus, Puerto Rican radical ethnic nationalists initiated systematic efforts to make the psychic break from whiteness. Moreover, they conspicuously celebrated Puerto Rican culture and identity that was "Third World" and thus, in effect, not white. This was a fundamental departure for the Puerto Rican nationalism and represented a significant break from earlier leaders and movements.

The Young Lords, as the first Puerto Rican radical ethnic nationalist group with a national appeal, denounced racism, while simultaneously calling for greater emphasis on their African and Taino histories. Juan Gonzalez, the minister of information for the Young Lords, explained the history of Puerto Rico, where the earliest census records showed that blacks and Indians comprised the majority while "whites were always the smallest part of the population."[60] This message offered a cultural nationalist challenge to how Puerto Ricans viewed themselves, while still adhering to the fundamental tenets of revolutionary nationalism. Although over 90 percent of Puerto Ricans on the mainland classified themselves as white at this time, the Young Lords commonly referred to whites and Puerto Ricans as separate and distinct. Cha Cha Jimenez and other Lords were careful to refer to the range of colors among Puerto Ricans as an instructive tool to inveigh against race-only discourse, while celebrating an identity that was not white. Jimenez, for example, would not make reference to even the lightest Puerto Ricans as "white." In discussing the importance of class struggle, he insisted that "we relate to the class struggle because there's Puerto Ricans that are real black, then there's Puerto Ricans that are light-skinned like myself."[61] Though he would refer to Puerto Ricans as "black," "red" and "yellow," the lightest were simply "light-skinned." He also insisted that it was inefficacious to insist on more "Puerto Rican" police to replace "white" police, when the fundamental job of the police was to operate as "bodyguards for the capitalists."[62] Here, Jimenez implied that, unlike the Poles, Italians, or Irish in Chicago, Puerto Ricans as a group were distinct from European (read as "white") ethnic groups. He acknowledged the real ramifications of race, yet race itself was a social construct that, with its slippery contours, included yet rejected Puerto Ricans as "others" in American racial politics.[63]

The Young Lords and other Puerto Rican militants unequivocally celebrated their Puerto Rican identity with great zeal. And though they were nationalists they were careful to transcend the debilitating xenophobia that often typifies nationalist movements. Alliances with other people of color as well as whites were central to the YLO. Even when highlighting Puerto Rican culture and history, the Lords tended to be broad. In referring to the creation of a Puerto Rican cultural center, Cha Cha Jimenez noted that it must "include some black culture, cause we got some blacks; we want to include some Chicano culture too, cause we want to include all Latins. We want to invite the people from the white community. We'll educate them." Unable to embrace a narrow form of nationalism, the YLO chairman explained, "[w]e feel that we are revolutionaries and revolutionaries have no race."[64]

Still, what is striking about the ethnic/national emphasis of the Young Lords is that the organization was never homogenous. Though mostly Puerto Rican, the Lords had Chicano members from its earliest years as a street gang. When it evolved into a radical ethnic nationalist organization, many non-Puerto Ricans adopted its special attention to Puerto Rican independence. In fact, Omar Lopez, a Chicano member, coined the Lords' slogan, "Tengo Puerto Rico en mi corazon" ("I have Puerto Rico in my heart").[65] On the East Coast the Young Lords had members who were Cuban, Dominican, Panamanian, and Colombian. An estimated 25 percent of the Young Lords membership was African American. Despite the explicit emphasis on Puerto Rican politics and welfare, the organization was broad enough to include serious support for "power to all oppressed people," which included all "Third World people." Some non-Puerto Ricans even held prominent positions in the organization, like Denise Oliver, an African American who was the first woman on the Central Committee and who served as the minister of economic development from 1970 to 1971.[66]

Although Puerto Rican identity reflected a protean quality, then, it was not entirely unique. Chicanos similarly shifted identities. And the Young Lords were not the only radical ethnic nationalist group with a heterogeneous membership. But, as much as the Young Lords helped rearticulate ethnic identity, they also addressed deep-seated psychological issues. On several occasions, for instance, Young Lords leaders indicated that one of their goals was to reject the notion of Puerto Rican passivity. Cha Cha Jimenez was careful to anchor YLO radicalism in a tradition of Puerto Rican struggle, not as an aberration from obsequiousness: "People consider Puerto Ricans as passive ... but as recently as 1950 there was a revolution in Puerto Rico. Lots of revolutionaries have come out of Puerto Rico." Despite the "Uncle Toms" who oppressed the people of Puerto Rico, Puerto Ricans were not unfamiliar with resistance, he explained.[67] And yet many Puerto Ricans found the Lords to be truly unique. "Puerto Ricans had been psyched into believing this myth about being docile," said Pablo Guzman. "A lot of Puerto Ricans really thought that the man in blue was the baddest thing going." Indeed, Guzman was shocked to learn in the Black Panther newspaper about the militancy of the Lords for the first time: "Cha Cha was talking about revolution and socialism and the liberation of Puerto Rico and the right to self-determination and all this stuff that I ain't *never* heard a spic say. I mean, I hadn't never heard no Puerto Rican talking this—just black people were talking this way, you know. And I said, 'damn! Check this out.' That's what really got us started."[68]

The Young Lords' conspicuous demonstrations of courage, militancy, and discipline, according to Guzman, provided models of revolutionary strength to the people in *El Barrio*. And, there were palpable changes in the self-awareness among Puerto Rican youth as well as among the police assigned the task of controlling them. "Before the Young Lords Party began people used to walk with their heads down ... and the pigs would walk through the colonies, man, like they owned the block. They'd come in here with no kind of respect in their eyes." But after the appearance of their revolutionary examples, the Lords claimed, the people had been psychologically empowered. They began to shed the fear that theorist Frantz Fanon said crippled the colonized. Police officers, no longer taking Puerto Rican deference for granted, treaded with greater caution. The people were now "fighting toe to toe" with the oppressor. In Guzman's view at the time, "the people now have hope."[69]

Gender and Nationalism

Despite their militant—indeed, military—posture, the Panthers proved to be largely ineffective in defending themselves against the massive assault mounted against them by the state in the late 1960s and early 1970s. Still, they provided perhaps the most potent model for young people of color longing for liberation during this period. And they especially appealed to men of color, who experienced the historic weight of the pervasive humiliation and marginalization of their manhood. The response was often a boldly masculinist one.

Machismo was palpable for Chicano militants. A clear masculine trope ran through the language of Chicano power, which bore a striking similarity to the language of Black Power. Chicano students in California warned that they would vigorously resist the "emasculation" of Chicanos. Others wrote poetry about liberating Chicano manhood.

> Until yesterday you called me a good Chicano . . . I was meek, humble, goddamned ignorant.
> I was young, passive. I was a good american.
> I licked the hand that fed me crumbs.

However, in transition, a new Chicano had emerged from the despair:

> A man- re-born a man, has learned to stand up, bear the burden of his people on his back.
> I — no longer dead. I — alive. See my people rising, my peasant blood sings with pride.
> See my people refuse to bend, prostitutes for an anglo dog.
> See a multitude of clenched fists, casting off shackles of death.
> See brothers join hand in hand, muscular and strong, march before the sun.[70]

In using such language Chicano nationalists attempted to forge a new identity as "liberated" men, rendering women rhetorically invisible. Women in the Brown Berets were active in all of the group's functions, which included military drills and protests; however, their role remained largely secondary. Women wrote for the organization's newspaper, *La Causa*, but their articles rarely focused on sexism, in society or among the Berets. Typically, the liberation of La Raza was the primary goal, while women's liberation was often viewed as a white women's movement. In 1969–1970 Grace Reyes wrote on subjects of particular concern to women in *La Causa*. The birth control pill had special significance for women who could more effectively choose when to give birth, and feminists typically viewed it as liberating. But, like many Black Nationalists of the day, Reyes saw the pill as an insidious attempt to curb the birth rate of people of color, not to empower women.[71] Reflecting the rising tide of feminism at large, though, by 1971

Chicana feminists demanded that women be moved to the center of Beret activities. In one *La Causa* article the writer complained that Chicanas had been active in all of the group's functions, but had no leadership role. Women were simply "working for the Beret guys" and not realizing their complete talents and skills.[72]

Women insisted that a successful revolution "must have full involvement from both Chicanos and Chicanas." But, to avoid any confusion with the burgeoning women's liberation movement, they declared that "we're not talking about women's liberation because, like that's not ours. That's a white thing. We're talking about our Raza's liberation." Perhaps in part for that reason, though Chicanas voiced their frustrations via the official organ of the Berets, a recalcitrant male leadership made no substantive changes regarding the organization's relationship with women.[73] A similar movement to challenge patriarchy occurred within the Puerto Rican Young Lords Organization, but that challenged produced very different reactions.

The YLO, in fact, experienced a fissure between its New York chapter and Chicago in 1970. The East Coast chapters under the direction of New York leadership became the Young Lords Party (YLP), which launched its bilingual paper, *Palante!*, in May 1970. *Palante!* reflected the hypermasculinity of the Puerto Rican nationalist movement, with acclamations that "machismo must be revolutionary."[74] Moreover, the organization excluded women from leadership roles, despite a general policy that granted all members access to all organizational activities. Already, in 1969, several female members had formed a women's caucus in reaction to Lords' machismo.[75]

Caucus members shared stories of confronting on a regular basis their comradres' sexism, thus forcing the male leadership to respond. Denise Oliver explained that equality for women was revolutionary and that machismo infected both men and women. For not only were the "brothers off the street" unaccustomed to gender equality, many women had been similarly convinced of their role as helpers of men. "In Puerto Rican society," Oliver stated, "the woman is taught to cater to the . . . demands of her father or husband. She is taught that she is inferior in her own ways."[76] The women's caucus issued demands for an end to sexual discrimination and the full inclusion of women into the leadership. The Central Committee reacted swiftly by promoting Denise Oliver and Gloria Fontanez to the Central Committee. The Lords also adopted a new slogan, "Abajo con machismo!" (Down with machismo!), which appeared in the newspaper and in other official YLP releases. They even made changes to the Party's thirteen-point program, in which they denounced sexism in point five: "Puerto Rican women," the Young Lords proclaimed, "will be neither behind nor in front of their brothers but always alongside them in mutual respect and love."[77] For many Lords, attacking sexism became a key step in the movement toward liberation. Indeed, men even formed a male caucus to discuss patriarchy and ways to resist it. Some men who considered themselves openminded and progressive realized just how ubiquitous sexism was in society generally. Pablo Guzman insisted that sexism was "impractical" to revolutionary struggle and he welcomed the women's liberation agenda, though he pointed out that the struggles of "Third World women" differed from those of white women, who "have been put on a pedestal," while white men raped and otherwise exploited women of color.[78] Others agreed that there were fundamentally different concerns between women of color and white women in the women's liberation movement. Iris Morales, a Central Committee member, noted later that "we were critical of that movement for purporting to speak for all women when it represented primarily white, middle-class women. It never successfully addressed the concerns of women of color and poor women."[79]

Some have argued that the Black Power movement and its adherents like the Black Panther Party were particularly sexist.[80] The movement clearly lionized black men as hypermacho leaders, fighters, and defenders of black people, and the bravado, militant rhetoric, and general character of Black Power were decidedly male-oriented. But, while Black Power advocates and Puerto Rican ethnic nationalists used hyperbolic language to express their politics, the movement was not monolithic. In 1968, the Panthers adopted the "eight points of attention" (largely derived from Mao's "Little Red Book"). Former Panther Safiya Bukhari-Alston marked the stricture against "tak[ing] liberties with women" as a "monumental step forward in addressing the issue of the treatment of women." Bukhari-Alston correctly noted that the Panthers were born in a sexist society and not above its predilections. But "the simple fact that the issue was placed in/on the books was a step forward. Now we had to make it a part of our everyday lives, the everyday lives of the lumpen who were the majority element of the Black Panther Party."[81]

Elaine Brown echoes this perspective when she asks, "Did these brothers drop from 'revolutionary heaven'? Of course not. We were working through issues [like sexism]."[82] Clearly there were cases of sexual abuse of women, as

Brown details in her own autobiography. But some Panthers argue that the experiences of the West Coast Panthers (such as Brown) were not the norm for the country. Akua Njeri recalls that she did not feel marginalized as a Panther woman in Chicago. "Men did not try to take advantage of sisters in our chapter. We had respect. Men and women both cleaned and cooked for the children. We also trained together. We were all Panthers."[83] Lee Lew-Lee, a member in Harlem, notes that Afeni Shakur, "basically led the chapter after the Panther 21 trial ended in acquittal. Women and men worked together without the very rampant type of sexism that was found on the West Coast."[84]

Despite the relative prominence of some Panther women and the tolerance that many enjoyed, however, the Party was not free of sexism. Most of its leaders were men, though it seems women made up roughly half of the membership.[85] Even prominent women such as Kathleen Cleaver experienced macho recalcitrance in their male peers. As Ericka Huggins, a celebrated national Panther, recalled: "There were men who thought that women were to be slept with. I dealt with male chauvinism." Clearly, women experienced similar sexual encounters outside the Party in places of employment and even churches. This did not, however, excuse abusive actions inside the Party. Eldridge Cleaver explained to men that their freedom could not be won at the expense of women's liberation. "The women are our half. They're not our weaker half; they're not our stronger half. They are our other half." And several articles written by female Panthers appeared in the *Black Panther* extolling Cleaver's position while calling to task recalcitrant male members for their continued sexism.[86]

In 1970, the Black Panther Party became the first major black organization to align itself with the women's liberation movement, as well as with the gay liberation movement. The Panthers also denounced sexism on several occasions and appointed women to key positions of leadership throughout the country. This move included appointing Elaine Brown as chair, and she effectively led the organization for four years.[87] The former minister of culture Emory Douglas recalls that stubborn men had no choice. Rules were rules. They either followed them or left the organization.[88] Though this challenge to chauvinism was tempered by the evident sexism of Huey Newton and others even as the Party moved into alliances with feminists, it is clear that the history of women in the organization is complex.[89]

The Young Lords similarly accepted the challenge to transcend the narrow confines of patriarchy and in so doing made substantive changes to their organization's rhetoric and style. Clearly, the liberation of a nation could not tolerate the oppression of half of its people. Still, it is equally clear that there was no formula or model for ethnic nationalists to respond to sexism. Latino Americans, like white and black Americans, lived in a patriarchal culture that often openly endorsed male domination. Mainstream African American and Latino organizations reflected patriarchal traditions without considerable challenges and upheaval. The national leadership of more mainstream organizations like the NAACP, the League of Latin America Citizens, and the Democratic and Republican parties were certainly more male-dominated than either the Panthers or the Lords. But it was the passion for total liberation that raised the expectations of struggle for many radical ethnic nationalists. Despite their criticism of the white-oriented women's movement, the radical ethnic nationalists were aware that women's liberation was intrinsic to national liberation. Some, like the Brown Berets, were less successful than others, like the Lords or Panthers, in denouncing sexism, but that these revolutionaries struggled with the issues there can be no doubt.

Conclusion

Like African Americans who lived in a virulently anti-black world and had to overcome psychological oppression, Latinos had to resist the culturally hegemonic forces of white supremacy as well as the de facto policies that discriminated against them. In the midst of this rejection of cultural orthodoxy, there emerged the opportunity to openly criticize and change traditional gender roles in ways that many mainstream organizations had not. This willingness to consider new challenges and ideas made these ethnic nationalist organizations attractive to young people. Why the Berets were less successful than some others in challenging sexism is unclear. Patriarchy has been historically pervasive in Mexico, as it has been in the United States and Puerto Rico. And women in the Berets did resist sexism and patriarchy. However, male obstinacy, it appears, was simply greater than that resistance.

At the same time, the radical ethnic nationalism of the Lords and Berets reflected a conscious effort to culturally affirm people who languished under a dehumanizing system of racial oppression, while these movements also refused to pander to the convenient race-only discourse that attracted many. The proponents of radical ethnic nationalism gloried in their ethnicity while they eagerly embraced a polysemic nationalist framework that pulled from

Fanon, Marx, Che, and Mao. In that way, they were significantly influenced by the political analysis of the Black Panther Party. But as seen above, Black Power's influence on non-African Americans altered the popular discourse and public discussion of identity and equality in the United States in sometimes unexpected ways. Outside and inside radical ethnic nationalist communities, militants rebuked whiteness and its implications, such as forms of status dependent on the subjugation of nonwhites, thus deligitimizing white superiority by stripping whiteness of its cultural prestige. Their open ridiculing of whites—for their smell, lack of rhythm, lack of hygiene, lack of morality, lack of beauty, and, at bottom, lack of humanity—may seem contrary to the practices of both the nonviolent integrationists and the anti-racist Panthers. But such ridicule of whites was an attempt to replace generations of self-hate with self-love.

Beyond the cultural and psychological effects that radical ethnic nationalism introduced to the New Left of the late 1960s and early 1970s, the movement was truly a unique phenomenon. There are no other major examples of ethnic nationalist movements establishing alliances as was done by the young radicals of the Black Power era. African American, white, Puerto Rican, Chicano, Asian, and Native American radicals merged ethnic nationalist rhetoric with a struggle that emphasized class conflict and interracial coalitions. When the Panther Party coined the slogan "All Power to the People," it was attempting to go beyond the call for Black Power by transcending race. Unique among political movements anywhere, this was an example of radicalism that adapted to the highly racialized climate of the United States while adhering to the fundamental principles of Marxism-Leninism that generally criticized nationalism as a bourgeois effort to subvert true radicalism. And yet, the Panthers were at the center of a Black Power movement that provided the earliest examples of cultural nationalism and mobilization around ethnic nationalist causes. More specifically, the Panthers offered a paradigm of radical ethnic nationalism, a vanguard party for a capacious revolutionary nationalist movement, and an unprecedented activist appeal in the annals of radical struggle.

Latino radical ethnic nationalism did not, however, depend solely on the Black Panthers for symbolism, political direction, or motivation. In fact, the various organizations necessarily influenced each other in alliances, networks, conferences, and general dialogue. To paraphrase integrationists who stressed the need to work with white liberals, black people could not go it alone. Chicano and Puerto Rican allies, as well as those from white, Asian, and Native American groups, were essential to forming a broad-based and effective movement to realize the liberation that the Panthers envisioned. In addition, the international dynamics that influenced Black Power similarly informed Latino and Asian struggle in the United States. If Mao Zedong served as an inspiration to the Panthers as well as to the Red Guards, then the Brown Berets and Young Lords had a particular affinity for Che Guevara, whom the Panthers also adored. The Black Power movement in general and the Panthers in particular, then, aided in a social and cultural transformation that would have substantive effects on the cultural and political landscape — a transformation that was, however, incomprehensible outside their interaction with Latino radicalism.

Notes

1. The connections between the Black Power movement in the United States and the period's global events were many. See "Black Power Studies: A New Scholarship," edited by Peniel Joseph, special issue, *Black Scholar* 31.3–4 (2001); William Van Deburg, *New Day in Babylon* (Chicago: University of Chicago Press, 1992); Ogbar, *Black Power: Radical Politics and African American Identity* (Baltimore: Johns Hopkins University Press, 2004).
2. Tony Castro, *Chicano Power: The Emergence of Mexican America* (New York: Saturday Review Press, 1974), 116.
3. Race, as understood in the nineteenth-century United States, granted European-descended people access to jobs, land, suffrage, education, and other privileges denied to black and Indian people. Indians, except for those in the western regions, had generally dropped from the national discussion of race by the mid-nineteenth century. The resultant racial binary of white-black relations would characterize popular racial discourse throughout the twentieth century, although laws would also prevent Asians and Latinos from access to the benefits of whiteness. For an examination of the shifts in Chicano racial identity generally, see Ian F. Haney Lopez, *Racism on Trial: The Chicano Fight for Justice* (Cambridge, Mass.: Belknap Press, 2003); Neil Foley, "Straddling the Color Line: The Legal Construction of Hispanic Identity in Texas," in *Not Just Black or White*, edited by Nancy Foner and George Frederickson (New York: Russell Sage Foundation, 2004). For more general discussions, see Ian F. Haney Lopez, *White by Law: The Legal Construction of Race* (New York: New York University Press, 1998); Sharon M. Lee, "Racial Classifications in the U.S. Census: 1890–1990," *Ethnic and Racial Studies* 16 (January 1993): 75–94; David R. Roediger, *The Wages of Whiteness: Race and the Making of the American Working Class* (London: Verso, 1991).
4. Rodolfo Acuna, *Occupied America: A History of Chicanos*, 3rd ed. (New York: HarperCollins, 1988), 180, 254–55.

5. Albert M. Camarillo, "Black and Brown in Compton: Demographic Change, Suburban Decline, and Intergroup Relations in a South Central Los Angeles Community," in Foner and Frederickson, eds., *Not Just Black or White*, 346.
6. For simplicity and clarity I refer to whites—who are, of course, composed of various ethnicities—as an organic group as they were socially, politically, and economically understood to be in California at this time. Though Chicanos are not considered a "race," state law and custom have racialized them as separate and distinct from Anglo whites.
7. See "Border Crossings," *L.A. Weekly*, 24–30 June 1988, 22; "The Los Angeles Chicano Area-Cultural Enclave," *San Francisco Chronicle*, 10 October 1970, 12; Ernesto Chavez, *"Mi Raza Primero!": Nationalism, Identity, and Insurgency in the Chicano Movement in Los Angeles, 1966–1978* (Berkeley: University of California Press, 2002), 10; "Chicano Militancy," *Guardian*, April 1970.
8. Lopez, *Racism on Trial*, 161.
9. F. Arturo Rosales et al., *Chicano! The History of the Mexican American Civil Rights Movement* (New York: Arte Publico Press, 1996); Doug McAdam, "'Initiator' and 'Spin-off' Movements: Diffusion Processes in Protest Cycles," in *Repertoires and Cycles of Collective Action*, edited by Mark Traugott (Durham: Duke University Press, 1995).
10. The Watts Rebellion erupted on 11 August 1965, after reports of police brutality against a black woman spread through the black community. Six days of unrest, resulting in thirty-four deaths, made it the most destructive case of civil unrest since the infamous Tulsa, Oklahoma, "riot" of 1921. See Gerald Horne, *The Fire This Time: The Watts Uprising and the 1960s* (Charlottesville: University Press of Virginia, 1995).
11. Chavez, "Mi Raza Primero!" 43–45; "Hail 'La Raza' and Scorn the Establishment," online at http://www.brownberet.org/bbraza.html.
12. Bobby Seale, *Seize the Time: The Story of the Black Panther Party and Huey P. Newton* (New York: Vintage Books, 1970); Huey P. Newton, *To Die for the People* (New York: Vintage Books, 1972); Charles E. Jones, ed., *The Black Panther Party [Reconsidered]* (Baltimore: Black Classic Press, 1998); Judson Jeffries, *Huey P. Newton: Radical Theorist* (Jackson: University Press of Mississippi, 2002).
13. Marguerte Viramontes Marin, "Protest in an Urban Barrio: A Study of the Chicano Movement" (Ph.D. diss., University of California, Santa Barbara, 1980), 123–24.
14. Ibid., 124–25; Rosales, *Chicano!*, 187–88.
15. More recent accounts downplay any conscious effort to model the Berets after the BPP. Johnny Parsons, who helped design the uniform, is remembered as saying that the French Resistance and Spanish antifascists wore the beret in the 1940s and 1930s (Chavez, "Mi Raza Primero!," 46). But Huey Newton and Bobby Seale also claim to have gotten the idea from a film featuring the French Resistance.
16. Seale, *Seize the Time*, 115.
17. "Hail 'La Raza' and Scorn the Establishment."
18. Elaine Brown, *A Taste of Power: A Black Woman's Story* (New York: Doubleday, 1994), 155.

19. Lopez, *Racism on Trial*, 183–87; Marin, "Protest in an Urban Barrio," 128.
20. *La Causa* (December 1970).
21. Seale, *Seize the Time*, 4.
22. Eldridge Cleaver, *On the Ideology of the Black Panther Party* (San Francisco: Black Panther Party, 1968), 7.
23. Chavez, "Mi Raza Primero!," 57–58; Newton, *Revolutionary Suicide* (New York: Harcourt Brace, 1973), 127–31.
24. Quoted in Lopez, *Racism on Trial*, 162.
25. Castro, *Chicano Power*, 13.
26. Quoted in Lopez, *Racism on Trial*, 162.
27. "Revolutionary Heros," *Black Panther*, 11 May 1969, 4; "Free the Latino Seven," *Black Panther*, 28 June 1969, 2; "Rodolfo Martinez, Father of Antonio and Mario Martinez of Los Siete de La Raza," *Black Panther*, 2 August 1969, 6.
28. *La Causa* (May 1969): 1.
29. Stemming from a number of sources (personal animosities, prior gang affiliations, ideological disagreements, as well as FBI provocation), the two groups engaged in physical attacks, leaving members injured or dead in both organizations. See Scot Brown, *Fighting for US: Maulana Karenga, The US Organization, and Black Cultural Nationalism* (New York: New York University Press, 2003); Ogbar, *Black Power*. For Chicano/Beret references, see *La Causa* 1.1 (23 May 1969), 1; Castro, *Chicano Power*, 13–16; Marin, "Protest in an Urban Barrio," 131–34; Lopez, *Racism on Trial*, especially chapters 7 and 8. (See, too, Lopez, *Racism on Trial*, 164–70; Marin, "Protest in an Urban Barrio," 129–34.)
30. Marin, "Protest in an Urban Barrio," 131.
31. Ibid., 135.
32. Ibid., 55.
33. Ibid., 143; Castro, *Chicano Power*, 12–14.
34. Acuna, *Occupied American*, 337–38.
35. "Chicano Militancy," *Guardian*, January 1970.
36. Castro, *Chicano Power*, 13–17; "In Memory of 1970 Protest," *Los Angeles Times*, 31 August 1980.
37. "FBI," *Los Angeles Times*, 19 July 1978; Lopez, *Racism on Trial*, 203; and, more generally, Ward Churchill and Jim Vander Wall, *Agents of Repression: The FBI's Secret Wars Against the Black Panther Party and the American Indian Movement* (Boston: South End Press, 1989).
38. Young Lords Organization flyer, November 1971, Box 18, Folder 33, Special Collections, University of California, Berkeley.
39. James F. Short and Fred L. Strodtbeck, *Group Process and Gang Delinquency* (Chicago: University of Chicago Press, 1974); David M. Downes, *The Delinquent Solution: A Study in Subcultural Theory* (New York: Free Press, 1966); James Diego Vigil, *Barrio Gangs: Street Life and Identity in Southern California* (Austin: University of Texas Press, 1988).
40. Truman initiated the Point Four Program in 1949 as a tool to extend industrial

capitalism into underdeveloped countries, with Puerto Rico employed as a model. Incentives, such as lower fares to the mainland, were offered to impoverished Puerto Ricans who had been courted by labor scouts.

41. http://www.gangresearch.net/latinkings/lkhistory.html.
42. David Dawley, *A Nation of Lords: The Autobiography of the Vice Lords* (New York: Anchor, 1973), 113, 118–19.
43. Ibid., 113–15; Dawley, interview by the author, 16 May 2003; "Interview with Cha Cha Jimenez," *Black Panther*, 7 June 1969, 17.
44. Young Lords flyer, n.d., Box 18, Folder 33, Special Collections, University of California, Berkeley.
45. Newton, *Essays from the Minister of Defense* (1967), 11.
46. "Interview with Cha Cha Jimenez," *Black Panther*, 7 June 1969, 17.
47. "From Rumble to Revolution: The Young Lords," *Ramparts*, October 1970; Young Lords flyer, n.d., Box 18, Folder 33, Special Collections, University of California, Berkeley. See also David Hilliard and Lewis Cole, *This Side of Glory: The Autobiography of David Hilliard and the Story of the Black Panther Party* (Boston: Little, Brown, 1993), 229.
48. "Yellow Power," *Giant Robot*, no. 10 (spring 1998): 71; Seale, *Seize the Time*, 72–73, 79.
49. "Interview with Cha Cha Jimenez."
50. "From Rumble to Revolution." Young Lords flyer.
51. For the Young Patriots, the Confederate flag was a symbol of their poor southern roots, not racism, which they denounced as an evil. Newton, *Essays*, 11; "From Rumble to Revolution"; Young Lords flyer; Hilliard and Cole, *This Side of Glory*, 229.
52. Pablo Guzman, "La Vida Pura: A Lord of the Barrio," in *The Puerto Rican Movement: Voices of the Diaspora*, edited by Andres Torres and José E. Velázquez (Philadelphia: Temple University Press, 1999), 156.
53. Ibid., 156–57; Young Lord Party and Michael Abramson, *Palante* (New York: McGraw-Hill, 1971), 75–77; "Palante Siempre Palante! A Look Back at the Young Lords," online at http://netdial.caribe.net/7Edfreedma/beginnin.htm.
54. Guzman, "La Vida Pura," 154–57; Iris Morales, "Palante, Siempre Palante: The Young Lords," in Torres and Velázquez, eds., *The Puerto Rican Movement*, 213–14; Young Lords Party and Abramson, *Palante*, 69–70.
55. Guzman, "La Vida Pura," 159–60; Morales, "Palante, Siempre Palante," 213–14; Young Lords Party and Abramson, *Palante*, 69–70; "Palante, Siempre Palante! A Look Back at the Young Lords."
56. Komozi Woodard, *A Nation within a Nation: Amiri Baraka (LeRoi Jones) and Black Power Politics* (Chapel Hill: University of North Carolina Press, 1999), 138–40.
57. On Puerto Rican notions of race, see Mariam Jimenez Roman, "Un Hombre (negro) del pueblo: Jose Celso Barbosa and the Puerto Rican 'Race' Toward Whiteness," *CENTRO: Journal of the Center for Puerto Rican Studies* 8.1–2 (1996): 9; Jorge Duany, *Puerto Rican Nation on the Move: Identities on the Island and in the United States*, (Chapel Hill: University of North Carolina Press, 2002), 248–55.

58. The psychological benefits translated into social and cultural, if not material, capital. See Roediger, *Wages of Whiteness*.

59. The Puerto Rican Civil Rights Commission in 1959 and 1972 found the explicit discrimination against darker-skinned Puerto Ricans to be pervasive on the island. Kelvin Santiago-Valles, "Policing the Crisis in the Whitest of all the Antilles," *CENTRO: Journal of the Center for Puerto Rican Studies* 8.1–2 (1996): 46.

60. Young Lord Party and Abramson, *Palante*, 60.

61. "We're Fighting for Freedom Together. There Is no Other Way," *Black Panther*, 2 August 1969.

62. "Interview with Cha Cha Jimenez."

63. It must be noted that although virtually all Puerto Ricans in the United States were classified as "white" in 1970, many of them, particularly in large, contiguous Puerto Rican communities on the East Coast, saw themselves as distinct from white Americans in a colloquial sense. Despite the history of prestige that many Puerto Ricans may have associated with being considered white, there is ample evidence that many, if not most, saw themselves as embodying more than just a variant of whiteness. On the census, for example, there was no option for "Hispanic" until 1980. Once given the choice, the percentage of Puerto Ricans who reported being white dropped from 92.9 in 1970 to 48.3 in 1980 (Duany, *Puerto Rican Nation on the Move*, 253–57).

64. "We're Fighting for Freedom Together."

65. Guzman, "La Vida Pura," 157.

66. Carmen Teresa Whalen, "The Young Lords in Philadelphia," 121, and Morales "Palante, Siempre Palante," 215, both in Andres, ed., *The Puerto Rican Movement*; Raquel Z. Rivera, "Boriquas from the Hip-Hop Zone: Notes on Race and Ethnic Relations in New York City," *CENTRO: Journal of the Center for Puerto Rican Studies*, 8.1–2 (1996), 208.

67. "We're Fighting for Freedom Together."

68. Quoted in Young Lord Party and Abramson, *Palante*, 75 (emphasis in original).

69. Quoted in ibid., 82.

70. Adelante Tigeres Angelines, flyer, Mexican American Student Confederation (MASC), March 1968, Box 18, Folder 30, Special Collections, University of California, Berkeley.

71. *La Causa* 1.2 (10 July 1969): 3.

72. Quoted in Marin, "Protest in an Urban Barrio," 144. Space constraints prevent a deeper, more detailed analysis of women, sexism, and the Brown Berets. The subject constitutes a lacuna in the scholarly literature.

73. Quoted in ibid., 144–45.

74. Young Lord Party and Abramson, *Palante*, 75, 82.

75. Though a similar group of women calling themselves the Clique had emerged in the Los Angeles BPP, there was no communication between them and New York Lords. Elaine Brown, interview by the author.

76. Young Lord Party and Abramson, *Palante*, 50–52.

77. *Palante Siempre Palante: The Young Lords*, written, produced, and directed by Iris Morales (New York: Latino Education Network, 1996); Young Lords Party, *Palante* (New York: Young Lords Party, 1971), 117.
78. Quoted in Young Lords Party and Abramson, *Palante*, 46, 54.
79. Morales, "Palante, Siempre Palante," 219.
80. The notion that the Panthers were particularly hostile to feminism is pervasive. In *Too Heavy a Load: Black Women in Defense of Themselves: 1894–1994* (New York: Norton, 1998), for example, Deborah Gray White discusses Elaine Brown's own frustrations with male chauvinism in the Party. White quotes from a story in Brown's autobiography where she and other women are told to wait to eat until the men get their share of food, although women were responsible for cooking and cleaning up after everyone was finished. The story is not about the Panthers, though, but a visit Brown made to a US Organization function in San Diego (not in Los Angeles, as White misreports it). Further, White asserts that for their several years in the Party "[Elaine Brown] and other black women were regularly beaten by black men in the name of 'black manhood,'" while a black feminist Panther was considered "an enemy of black people." White makes no mention of the powerful rhetoric of Panther men and women in support of feminism, nor does she note that Brown became chair of the Party and brought large numbers of women into major positions in it. Moreover, some men, such as her chief of staff Larry Henson, demonstrated unwavering loyalty to her. And while violence was a tragic and destabilizing part of Panther punishment, men too were beaten, sometimes by women or under the direction of women, including Brown. Still, violence against fellow members, men or women, was rare and was far from acceptable. And although misinterpretations and misinformation have cultivated an image of the Party as virulently sexist, closer examination reveals that while sexism existed in the ranks it was no more virulent than it was in society at large. Finally, few organizations at the time made as explicit attempts to challenge sexism as did the Panthers. Tracye Matthews offers the most balanced analysis of Party gender dynamics in her essay "No One Ever Asks What a Man's Place in the Revolution Is," in Jones, ed., *Black Panther Party*. See also Gray, *Too Heavy a Load*, 219–20; Brown, *Taste of Power*, 108–9, 357–58, 369–71.
81. Safiya Bukhari-Alston, "On the Question of Sexism Within the Black Panther Party" (1992), online at www.blackpanther.org.
82. Elaine Brown, interview by the author, 26 September 2003.
83. Akua Njeri, interview by the author, 14 August 1995.
84. Lee Lew-Lee, interview with author, 31 May 1997.
85. No records of national Panther membership have survived (outside the counts done by the FBI). In my interviews, however, former Panthers have always given estimations of female membership at over 40 percent. Bobby Seale asserts that by mid-1968 about two-thirds of Panther membership was female. Interviews by the author: Bobby Seale (22 October 1998); Omar Barbour (22 October 1996); Lee Lew-Lee (22 October 1996); Akua Njeri (22 October 1996).

86. "Roberta Alexander at Conference," *Black Panther*, 2 August 1969, 7; "The Role of Revolutionary Women," *Black Panther*, 4 May 1969, 9.
87. Brown replaced Seale, who left the Party in 1973; a year later, Newton went into exile, leaving Brown in control of the organization until his return in 1977.
88. "Comrade Sister," in Paula J. Giddings, *When and Where I Enter: The Impact of Black Women on Race and Sex in America* (New York: HarperCollins, 1996), 317; Douglass, interview with author, 8 November 1996.
89. Hugh Pearson's *The Shadow of the Panther: Huey Newton and the Price of Black Power in America* (Reading: Addison-Wesley, 1994), provides a detailed discussion of Newton's violence against women. As Pearson also details, Newton was even more violent toward men. In fact, the Panther leader's rage was not discriminating. To call him a "misogynist" may be a simplistic take on Newton's violent character, which was not particularly directed at women.

PART FIVE Revolutionary Politics: The Black Panthers in the American Imagination

Introductory Comment

"Culture Is a Weapon in Our Struggle for Liberation": The Black Panther Party and the Cultural Politics of Decolonization

DAVARIAN L. BALDWIN

As an "Affirmative Action baby" growing up in small-town Middle America, I was historically distant from the Black Panther Party (BPP). While I grew up with "black history," outside of family stories it was usually presented as a mere collection of names, dates, and events without historical context. In the case of the BPP, I was simultaneously captivated by and somewhat fearful of the iconography of black berets, leather jackets, and big guns. I would only later come to understand that my access to the group, both real and imagined, was mediated by white control of what those in the Frankfurt school called the culture industries (film, television, radio, and recording).[1] So, despite my best intentions, some "slippage" occurred, where the "f" in Panther defiance turned into the "v" of Panther deviance.

My initial experience with the BPP thus reinforced all of the archetypal narratives that bedevil my position as part of Generation X, where connections to past (and present) realities are mediated by the corrosive force of the mass marketplace, where reality itself is converted into decontextualized commodities of pixels, sound bites, voiceovers, and video clips. But, there are also the unintended consequences of consumer capitalism. My ability to sift through the layers of fear, misinformation, and simple ignorance was made possible by the lower frequencies on the very same circuits of the dominant culture industries. The sonic force of the hip-hop group Public Enemy, for example, and especially the black radical history lessons disseminated on their album jackets, along with the video clips of local BPP member Michael McGee on Donahue and at my college campus, introduced me to an alternative history of the organization and the larger "1968 moment." Still, my encounter with the BPP underscores the homogenizing, alienating force of a now global mass culture. And yet that very same terrain also is the conduit for the global expression of local struggles, past and present, while planting the seeds for new political ideas.

When I finally came to terms with this dialectic of representation to uncover a more humane and complicated, if still cultural-industrial, image of the Panthers, it was their cultural politics that stood out. For, more than any other contemporary group, they understood that the framing of each historical moment arises from diverse and competing interests struggling over representational legitimacy. That process became readily apparent at a recent meeting of my faculty about a local showing of the photographic exhibit titled Reflections in Black. When one of my "reformed" radical colleagues saw that pictures of Panthers were to be included, he vigorously protested, as "someone who was there," the inclusion of images of "rapists and murders" in a university exhibition. Forced to respond, I realized that, while I was not able to wield the authority of having "been there," I have benefited from the cultural politics of the 1968 moment. This realization drew me to how and for what purposes contemporary cultural representations link that moment to the Black Power era, as well as to our own. Indeed, such pointed rememories of "the sixties" are precisely the ground on which current social and political anxieties are still being worked out.

For the right, the color-blind solidarity of Martin Luther King Jr. and his "content of your character" politics was hijacked by unruly bands of urban black guerrillas (read: gorillas). Because such man-children refuse to grow up, the story goes, they continue to hold American civilization hostage to their identity-based victim ideology, especially in the university and in the liberal media. At the same time, many on the Left argue that a national popular front of proletarian politics was eroded by the false consciousness of identity politics in general and of the "bogey of race" in particular. Thus, when well-meaning white radicals were taken on this errand into the wilderness of divisive cultural nationalism and irrational violence, they became the unwitting conduits for the right's current "family values," free-market fundamentalism. Meanwhile, some cultural/postcolonial studies renditions argue that the "Black" in 1968 Black Power has blinded us to the dynamic, hybrid, and international routes of identity and cultural politics.[2] Whether the goal is a national cultural consensus, laborist ideology,[3] or postcolonial cultural politics, the common criticism is the allegedly problematic "cultural turn" to Black Power.

We are at a stage where it is hip to consume black culture, but it is no longer hip to be black. Black thinkers/scholars are in vogue when their ideas can be abstracted, universalized, and then expunged of their provincial black experiential roots/routes. Consider the postcolonial celebration of C. L. R. James, robbed of his Black Nationalism, or the dismissal of Frantz Fanon's radicalism because of his "unique" misogyny. We love conversion stories where old race radicals become colorblind and/or class conscious ("I once was black, but now I see"). At the same time, the culture industries trade in black cultural products, selling *Everything but the Burden*, while a few years back the U.S. academy hosted what some called another "British invasion," with scholars of the Birmingham-trained cultural studies variety chastising U.S. black studies for its provincial, policing, and politically repressive notions of race, nation, and identity. Concurrently, students left black studies behind for American cultural studies programs to complete their graduate training. In some ways, this was a necessary turn of events, where younger students felt alienated from a particular version of a "sixties model" of social protest and academic inquiry that did not seem commensurate with current conditions. My degree in American studies places me squarely within this shift.[4]

However, this process of racial purging, especially within the academy, has ignored the critiques of biological, national, and culturally rigid visions of blackness in the legacy of black studies within its Black Power social context. In fact, many young scholars have found academic homes in some version of black studies not cultural studies, and in the United States not in the United Kingdom. But perhaps these worlds might be bridged by making visible counternarratives of "black worldliness" within the movement culture of Black Power. Perhaps, the work of postcolonial and subaltern studies — which, until recently, drew primarily from the South Asian experience — and the older African diaspora studies can be joined by attending to, for example, how and why non-"black" African and Asian Jews in Israel and the Dalit "untouchables" in India found liberatory possibilities in modeling themselves after the BPP.[5]

It is in this larger context that the Black Panther Conference at Wheelock College occurred. As I moderated the "Art and Arts" panel, I could see ex-Panthers in the audience cringing at the cultural studies analysis of some panelists who spoke of politics as "performance," which recognizes the self-conscious, constructed, and contested nature of ideologies and identities in everyday life. Protests that "it wasn't performance, it was real" does suggest that we have too much culture and not enough politics in our current cultural politics. But, part of the problem was a generational difference in language where performance seems to suggest the term "fake." Though the discussion did include some sympathetic reception to cultural studies, there was also the expressed worry that the art of deconstruction had left Black Power history and politics unreconstructed and open to attacks of illegitimacy from the mass cultural mediums of both the Right and the Left.

This tension between mass culture as industry and mass culture as politics brings together the two essays in this section and sheds light on our received knowledge about the BPP. Tim Lake's "The Arm(ing) of the Vanguard, Signify(ing), and Performing the Revolution" offers some suggestions about how to construct a more comprehensive memory of the Panthers by reconsidering their "performance" of politics within the mediated spaces of the culture industries. On the other hand, Ted Morgan's "Media Culture and the Public Memory of the Black Panther Party" utilizes a culture industries approach to examine the Panthers' losing battle in their struggles with media culture, where the legacy of the BPP image in the white mind leaves us with the sensational over the substantive.

Beginning his analysis precisely where Morgan charts the decline of Panther politics, Lake offers a decidedly theoretical approach by using "social movement theory, the modern avant-garde tradition and language theory" to offer a reconsideration of the BPP's revolutionary identity. Robin Kelley's critique of how we currently evaluate social movements is deployed by Lake to focus on Panther strategies for creating revolutionary lives as opposed to their success in upending power relationships. Thus, the very presumption of a fixed notion of "real" revolutionary politics, and therefore radical ideas, becomes the site of investigation. For Lake, the revolutionary nationalist position that an individual identified with when joining the BPP was never a stable category but was "contingent, historically specific, and relational," to both external and internal forces.

From this perspective, the relationship between visual expression and radical ideas represents more than a story of co-optation; rather, it is part of an ongoing re-creation of political meaning in the black radical tradition. Lake asserts, using the logic of post–World War I avant-garde movements, that the visual display of BPP protest aesthetics—newspapers, artwork, leather clothing, guns, raised fists, military drill formations—"harnessed the power of art to arrest the imagination and to communicate an incendiary message intended to initiate social change." The convergence between art and revolutionary politics here, then, altered the perception of what was possible in everyday life. For example, Lake says, BPP members used their guns as a visual expression of police intimidation and as a way of drawing community admiration, not as means to sanction lawless violence. As he points out, "the guns themselves were not the revolution but a tool for raising the revolutionary consciousness of the people." The debates between Huey Newton and Eldridge Cleaver over self-defense versus aggressive violence helps further to clarify this point. Their differing interpretations of the use of the gun demonstrated competing visions about how revolution could be *performed*. Thus, Lake concludes, a "revolutionary" identity is not an a priori entity, but rather revolutionary consciousness is realized by "performing revolutionary acts." In his view, the BPP's sensational displays of resistance and defiance helped diverse groups of people identify with a new way of seeing the world and to imagine their place within it.

By blending media theory with empirical data, Morgan offers a rich account of the BPP's mass-mediated (mis)representation as a warning to present-day scholars/activists concerned with media culture. He asserts that current media recollections of the "turbulent" sixties almost exclusively draw from the media culture of that era, creating an exclusionary matrix of representation that prizes iconography over social and political context, thus demonstrating the dangers of mass-mediated archives as the source of public memory. With the "ideologically bound range of discourses and dichotomies" of mass media defining legitimate and illegitimate dissent in the interests of a culture-owning elite, the images and ideas of the sixties that sought to undermine the authority of this elite are simplified and/or sensationalized. Thus, events of protest are not silenced; rather, they are recodified and given new meaning within the public sphere of the mainstream media. In this context, the televisual or textual dramatization of protests, slogans, and defiant behavior become a spectacle, because that meets the needs of commercial marketing to a "youth market and its more flamboyant modes of expression."

In Morgan's formulation, media culture focuses on expressive imagery while constraining ideas within a rigid evaluative framework of the credible/

incredible. Because the BPP understood how to get attention through the mass media, he suggests, their "inflammatory" verbal expression and confrontational visual displays fell into the trap of the dominant logic. Their gun-toting paramilitary behavior was consistently represented as illegitimate social action dichotomously contrasted with, for example, the pre-1967 Martin Luther King Jr. When the Panthers garnered mainstream support, Morgan notes, they were caricatured and their supporters delegitimized as the "'Effete' Liberal Elite" and the "Liberal Media." Not even the "New Journalism" style of reportage offered reprieve, as its focus on the "inner life of event participants" conflated the politically "real" with the flamboyant and colorful. In the end, encounters with mainstream mass media reinforced the BPP's penchant for symbolic action — or what Morgan calls "the 'performative' nature of much late-1960s politics."

In the face of such "media assassination," or revolution as "performance," many of those attending the Wheelock conference understandably desired a more positive or more authentic image of the BPP with which to build a unified space of oppositional politics. Performance seemed like an unsatisfactory strategy for recuperating the past to meet contemporary realities. Given the already-marginalized status of radical experience today, could we afford to allow every contested account or memory to enter the discussion? Meanwhile, current cultural representations of the BPP leave us with a collection of angry men, black fists, and gun battles, without the survival programs, radical theory, and blueprints for the future. But, though some have succumbed to the scholarly dead end of finding resistance everywhere while others see the dominant culture as purely hegemonic, it seems important to bring together the performative politics of culture and the oppositional culture of politics as they existed under the globalizing sign of Black Power.[6] The current specter of Black Power makes it difficult to see the global within the local, the political within the cultural, the substantive within the sensational, the international within the national, and the progressive alongside the reactionary. However, as we look back, the emerging rubric of globalization is quite useful in reconciling the seeming contradictions between culture and politics under the sign of Black Power.[7]

In his latest work, cultural studies scholar Michael Denning provocatively argues that current critical interest in globalization is at least partly about trying to understand the ending of an era he calls the age of three worlds (capitalist, communist, and decolonizing). What were once seen as alternative and competing visions of modernity, he suggests, have been flattened out by the monolithic "global cultural flow[s]"[8] of Americanization, where dissent is oversimplified into a "holy war" between civilization and barbarism. Some globalization studies capture, on one hand, the unholy alliance between neocolonial states and multinational corporations in the production of an overlapping world economy with an international division of labor and global mass culture. On the other hand, these works focus on the global articulation of local struggles in examining how the making of transnational social movements is partially worked out through the cultural spheres of commodity and communication. For Denning, the central phase of this era was the 1968 moment when social movements around the globe simultaneously articulated a politics of culture.[9] In many ways, the Panthers' engagement with the U.S. empire of transnational capital took place precisely through their manipulation and production of mass cultural products and ideas at that particular moment. In their hands, blackness became the conduit for a cultural politics of decolonization, connecting black ghettos to the Third World.

Thus, the very critiques of the seemingly messy anomaly of convergence between culture and politics within the BPP, as an avant-gardist, politically inconsistent, damaging influence on the moment, encourage us to resituate the BPP within Denning's "three worlds" context of cultural politics. The age, he notes, spans, on one end, the inception of the Cold War, the beginnings of a global marketplace, anticolonialism, and the rise of a "third" way in the world. The other end, 1989, marked by the fall of the Berlin wall and the beginning of the end of South African apartheid, also witnessed metropolitan racial violence in the United States and Europe. In labor relations, we see accelerated outsourcing (and devalued insourcing) to sweatshops, temporary/adjunct agencies, tourism and travel management, public/private security force units, nonunion "reality" entertainment venues, and incarceration workstations. There has also been the suppression of any "rainbow coalition" possibilities in U.S. politics, as a transnational outcry of the "silent (moral) majority" seeks to reshape the bounds of civil society. With the early stages of a WTO/IMF/World Bank "structural adjustment" hegemony has come the white recolonization of urban spaces through tourist economies of multicultural tragic hipness, sports entertainment, and historic preservation.

Most critical was what happened in between these two historic moments.

At midcentury, the "Greater Migration" of peasant displacements and dissensions all over the world fostered the making of the so-called "second ghetto" across the United States, with parallel shantytown and barrio formations around the globe. A growing gap emerged between a new "knowledge proletariat"[10] of university students and bureaucratic laborers in the culture industries, on the one side, and a rising "lumpen" in an era of "deindustrialization" on the other. Meanwhile, the ongoing economic boom in Keynesian market management fueled U.S. imperial advance into Asia, Africa, the Caribbean, and Latin America. This set the stage for an accelerated transnationalization of commodified culture that emblazoned the IBM, ITT, Hollywood, and the already international Coca-Cola and Ford corporations onto the global imagination. This hemispherically uneven division of labor was further rationalized through the neo-anthropological logic and language of modernization and development, alongside the state-led U.S. urban "white flight" and the ensuing criminalization of, and war on, poor people.

However, the transnationalization of culture was also taken up at the 1955 Bandung Conference of nonaligned nations, which was widely recognized as the first formal pronouncement of Afro-Asian solidarity and an emerging Third World consciousness of decolonization. However, the conference merely signaled a larger convergence of points of resistance against colonialism and racial violence. This initial stage encompassed national liberation in India and Pakistan (1947), the Chinese revolution (1949), the battles of Algiers and Dien Bien Phu (1954), the Kenyan Mau Mau rebellions, the Montgomery bus boycott (1955), the North Carolina armed self-defense group of Robert Williams (1957), the Sharpesville massacre (1960), the Birmingham confrontations (1963), and guerrilla skirmishes throughout Africa, alongside Ghanaian independence (1957) and the Cuban revolution (1959).

These social movements also encouraged Third World intellectuals to begin rereading politics through the culture of a decolonizing global landscape. On his trip to India in 1959, King commented on the "bond" of solidarity among "minority and colonial peoples in America, Africa, and Asia struggling to throw off racism and imperialism." The volume *Quotations from Chairman Mao Tse-Tung* offered a useful Third World interpretation of Marxist revolutionary thought when in 1963 Mao explicitly located the African American freedom movement within the larger struggle against colonial imperialism. Frantz Fanon's *Black Skin, White Mask* (1952), along with his theory of epidermalization, deconstructed the superstructural imposition of white supremacy on the social psyche of everyday colonial life and culture. Then, his *Wretched of the Earth* (1961) connected decolonization to revolutionary violence in both the First World and the Third World.

In the Western Hemisphere, E. Franklin Frazier offered a scathing critique of the consumer culture of the black bourgeoisie (1957) and the "make believe" quest for black autonomy. A year after Trinidadian independence, however, C. L. R. James's *Beyond a Boundary* (1963) examined the mass cultural sport of cricket as a key site of anticolonial consciousness. In 1962, Harold Cruse wrote that black radical thought in the United States and its understanding of the Negro as a "colonial being" was heavily influenced by the revolutionary ferment in Africa, Asia, and the Caribbean. In *The Crisis of the Negro Intellectual* (1967), he added that the political foundation for decolonizing the "nation within a nation" that was Harlem would be found in the relationship between culture and industry, or what he called (borrowing from C. Wright Mills) the black cultural apparatus.[11]

However, nothing helped more to foster a culture of decolonization linking black American life to the Third World than the over three hundred urban uprisings from 1964 in the United States, in addition to, for example, the Jamaican (Walter) Rodney riots (1968) and the Soweto race riots (1976) abroad. The range of events in this period, then, helps frame the larger 1968 moment of Third World resistance when the ordinary recognized the "war zone" parallels between the uprisings in Birmingham, Harlem, Detroit, and Newark, and U.S. imperialist incursions in places like the Congo and, especially, Vietnam. This moment of collective insurgency instigated what Nikhil Pal Singh calls a "geopolitics of pride and shame."[12]

The polarity between national guardsmen/police and everyday residents highlighted the ghetto as a space of colonial occupation, as an internal colony within the United States. In *Black Power*, Kwame Ture and Charles Hamilton observed that "institutional racism has another name: colonialism." Looking abroad, James Baldwin observed that as "darkest" Africa and the "oriental" Far East were engaged in nation-building, the black "image" would no longer signify lack, void, negation, a longing psychosis or, to paraphrase Franz Fanon, the permanent Other to the White Self. Alongside this physical struggle, *Decolonizing the Mind* was paramount—in the vernacular of funkster George Clinton, people believed, "free your mind and your ass will follow." Turning blackness as deviance into blackness as pride was part of the larger culture of decolonization in a similar vein as Gabriel García Márquez's magical realism reimagined the colonized world. Moreover, urban centers that had been racialized as concrete symbols of fear, shame, and black deviance became spaces of black anticolonial liberation with the right to self-determination as part of what the Revolutionary Action Movement (RAM) appropriately called the "Bandung World." People heard it on the streets, "I'm from Watts, baby!" and on airwaves, "We Live in Brooklyn, Baby!" (1971).

The ghettos and the uprisings within them were celebrated as another site of anticolonial internationalism; metaphors of ghetto and colony went both ways, as the radical thinkers and activists James Boggs and Grace Lee Boggs claimed the ghetto as the "black man's land," while the musical group named War sang *The World Is a Ghetto* (1971). Moreover, not only were riots renamed revolts, but, in the spirit of Fanon's analysis of the lumpen proletariat, rioters were celebrated as revolutionary. The "pimps, [the] hooligans, [the] unemployed and [the] petty criminals," demonized as instigators of the riots, were now transfigured as the advanced guard of Third World decolonization in the overdeveloped world. The RAM leader Max Stanford suggested that black students become a "revolutionary intelligentsia," while gangs "serve as the liberation force in the black revolution."[13]

From outside of the United States, Mao defined the riots after King's assassination in 1968 as resistance against the "barbarous rule of the monopoly capitalist class." This helped those in the mainstream New Left — ranging from the Students for a Democratic Society (SDS) in the United States to the Situationist International in Paris — to see the "darker peoples" as the revolutionary segment of the working class and Black Power as a political symbol of "imaginary equivalence" that could be accessed by other social movements.[14] Moreover, the symbolic importance of the Great Proletarian Cultural Revolution in China helped legitimize culture as a site of revolutionary struggle throughout the Third World.

In many ways, the Panthers' cultural politics was a consolidation of this larger 1968 moment, for what was arguably unique about them was their ability to create an imagined community of blackness, as anticolonial solidarity, that could speak to the everyday experiences of the urbanizing globally oppressed. Members read the anticolonial works of Che Guevara, Mao, and Fanon. They were also directly influenced by the armed self-defense and anticolonial visions of Robert Williams's *Negroes with Guns* and the "internationalism" of his "Radio Free Dixie" broadcasts from exile in Cuba, as well as by Malcolm X, who traveled to the Third World, appealed to the United Nations on behalf of U.S. blacks, and launched his new Organization of Afro-American Unity (modeled on the Organization of African Unity). These international contexts, alongside the Bandung humanism/black internationalism of RAM, preceded the BPP's more popular reconfiguration of blackness and black ghettos as key sites in a culture of decolonization—or, what Newton would call by 1970, "intercommunalism." On the home front, they sparked provisional rainbow coalitions with gay and women's liberation organizations, the Puerto Rican Young Lords and the Chicano Brown Berets, the American Indian Movement, and the Asian American Red Guard and I Wor Kuen. This interface between culture and social movements did not simply instigate new political organizations but ignited new ways in which political struggles were waged. On a philosophical level, the rise of a Third Way among the "darker races" was partially attractive because it collapsed the Cartesian divide between mind and body, or, in mass cultural parlance, between ideology and spectacle.[15]

As Erika Doss has pointed out, if we take Huey Newton's observation that "the Black community is basically not a reading community" beyond its potential suggestion of racial essentialism, we can begin to better understand the BPP's cultural politics. Here, too, we can join the apparently competing notions of performance as addressed by Lake and by Morgan. For the Panthers, cultural politics included both meanings of performance that these authors attribute to them: the execution and accomplishment of a plan and formal exhibition or self-conscious theatricality. The Panthers were able to turn the streets and the mass media into literal theaters of war—as sites of struggle in the remaking of blackness into what they called a revolutionary consciousness. Their self-presentation of black clothing and paramilitary formations, combined with a vernacular intellectual style of address ("Power to the People," "Off the Pigs"), helped materialize their larger "white mother country/black internal colony" metaphor of social difference. Most provocatively, they understood their guns (loaded or not) as a powerful "recruiting device" for the lumpen "street brothers."[16]

Moreover, their armed confrontations over the law were consistently positioned as a method to "teach security against the police" and shed light on the practitioners of the rampant police brutality plaguing black communities. Most remember, whether with pride or shame, the spectacle of "Black men, armed with guns and a knowledge of the law," exhibiting a "highly visible oppositional appearance." However, most forget that part of the brilliance of these provisional community events is that to be effective they had to stay within the bounds of the law. It is telling that Newton called these encounters "shock-a-buku," for the word *kabuku* means "to be off balance." Significantly, the term would come to refer to one whose social unconventionality was expressed in unorthodox, excessive, or extravagant dress and behavior, as found in Japanese Kabuki theater. The BPP's adherence to the law, in the context of such an arresting display of unconventional defiance in dress and behavior, created a formal exhibition of role reversal. In these moments, police abuse was marked as criminal and subject to a higher authority that demanded they protect and serve black lives. In this small example, we can see how the BPP attempted to create politics through the lens of black popular culture and everyday life.[17]

That effort is evident in the work of the Panther minister of culture Emory Douglas, who "crafted a protest aesthetic aimed at convincing audiences of black power." Alongside Huey Newton reciting political poetics as he chanted down police brutality from the rooftops of cars, Douglas's artwork depicted the police as pigs and offered images of black people with guns kicking down prison gates. Douglas helped convert everyday life into art by making the black ghetto his "museum," with pictures plastered on barbershop walls, in alleyways, and on telephone poles. As a product of his era, Douglas transformed the commercial style he learned at New York's City College into a revolutionary art aesthetic disseminated all over the world through the Black Panther newspaper.[18] And, when the BPP sent a contingent to the 1969 first Pan-African Cultural Festival in Algiers, Algeria, where President Houari Boumedienne argued that "culture is a weapon in our struggle for liberation," Douglas was prominent.[19] He and other Panthers convened with U.S. black artists and musicians, liberation activists from South Africa and Zimbabwe, the Palestinian Al Fatah, Vietnam's National Liberation Front, and the PAIGC leader Amilcar Cabral.[20] The BPP's cultural politics of convergence between the visceral and cerebral, the visual and the ideological, was thus key for reconstructing abject representations of the black subject throughout the decolonizing world. Concurrently, radical black feminists like Patricia Haden, Donna Middleton, and Pat Robinson (1969), along with the later Combahee River Collective (1974), quickly pointed out that consistent reliance on the traditional tropes of militant violence and physical defiance tied black liberation to images of virile masculinity.[21] From the outside, such images reinforced an already-stereotyped black rage, and from the inside limited the possibilities for a Black Power. Still, the vision of Black Power had, for better or worse, helped to cohere a culture of decolonization in the Bandung World.

Further, these "interesting times" had an equally profound effect on decolonizing aesthetic forms within mainstream mass culture industries. The Black Arts movement, dubbed "the aesthetic and spiritual sister of the Black Power concept," solidified the networks of theater and literature among, most notably, Amiri Baraka's Black Arts Repertory Theatre / School and *Umbra Magazine* (New Youk City), the *Journal of Black Poetry* and the *Black Scholar* (Bay Area), *Negro Digest / Negro World* and Third World Press (Chicago), Lotus Press (Detroit), and Drum and Spear Press (Washington, D.C.).[22] This collection of cultural workers also helped to produce paradigm-forming anthologies, including *The Black Aesthetic* and the pioneering "womanist" project, *The Black Woman*. This period also provided the context for a vernacular literary style found in the "ghetto realism" of Iceberg Slim (1967) and Donald Goines (1970). In turn, these U.S. formations found hemispheric compliments in the postcolonial *Présence Africaine* and Caribbean Arts movements and the Brazilian *bloco afros*.

This moment also included the "Third Cinema" of *cinema novo* (Brazil), *Grupo Cine Liberaçion* (Argentina), the film work of the Senegalese writer Sembene Ousmane, the early Melvin Van Pebbles's "blaxploitation" opus, *Sweetback's Baadasssss Song!*, Jimmy Cliff's *The Harder They Come*, and UCLA's School of Black Cinema critique. Their soundtrack counterparts include the "Trenchtown Rock" of Bob Marley's Rastafarian reggae. Similarities in spirit, if not in sound, were the Brazilian tropicalismo of Gilberto Gil, the Zimbabwean chimurenga of Thomas Mapfumo, and Fela Kuti's Nigerian Afropop. In the United States alone could be heard the Afro-Latino hybridity of Nuyorican Boogaloo, the *Ascension* of "free jazz," and the sonic black radicalization of U.S. Soul Power in the "Black and Proud" moment. Out of soul quickly came the migrant Afro-futurism of funk music in minimetros like Dayton, Ohio, and Tulsa, Oklahoma, pointedly offering the chocolate city / vanilla suburb geographical imagination.[23]

Even television came under siege, from *Julia* (1968–1971) and the every-(black)man Watts, Los Angeles junk dealer (*Sanford and Son*, 1972–1977), who literally paved the way for the Malcolm X-reading, cocaine-snorting

Bicentennial Nigger (1976) and his brilliant (but short-lived) self-titled *Richard Pryor Show* (1977).[24] And, finally, the mass cultural realm of sport became the unintended showcase for Black Power on the national and global stage. In 1966, the football star and activist Jim Brown formalized a relationship between black athletes and economists into the Negro Industrial and Economic Union (NIEU) to support community entrepreneurship. The 1968 Mexico City Olympic Games displayed the "bare feet and black fists" protest of Tommie Smith and John Carlos on the medal-recipient platform as part of Harry Edwards's Olympic Project for Human Rights (OPHR). In boxing, Muhammad Ali's conversion to Islam and his meetings with African leaders, controversial anti–Vietnam War stance, and paradigmatic Third World boxing showcase, "The Rumble in the Jungle," made him arguably the most potent Black Power symbol for the Bandung World.[25] Clearly, these Third World negotiations of mass culture were not unified in vision, but we can see how they constituted a culture of decolonization with both local and global interventions.

So what we see today as simply an academic exercise in cultural studies, divorced from "real" politics, in reality began on the ground where everyday life and culture were the sites of struggle over the representations of race, nation, and freedom in creating a better world. The black culture of decolonization in the Bandung World ought not to serve as an obituary but as an opportunity to make better sense of cultural politics. The knee-jerk reaction against too much culture is not necessarily a groping for more radical politics but rather represents the concession that an inadequate sense of everyday life, in all of its contradictory splendor, has been our loss. In this sense, the agents of "conservatism" have been better investors in cultural politics.[26] For those who would understand the Panthers and their historical moment, the politics of poetry, performance, and popular culture ought to be brought closer to the art of choices, decisions, and resistance in our critical memory of the past and our imagination of a revolutionary future.

Notes

1. Theodor Adorno, *The Culture Industry* (London: Routledge, 1991); Andrew Arato and Eike Gebhart, eds., *The Essential Frankfurt School Reader* (New York: Urizen Books, 1978).
2. Jeremy Varon, *Bringing the War Home: The Weather Underground, the Red Army Faction, and Revolutionary Violence in the Sixties and Seventies* (Berkeley: University of California Press, 2004); Mark Kurlansky, *1968: The Year That Rocked the World*

(New York: Ballantine Books, 2003); Max Elbaum, *Revolution Is in the Air: Sixties Radicals Turn to Lenin, Mao and Che* (London: Verso Press, 2002); Jules Witcover, *The Year the Dream Died: Revisiting 1968 in America* (New York: Warner Books, 1998); Alice Echols, *Daring to Be Bad: Radical Feminism in America, 1967–1975* (Minneapolis: University of Minnesota Press, 1989); Ward Churchill and Jim Vander Wall, *Agents of Repression: The FBI's Secret Wars against the Black Panther Party and the American Indian Movement* (Boston: South End Press, 1988); Ronald Fraser et al., eds., *1968: A Student Generation in Revolt* (New York: Pantheon Books, 1988); George Katsiaficas, *The Imagination of the New Left: A Global Analysis of 1968* (Boston: South End Press, 1987); Todd Gitlin, *The Sixties: Years of Hope, Days of Rage* (New York: Bantam Books, 1987); Stuart Hall et al., eds., *Policing the Crisis: Mugging, the State and Law and Order* (New York: Holmes and Meier, 1978).

3. Daniel Bell, *The End of Ideology: On the Exhaustion of Political Ideas in the Fifties* (New York: Free Press, 1962).

4. Some suggest that the popularity of Paul Gilroy's *The Black Atlantic: Modernity and Double Consciousness* (Cambridge, Mass.: Harvard University Press, 1993) was a product of this moment that, in effect, rendered invisible earlier U.S. black intellectual projects, including Cedric Robinson's *Black Marxism: The Making of the Black Radical Tradition* (London: Zed, 1983). See, too, *Found Object* (fall 1994); Greg Tate, ed., *Everything but the Burden: What White People Are Taking from Black Culture* (New York: Harlem Moon, 2003).

5. On "Black worldliness, see Nikhil Pal Singh, "Culture/Wars: Recoding Empire in an Age of Democracy," *American Quarterly* 50 (September 1998): 471–522. See, too, Laus Benesch and Genevieve Fabre, *African Diasporas in the Old and New Worlds: Consciousness and Imagination* (Amsterdam: Rodopi, 2003); Gayatri Spivak, *A Critique of Postcolonial Reason: Toward a History of the Vanishing Present* (Cambridge, Mass.: Harvard University Press, 1999); Brent Edwards, *The Practice of Diaspora: Literature, Translation, and the Rise of Black Internationalism* (Cambridge, Mass.: Harvard University Press, 2003); Dipesh Chakrabarty, *Habitations of Modernity: Essays in the Wake of Subaltern Studies* (Chicago: University of Chicago Press, 2002); Tiffany Ruby Patterson and Robin D. G. Kelley, "Unfinished Migrations: Reflections on the African Diaspora and the Making of the Modern World," in "Special Issue on the Diaspora," *African Studies Review* 43 (April 2000): 11–50. On the BPP abroad, see Vijay Prashad, *Everybody Was Kung Fu Fighting: Afro-Asian Connections and the Myth of Racial Purity* (Boston: Beacon Press, 2002); Michael L. Clemons and Charles E. Jones, "Global Solidarity: The Black Panther Party in the International Arena," in *Liberation, Imagination, and the Black Panther Party*, edited by Kathleen Cleaver and George Katsiaficas (New York: Routledge, 2001).

6. T. J. Jackson Lears, "Power, Culture, and Memory," *Journal of American History* 75 (1988): 137–140; Meaghan Morris, "Banality in Cultural Studies," *Discourse* 10.2 (1988): 3–29.

7. Robin D. G. Kelley, "'Roaring from the East': Third World Dreaming," in *Freedom Dreams: The Black Radical Imagination* (Boston: Beacon Press, 2002); Robin D. G.

Kelley and Betsy Esch, "Black Like Mao: Red China and Black Liberation," *Souls* 1.4 (fall 1999)): 6–41; Clemons and Jones, "Global Solidarity"; Kathleen Cleaver, "Back to Africa: The Evolution of the International Section of the Black Panther Party (1969–1972)," in *The Black Panther Party [Reconsidered]*, edited by Charles E. Jones (Baltimore: Black Classic Press, 1998).

8. Denning takes this term from Arjun Appadurai, *Modernity at Large: Cultural Dimensions of Globalization* (Minneapolis: University of Minnesota Press, 1996), 4.

9. Denning, *Culture in the Age of Three Worlds* (London: Verso, 2004). See also Fredric Jameson and Masao Miyoshi, eds., *The Cultures of Globalization* (Durham, N.C.: Duke University Press, 1998); Anthony D. King, ed., *Culture, Globalization, and the World System: Contemporary Conditions for the Representation of Identity* (Minneapolis: University of Minnesota Press, 1997); Lisa Lowe and David Lloyd, eds., *The Politics of Culture in the Shadow of Capital* (Durham, N.C.: Duke University Press, 1997); Amy Kaplan and Donald Pease, eds., *Cultures of United States Imperialism* (Durham, N.C.: Duke University Press, 1993).

10. Nick Dyer-Witheford, *Cyber-Marx: Cycles and Circuits of Struggle in High Technology Capitalism* (Urbana: University of Illinois Press, 1999).

11. The work of James and Cruse, and their "organic" place in the New Left and liberation movements of 1968, are essential in understanding the emergence of cultural studies and black studies, respectively.

12. Singh, "The Black Panthers and the 'Undeveloped Country' of the Left," in Jones, ed., *The Black Panther Party*, 74–75.

13. James Boggs and Grace Lee Boggs, *Racism and the Class Struggle: Further Pages from a Black Worker's Notebook* (New York: Monthly Review Press, 1971), 39; Franz Fanon, *The Wretched of the Earth* (New York: Grove Press, 1968), 130; Max Stanford, "Revolutionary Nationalism and the Afroamerican Student," *Liberator* 5.1 (January 1965): 13–14.

14. Kobena Mercer, "1968: Periodizing Politics and Identity," in *Cultural Studies*, edited by Lawrence Grossberg et al. (London: Routledge, 1992), 433–34.

15. Michel de Certeau, The Practice of Everyday Life (Berkeley: University of California Press, 2002 [1974]); Cruse, *The Crisis of the Negro Intellectual* (New York: William Morrow, 1967); Guy Debord, *Society of the Spectacle* (Cambridge: Zone Books, 1995 [1967]); Henri Lefebvre, *Critique of Everyday Life* (London: Verso, 1991 [1947]); Henri Lefebvre, *Critique of Everyday Life*, vol. 2 (London: Verso, 2002 [1962]). It is no coincidence that studies of the "politics of the everyday" with a consumer culture focus arose in this larger moment.

16. Erika Doss, "'Revolutionary Art Is a Tool for Liberation': Emory Douglas and the Protest Aesthetics at the *Black Panther*," in Cleaver and Katsiaficas, eds., *Liberation, Imagination, and the Black Panther Party*; David Hilliard and Donald Wiese, eds., *The Huey P. Newton Reader* (New York: Seven Stories Press, 2002), 143, 48.

17. Hilliard and Wiese, *The Huey P. Newton Reader*, 60; Mercer, "1968: Periodizing Politics and Identity," 433. Singh offers a similar reading of the BPP's "performance" of sovereignty in his *Black Is a Country: Race and the Unfinished Struggle for Democracy* (Cambridge, Mass.: Harvard University Press, 2004).

18. Doss, "'Revolutionary' Art," 175, 184.
19. Quoted in Eric Pace, "African Nations Open 12-Day Cultural Festival with Parade Through Algiers," *New York Times*, 22 July 1969, 9.
20. Cleaver, "Back to Africa." The acronym PAIGC stands for the African Party for the Independence of Guinea-Bissau and Cape Verde Islands.
21. Patricia Haden, Donna Middleton, and Patricia Robinson, "A Historical and Critical Essay for Black Women," in *Words of Fire: An Anthology of African-American Feminist Thought*, edited by Beverly Guy-Sheftall (New York: New Press, 1995); *Combahee River Collective*, "A Black Feminist Statement," in Guy-Sheftall, ed., *Words of Fire*.
22. Quoted in Kaluma ya Salaam, "Historical Overviews of the Black Arts Movement," in *The Oxford Companion to Women's Writing in the United States* (New York: Oxford University Press, 1995).
23. For accounts of the Third World politicized reception of U.S. soul and funk music culture, see Manthia Diawara, *In Search of Africa* (Cambridge, Mass.: Harvard University Press, 1998); Monique Guillory and Richard Green, *Soul: Black Power, Politics, and Pleasure* (New York: New York University Press, 1998).
24. Christine Acham, *Revolution Televised* (Minneapolis: University of Minnesota Press, 2004).
25. On the 1968 Olympics, see Amy Bass, *Not the Triumph but the Struggle: The 1968 Olympics and the Making of the Black Athlete* (Minneapolis: University of Minnesota Press, 2002); on Muhammad Ali as a "vernacular intellectual," see Grant Fareed, *What's My Name: Black Vernacular Intellectuals* (Minnesota: University of Minnesota Press, 2003).
26. A counter-reading might be the radical politics/analysis galvanizing around the culture of "incarceration," or more broadly "surveillance" or discipline. Denning even suggests that Michel Foucalt's *Discipline and Punish* "itself had its origins in the prison revolts at Attica, New York." In the notion of incarceration, there are direct links to the era that inspired the metaphor of internal colonization. Singh points out that the wrongfully imprisoned boxer Rubin "Hurricane" Carter suggested that black existence within the United States constrained the status of the nation to a "penitentiary with a flag." Carter, quoted in Bruce Franklin, *Prison Literature in America* (New York: Oxford University Press, 1978), 242. In the early 1990s, many commented on the prison aesthetic of hip-hop culture (baggy jeans, no belt, orange jumpsuits). At the same time, the Black Power activist and scholar Angela Davis has become a major force in the global prison abolition movement, while the Vassar College literary scholar Tyrone Simpson's work on ghettos as "carceral spaces" not surprisingly pulls directly from internal colony thought as a conceptual foundation overlooked within the genealogy of the current vogue in critical geography studies. The most prominent work in this field, that of Michel Lefebvre, also gained currency in the 1968 moment. See Angela Davis, *Are Prisons Obsolete?* (New York: Seven Stories Press, Open Media Series, 2003); Angela Davis, *The Prison Industrial Complex* (video recording) (Oakland: AK Audio, 2000). See also, Henri Lefebvre, *The Production of Space* (Malden, Mass.: Blackwell, 1991 [1974]).

The Arm(ing) of the Vanguard, Signify(ing), and Performing the Revolution: The Black Panther Party and Pedagogical Strategies for Interpreting a Revolutionary Life

TIM LAKE

In order to develop creative pedagogical strategies for reimagining ways in which the Black Panther Party (BPP) might continue to instruct us in how to live revolutionary lives, scholars need to think about how social movements function and to explore ways to bring the BPP into relationship with other modern movements. Scholars with an unbending fidelity to traditional historical methods will be challenged by this approach because it gives grounds to theoretical concerns that are usually occupied by matters of periodization and the excavation of primary documentation. In contrast, this essay emphasizes the interpretation of events associated with the Panthers as sites of social discourse and not the rigorous chronicling of the events themselves. My goal here is to demonstrate that social movement and language theory, and the modern avant-garde tradition, are suitable pedagogical tactics for appraising the BPP's revolutionary identity.

Robin D. G. Kelley argues that the problem we face today in understanding past social movements is that our "standards for evaluating" them are inappropriate. According to Kelley, we evaluate social movements based on whether or not they achieved their expressed goals and not "on the merits or power of the visions themselves." Indeed, by such a standard nearly every radical revolutionary movement comes up short, "because the power relations they sought to change remain pretty much intact."[1] But this standard of evaluation is rather shortsighted when it comes to measuring the alternative visions of groups such as the Black Panther Party. The freedom dreams of the

BPP serve as inspiration for new generations to continue to struggle for change.

It is unusual for a social movement to spring up without any relation to an antecedent tradition. In fact, the Panthers' revolutionary vision was not without precedent within the African American tradition of struggle for dignity and decency. George Katsiaficas reminds us that the black protest tradition includes a call to radically remake the social order.[2] From the early African American colonizationist organizations and missionary societies to Du Bois's pan-Africanism to Malcolm X's attempt to create a transnational freedom organization, African American political protest has always been transnational in vision. Michael L. Clemons and Charles E. Jones detail the extent to which the BPP fits within this global character of black protest. They argue that while the Party was influenced by socialist philosophies of noncapitalist nations, the Panthers nonetheless also "catalyzed indigenous insurgent organizations in at least five nations."[3]

The BPP was thus part of a long albeit episodic tradition of radical political struggle with a global connection. The emergence of the Black Panther Party in 1966 in fact attests to the enduring vitality of African American freedom dreams to inspire others to live courageous lives in the quest for full recognition of and respect for the humanity of all people. As Kelley points out, our failure to appreciate the power of the vision promulgated by such freedom fighters lies not in their success or failure but in our standard of evaluation.

The BPP, then, challenges us to rethink how social movements function. Belinda Robnett argues that social movements occur when a critical number of individuals who share a "collective identity" decide to take action toward some common objective. This collective identity can be formulated along the lines of any social marker—for example, a common history, race, gender, or class—strong enough to draw people together to act in ways that promote a particular vision. For Robnett, collective identities are fluid categories that are responsive to external (political) and internal (cultural and organizational) changes. In addition, Robnett describes social movements as having a relational character because they function within an unstable set of categories—again, historical, race, gender, or class consciousness—that respond to the interplay between external and internal forces.[4]

Robnett's relational approach toward understanding social movements helps us to understand, and perhaps to teach, in a new way the infamous 1970–1971 split in the BPP.[5] Her approach moves the discussion past simplistic questions of whether the New York Panthers stayed true to the revolutionary vision of the Party, or whether the Oakland leadership became moderate reformers.[6] The internal fractioning, external manipulation, deadly assaults, and rampant megalomania that marked this period blur the radical vision that makes the BPP such an important phenomenon.[7] Instead, aided by Robnett's relational approach, we can to use the split to shed light on the nature of revolutionary visions.

First, as Robnett instructs us, social markers that form the collective identities of those within social movements are social constructions, and as such are subject to political and cultural manipulation. While, as already noted, these social markers do not have fixed meanings, external (political) and internal (inner-group dynamics) forces help determine those meanings. Moreover, any alteration in the meaning of a social marker affects the collective identities and cohesion within a social movement. The point is not that race, gender, and class are meaningless categories; it is, rather, that whatever meaning is ascribed to them is contingent, historically specific, and relational. Therefore, the degree to which these social markers are meaningful has a direct bearing on the collective identities within a particular social movement.

Second, employing a relational approach as a pedagogical device makes it possible to teach the Party split as an example of how a category of collective identity can serve to galvanize people into a social movement and also undo that same social movement. How, precisely, does this work? In the case of the Black Panthers, what was peculiar about them was not their vision of a self-determining and self-governing African American community. Rather, what made them distinctive was their willingness to resort to armed struggle to bring that vision into existence.[8] "I did not join a movement for fortune or fame," asserts Geronimo ji Jaga (né Elmer Pratt), "I joined a movement to win. And that's the bottom line." Jaga confesses that he "joined . . . to help build a Ministry of Defense."[9] For people like Geronimo, becoming a Black Panther meant, among other things, that he was identifying himself as a revolutionary nationalist. In this sense, being a revolutionary nationalist became a necessary category for collective identity formation within the BPP.

However, again, collective identities are unstable—they blur and they blend—because they are social constructs whose meaning and value are derived from political, cultural, and organizational shifts. So, while a revolutionary nationalist identity may have been necessary for attracting persons to join the BPP, it was not a stable category of collective identity formation. Therefore, as internal forces (organizational developments) and external forces (repressive acts of the state) worked on the Party, its revolutionary identity began to shift and the collective identity needed to build a social movement started to unravel—as did the BPP.

Third, the relational approach presents the revolutionary dream that formed a base for collective identity in the BPP, allowing our inspection of it on its on merits. As Robin Kelley notes: "Revolutionary dreams erupt out of political engagement; collective social movements are incubators of new knowledge."[10] At its best, the BPP was a socially and politically engaged revolutionary organization that was responsive to the needs of the people— as, for example, in its establishment of community programs in the late 1960s. What made its revolutionary dream both radical and attractive was its contiguous relation with the people's dreams. It was the BPP's engagement with a tradition of struggle, connecting its vision with that of Malcolm X and, by extension, Marcus Garvey and the classical Black Nationalist tradition, that in turn opened up new possibilities, new knowledge, and new imaginings of a better future. As Kelley writes, "The most radical ideas often grow out of a concrete intellectual engagement with the problems of aggrieved populations confronting systems of oppression."[11]

Following the relational approach, then, broadens our understanding of social movements and dislodges the Black Panther Party from narrow biographies of its leading personalities, focusing instead on the nature of social movements. Further, such an approach guards against a fixation on measuring its meaning by traditional standards of success or failure. The BPP was more than Newton's drug addiction, Seale's thespian aspirations, the guns, the black berets and black leather jackets, or the raised clenched fists. It was, at its salient best, about a tradition of struggle to make real the revolutionary dream of an aggrieved and downtrodden people to exercise control over their individual lives and collective destiny. In short, it is possible to "read" the Panthers as a bid for an alternative way of conceiving reality so that new democratic possibilities might emerge—new ways of thinking about the nature of our social and political relationships. "It's not what I say, but what the people say," contends Jaga, "that's the epitome of democracy. And if we are denied that, then it is they who are being anti-democratic. We have the right to fight against that!"[12]

The BPP and the Modern Avant-garde Tradition

Invoking the work of social movement theorists is a beneficial pedagogical strategy because it allows us to interrogate the behaviors of individual actors while remaining cognizant of the character of social movements themselves. Here, we see social movements as relational—responding to external and internal forces. Moreover, social movements are comprised of individuals who appear to share a general vision of how the world should be. The African American struggle for freedom, dignity, and self-governance has been rooted in a particular historical reality that has shaped its expression and dictated the terms of its manifestation. However, there is no denying the fact that freedom is the goal of all oppressed people, and that history is replete with marked traditions of collective struggle inspired by a vision of freedom of one sort or another. This seems a rather straightforward point; what is not so clear is what the result would be of bringing together two apparently disparate social movements traditions. It is possible that such an effort would yield new knowledge about the nature of social movements. But, going further, it might be useful to remember that we are concerned here with the exploration of new pedagogical strategies aimed at producing alternative interpretive and evaluative perspectives on the revolutionary legacy of the Black Panther Party.

One pedagogical strategy that allows for a nuanced appraisal of the Panthers' revolutionary stance and a possible explanation of why that stance could not be sustained is to "read" the Party within the tradition of the post–World War I artistic and literary avant-garde movements. Erika Doss has examined the role of art as means for spreading the BPP's vision and emboldening its members in the revolutionary struggle. She describes the "protest aesthetics" of Emory Douglas, former BPP minister of culture, as "aimed at convincing audiences of black power."[13] Panther artists like Douglas understood the power of images to convey their message. "With their black berets and leather jackets, their Afros, dark glasses, raised fists, and military drill formations, the Panthers made great visual copy," writes Doss.[14]

Panther protest aesthetics—the deployment of art in the service of revolution—harnessed the power of art to arrest the imagination and to communicate an incendiary message intended to initiate social change. Douglas, for example, sought to produce art that would raise the revolutionary consciousness of his audience as well as to assist in the destruction of oppressive systems and the demise of the ideological status quo. But, in doing so in the late twentieth century, he shared goals expressed by members of the artistic and literary movements in the early part of the century, specifically the Dadaists and surrealists. As Sadie Plant points out, these movements must be understood as products of a political moment: "Both Dada and surrealism arose in response to the enormous political events of the early decades of the twentieth century."[15]

As Plant relates, Dada, "a nihilistic art" that is "impossible to define," was started by "a group of deserters, dissenters, and refugees who had gathered in Zurich," during World War I. Among the leading figures in this artistic movement were Hugo Ball and Marcel Janco. Having lost "confidence" in their culture, Ball and Janco formed the Dadaist Cabaret Voltaire in 1916. The Dadaists charged that the war had been caused by bourgeois culture, which they sought to destroy. Indeed, the word "Dada" itself was meant to underscore their attack on "established meanings." Though the word is nonsensical and meaningless, "its impact was such that it could not be ignored." And, although the movement claimed to be without purpose, "Dada displayed overt political commitments and expressed the hope that new possibilities of living would emerge from the wreckage it left in its wake." Dada artists thumbed their noses at all conventions, rules, and the proper aesthetics of the art world. The best-known case of this is Marcel Duchamp's "ready-mades." "The most famous of these pieces" Plant notes, "was a urinal, turned on its back and signed 'R. Mutt.'"[16] Duchamp titled the piece *Fountain*, and entered it (unsuccessfully) for exhibition in 1917. In the end, Dada was unable to confront or step outside of the culture it despised. "The movement simply could not survive without some larger social movement to effect the destruction of which it dreamed, and Dada was gradually forced into a dilemma of suicide or silence," concludes Plant.[17] The movement that was not a movement thus abolished itself. But the Dada artists did influence the surrealists, who emerged in Paris in 1924.

The leading surrealists, such as André Breton and Louis Aragon, were aware of Dada as early as 1920. Whereas the Dadaists wanted to negate all values, the surrealists wanted to rebuild them. "Instead of struggling in vain to stay free from the influence of despised cultural codes," Plant explains, "the surrealists assumed the role of an artistic and literary movement with the intention of subverting convention from within."[18] For the surrealist, the dreams and desires of ordinary persons contained privileged moments of objective chance when the "imagined world fused into the real."[19] For Breton and Aragon, the streets of Paris provided an endless array of scenes and objects for the surrealist exploration of signs that pointed to other worlds and possibilities for existence. Breton's novel *Nadja*, for instance, is packed with picturesque scenes and signs of life on the streets of Paris. It is as if Breton takes the reader on a stroll down a familiar street, pointing out the "marvels of objective chance and surreality" along the way, for the avante garde "wanted to distinguish between revolutionary politics and cultural criticism" so as to obliterate the distinctions between art and real life.[20]

Breton's thinking about the role of art in altering perceptions about what is possible is similar to that of the revolutionary artists in the BPP. "The primary thing about a revolutionary artist is that he is a revolutionary first," explained Panther artist Brad Brewer in 1970. The revolutionary artist holds the brush in one hand, and the gun in the other. "They aren't involved in dealing in life style but rather [in] offering solutions," Brewer asserted.[21] The desire to wed art to revolutionary politics in the service of changing how people perceive everyday life is thus reflected in both of these social movements. While the surrealists and the Black Panthers hardly held identical views about what constituted revolutionary social disruption, the distinction here is not great. The surrealists emphasized a revolution of consciousness — a rejection of prevailing capitalist value structures that mediated perceptions of the world — as the means by which society was to be transformed. For the Panthers, heightened consciousness was a step toward armed insurrection leading to the transformation of society. Nevertheless, the difference does constitute more than a simple privileging of militarism over consciousness in producing revolution. Rather, it is — at least it was for Panther artists — a refusal to accept the alteration of consciousness as authentically revolutionary in and of itself. A change in consciousness had to be met with revolutionary action "on the ground," as it were.

But between the surrealist and Panther moments, a new artistic group did emerge as a kind of corrective to surrealism, the Situationist International (SI). Their appearance in the late 1950s, in fact, collapses the distinction between the protest aesthetic of the avant-garde artistic movements and that of the BPP. In 1957, Guy Debord and Isidore Isou formed the SI in reaction to Breton's drift away from the aims of Dada — that is, the annihilation of status quo values — and toward mysticism. Debord and Isou wanted to return poetry to people's lives. When poetry was returned to people, they believed, they would be able to break the mind-numbing, imagination-stilting effects of capitalism that divided actors from spectators, producers from consumers. The Situationists sought to transform consciousness by transforming the here and now. They supported vandalism, wildcat strikes, and sabotage as ways of disrupting and defeating the commodity economy.[22] The Situationist critique was thus directed toward both art and revolutionary projects in general. For the SI, modern art and revolutionary politics were dead and their "revival" depended on "surpassing" them. The artist and the revolutionary had to go beyond both art and politics in order to come to the "realization of what was their most fundamental demand."[23]

Here, the fundamental demand of art and politics was the liberation of the individual from the homogenizing influence of dominant society in the service of capitalism. However, art and politics had been separated, and their unifying aims muted and radicality dulled. In order to resuscitate the radicalism of art and politics, they both had to be surpassed. That is, art and politics were to be demystified so that it became clear that modern art and revolutionary politics were no longer alive. Through their "radical gestures," then, the Situationists aimed to reunite art and politics into a coherent revolutionary program.

An example of a radical gesture that fit within the Situationist revolutionary movement occurred in Caracas, Venezuela, in January 1963 when students there captured five paintings from a French art exhibit and offered to return them in exchange for the release of political prisoners. Although a shootout with the police resulted in the recovery of the paintings, in retaliation the students bombed the police van transporting the recovered paintings in an unsuccessful attempt to destroy them. As Debord stated in reference to the entire event: "This is clearly an exemplary way to treat the art of the past, to bring it back into play for what really matters in life."[24]

For the Situationists, art was political and the political was art; at their best, they both pursued the objective of a revolutionary movement against exploitation. Panther protest artists understood the relationship between art and politics in a like manner. Emory Douglas's critique of the social realism in the work of African American visual artists of the 1950s and the soul aesthetic in the music of the 1960s is particularly revealing of a perspective akin to that of the Situationists. Douglas criticized Charles White's drawings, for example, for being "civil rights art."[25] While White used his art to expose the social condition of the African American masses, according to Douglas he did not show the people's "raising revolutionary consciousness."

Indeed, it is one thing to draw a black woman scrubbing a floor, but it is a different thing altogether to draw an image of a woman carrying both her child and a rifle, as Douglas did.

Doss tells us that Douglas also dismissed black musicians like Aretha Franklin and B. B. King for singing about what he took to be "cultural nationalism" as opposed to singing about "anything that TRANSCENDS COMMUNITIES and creates revolution."[26] For Douglas, social realism and the soul aesthetic separated art from its fundamental demand of revolution, and that what results is art that is "toothless and soft." Yet, Debord inveighed against the same thing, as "cheap and mendacious." In this way, the protest aesthetic of the BPP and the avant-garde stance of the Situationists were ideologically connected. They both saw the need to reunite art and politics in the service of social revolution. There is little doubt, for example, that the Situationists would have counted the arrests of Bobby Seale and Huey Newton for their impromptu recitation of poetry on a public sidewalk in Berkeley, California, as an appropriate radical gesture. According to Seale, he was standing on a chair on Telegraph Avenue reciting the poems "Burn, Baby, Burn" and "Uncle Sammy Call Me Fulla Lucifer" when a crowd started to gather around him. Almost immediately, a white "uniformed pig cop" appeared, and in hearing the subversive words of the poems he placed Seale under arrest for "blocking the sidewalk." The result was mayhem. Seale, Newton, and several others physically engaged the officer, along with two other "paddies," and a small riot ensued.[27]

The Situationists also shared the Panthers' Marxist values. However, the Situationists believed that through their "unorthodox rebellion" they could use propaganda to affect the "central task of a revolutionary organization."[28] They described late-capitalist society as a hyperreality. In Debord's language, it was a "society of the spectacle"; that is, in contemporary society, alienation had been replaced by the realization of commodity relations. "The Spectacle is a permanent opium war waged to make it impossible to distinguish goods from commodities, or true satisfaction from a survival that increases according to its own logic," he explained. "Consumable survival must increase, in fact, because it continues to enshrine deprivation. The reason there is nothing beyond augmented survival, and no end to its growth, is that survival itself belongs to the realm of dispossession: it may gild poverty, but it cannot transcend it."[29]

It is possible to read the Black Panthers as also having comprehended that

Debord's "consumable survival" was a nonrevolutionary station. Although they initiated a number of so-called survival programs aimed at providing commodities and services to the African American community, they seemed to understand that true revolution required a dismantling of the economic structure that provided the commodities and services that the people so desperately needed. "We're not saying that the survival programs are really revolutionary," confessed Seale later, "but the survival programs are tools and institutions by which we unify our people."[30]

The BPP's survival programs included a children's breakfast program, a free clothing program, a medical care program, and an education program. Eldridge Cleaver directly connected such programs and revolution by associating them with a nationalist agenda. For Cleaver, the distinction between understanding "Breakfast for Children" and understanding a "People's Government" was fractious if measurable at all.[31] However, Newton loosened the tether between the survival programs and the very goal of revolution itself. "We must not regard our survival programs as an answer to the whole problem of oppression," he explained, "revolutions are made of sterner stuff." Newton thus understood the survival programs in pragmatic terms. The survival programs had been created to ensure the availability of a healthy revolutionary army once the people determined that they were (to borrow a phrase from Kwame Ture, né Stokely Carmichael) "ready for the revolution." If there is one thing that is absolutely necessary to any revolution it is for the people to survive in order to make revolution a possibility. "If the people are not here," warned Newton, then the "revolution cannot be achieved."[32] The survival programs served the needs and interests of the people to ensure their survival under oppressive conditions. For Newton, revolution was a process that required the people's survival and their healthy development so that they might eventually reach the point of being ready to engage in the "serious business" of revolutionary struggle.[33]

Signification and Performance of Revolution

Incorporating a poststructuralist analysis into our deployment of social movement theory and avant-garde tradition augments our pedagogical strategy for interpreting the history and legacy of the Black Panther Party. Again, this augmentation presents an opportunity to gain new insight into the Panthers' revolutionary identity without resorting to a success-or-failure standard for evaluating the Party. According to Jacques Derrida, language (and indeed all representations of the world) is a tool for the signification of reality.[34] For Derrida, words were inherently ambiguous symbols. This does not mean that words are necessarily meaningless; however, as symbols (signifiers), words do not in and of themselves contain meaning, nor are they intrinsically referential. That is, words are not connected to any transcendent truth or ultimate reality. Rather, language — words with syntax and grammar — call our attention to certain symbols, sounds, or gestures that we must then interpret or translate into our own private language. And we interpret or translate words by way of other words. In this way, words refer to other words and, therefore, it is through the association of words with other words that meaning is derived (or, that the sign is produced). We use language — the association of symbols with other symbols governed by certain rules and structure — to guide us through the chaos of images and impressions that constantly bombard us. In short, language is the vehicle or tool we use to signify — or stand in for — a particular vision, attitude, or idea.

To illustrate Derrida's theory of signification, consider the letters "F-I-S-T" and their relationship to an actual clenched hand. The letters, "F-I-S-T," function as the signifier and the actual clenched hand that is being signified. In other words, the letters, "F-I-S-T," substitute for the object itself. And, finally, the sign is the meaning we attach to or derive from the symbol, gesture, or utterance (the signifier) that is standing in for the actual object (in this case a clenched hand). When members of the Black Panther Party raised their fists in public, they presented a symbol that elicited a variety of possible interpretations: black revolutionary insurgency, black love and self-respect, solidarity. Multiple interpretations are possible here, because signifiers never get it quite right; they do not exactly match that which is signified. Therefore, when we see images of Panthers standing in line wearing black berets, blue shirts, and black jackets with their fists thrust into the air, we cannot be exactly sure what the sign (or meaning) is.[35]

Again, this appreciation for the ambiguity of language allows us to avoid dead-end success-or-failure standards for evaluating the BPP as a revolutionary organization. Instead of asking if the Party achieved its goal of supplanting the existing social order or tracing intergroup factionalism for proof of revolutionary authenticity, the focus here is the inherent instability of an expressed revolutionary identity. In "On the Defection of Cleaver from the Black Panther Party and the Defection of the Black Panther Party from the Black Community" Newton acknowledged the "contradictions" inherent in his understanding of revolution and the understanding held by Eldridge Cleaver. "I had asked Eldridge Cleaver to join the Party," Newton explained in this pivotal document, "but he did not join until after the confrontation with the police in front of the office of *Ramparts* magazine, where the police were afraid to go for their guns." According to Newton, Cleaver interpreted the willingness of the BPP (at that time called the Black Panther Party for Self-Defense) to display arms in open view of the police as "*the* Revolution and *the* Party." What is revealed here is a contradiction within the Party between the possession of guns and an identification of the BPP as the revolutionary vanguard. However, the fundamental contradiction that ultimately surfaced in the Panther movement was of two different meanings of revolution itself. This contradiction made it necessary for Newton to try to clarify his understanding of *the* Revolution and *the* Party. "The gun by all revolutionary principles is a tool to be used in our strategy; it is not an end in itself," he wrote. For Newton, only "the people," and not the Party, "can make the revolution," because "revolution is a process" and not a spontaneous event.[36] As for the 21 February 1967 *Ramparts* incident, Newton states that the Panthers were only there to protect Betty Shabazz.[37] They were not signifying a revolution as such.

Whatever can be made of Newton's later assessment of the original revolutionary identity of the BPP, it is clear that as early as 1969 a serious contradiction had manifested itself within the Party. For Cleaver, the Panthers' experience in developing "coalition[s] for working with revolutionaries in other communities, must now be transferred over, not into the political arena but strictly into the military arena where politics have been transformed into warfare."[38] This is where Cleaver believed the liberation movement was heading, and it was on this basis that he interpreted all revolutionary actions: "I feel that all revolutionaries in the United States should be dedicated to — to recognize that we have to fight a revolutionary struggle for the violent overthrow of the United States government and the total destruction of the racist, capitalist, imperialist, neo-colonialist power structure."[39]

For Cleaver, then, the revolution was at hand. The critical question was how to organize the "revolutionary forces in every community" into what he envisioned as "the North American Liberation Front."[40] While he interpreted the increased repression of the BPP and other vanguard organizations as evidence of revolutionary momentum among the masses, Newton's interpretation of the situation was altogether different. He saw the stepped-up repressive measures of the state as having the effect of isolating the BPP from the people.[41] "The only time an action is revolutionary is when the people relate to it in a revolutionary way," he declared. An overemphasis on the gun as the essence of the revolution had failed to inspire the people toward revolutionary actions. Accordingly, "if [the people] will not use the example you set, then no matter how many guns you have your action is not revolutionary."[42]

As the political scientist Judson Jefferies points out, from the start Newton assumed that "armed resistance would have two effects: the Black Panther Party would put fear in the hearts of the police, making them apprehensive about brutalizing African Americans, and it would earn the respect and admiration of the African American community."[43] With the respect and admiration of the people, the BPP would serve as the organizational structure through which the people would create the revolution. For Newton, the guns themselves were not the revolution but a tool for raising the revolutionary consciousness of the people and establishing a positive relationship between them and the BPP. For Newton, Eldridge and others misinterpreted a courageous willingness to use guns against the state, and the ensuing repression, as the revolution itself. Consequently, they viewed any unwillingness to pick up the gun as cowardice. And, in Newton's absence in jail, their view had led the Party astray. "Eldridge Cleaver influenced us to isolate ourselves from the Black community so that it was war between the oppressor and the Black Panther Party, not war between the oppressor and the oppressed community," surmised Newton.[44]

The point here is not that Cleaver's understanding of *the* Revolution or *the* Party was less authentic than Newton's. That, of course, would be to fall into precisely the success-or-failure trap in evaluating social movements that Kelley cautions against. The point, rather, is that a poststructural pedagogical approach sharpens our appreciation of the different interpretations (significations) of what the gun might mean (sign) for the revolution (signified) and the BPP (signifier). What we learn through this approach is that our tools for representing reality—words, gestures, and symbols—are inherently ambiguous, and, therefore, in terms of what it means to be a revolutionary, a single meaning is nearly unachievable. This approach, then, in examining the ever-shifting revolutionary identity that went on in the Party, provides the opportunity to interrogate, and learn from, the marvelous militancy of the BPP.

Though somewhat unfair, given that Derrida did not deal with the issue of revolutionary insurgency, we might also fruitfully consider the implications of his claims about language, its ambiguity and shiftiness, for understanding how collective identities are formulated within social movements. Judith Butler, who builds upon Derrida's theory and argues for the performative nature of language, offers help in this endeavor.[45] Butler accepts Derrida's idea that words make sense through their association with other words (i.e., signifiers). However, for Butler, words are also associated with our performance of the meaning we intend for them to convey. Words do not embody truth or reality; rather, they signify a behavior, attitude, idea, or disposition that we want to project. In short, language is a system by which we sign (make meaning out of) certain performances.

Butler's understanding of the performative character of language allows for a reframing of the issue of plural interpretations of the Panthers' revolutionary identity. In her account, a person comes to see himself or herself as a revolutionary by performing revolutionary acts. Following Butler, then, we can understand that revolutionaries do not actually exist. Instead, people can and do engage in revolutionary performance. So, in the end, the distinction between Cleaver and Newton rests, in large measure, in how they performed revolution, as opposed to their desire for revolution. For they both desired the transformation of everyday life and envisioned the BPP playing a leading role in helping to radically transform society.

The Black Panther Party was, in part, a vehicle for the performance of revolution as a means of creating alternative visions of the social order. Take, for example, the notorious example of the events in Sacramento, California, in spring 1967, which garnered the group national, even international, exposure for the first time. On 2 May a group of Panthers attempted to exercise their right to witness the California state legislature debate a bill that, if passed, would have made carrying firearms in public illegal. According to Seale, the best members of the BPP went there "loaded down to the gills" with guns.[46] While this was a sensational event, it was not the revolution but an act of revolutionary performance. Such a reading of the Sacramento event is supported by the fact that Huey was left behind for fear of arrest, and also by the fact that the guns were never aimed at anyone—let alone fired. Finally, no "laws" were violated.

Here, then, courageous members of the Black Panther Party constructed a revolutionary identity that used signifiers (guns) to ascribe new meanings to conventional signs (legal rights) in order that new ways of understanding the world (black self-defense) could be dreamt of and pursued. More broadly, in their many activities, the Panthers engaged in revolutionary performance in acting out in ways that created space for critical reflection about the mean-spirited and cold-heartedness of a capitalist economic structure that held poor people of all colors in a condition of perpetual exploitation. Thus, the slogan "All Power to the People" was not simply a reinterpretation of the cry for "Black Power." Rather, it was a call to redistribute power so that brown, red, poor white, and black people would have power to shape their own destinies.

Pursuing a historiographical and pedagogical strategy that incorporates social movement theory, the avant-garde tradition, and theories of language, then, allows us to understand the Black Panthers' revolutionary identity as the performance of everyday acts of social transformation. In the end, those acts did not produce a successful social revolution. But this is not the point. Though the BPP met an untimely demise, its imaginative insights, generated in the heat of struggle, about how to live a progressive life continue to signify the performance of revolution.

Notes

1. Robin D. G. Kelley, *Freedom Dreams: The Black Radical Imagination* (Boston: Beacon Press, 2002), vii.
2. George Katsiaficas, "Introduction," in *Liberation, Imagination, and the Black Panther Party: A New Look at the Panthers and Their Legacy*, edited by Kathleen Cleaver and Katsiaficas (New York: Routledge, 2001), vii.
3. There were Black Panther-inspired organizations in England, Bermuda, Israel, Australia, and India. Clemons and Jones, "Global Solidarity: The Black Panther Party in the International Arena," in Cleaver and Katsiaficas, eds., *Liberation, Imagination, and the Black Panther Party*, 20–39.
4. Belinda Robnett, "External Political Change, Collective Identities, and Participation in Social Movement Organizations," in *Social Movements: Identity, Culture, and the State*, edited by David S. Meyer Whittier and Belinda Robnett (New York: Oxford University Press, 2002), 266.
5. Following Huey Newton's release from prison, while Eldridge Cleaver was still in exile, a rift occurred between the New York Panthers and the Oakland national leadership over, among other things, the revolutionary direction that the Party should take. The results were bloody and destructive — so much so that some scholars and former Party members trace the end of the group's revolutionary phase to that moment.
6. Akinyele Omowale Umoja, "Repression Breeds Resistance: The Black Liberation

Army and the Radical Legacy of the Black Panther Party," in Cleaver and Katsiaficas, eds., *Liberation, Imagination, and the Black Panther Party*, 13–19.
7. Donald Cox's "The Split in the Party" (in Cleaver and Katsiaficas, eds., *Liberation, Imagination, and the Black Panther Party*, 118–22) is a moving and graphic account of the depths of inhumanity to which some members of the Party sunk during the split.
8. Nonmilitaristic examples of classical Black Nationalism are Henry Highland Garnet's African Civilization Society (1850s), Alexander Crummwell's American Negro Academy (1897), Marcus Garvey's Universal Negro Improvement Association (1914), and W. D. Fard's Nation of Islam (1930s). See Wilson J. Moses, ed., *Classical Black Nationalism: From the American Revolution to Marcus Garvey* (New York: New York University Press, 1996).
9. Geronimo ji Jaga, "Every Nation Struggling to Be Free Has a Right to Struggle, a Duty to Struggle," in Cleaver and Katsiaficas, eds., *Liberation, Imagination, and the Black Panther Party*, 71–77.
10. Kelley, *Freedom Dreams*, 8.
11. Ibid., 9.
12. Jaga, "Every Nation Struggling," 73.
13. Erika Doss, "Revolutionary Art Is a Tool for Liberation: Emory Douglass and Protest Aesthetics at the *Black Panther*," in Cleaver and Katsiaficas, eds., *Liberation, Imagination, and the Black Panther Party*, 175–87. For an expanded version, see Doss, "Imaging the Panthers: Representing Black Power and Masculinity, 1960s-1990s," *Prospects: An Annual of American Studies* 23 (1998): 470–93.
14. Doss, "Revolutionary Art," 178.
15. Sadie Plant, *The Most Radical Gesture: The Situationist International in a Postmodern Age* (London: Routledge, 1992), 40.
16. Ibid., 44.
17. Ibid., 47.
18. Ibid., 48.
19. Ibid., 49.
20. Ibid., 50, 56.
21. Brad Brewer, "Revolutionary Art," *Black Panther*, 24 October 1970, 17, quoted in Doss, "Revolutionary Art Is a Tool for Liberation," 181.
22. Peter Marshall, "Guy Debord and the Situationists," in *Demanding the Impossible: A History of Anarchism* (London: Fontana Press, 1992).
23. Debord, "The Situationists and the New Forms of Action in Politics or Art," in *On The Passage of a Few People Through a Rather Brief Moment in Time: The Situationist Internationale, 1957–1972*, edited by Elizabeth Sussman (Cambridge, Mass.: MIT Press, 1991), 148–53.
24. Ibid., 150.
25. Douglas's take on African American social realist artists overlooks the fact that many of these artists were politically engaged. For example, Elizabeth Catlett once stood on the steps of the Supreme Court building with a hangman's noose around her

neck as part of an organized protest against the practice of lynching. Also, Charles White's *Native Son No. 2*, the painting of Richard Wright's Bigger Thomas, shows Bigger brandishing a weapon. Likewise, Aretha Franklin was involved in the political activities in Detroit, Michigan, of her father, the Reverend C. L. Franklin. For an excellent explication of the influence of social realism on African American cultural workers, see Stacy I. Morgan, *Rethinking Social Realism: African American Art and Literature, 1930–1953* (Athens: University of Georgia Press, 2004).

26. Doss, "Revolutionary Art Is a Tool for Liberation," 181.
27. Seale, *Seize the Time: The Story of the Black Panther Party and Huey P. Newton* (New York: Random House, 1970), 28.
28. Plant, *The Most Radical Gesture*, 1–2.
29. Debord, *The Society of the Spectacle*, translated by Donald Nicholson-Smith (New York: Zone Books, 1995), 30–31.
30. Seale, speaking at a rally recorded by Stenna McLean in the documentary film *Still Revolutionaries* (University of California Extension Center for Media and Independent Learning, 2000).
31. "On Meeting the Needs of the People," *Black Panther*, 16 August 1969, quoted in Philip S. Foner, ed., *The Black Panthers Speak* (New York: Da Capo Press, 1995 [1970]), 167.
32. Huey Newton, "Speech Delivered at Boston College: November 18, 1970," in *The Huey P. Newton Reader*, edited by David Hilliard and Donald Wiese (New York: Seven Stories Press, 2002), 161.
33. Newton, "On the Defection of Eldridge Cleaver," in Hilliard and Wiese, eds., *The Huey P. Newton Reader*, 206.
34. It is a curious historical fact that Seale and Newton founded the Party in the same year that Derrida first presented his theory of deconstruction to an American audience in his 1966 Johns Hopkins University lecture, "Structure, Sign and Play in the Discourse of the Human Sciences." See his *Writing and Difference*, trans. Alan Bass (Chicago: University of Chicago Press, 1978), 278–94.
35. The three elements of Derrida's theory of language—signifier, signified, and the sign—influenced the poststructural writers. The works of Gertrude Stein, such as *Tender Buttons*, George Bataille's *Story of the Eye*, and William S. Burroughs's *The Naked Lunch*, might be considered examples of challenges to our literary sensibilities in ways that reflect Derrida's subsequent theories.
36. Newton, "On the Defection of Eldridge Cleaver," 204.
37. Panthers had been assigned the responsibility of protecting Betty Shabazz, the widow of Malcolm X, while she was in San Francisco to deliver the keynote address at a memorial for her slain husband on the first anniversary of his death. It was while escorting Shabazz from an interview with Cleaver at the office of *Ramparts* magazine that the now-legendary exchange between Huey Newton and the white police officer occurred. It is here that Newton and other Panthers, armed with guns, faced down the police. Cleaver witnessed the exchange and was, allegedly, motivated to join the Party. For accounts, see Seale, *Seize the Time*, 125–32; Cleaver, "The Cour-

age to Kill: Meeting the Panthers," in *Eldridge Cleaver: Post-Prison Writings and Speeches*, edited by Robert Scheer (New York: Random House, 1969), 31–36; Newton, *Revolutionary Suicide* (New York: Writers and Readers Publishing, 1995 [1973]), 130–32.
38. Lee Lockwood, *Conversations with Eldridge Cleaver: Algiers* (New York: Dell Publishing, 1970), 54–55.
39. Ibid., 54.
40. Ibid.
41. Ward Churchill argues that all dissident groups suffered under government-backed COINTELPRO operations in the 1960s, but that the BPP was "sledgehammered" by them. As he writes, "Of the 295 counterintelligence operations the [FBI] has admitted conducting against black activists and organizations during the period, a staggering 233, the majority of them in 1969, were aimed at the Panthers" ("To Disrupt, Discredit and Destroy: The FBI's Secret War against the Black Panther Party," in Cleaver and Katsiaficas, eds., *Liberation, Imagination, and the Black Panther Party*, 82).
42. Newton, "On the Defection of Eldridge Cleaver," 204.
43. Judson L. Jefferies, *Huey P. Newton: The Radical Theorist* (Jackson: University Press of Mississippi, 2002), 16.
44. Newton, "On the Defection of Eldridge Cleaver," 206.
45. Butler is a gender theorist who argues that male and female sexual identities are not ontological or even biological, but rather are brought into existence by language. We are "male" or "female" because that is what we are called, and having been so called, we perform the corresponding role. For her, the material difference between male and female bodies makes little sense without them being interpreted differently as sexed bodies. This is not proof of a material difference between the male and female body; rather, it reveals a difference between the perceived materiality of their bodies as natural attracting bodies for the purpose of reproduction. Furthermore, the process of materialization is largely a social construction that requires the performance of sexual norms that are always already present. The aim here is to apply Butler's notion that identities are performed to the BPP's revolutionary identity in order to complicate readings of the conflict between Cleaver and Newton over the meaning of *the* revolution and *the* Party. See Butler, *Bodies That Matter: On the Discursive Limit of "Sex"* (New York: Routledge, 1993), and *Gender Trouble: Feminism and the Subversion of Identity* (New York: Routledge, 1989).
46. Seale, "Seize the Time," speech at MIT, Cambridge, Mass., 20 February 1995 (audiotape).

Media Culture and the Public Memory of the Black Panther Party

EDWARD P. MORGAN

Ever since I was first taught about the civil rights movement, I've heard of the Black Panthers. It has always been in a negative aspect, and every picture I can remember shows black men angrily standing with guns.

— A student in my "Movements and Legacies of the 1960s" class

In a widely viewed popular culture reference to the Black Panther Party, the sympathetic figure of an innocent Forrest Gump happens across his friend Jenny amid a secret meeting of 1960s revolutionaries — most notably, a threatening group of black-leather-jacketed, afro-ed, and gun-toting Black Panthers who defiantly spit their manifesto against racist America in Gump's face. Forrest's attention is diverted when Jenny's boyfriend slugs her in the face with his fist. Forrest instinctively attacks the boyfriend, pummeling him until he is pulled away. Seemingly embarrassed, and innocent of the gathering's political significance, he withdraws, apologizing to the Panthers for crashing their "party."

I draw attention to *Forrest Gump* not only because it stereotypes the Panthers but because it appeared amid a broader revision of 1960s history in late-twentieth-century mass media culture; its "realism" cast against a backdrop of a turbulent era neatly dichotomized between an early "good 1960s" and a late "bad 1960s."[1] The *Washington Post* columnist Jonathan Yardley captured the view in 1987, when he wrote: "During the 'Sixties' — which began around 1965 and ended about a decade later — little of lasting value was accomplished either politically or culturally; for all their noisy rhetoric and noisy music, the Sixties contributed nothing to the national heritage, at least nothing anyone in his right mind would care to treasure." Curiously, given his disregard for the decade's calendar bookends, Yardley then asserts that "apologists for the time like to claim . . . that the civil rights movement was part of the Sixties, when . . . it had begun long before then."[2] In fact, that movement provided both an experiential grounding and a powerful inspiration for racial and ethnic minorities, women, and sexual minorities who struggled against their effective exclusion from the wider society and participated in the reconstruction of their own social identities. At the same time, experientially linked movements attacked political and economic institutions, in the grassroots struggle against poverty and opposition to the Vietnam War, in the counterculture, and in the ecology movement. Together, such protest movements forced the nation to address problems previously off the public agenda.

But the context of these struggles have largely disappeared from the public history retained in mass media culture. The icons that remain — a glamorous young president; Martin Luther King Jr. as the national conscience; betrayed American soldiers; a generation in revolt; black revolutionaries and militant New Leftists; the Woodstock nation — are repeatedly exploited to bolster the ideological campaigns of the Right and to play on the nostalgia of the middle-aged for financial gain. For this, propaganda attacks and popular culture representations draw heavily on the images and texts popularized by the mass media in the 1960s. Mass media "history," then, is a reflection of past mass media coverage.

Within this discourse, the Black Panthers stand out as the most provocative of 1960s icons, the subject of a rewriting that reduces them to their most inflammatory behaviors by highlighting criminal activity. This body of work includes, for example, the anti-Panther polemics of David Horowitz, who has influenced the long wave of propaganda attacks against the 1960s, and the work of the journalist Hugh Pearson, whose historical study *Shadow of a Panther* focuses largely on the media-hyped Oakland Panthers and the violent life of Huey Newton.[3] Though these two authors differ sharply in their tone of writing and their respect for empirical evidence, both focus on violence, criminality, and personality disorders, particularly in the Oakland chapter's later years when Newton exhibited manifestations of paranoid megalomania, surrounded by a coterie of thugs carrying out his commands, in the manner of a deranged Mafioso boss.[4] As history, the portrait is inseparable from media culture's "sixties," then and now.

A Model of Mass Mediated Politics

The forces that produced the sixties turbulence are complex, of course, reflecting wide-ranging grievances, personal predispositions, the responses of the politically powerful and their law enforcement agents, and the way these were communicated through capitalism's mass media. In whatever form, political protest arises because of a perceived inability to redress grievances not seen as part of the legitimate government agenda. Thus, the first aim of protest is to inject them onto that public agenda, to make them part of public discourse. To be effective, protesters must make the protest audience feel psychologically "closer" to the protesters than they do to the target of the protest—typically through political organizing and the mass media. Conversely, targeted power must increase the psychological distance between protesters and the wider audience—usually through propaganda that wraps power in consensual values and denigrates protesters by embellishing whatever negative features might be visible in the media.

Radicals face profound obstacles in this dynamic.[5] The powerful, drawing on years of indoctrination, social myths, and a degree of public satisfaction with institutional performance, make protesters seem like threatening "outsiders." For their part, protesters must overcome widely held perceptions, making institutions appear more alienating to public audiences than the protesters themselves. As protesters typically reach wider audiences through the mass media, the ways media treat issues are critical. Media, reflecting elite interests and the market imperative of shaping conventional perceptions of mass publics, interpret the meaning of events in ways that systematically reinforce ideological hegemony, though within the bounds of conventional discourse, conflicting views compete, sometimes stridently.[6] In this sense, the national media—particularly the *New York Times* as the "paper of record"—act as the arbiters of the boundaries between legitimate and illegitimate dissent. The advent of mass communications also produced the tendency to present news events in simplified, dichotomous form, in part reflecting the rise of journalism's professional norms of impartiality and balance.[7]

Two other characteristics of mass media—news as a form of dramatic entertainment and consumer culture's co-optive responses to resistance—evolved in response to the tumultuous events of the 1960s. From civil rights protests and assassinations to late-1960s turmoil, the sixties were full of dramatic televisual political spectacles that served the market imperative of attracting and holding audiences, with increasingly personalized news stories producing a culture of public celebrities. At the same time, commercially driven media became attentive to the youth market and its more flamboyant modes of expression. In the 1960s, the media flattered participants in social movements with the light of public recognition, establishing a dynamic that has since been emulated by advertising and entertainment TV, with co-optive effect.[8]

If protest can garner sufficient numbers and provide potent visual imagery, it gains media attention. In turn, the media highlight those aspects of protest that will arouse the curiosity and hold the attention of potential audiences; they focus on the behaviors, appearances, and personal stories of the protesters and on any dramatic conflicts. Simultaneously, media interpret the meaning of protest. Legitimate protest resonates with conventional ideological assumptions expressed by "credible" spokespersons. But if the "agitators" oppose the status quo, like Martin Luther King Jr. did, the voice of legitimate expression is not the King who denounced the war in Vietnam as immoral nor the King who linked poverty to the imperatives of capitalism but rather the Baptist preacher who advocated racial integration in the South. All else gets minimal coverage — typically highlighted by the chanting of slogans, the occasional poster or symbol, and possibly a speech soundbite.

In effect, then, the arena of public discourse — the mass media — is closed off to the arguments of outsiders, even as outsiders are invited to express themselves in ways that attract media cameras. Instead of a public conversation between different arguments, the public witnesses a drama that invites little more than the subjective response of feeling sympathetic to one side or the other. They may feel encouraged to emulate the protesters' behaviors, or feel sympathy for those who seek to denigrate the protests, but the media spectacle offers little else. Scholars have noted the co-optive effect this had on radical political critics like the Panthers:

> Not only are certain actors given standing [in the media] more readily than others, but certain ideas and language are given a more generous welcome. It is not simply that certain ideas are unpopular — some are rendered invisible. . . . The media speak mainstreamese, and movements are pushed to adopt this language to be heard since journalists are prone to misunderstand or never hear the alternative language and its underlying ideas. But it is a common experience of movement activists to complain that something has been lost in translation. Movements that accept the dominant cultural codes and do not challenge what is normally taken

for granted will have less of a problem, but *for many movements, this would involve surrendering fundamental aspects of their raison d'être* (emphasis added).[9]

In part because of this dynamic, the underground press — including the Panthers' newspaper, the *Black Panther* — flourished in the latter part of the 1960s.

Instead of including the arguments of radicals, then, late-sixties media discourse increasingly focused on the most flamboyant actions, sights, sounds, and rhetoric of the "outsider." Drama made political activity newsworthy; it helped to sell news programming to wider audiences as the "society of spectacle" was coming of age. Thus, because the Panthers' arguments were largely excluded from the mass media while their dramatic actions were noticed, their encounter with media reinforced their path toward symbolic action as a way of gaining a voice in the wider culture — thus, the "performative" nature of much late-1960s politics.[10] In the absence of any serious consideration of radical ideas within mainstream discourse, "radical" came to be defined, in short, by militant behavior.

Panther Radicalism and Militancy

The Black Panther Party, in posing a radical argument in especially militant fashion, constitutes a particularly revealing case study of mass-mediated politics at work, both during and since the 1960s.[11] As self-proclaimed "heirs of Malcolm," the Panthers expressed the newly emboldened black masculinity of the Black Power movement, embodied especially in the volatile and complex personality of founder Huey Newton. Moreover, the Ten-Point Platform and Program of October 1966 included demands for black self-determination, full employment, an "end to robbery by the white man" of the black community, trial by peer juries, and freedom for all black men in jails across the county — all echoing the language and politics of contemporary black militancy. Over time, however, and influenced especially by what they saw as an imperial war in Vietnam, the Panthers increasingly expressed more radical condemnations of the American system. Newton's 1970 articulation of "intercommunalism," for example — a kind of solidarity among peoples of the world subjected to American imperialism — reflected that evolution in Panther radicalism.

Though Panther strategies varied significantly over time, their verbal expression tended to be inflammatory, at least until the internecine fighting that produced a bloody "split" in early 1971. By 1968, Panther activities included a variety of community service projects — free breakfasts for school children, followed by free health clinics, free clothing drives, and liberation schools that taught black history and black pride. Even in 1967, they had launched their own newspaper, started a drive for decentralized police departments, and engaged intermittently in electoral campaigns. But organizing popular support for the "revolution" — whatever form that might ultimately take — was always a significant element in Panther leaders' thinking. Even their early, highly provocative actions reflected a desire to expand their base in the black community and to use the media to reach a wider audience.

Point seven of the Ten-Point Program minced no words: *"We want an immediate end to POLICE BRUTALITY and MURDER of black people."*[12] Nothing crystallized the powerlessness of the inner-city population — particularly among young black males — as graphically as their abusive treatment at the hands of an overwhelmingly white police force. And so, the Panthers' crucial initial action was their institution of police patrols. Drawing on Newton's law school courses, the patrols were carefully trained in constitutional rights and California state law. Starting in late 1966, the Panthers began to follow police cars patrolling the streets of inner-city Oakland. When the police stopped the Panthers also stopped, got out of their car, ostentatiously loaded their guns, and observed the police to make sure no rights were violated. The immediate target of the initial Panther action was, in short, police brutality; their intended audience was the inner-city black community itself. By their bravado, their insistence on the right to carry guns and, if necessary, to use them in self-defense, the Panthers hoped to embolden and empower the inner-city black population.[13]

Not surprisingly, however, the Panthers' inflammatory rhetoric and open embrace of armed self-defense was immediately viewed as illegitimate by Oakland police and California state officials, notably Governor Ronald Reagan. The path toward national media attention and state repression — often working hand in hand — began with an effort to change the California gun laws to prohibit carrying loaded weapons, which in turn attracted a delegation of armed Panthers to the corridors of power in the Sacramento state legislature in 1967. By 1968 the FBI's counterintelligence program, COINTELPRO, targeted the Panthers by employing widespread surveillance, infiltration, agents provocateur, and even seeding open warfare between the Panthers and other black militant groups or city gangs. Most important, perhaps, by "orchestrating false and derogatory stories" and racial stereotypes in the news media, via a network of some three hundred "cooperating journalists," COINTELPRO aimed to discredit the Panthers in the eyes of the broader public.[14] Thus, as the Panthers sought to express their political voice in a hostile environment and the state sought to "neutralize" it, the media helped produce the meteoric rise, repression, and fall of the Black Panther Party.

Covering the Panthers in the 1960s and 1970s

Surprisingly, there has been little systematic study of the mass media coverage of the Black Panthers.[15] Among the few efforts of any value is a 1997 article by Michael Staub in the journal *Representations*, which reviewed samples of late-1960s and early-1970s coverage in the *New York Times*, in selected newsmagazines, and in the "New Journalism" in *Esquire* and *New York*.[16] Here, I have expanded on Staub's work, in light of the media-protest dynamic outlined above, by examining all articles about the Panthers appearing in major national magazines between 1966 and 1976, focusing primarily on three weeklies, *Time, Newsweek*, and *U.S. News and World Report*.[17] I have supplemented that coverage with daily accounts in the *New York Times* and the participant-observer pieces in *Ramparts, Saturday Evening Post*, and the *New Yorker*.[18] The search netted 163 articles, 67 of which were in the three newsmagazines. A preliminary yearly count (table I) confirms the surge in Panther interest referred to by Staub, especially as 10 of the 28 articles in 1969 appeared after the police slayings of the Chicago Panthers Fred Hampton and Mark Clark in December of that year.[19]

Strikingly, over this eleven-year time span there isn't a single article that focuses primarily on what might be called the community-building aspect of the Panthers, namely their programs like free breakfasts, free health clinics, and free clothing. Yet, as Yohuru Williams has argued, "community organizing efforts came to the forefront of Panther activity" in Oakland in April 1967, and, following the police shoot-outs resulting in Huey Newton's incarceration and Eldridge Cleaver's exile, the Panther leaders Bobby Seale and David Hilliard reemphasized the Panthers' "Serve the People" program.[20] Nonetheless, only a handful of the articles in my survey even mention the community-building aspect, and those that do consistently frame it in pejorative ways.

Similarly, with few exceptions beyond repeated catchall phrases, the newsmagazines paid no substantive attention to the Panthers' political ideology.

Table I: National Magazine Articles on the Black Panthers

	1966	1967	1968	1969	1970	1971	1972	1973	1974	1975	1976
news magazines	0	1	6	10	29	15	2	1	0	1	2
all magazines	0	2	16	28	66	28	5	8	0	1	5

Stories paraded the usual Panther slogans about revolution or killing "pigs," while some linked the Party to leftist traditions like Marxism-Leninism and Maoism. For example, in its second article on the group, following Newton's manslaughter conviction in September 1968, *Time* characterized the Panthers as "the most extreme of the black extremists," noting simply that, "committed to revolution, devoted to some hard line Chinese Communist double-talk, they are gathering notoriety as an American Mao-Mao."[21]

For the most part, the national newsmagazine coverage was preoccupied with the violence-connected aspects of the Panthers: their clashes with police, the highly publicized travails of their leaders, the "New York 21 conspiracy" trial, and various Panther incarcerations. Even the relatively few articles that purported to examine other aspects of the Panthers were framed by references to violent rhetoric, guns, and police battles. The cumulative effect of leafing through such material is overwhelming: the Panthers are reduced to a single, dominant essence — they are about violence and criminality, period.

The Early Years: 1966 to September 1969

The perceptions of the Panthers as a violence-prone, anti-white group grew out of the earliest encounters between them and the news media from 1966 to 1969, prior to the "moral panic" phase that Staub found decisive. During these years, the portrait of the group was one-dimensional: violent, criminal, aggressive. In addition, most of the articles focused disproportionate attention on at least one of three Panther celebrities: Newton, Seale, or Cleaver. Readers would have to turn to other sources — the Panthers' own newspaper or more in-depth magazine articles — to understand the context of the group's emergence or the nature of their politics.

The earliest Panther activities — police patrols, efforts to politicize inner-city ghetto youth, a dramatic standoff between Oakland police and Huey Newton during a visit by Malcolm X's widow Betty Shabazz[22] — failed to attract any attention from the national newsmagazines or from the *New York*

Times. The national limelight first illuminated the Panthers when they staged their armed protest in Sacramento on 2 May 1967.[23] In its first recognition of the Oakland-based Panthers, the *Times* opened its news article by observing, "With loaded rifles and shotguns in their hands, members of the *anti-white* Black Panther party marched into the state Capitol today" (emphasis added).[24] Four days later, the paper editorialized against "the spirit of lawlessness" exhibited by the Panthers, Stokely Carmichael, and a defiant Governor Lurleen Wallace of Alabama. Reflecting its centrist assumptions, the *Times* noted that the "laws of a free society" prevailed in the United States and "no individual or group is without legal and political redress for his grievances."[25]

Once the national media noticed the Panthers, their attention took on predictable characteristics.[26] The media came to define the Panthers by their appearance and rhetoric as a violent, largely criminal, paramilitary group. In doing so, they were reflecting the potency of visual media; the emphasis on dramatic action, personalities, and conflict; and the mass media's ideological framing. Further, the media here exemplify what some have called the mainstream journalists' inability to hear the Panthers' "alternative language" and "underlying ideas."[27] The negative image of the Panthers, then, became the prevailing mass media portrayal of them.

The first event to attract the attention of *Time* and *Newsweek* was an April 1968 shoot-out between the police and the Oakland Panthers, which resulted in the death of the seventeen-year-old Panther treasurer Bobby Hutton. Both magazines briefly included the two sides' conflicting accounts of the shoot-out, but both framed the Panthers in ways that anticipated all future accounts, clearly suggesting that the Panthers were the aggressors. *Time* led its story with a statement about the "maelstrom of looting and arson" across the United States following the earlier murder of Martin Luther King Jr. And, without mentioning the Panther efforts that kept Oakland cool in the aftermath of the King assassination, *Time* noted that "Oakland's police were deeply involved in a bitter private race feud of their own. Ranged against them was a strutting band of hyper-militants, styling themselves the Black Panther Party for Self-Defense. The Panthers, armed and angry, are defiantly demanding a facedown." *Time* then simply noted that "routine police procedure provided the invitation to bloodshed."[28] Police accounts of the shoot-out were followed by a brief mention of "Black Power spokesmen" who "shrilled murder, claiming Hutton's hands were raised." The balance of the article highlighted the arrest records of Cleaver, Newton, and Seale, and referred to Cleaver's *Soul on Ice* and rhetoric that "bares the pent-up black rage that inspires the Panthers' snarling intransigence."[29]

The somewhat more liberal *Newsweek* sought to convey a broader sense of who the Panthers were, though their coverage was hardly less hostile than that of *Time*. Under the heading "Panther Hunt," the article began: "In the workaday world of Oakland, Calif., the Black Panthers loom as a particularly bizarre bunch [of] militant Negro extremists who model themselves after Malcolm X and take their motto from Mao Tse Tung, 'Political power comes through the barrel of a gun.'"[30] The piece then briefly reviewed Panther history: their "pouncing" into the national spotlight in Sacramento; the Oakland street patrols and ready use of guns; the murder charge against Huey Newton; the efforts to connect with leaders of the Student Nonviolent Coordinating Committee (SNCC) and take over the New Left. It culminated with an exclusively police-based report on the Oakland shoot-out that resulted in Hutton's death. The accompanying photos show an armed policeman crouching behind a police car, a manacled Cleaver being wheeled away in a wheelchair, and three Black Panther Party buttons.[31]

The Panthers' next appearance in national newsmagazines occurred in fall 1968, in conjunction with Huey Newton's trial. *Time*'s second Panther article highlighted the manslaughter verdict, while continuing to flesh out the "state of war" spreading to other American cities by, as *Time* cast it, Panther aggression ultimately producing a "get tough" reaction from police. The article included the iconic photograph of an enthroned Huey Newton on an African wicker chair holding a rifle and a spear, and it gave passing references to Cleaver's campaign for president as the "Peace and Freedom Party" candidate, Cleaver's *Soul on Ice*, and the "ten-point manifesto." It concluded by observing that though "a heavy majority of Negroes reject this sort of thing as ridiculous mumbo-jumbo," many "moderates" are "too intimidated by the Panthers to speak out."[32]

Newsweek's coverage preceded that of *Time* by a few days and therefore anticipated rather than reported on the end of Newton's trial: the article's focus was on the Panthers' potential response to what *Newsweek* implied was a likely guilty verdict. First, the magazine noted Newton's position as "defense minister" of the Panthers, who, readers were reminded, were the "cop-hating organization viewed by its admirers as a dedicated band of Robin Hoods, by its opponents as a collection of hate-mongering, crime-prone psychopaths — and by much of the rest of the U.S. as one of the more baffling and vexing manifestations of the nation's racial tensions."[33] So much for informative news reporting by the "objective mainstream press." The remainder of the article returned to the dichotomous, "neutral," coverage of Newton's case by asking a number of "unresolved" questions: "Did Newton pull a gun from his shirt and fire it at Officer Frey, as the prosecution contended and the defense denied? Did Frey draw his pistol against Newton and somehow in the ensuing scuffle manage to shoot himself five times, presumably with his own weapon?"[34] I will return later to the subjective effects of this kind of dichotomous reporting.

A week later, *Newsweek* followed up with an account of two Oakland policemen who shot up Panther headquarters after the jury's "compromise verdict" — manslaughter instead of first-degree murder. It would seem that the article's title, "On the Prowl," though suggestive of prowling Panthers, was actually a reference to the two cops, as the headquarters barrage was the only news reported in the short piece. However, the article framed an act that could be construed as evidence supporting Panther claims about police aggression in a manner that nonetheless put the onus on the Panthers. It began by noting that "ever since 'Defense Minister' Huey P. Newton was arrested last autumn on charges of murdering one policeman and injuring another, his pack of supporters has threatened to blow Oakland apart if he were not freed," and then observed that the "special alert by the Oakland cops seemed a fair enough precaution." The article went on to introduce the police attack by acknowledging that these "emergency measures" adopted by the police seemed "a bit misplaced," then commenting that the policeman who pumped several rounds into the "postered walls and windows" were "no doubt reflecting disappointment on the Oakland police force that the jury failed to return a first-degree murder verdict" — no such context for Panther police patrols ever appeared in the newsmagazines. Noting that Oakland's police chief was "desperately trying to keep the lid on an edgy city," *Newsweek* acknowledged that Newton "put out the word to 'cool it' while his appeal runs its course," adding that his plea did not "stop the Panthers from chortling over the latest police incident" as a "clear vindication of their view that the Oakland cops have been out to get them all along." The article then quoted Bobby Seale denouncing the "jive-assed, scared-assed brothers and sisters" in the media for saying the Panthers were crazy for calling the police "pigs." *Newsweek* concluded that "the militant Panthers are also expected to turn the police attack to practical advantage" — that is, recruitment.[35]

A week later, *Time* briefly reported on two court actions affecting Panther leaders Newton and Cleaver. In one, an Oakland judge denied a motion to free Newton—the "handsome, light-skinned leader of the hypermilitant" Panthers—on bail while his case was appealed, and then ordered him imprisoned for two to fifteen years. Separately, Cleaver's parole was revoked for his involvement in the April "firefight" ending in Hutton's death, with Cleaver charged with "assault with intent to commit murder." *Time* noted that although Cleaver was granted sixty days for appeals, the court ruling came "at an embarrassing moment" for "the presidential candidate for the antiwar Peace and Freedom Party." *Time* concluded that "with two of their leaders on ice, it was a time of barely throttled fury" for the Panthers.[36] Mass audiences, in other words, were left to anticipate the next Panther attack.

In fact, Newton's 1968 trial and imprisonment provided the Panthers with a cause célèbre that helped trigger the rapid national growth of the Party.[37] Until his own incarceration, Cleaver provided significant national leadership—including his presidential candidacy—for the Panthers' growing national visibility. After Cleaver's parole was revoked, however, and he fled the country, Seale and Hilliard sought to bring order to a fragmented national organization through a reemphasis on community-based work.[38] The breakfast program, for example, engaged the Panthers in classic community organizing–providing a basis for raising public consciousness about hunger and its link to the widespread poverty in the United States and the Third World, and exposing Panther members to related community issues like the need for adequate winter clothing.[39] Late fall 1968 was also the moment when the rapidly growing Black Panther Party was added to the FBI's COINTELPRO efforts to eradicate the New Left and Black Power movement. The following spring, the FBI dispatched a memo to its field offices targeting the Panther breakfast programs for destruction; a 15 May FBI airtel to twenty-seven field offices noted that the free breakfast program was the "best and most influential activity going for the BPP and as such, is potentially the greatest threat to efforts by authorities . . . to neutralize the BPP and destroy what it stands for."[40]

Around the same time that the FBI was demonstrating alarm about such threatening programs, the national media also began to take notice of this "new" aspect of the Panthers. *Newsweek*'s "Guns and Butter" article of 4 May 1969 marked the first mention of the Panthers' breakfast for children program in any of the newsmagazines. Like the "butter" in the title, *Newsweek* framed this "good side" of the Panthers with an initial paragraph that began,

"They were all of white America's nightmares of the black revenge come chillingly to life—an armed, angry guerrilla cadre uniformed in black berets, black leather black looks and devoted almost obsessively to guns." After revisiting the gun-toting incident in Sacramento and the recent arrest of the New York Panther 21 for allegedly "plotting to blow up five Manhattan department stores," *Newsweek* glibly suggested that the Panthers were "busily escalating to phase two: dishing up free hot breakfasts, amiably as you please, to the ghetto's poorest, hungriest children." The article asked, "Had the Panthers turned pussycat?" Hardly. Observing that this "vanguard of an armed black revolution" had run into the "limits of the bellicose steel-and-leather imagery" while growing into a national organization, *Newsweek* maintained that the Panthers had "begun experimenting" with a form of "escalation" that was "decidedly unrevolutionary"—presumably because it was not violent. The article concluded with Seale observing that "breakfast for children is a very socialist program," along with "Kathy" Cleaver adding, "Panther style," to which *Newsweek* added ominously, "but Panther-style hasn't lost its edge of menace. 'You'll hear more of us during the summer,' said a Detroit Panther—and he wasn't talking about breakfast for the kiddies."[41]

Given that previous national media coverage failed to acknowledge any Panther political strategy other than violent warfare with police, the mass media were left to interpret the breakfast program as a kind of desperate shift in Panther public relations. In contrast to the "pussycat" and "unrevolutionary" media framing, the FBI took note of the program's political impact. After observing that churches and other black organizations were responding supportively to the Panther breakfasts, J. Edgar Hoover responded with a series of May 1969 memos targeting the "serve the people" programs for FBI "eradication." The one-time counterintelligence director William C. Sullivan suggested that COINTELPRO efforts should misrepresent the breakfast program as a means by which children were being indoctrinated with "violent . . . anti-white propaganda" and encouraged to "hate police."[42]

The next newsmagazine article to appear, in the July 1969 issue of *U.S. News and World Report*, suggests a more direct linkage to the FBI's COINTELPRO efforts to influence the media. As the second of two *U.S. News* articles during this entire period, the magazine curiously singled out for coverage "a booklet that shocked Congress," the twenty-three-page Panther pamphlet titled "The Black Panther Coloring Book," which showed youths attacking police represented as "boar-toothed pigs." The brief article followed a longer alarmist piece titled "Racial Outbreaks: A Long Hot Summer After All?" that referred to racial strife in Omaha, Harrisburg, and elsewhere, and a second article that reported on a slowing in the growth of the nation's crime rate—a "sign of Hope in War on Crime." Accompanied by a cartoonlike illustration from the pamphlet, the article opened by stating: "One Senator called it a 'blueprint for murder of policemen in the hands of children.' Others said they were 'shocked and appalled.'" In the end it concluded with a brief reference to Seale's comment that the booklets were "unauthorized" and that distribution had been stopped."[43] Despite the Panthers' efforts to destroy the coloring book, an FBI infiltrator-turned-agent provocateur printed one thousand copies for distribution.[44]

It is also noteworthy that during this period, the widely read, conservative *Reader's Digest* published in October 1969 its only article on the Panthers, an "Intelligence Report on Today's 'New Revolutionaries.'" Focusing on the Students for a Democratic Society in addition to the Panthers, the article reads as a virtual replication of the kinds of charges that the FBI and the Nixon administration, in particular, were generating against both groups —backed by quotations from Professor Harvey Mansfield of "strife-torn Columbia" and Senator John McClellan, whose Senate Investigative Committee's hearing produced "cold, irrefutable facts" that the public "now deserves to be acquainted with."[45]

The previous August *Newsweek* provided the public with a glimpse into Panther ideology; however, instead of discussing the content of the Panthers' positions it focused on offering a who's who among the "clans" that gathered at a 1969 conference in Oakland—ranging from "shaggy-haired campus revolutionaries" to "balding Troskyites," and from "leather-jacketed whites of the Young Patriots" to the "Spartacist League." Other than representing the gathering as an effort to organize a "United Front Against Fascism"—which presumably made no sense to the majority of *Newsweek* readers—the magazine's substantive discussion of the three-day conference was limited to a single and familiar issue: community control of police. After mentioning the strategy of introducing that option on the November ballot, the latter half of the article returned to the familiar theme of past Panther-police battles and the prosecution of Panther court cases. The concluding paragraph took note of Hoover's proclamation that the Panthers represented the "greatest threat to the internal security of the country," a comment seemingly buttressed by

Newsweek's conclusion about the Panthers' "growing prominence" within the "radical movement as a whole"—a tone that clearly anticipated the "moral panic" that Staub discerned after the Hampton-Clark killings of December 1969.[46]

Newsweek's final Panther article before that event focused on the "Panther Hunt" that followed the spring discovery of Alex Rackley's mutilated body in Connecticut. Beginning with a description of the "brutal marks of interrogation by torture and death by execution," and noting that eight Panthers had been arrested (including George Sams Jr., very likely a government agent), the article drew on police sources to trace connections between the Rackley killing and an alleged "Panther plot to dynamite five department stores and a police station" in New York. The FBI investigation of that plot provided the rationale for police raids in Chicago, Denver, Salt Lake City, and Prince Georges County in Maryland.[47] *Newsweek*'s narrative then seguéd to Seale's arrest and incarceration on murder charges in connection with the Rackley killing. Noting that the Panther leadership was "in considerable disarray," the article included a Justice Department denial that there was a campaign to "bust up the Panthers," and a comment by Seale that the Panthers were being "attacked" because "we're doing something that's good for the people. . . . The power structure is trying to get rid of the whole party." In conclusion *Newsweek* remarked that Seale's arrest would "likely mean new posters, more contributions and an increased sense of unity and determination for the Panthers."[48]

Prior to December 1969, then, suggestions of a concerted effort to "get the Panthers" were being aired in the media, along with official denials and plenty of information and government propaganda suggesting that the Panthers were a growing national threat. In addition, legal charges had been levied against two large groups of Panthers, in New York and New Haven, and both sets of charges were to evolve into sensational trial coverage in 1970 and 1971. While the overall pattern of newsmagazine coverage remained the same, there was one significant change. "Credible" voices expressing support for the Panthers could now be found within these media, legitimizing and broadening the Panthers' potential appeal. In short, largely through growing perceptions of governmental repression—heightened by the alarming Hampton-Clark shootings—the Panthers finally succeeded in reaching a broader audience within the ideological boundaries of mainstream media culture—namely, among liberals. Reports in the media conveyed a highly plausible impression of the Panthers under government attack, although it was not until congressional hearings in the mid-1970s that the full scale of government repression came to light.

Together with events that suggested that the Panthers were being victimized, the chorus of authoritative, credible voices legitimizing the perception of the Panthers as victims appears to have triggered the spread of what Staub termed a "moral panic" in media coverage. In fact, rather than "panic" about the Panthers, the new tone was more of a backlash against liberal voices in the media and, ultimately, the liberal media themselves — a backlash that was to grow and broaden in ensuing years. The leading edge of this panic emanated from a rightist response attacking these voices for giving legitimacy to the illegitimate. Ultimately, the attack succeeded in returning the Panthers to their one-dimensional profile as criminal outsiders.

Panther Panic: 1969 to 1971

The shift in media attention toward the Panthers also followed the massive, violent insurrections in Newark and Detroit, the antiwar movement's shift "from protest to resistance," the murders of Martin Luther King Jr. and Robert Kennedy, and the police riot at the Democratic National Convention in Chicago.[49] The United States was sharply polarized and violent, and the electoral option appeared increasingly hopeless to many on the Left in 1968. Amid escalating COINTELPRO activity against the Black Panthers, SNCC, the American Indian Movement, and the white New Left, Hoover's repeated declarations that the Panthers were the "greatest threat" to the nation's security gave them particular visibility within this growing maelstrom.

THE CHICAGO ASSAULT

The news coverage of the 4 December 1969 slaying of Fred Hampton, the charismatic twenty-one-year-old deputy chairman of the Illinois Panther chapter, initially followed the "shoot-out" storyline adopted in earlier Oakland clashes between the Panthers and the police. The only newsmagazine article to focus explicitly on the police raid was a 15 December *Newsweek* article titled "The Panthers: Shoot It Out," which featured a photograph of "war casualty" Fred Hampton and juxtaposed the police account of a peaceful raid met by Panther gunfire with Panther claims, buttressed by the attorney Charles Garry's contention that the raid (as *Newsweek* put it) "brought to 28 the number of Panthers killed by police this year (*sic*)."[50] In subsequent articles focusing on the Hampton-Clark killings, *Newsweek* distanced itself from the *Chicago Tribune* coverage that "backed up the police version." Rather, the weekly magazine, while noting that a coroner's jury had found the police action "justifiable," reported on Judge Saul Epton's finding of inadequate state evidence for murder charges against seven Panthers; reported on a federal grand jury report that chastised but declined to indict Chicago policemen along with the department's demotion of three of its members; and, finally, more than a year later reported that "on orders from the Illinois Supreme Court, a Chicago judge released a long-suppressed grand jury indictment that charged fourteen lawmen, including Mayor Daley's designated prosecutor, the state's attorney Edward V. Hanrahan, with conspiring to obstruct justice in the aftermath of the police raid."[51]

Time's four articles focusing on the Chicago case began with the ominous "Police and Panthers at War" on 12 December 1969, and later revisited the case with "Black Panthers: Questions Remain" on 25 May 1970, "The Hanrahan Indictment" on 6 September 1971, and "Trials: Victory for Fast Eddie [Hanrahan]" on 6 November 1972.[52] *U.S. News* published no articles featuring the Chicago raid and its aftermath. More telling, especially after a police-Panther shoot-out in Los Angeles only days after the Chicago police raid, is the fact that the newsmagazines began to publish broader assessments of the Panthers and the phenomenon of police-Panther "warfare."

Such was the intensity of media attention in the aftermath of the Chicago raid, however, that only by attending to daily news reporting can the rapid chain of events and the entry of new voices coming to the Panthers' aid be discerned. In the month immediately following the Chicago raid, for example, thirty-five items directly pertaining to the raid and its aftermath appeared in the *New York Times*. These included three news articles about the raid itself, four detailing Panther claims about their numbers killed in the preceding year, six about different groups decrying the killings and calling for official inquiries, five about various official, investigatory responses, five letters to the editor criticizing the police action, an op-ed by the *Times*' liberal columnist, Tom Wicker, a cartoon, and a *Times* editorial.

The initial report by the *Times* relied exclusively on police accounts of the shoot-out, "balanced" by the final sentence of the story that noted that "Bobby Rush, Black Panther deputy minister of defense, charged later that Hampton was 'murdered' while he slept in bed in a 'search and destroy mission' by the Administration." At the same time, after recounting preliminary facts, the *Times* reported on Charles Garry's claim that Hampton and Clark were "the 27th and 28th Black Panthers killed in clashes with the police since January of 1968." It then observed that "Hampton was regarded as one of the most effective Panther leaders still in circulation," noting the decimation of the Party's leadership by a "wave of arrests and police actions."[53]

In the next day's paper, the *Times* reported that "three [Chicago] alderman, the Afro-American Patrolmen's League, the Illinois division of the American Civil Liberties Union and black community groups called today for independent investigations of the slaying of two Black Panthers in a police raid," and included the reporter's observations from tours of the Panther's apartment conducted by Party members.[54] Similarly, on 9 December the *Times* reported that the NAACP, the United Auto Workers, and the mayor of Fred Hampton's home town "joined dozens of black community organizations" in calling for an investigation into his death.[55] On 10 December, nine Democratic members of Congress urged the National Commission on the Causes and Prevention of Violence to investigate the police raid.[56] On 16 December, the *Times* reported on a different kind of response: a "coalition of black community organizations" in Chicago announced a [short-lived] overnight curfew on whites in the city's black neighborhoods.[57] On 21 December, five "negro congressmen" toured the Hampton apartment and announced the prospective inauguration of their own investigation into clashes between the police and the Panthers.[58] On 29 December, the American Civil Liberties Union issued a report on police harassment of Panthers in nine metropolitan areas, highlighting a "pattern of provocative and punitive harassment."[59] On 21 December, in a letter to the *Times*, future National Security Advisor Zbigniew Brzezinski suggested that "even if we accept the official version of the Chicago police to the effect that Black Panther leader Fred Hampton was shot while resisting arrest, there still remained considerable grounds for suspicion that a grave miscarriage of justice has taken place."[60]

News articles on 11, 13, 18, and 20 December detailed the consideration of an official investigation by the Justice Department, which was followed by the announcement of a "preliminary investigation" and subsequently a special grand jury inquiry. In a reflection of their mistrust of the Nixon administration, a collection of twenty-seven highly visible liberals, including Arthur J. Goldberg and Roy Wilkins, announced in the 16 December issue that they would be conducting an "independent" formal inquiry.[61] That same day, Tom Wicker crafted an op-ed on the link between public mistrust and calls for independent investigations into both the Panther deaths and the My Lai massacre.[62] On 3 January 1970, the *Times* reported on Hoover's year-end summary of FBI's operations "deploring attacks on police" by black militants around the country.[63]

The *Times*' editors themselves chimed in with an editorial on 17 December, noting that the police raid "raised anew the question whether the authorities there and elsewhere are engaged in a search-and-destroy campaign rather than in legitimate law enforcement." Observing that there were "many unanswered questions" to be resolved by the promised investigation of the Justice Department, the *Times* made sure its narrow intention was not misconstrued. "The doctrine and tactics of the Panthers are offensive, provocative, and neo-fascist; their members have on occasion engaged in acts of violence and intimidation, particularly within the black community; but none of this would excuse lawless, punitive measures on the part of the police."[64] The offense that particularly rankled the *Times* editors was the state's attorney, Hanrahan, giving the *Chicago Tribune* photographs of "evidence" of heavy Panther gunfire, when subsequent inspection by reporters revealed the "bullet holes" to be nail heads. Including the *Tribune* in its criticism, the *Times* noted that these actions violated a report on "free press versus fair trial" published the previous year by the Judicial Conference of the United States.[65]

THE NEWSMAGAZINES TAKE STOCK OF THE PANTHERS

On 19 December 1969, *Time* published a three-page article titled "Police and Panthers: Growing Paranoia." Interestingly, the article opened with a "balanced" but loaded glimpse of the Panthers' community service programs, one that again echoed COINTELPRO charges: "Every month they serve free breakfasts to some 10,000 needy black children, but they also teach the kids a song: 'There is a pig upon the hill, if you don't kill him, the Panther's will.' They have set up free health clinics for blacks in several cities, but the *Black Panther Coloring Book* shows a black man shooting a pig-faced policeman as a young girl looks on. The caption: 'Black Brothers Protect Black Children.'"[66] Here, each "positive" Panther activity was balanced against a specific negative incident, cited as if it, too, were a characteristic Panther policy. Perhaps this was *Time*'s glimpse of the Panthers' good side, because after reminding its readers of the Panthers' commitment to "organized violence," the magazine provided an account of the Los Angeles shoot-out — the fury of which was "right out of Vietnam"—based entirely on police reports. The article then returned to the Chicago raid, juxtaposing the Panther lawyers' contention that "the police burst in and began firing without warning" against Hanrahan's denunciation of the stories appearing in press and television accounts as "an orgy of sensationalism."[67]

After a closer look at claims and counterclaims, *Time* proceeded to examine the possibility of, in their words, a "Design of Genocide" by quoting charges to that effect by Ralph Abernathy of the Southern Christian Leadership Conference. The latter third of the article probed the BPP style and their grievances, framed by photographs of marching Panthers giving the black power salute (the caption read, "Jumpy men take no chances"), as well as shots of two Panthers arrested in the Los Angeles "shoot-out" and close-up photos of Huey Newton and Bobby Seale. Three paragraphs (out of a total of nineteen) provided a rare glimpse of the Panthers' own rationale for their weapons: the longstanding police hostility toward inner-city blacks; the fact that the police constituted an occupying army over a "colonized people"; and that their use of "Marxist-Maoist" terms linked them with historic struggles in China, Korea, and Russia.[68]

The tone of *Time*'s analysis seemed sobered by the chain of events. The magazine compared the Panthers' treatment by New York authorities (indicted for "plotting to kill policemen and dynamite police stations, stores and a railroad right-of-way" and then incarcerated for eight months on $100,000 bail) to that of four white radicals (arrested for "actually setting dynamite charges in Manhattan office buildings" held on $20,000–$50,000 bail). Nevertheless, this news account editorialized in a manner that framed the Panthers as aggressors and raised the specter of racial exceptionalism: "Society has a duty to defend itself against private armies; there can be no argument that Panther arms caches should be broken up just like those of the Mafia or the Ku Klux Klan or the Minutemen. But because of the special history of injustice to blacks, there is incipient tragedy in the use of conventional police tactics against them."[69] There was, of course, an argument for the Panthers' arms caches, having to do with self-defense, but it reflected a perspective clearly beyond the imagining of *Time*. Adopting a racial context for framing its conclusions about violence and a potential "police conspiracy," *Time* concluded: "To most whites, violence is not justifiable; to an increasing number of blacks it is. While there is no evidence of a police conspiracy to annihilate the Panthers, more and more blacks believe it to be so."

For its part, *Newsweek* published "The Panthers and the Law," a five-page special section on 23 February 1970. It began with the oft-used reference to "white America's nightmare" and employed rhetoric familiar to hip readers of the New Journalism:

> They were the Bad Niggers of white America's nightmares come chillingly to life — a black-bereted, black-jacketed cadre of street bloods risen up in arms against the established order. They were, they announced, the Black Panthers, and the name alone suggested menace. They swaggered, blustered, quoted Mao, preached revolution, flashed their guns everywhere and sometimes used them. They addressed white power in harangues that began with f——— and mother-f———. . . . . They are guerrilla theater masterfully done, so masterfully that at a point everybody began to believe them and to be frightened of them. . . . They are Media Age revolutionaries, gifted with words, good at sloganeering (POWER TO THE PEOPLE), irresistibly photogenic, scary on television, masterful at poster art from their first effort.[70]

Newsweek's curious juxtaposition of past and present tense here suggested that the threatening Panthers were no more, though their media performance was likely to continue. In effect, the magazine introduced the Panthers as a political threat that faded after a wave of state repression, reduced instead to media exploitation — a revolution turned into the "drudgery" of "running showcase breakfast-for-children programs and free medical clinics."[71] In this fashion, the Panthers' community-building efforts were themselves reduced to media-age public relations; the Panther view of the breakfast program is, once again, invisible.

The balance of *Newsweek*'s article pointedly suggested that with so many Panthers in jail or on trial, the organization's viability was in doubt. On the other hand, the article referred to Attorney General John Mitchell's belief that the Panthers were a continuing "menace to national security."[72] The article also included a gallery of photographs representing the Panthers' visible trajectory: three Panthers "waving the flag" at a Panther demonstration outside the Oakland courthouse; two Panther arrestees after the Los Angeles shoot-out ("cops take a pair of POW's"); gun-toting Panthers menacing the camera in a Panther headquarters ("Pantherismo: A Bogart Image?"); a manacled Bobby Seale in prison; Eldridge Cleaver and Kim Il Sung on the cover of the *Black Panther*; a Panther serving breakfasts, side-by-side with Fred Hampton's blood-soaked bed; the iconic enthroned Huey Newton poster adjacent to a shot of the Panther defender Charles Garry at a Panther rally; and finally, Mrs. Leonard Bernstein greeting the Panthers at the Bernstein's fund-raiser. Considering the likelihood of a Panther obituary, the article concluded that it was "no doubt premature," but concluded by quoting the ex-Panther Virtual Murrell: "Revolutionaries by the time they are 40 are either dead or in prison or lying on park benches. Frankly, I'm scared."[73]

THE NEW YORK AND NEW HAVEN TRIALS

The period from late 1969 into the early 1970s also saw a wave of media attention given to two celebrated Black Panther trials: the trial of the so-called Panther 21 bombing "conspiracy" in New York, and the trial of several Black Panthers, including Chairman Bobby Seale, for the murder of Panther Alex Rackley in New Haven. The Chicago Conspiracy Trial, in which Seale was bound and gagged and then removed from the "Chicago 8," figured prominently in the news of these months, too. As with the Chicago raid, newsmagazine trial coverage was more intensive than it had been for any single Panther event during the first three years of the Party's existence. *Newsweek* published five articles on the New York case and seven on the New Haven case (overlapping at times with Yale student protests in support of the Panthers). *Time* featured four articles on each trial. Additional articles about campus unrest in the aftermath of the U.S. invasion of Cambodia (including the Kent State killings) also made references to the Panthers' New Haven trial. *U.S. News* published one article focusing on the New Haven protests and campus turmoil prior to Kent State.

Much of this coverage reflected the newsmagazines' time-honored formula for reporting on the Panthers, particularly in playing the two sides off each other with the usual coloration provided by Panther flamboyance and court unruliness. But the trial reports contributed to the overall media coverage of the Panthers in significant ways.[74] Not only did the unprecedented newsmagazine coverage intensify the Panthers' visibility, but the reporting fit nicely with the mass media's tendency to personalize news and create a celebrity culture. They also played into the media's "balanced" dichotomous reporting, reducing the Panthers again to one side in a conflict over charges of criminality—the other side of which was repeatedly represented as more authoritative. Finally, along with the police raids, the trials themselves reflected the COINTELPRO effort to trigger internecine battles between the

Panthers and rival black militants and to prevent the rise of a new "black messiah" who could unite the black masses in revolt. The New York bombing conspiracy trial also drew highly inflamed accusations against the Panthers into print. A front-page *New York Times* story on 13 March 1970 focusing on the Panthers, the militant Weatherman group, and the Young Lords was headlined "[New York City Council President] Garelik says Terrorists Are Growing Peril Here."

THE THREAT OF LEGITIMATE EXPRESSION

In addition to the suggestive events recounted above, and as reflected in the *New York Times* analysis, a new voice — credible and legitimate within the mainstream — entered public discourse suggesting intentional and illegitimate government repression of the Panthers. On 14 December, the *Times* published a lengthy article by Earl Caldwell headlined "Declining Black Panthers Gather New Support from Repeated Clashes with Police." In other words, though the Panthers were badly pummeled after losing their battles with police, they were showing some signs of winning the propaganda war. They were gaining supporters, and some of the context for their militancy — police violence and government repression — was gaining visibility in the media. As was the case with the North Vietnamese "propaganda victory" during the Tet Offensive early the previous year, nothing seemed to alarm and infuriate the U.S. government and the right-wing more. Almost immediately, the credible liberal voice was countered by another. The very forces that gave the Panthers any semblance of legitimacy within mainstream media culture themselves became the targets of a backlash. This attack, in turn, helped to normalize mass media culture references to the Panthers in ensuing years, returning them to the one-dimensional band of violent, albeit colorful, criminals that they appeared to be prior to December 1969.

The first groups to come under fire were those credible liberals who expressed sympathy for the Panthers in the aftermath of the Hampton-Clark slayings. The opening shot was fired from the Right in a 30 December 1969 editorial in the *National Review* titled "The Persecution and Assassination of the Black Panther Party as Directed by Guess Who." The *Review* opened by noting, "What happened in that police raid on a Black Panther coven in Chicago is unclear — except that two Panther leaders died, and that the Black Panther Party has overnight become Liberal Cause Number One." Without reviewing the reasons for their complaints, grounded in the post-attack revelations, the editorial cited the public condemnations of police conduct "by the Illinois NAACP ('a modern-day lynching'), the local United Auto Workers civil rights council ('a brutal and unwarranted slaying'), Roy Wilkins ('a vendetta by police authorities') and scores more liberal individuals and organizations."[75]

After referring to the "hastily gathered commission of private citizens ranging from Wilkins and Arthur Goldberg leftward to Julian Bond and Sam Brown," the *Review* resorted to sarcastic ridicule of the liberals. "Mind, all these good people reject the Panthers' Maoist ideology and violent methods," reasoned the *Review*, going on to quote Roy Wilkins on Fred Hampton: "Although he strayed from the NAACP way, he was a fine young man who wanted for his people only what we want for everyone."[76] The *Review* pointedly asked, "Was Hampton (and by extension Eldridge Cleaver, Bobby Seale and the rest) a sweetly reasonable NAACP-style integrationist? Are the Black Panthers meliorists committed to working within the system, like the SCLC and the Urban League?" The liberals, apparently, had slipped into a state of irrationality, especially as the balance of the column — eight of eleven paragraphs — recounted a host of Panther excesses, noting that "the Panthers' abstract principles [the platform] translate into such calls to action as 'Dynamite! Black Power! Use the gun! Kill the pig everywhere!'"[77]

No Panther-supporting event drew more attention than the Upper East Side reception hosted by Leonard Bernstein and his wife to help raise funds for the Panthers' growing legal defense costs. Later immortalized by Tom Wolfe in his *New York* magazine article, "Radical Chic: That Party at Lenny's," the fund-raiser was first reported by the *New York Times* fashion editor Charlotte Curtis under the ironic headline, "Black Panther Philosophy Is Debated at the Bernstein's."[78] Curtis's article highlighted humorous moments in a dialogue between the Panther's Donald Cox ("a tall, handsome man in a black turtleneck sweater and gray pants") and conductor/composer Bernstein ("who was wearing Black Watch tartan slacks, a turtleneck shirt and a blue blazer" and who responded to Panther assertions with comments like "I dig it completely"). It is difficult not to read Curtis's article as other than lightly satirical, spoofing the "effete snobs and intellectuals" gathered at the Bernstein's. Subsequent media commentary, however, was more pointed.

The next day, for example, a *Times*' editorial found the "emergence of the Black Panthers as the romanticized darlings of the politico-cultural jet set" to be "an affront to the majority of Black Americans." Like Gail Sheehy, John Fischer, and others, the *Times* attempted to drive a wedge between the "so-called party with its confusion of Mao-Marxist ideology and Fascist paramilitarism" and "those blacks and whites seriously working for complete equality and social justice."[79] The *Times* also juxtaposed the "group therapy plus fund-raising soirée" at the Bernsteins' with the legitimate voices of "a committee of distinguished citizens" recently formed to protect the constitutional rights of Panther members however reprehensible the latter might be."[80] Clearly, the *Times* perceived itself as the arbiter of lines between the legitimate and the illegitimate.

The *New York Times*' take on the event was echoed in *Time* magazine, the only newsmagazine that paid significant attention to the Bernstein event. On 26 January, its wittily titled "Upper East Side Story" offered a commentary that drew heavily on the *New York Times*' fashion piece, complete with a list of some of the "social notables" in attendance. After itemizing some of the monetary contributions made during the gathering, *Time* seemed to pick a fight with the *New York Times* by noting that the latter's editorial "missed at least part of the point" of the gathering—namely, quoting Bernstein, that the meeting "was for an extremely serious purpose that has nothing to do with the Panthers.... People wrote checks because the Panthers' civil liberties were violated." In the end, *Time* affirmed the same mainstream principles as did the *New York Times*, though not without including a dig at the *Times* from the movie producer Otto Preminger, who was present at the gathering: "I believe in this country and I would fight the Panthers if they tried to destroy it. But if there was discrimination in determining bail, then the people who believe in this country ought to correct the injustice. *The New York Times* is very old-fashioned—you can quote me."[81] And *Time* also had this to say about the Bernstein event: "Pop sociology is what it is all about—the sudden enthusiasm among the fun people to have their own Worst Enemies, Black Panthers, Grape Strikers and such, in for cocktails. Confrontation now!"[82]

Panther sympathizers were, in short, the "liberal elite" who were soon to become a distorted, though not entirely inaccurate, target of rightist Republican propaganda designed to win white working-class support. "Radical chic" entered the language of common discourse, to be resurrected as a pejorative metaphor in the *Times*' 1995 account of Mumia Abu Jamal, for example.[83] In the academy, "radical chic" became a watchword for a growing critique that equated the "identity politics" of the late 1960s and early 1970s with a narcissistic "therapeutic" preoccupation — in the hands of some critics at least, once again stripping the "northern radical movements" of any political legitimacy.[84]

The second target of the gathering backlash was the mass media's citation of the claim by the Panther attorney Charles Garry that the Hampton-Clark shootings were the "the 27th and 28th" police-related Panther deaths since 1968 — numbers that were instantly dismissed by the Justice Department as exaggerated.[85] *Newsweek*, *Time*, the *New York Times*, and the *Washington Post* referred to Garry's figures when discussing the growing violence between the police and the Panthers. Although Garry responded to public criticism by reducing the number to nineteen dead "at the hands of police," the figures themselves quickly became the flash point for an attack on the legitimate voices that decried government repression after the Hampton-Clark deaths. References to the controversy cropped up in a host of magazines, including *Senior Scholastic*'s "teacher's edition."

After more than a year of charge and countercharge, Edward Jay Epstein penned a lengthy article in the *New Yorker*, titled "The Panthers and the Police: A Pattern of Genocide?" in which he undertook a systematic analysis of the matter.[86] In effectively putting the matter to rest, the piece became the final word on Panther genocide in the mainstream media. Epstein began his ostensibly "objective" effort to set the record straight by reviewing a series of quotations from the *New York Times*, *Washington Post*, *Time*, and *Newsweek*. He constructed two meanings out of the Panther controversy. First, by leaving the impression that the stalwarts of the national print media had uncritically taken Panther attorney Garry at his word, Epstein established a record of media gullibility.[87] Yet, in several cases, Epstein's interpretation overstepped his evidence. Thus, for example, he noted that on 7 and 9 December, the "*Times* reported as an established fact, without giving any source for the figure or qualifying it in any way, that twenty-eight Panthers had been killed by police," when in fact these references were drawn from the 5 December *Times* report that attributed the figures to a "claim" by Charles Garry. Epstein also failed to note that a 14 December *Times* article had quoted a New York policeman who dismissed Garry's conspiracy charges as "the silliest thing I ever heard."[88]

The *Washington Post* repeated the *Times*' reporting pattern, first attributing the numbers to Garry then dropping the reference in a later report.

Interestingly, Epstein ignored the first *Post* citation, which referred to Garry in its fifth paragraph, but highlighted the unattributed claim buried deep in an article about investigations into the Hampton-Clark slayings. After Epstein's article appeared, the *Post* issued an apology for the second, unattributed use of the figure of twenty-eight Panther deaths. On 8 March 1971, *Time* reported on the *Post*'s "mea culpa," noting that both the *Times* and the *Post* had dropped their attribution. *Time* concluded with an ominous reference to the *Washington Star*'s observation that the press "should have learned to suspect the casual statistic from the bitter history of Senator Joseph McCarthy."[89]

Similarly, Epstein charged that "*Time* reported, on December 12, 1969, that 'a series of gun battles between Panthers and police throughout the nation' amounted to a 'lethal undeclared war,' and concluded, 'Whether or not there is a concerted police campaign, the ranks of Panther leadership have been decimated in the past two years.'" Yet the reference to a "lethal undeclared war" did not, in fact, target police practices as Epstein suggested; instead, it opened the article by drawing heavily on police accounts to introduce a battle between the police and the Panthers in the Hampton case. After recounting this episode and reviewing Panther claims, *Time* cited Garry's charge of twenty-eight dead Panthers. And, after noting support for a follow-up investigation from the ACLU and others, *Time* retipped the scales in its dichotomous account of the Hampton killing by observing that "police officials around the country and the Justice Department officials in Washington deny that there is any concerted nationwide drive against the Panthers, 'But we obviously keep an eye on them,' says an FBI source."[90]

Finally, the *Time* article did not conclude in quite the way that Epstein suggested. True, the final paragraph began with the "whether or not" sentence, but the "decimated" leadership it listed (with the exception of Bobby Hutton) had nothing to do with the infamous twenty-eight deaths. This was also the case with a *Newsweek* article Epstein cited. Instead, it referred to the incarcerated Newton, the jailed Seale, the overseas "fugitive" Cleaver, and the arrest of David Hilliard for delivering an "inflammatory and obscene speech" threatening the life of President Nixon. In fact, *Time* actually concluded the article by quoting Hilliard ("We will kill Richard Nixon. We will kill any mother—— that stands in the way of our freedom") and a defiant Raymond Masai Hewitt, the Panther minister of education ("We speak in the rhetoric of the ghetto and we're not going to change it to suit anybody's

Marquis of Queensberry rules"). With this inflammatory Panther rhetoric as a backdrop, *Time* added innocuously that "the police seem to feel just as violently about the Panthers." The apparent "balance" between violent Panther words and violent police deeds was, then, rebalanced to depict the Panthers, once again, as the aggressors. Yet this was the *Time* article that Epstein singled out as evidence of an irresponsible media attack on police violence. In sum, a careful inspection of the relevant articles makes it difficult to credit Epstein's conclusions, which became the final word on the liberal media as a gullible mouthpiece for Panther claims.

The Epstein article linked these alleged media abuses to the charges by various liberals of a campaign of police repression—charges that later evidence confirmed were accurate. Epstein proceeded to review each of eighteen deaths in question, having winnowed the list via an exchange with Garry. Interestingly, while reviewing claims and counterclaims in each of these records, Epstein presented the cases in a narrative style without clarifying for his readers who the factual sources for these narratives were. Four of the Panther deaths were attributed to the Panthers' rivals, the black militant group the US Organization. In hindsight, these deaths can arguably be linked to COINTELPRO efforts to provoke internecine warfare between the Panthers and US. While that evidence was presumably not available to Epstein in 1971, it helps to validate the perceptions of Panthers and their attorneys making the claims about these deaths.

The second meaning that flowed from Epstein's article was the dubious assertion that debate about a campaign of government repression could be narrowed to disputed numbers and thereby resolved. Contesting a *New York Times* report suggesting that the Nixon administration "contributed to a climate of opinion among local police . . . that a virtual open season has been declared on the Panthers," Epstein limited his discussion to the ten cases he acknowledged that involved Panthers killed by police and observed that five of these occurred before the Nixon administration took office. He failed to mention the government proclamations against the Panthers or the prosecution of Panther leaders, thereby concluding that the broader "conspiracy" charge was "historically inaccurate" and the greatly amended claim by Charles Garry was "false."[91]

In the context of Vice President Spiro Agnew's attacks on the media's "liberal elite," Epstein's piece engraved in stone the notion that a sympathetic liberal media uncritically parroted exaggerated charges about government repression made by the Panthers' attorney. Thus, a 1973 *National Review* article cited Epstein in its account of "The 'Black Genocide' Myth," noting that he "examined the nineteen cases cited by Garry and knocked them down one by one" and concluded that the Hampton raid was the "only incident where police action was questionable." The article also sought transcripts and audio recordings of television broadcasts and with limited results found, not surprisingly, that Garry's figures were cited along with the charges of several liberal notables as well as the claims of police defenders.[92] Fifteen years later, the centrist political columnist Richard Cohen cited the Epstein article and its conclusion that "the public was misled by a press that was unwilling to verify the facts for itself" as a prologue to his own critique of the media for uncritically using the word "epidemic" to describe the nation's drug scare of the late 1980s. By this time, of course, the campaign against the "liberal media" and "hysterical sixties" had been in full swing for years. The "sixties" had been largely emptied of meaning, with the liberal media blamed for giving undeserved publicity to leftist groups during the decade.

The mass media coverage of the Black Panthers consistently framed them as a group of angry black Americans prone to violence and criminality. In the post-Hampton era, the media boundaries relaxed enough to acknowledge, even to highlight, some of the context for Panther rage—namely, massive police violence. To that degree, the Panthers gained the support of legitimate voices within mainstream political discourse. The attack on those allies, however, quickly returned the Panthers to their status as utterly illegitimate outsiders. As in the period before the Hampton-Clark killings, the context of Panther emotions and actions disappeared. A similar "rethinking" occurred in the arena known as the New Journalism, which also influenced later perceptions of the Panthers.

THE PANTHERS' DEMISE AND VIRTUAL DISAPPEARANCE IN MEDIA CULTURE

By 1971 the Panthers had suffered serious erosion at the hands of criminal prosecution, government repression, and internecine conflict. Not surprisingly, the national media now reflected on the Party's meteoric rise and fall. A March 1971 report in *Newsweek* noted that the BPP was near disintegration, with its ranks "riddled by warfare with the cops, arrests, purges and desertions." *Newsweek* effectively dismissed the group as "a few homemade Marxists-Leninists at the top, a few hundred idealistic youth who did most of the drudgery [i.e., the "serve the people" programs], a few hundred more street bloods drawn by the Panthers' guns-and-leather look and their off-the-pigs lingo."[93] As in the mass media generally, most of this article focused on a highly personalized account of the late Panther split—Cleaver versus Newton—rather than the programmatic and strategic differences between the East Coast and West Coast contingents, which in fact resonated in chapters throughout the country.[94] Although the *Newsweek* article mentioned toward the end that a few locals were "still functioning," it implicitly suggested that the Panthers had self-destructed.

That same month, *Time* carried the story of the Panther split with an intriguing twist. Titled "Destroying the Panther Myth," the article probed the death of Panther Robert Webb, which was attributed to the Newton faction by the Cleaver faction, and explored the charges and countercharges between the two groups. Noting that a Harris poll taken for *Time* the previous year had demonstrated that "64% of all blacks surveyed" felt that the Panthers gave them a "sense of pride," *Time* concluded that the Panthers were in the process of destroying a "potent myth of their own creation."[95] For *Time*, it seemed, the Panther "mythology" involved the Panthers fooling mainstream African Americans into supporting them, when in fact they were only about violence.

What remained of the Panthers in the mainstream mass media culture were the largely reminiscent snapshots triggered by the notable actions, or deaths, of the Panther celebrities of yore. In 1972–1973 Bobby Seale ran for mayor of Oakland.[96] During the 1972 campaign, *Time* revisited the Panthers in an article titled "Tame Panthers?" It highlighted Seale's mayoral campaign and the "neatly dressed workers" in the Panthers' Oakland headquarters directing what *Time* suddenly discovered was "an impressive list of projects —breakfast for children of the poor, a free clinic, sickle-cell anemia tests, and a once-a-week prison bus service for relatives of convicts."[97] Apparently, for *Time*, participation in electoral politics legitimized activities once scarcely deemed worthy of recognition.

Later, *Newsweek* viewed the Seale campaign in a manner befitting a media-based icon, as evidence of a "new Bobby."[98] A 1975 *Newsweek* article focusing on Cleaver's move from Algeria to Paris depicted an "old Panther with a new purr."[99] A 1976 *Newsweek* article, titled "Purring Panthers," focused on the Party's "regrouping" under the new leadership of Elaine Brown, with an emphasis on community-building activities in Oakland.[100] *U.S. News*, which never seemed to pay any significant attention to the Panthers, published in 1976 an article titled "Whatever Happened to . . . The Black Panthers"? Totaling just one magazine column in length, the article summarily reviewed Panther origins ("power comes out of the barrel of a gun"), brushes with the law (citing government scrutiny and FBI charges as well as the fugitive status of both Cleaver and now Newton, too), the "muted anger" reflected in the Seale mayoral campaign, and the newly discovered community service dimension. However, the magazine remarked ominously that despite the Panthers' "'new look,' many observers continue to regard them as a potential source of violence. Says one Washington official, 'It is a tightly knit group waiting for some leadership again.'"[101] Echoing Cold War propaganda about the Communist threat, the media trumpeted the taming of the once-violent Panthers, but hastened to remind readers to stay vigilant all the same—thereby wittingly or not providing the rationale for ample budget allocations to fight the criminal menace.

The Panthers and the New Journalism

Largely because of the inability of the mainstream mass media to reflect the experiences, much less the degree of alienation, felt by many American youths after mid-decade, the sixties saw an enormous surge in alternative media, which included the Panthers' own organ, the *Black Panther*. Similarly, the New Left monthly *Ramparts* published thirteen articles on the Panthers over a four-year period, all of them either written by Panthers like Eldridge Cleaver, Bobby Seale, and Kathleen Cleaver, or by Panther sympathizers like Gene Marine, Jean Genet, and Tom Hayden, and most provided sympathetic explanations of Panther politics or detailed accounts of police persecution.

Meanwhile, within mainstream media discourse, the so-called New Journalism also reflected the inadequacy of the conventional mass media in explaining the tumultuous events of the era. Although typically colorful and engaged with 1960s "outlaws" of various types, the writings of the New Journalism reflected its authors' ideological view and publishing home within conventional parameters. In effect, the New Journalism helped make the world beyond the bounds of mainstream discourse more "real" for mass audiences, yet it did so without embracing a view that challenged the ideological foundations of that culture. While a few writers, notably Norman Mailer, were not only sympathetic to outsiders but also participated in the activities they wrote about, the New Journalism accounts about the

Panthers ranged from the disappointed sympathy of Donald Schanche,[102] to the embittered disappointment of Gail Sheehy,[103] to the strident mockery of Tom Wolfe.[104]

As early as late 1970, the Panthers were packaged as an assembly of images, cartoons, and personalities in a lightly mocking *Esquire* piece titled "Is It Too Late for You To Be Pals with a Black Panther?" Hip readers of this popular New Journalism magazine were invited to participate — to play the game by seeing how they reacted to seminal Panther images (berets, leather, afros, shades, guns), subjecting themselves to Panther rules designed to purge the Party of police agents and "lackeys," and then briefly considering the history of derogatory black images. Readers were given a host of examples to consider in weighing the conclusion that others had apparently come to—namely, that it was too late to be a Panther pal since these observers (presumably like *Esquire* readers) were "incapable of telling the difference between Panthers and imposters," having been "so influenced by the media" that they're incapable of penetrating the Panther's "image to understand his reality."[105]

Like the mass media generally, then, the New Journalism helped grease the skids on the disappearing realities that spawned the Black Panthers. The one-dimensional stereotype of the Panthers as violent but charismatic criminals was central to the subsequent popular revisionism of David Horowitz and Hugh Pearson. As with the New Journalism authors Don Schanche and Gail Sheehy, both accounts were cast as "second thoughts" on the part of those once drawn in by the magnetism of the fighters so highly publicized in the media.[106] Similarly, in a very early account in the national media, Sol Stern penned a lengthy *New York Times Magazine* article on the Panthers in 1967. While it appeared to distance itself from the Panthers' persistently violent rhetoric and fixation with guns, Stern's article was unusual in seeking to understand some of the reasons behind their controversial style. Thirty-six years later, in a Manhattan Institute *City Journal* article, Stern repented. Noting that "like other ex-sixties radicals," he made the "unfortunate mistake of thinking that the Black Panthers were a legitimate social protest movement," he came to understand, in a few years, that he "should have described Newton and his cadres as psychopathic criminals, not social reformers. By now, a torrent of articles and books, many written by former sympathizers, has voluminously documented the Panther reign of murder and larceny within their own community. So much so that no one but a left-wing crank could still believe in the Panther myth of dedicated young blacks 'serving the people' while heroically defending themselves against unprovoked attacks by the racist police."[107] Apparently, for Stern, there is no middle ground, no gray area, no good and bad within the Panther realm of its time. If these individuals were "taken in" by the media images of the Panthers, it seems the Panthers must have been "media creations," assisted by the projections of these misguided characters. Thanks to their corrective revisionism, the media culture finally got it right. And not only media culture, apparently, but popular history as well.

The Panthers as attacked by polemicists like Horowitz or as dismissively criticized by journalists like Pearson, Stern, or Coleman not only conform to the one-dimensional Panthers who flourished within mass media culture in the sixties, but have increasingly become the Panthers who are remembered in the "second wave" of 1960s historical surveys. Perhaps understandably, most provide brief snapshots that emphasize the Oakland chapter and the Newton-Seale-Cleaver triumvirate, along with the guns and the Panther flamboyance that captured media attention. Reflecting conventional framing, the revisionist history by Maurice Isserman and Michael Kazin, *America Divided: The Civil War of the 1960s*, which was hailed by Todd Gitlin as "the most comprehensive, comprehensible history of the American 1960s that I know," interprets the era as a "civil war" in the long-running historical competition between an American Left and Right. Except for two sentences in other parts of the book, the only reference to the Panthers in the text of *America Divided* features Huey Newton's deteriorating behavior and the Oakland chapter's "operating more as a protection racket for black businesses than as a revolutionary movement." Pearson's *The Shadow of the Panther* is the one Panther source the authors cite.[108]

Living History and Today's Media Culture

The lived history of the Black Panther Party has been reduced to a one-dimensionality that can safely be consigned to the black hole of public memory. Within the media culture, the Panthers' efforts to empower the "brothers and sisters on the block" have disappeared. Their "doctrine and tactics," as the *New York Times* simplified it, were "neo-fascist." Stripped of their experiential context in violent inner-city America in the mid-to-late 1960s, and detached from their political analysis of economic and racial exploitation, the Panthers are easy targets for the ongoing effort by the powerful to restore the hegemony threatened in the 1960s era. These Panthers are part of the panoply of images included in the mass media's characterization of the sixties — a time of "democratic distemper," in the words of a Trilateral Commission bent on restoring neoliberalism, or of liberal excess in the framing of rightist attacks that helped to usher in an alleged "right turn" in American politics. The Panthers have become synonymous with the "bad 1960s" and are discredited and dismissed. Given the nature of the American mass media and its ideologically bound public discourse; given the Panthers' understandable initial action using the show of arms to defend themselves and the inner-city community against police violence; given the understandable response of those in power to this action, it is hard to imagine a different outcome. The Panthers, in short, were frozen in their origins, both not able and not allowed *to* evolve into a broader, politically effective radical movement.

In this, of course, the Panthers are not much different from the other late-1960s movements of the New Left. No radical movement during or since the 1960s has been able to get its voice heard within the mainstream mass media. Instead, these movements — or, more accurately, the fragments loosely attached to broader social movements — have at best been able to muster appearances in the media by generating increasing militancy and flamboyance. And that is, of course, what most of America sees — in narrative fragments, packaged and interpreted for them by media opinion leaders and political propagandists alike. Within the mass media culture, state repression pays off twice. It adds to the likely visibility of militancy and violence, widely viewed as alienating by mass audiences, while it runs these radical fringe elements into the ground.

As W. Lance Bennett and the late Murray Edelman have pointed out, "recurring and stereotypical narrative accounts in the mass media . . . rationalize and distort the contradictions of our time," and, though "highly selective impressions of reality," they can "seem objective when applied uncritically to ongoing events. The daily life stories that embody the truths of social elites and their publics seem objective because they are confirmed time and again by self-fulfilling selection of documentary detail. Information that doesn't fit the symbolic mold can be ignored, denied, or rationalized out of serious consideration. When a ruling group promotes its cherished ideals at the expense of critical evaluations of actions taken in the name of those ideals, the telling of familiar tales becomes a comforting fantasy-escape from the otherwise unpleasant contradictions of life experience."[109] Such is the narrative of the Panthers that prevails in mainstream media and political discourse. Taking into account the bloodshed and violence, the history of the Panthers is a tragic one, especially because if their full history were known it might potentially inspire others to seek empowerment, albeit in more effective and lasting ways.

What, then, can we expect from efforts to revisit and learn from the full Panther history? We may briefly consider two approaches. One involves careful historical study within the free spaces of academic inquiry; the other involves utilizing the media of popular culture and entertainment—that of film, for example. But, how effectively can we reach wider audiences with authentic, potentially empowering history within this media culture?

This very volume is, in effect, an effort to realize the aim in the first approach. However, one clue to its potential reach may come from the mass media's response to the historical conference that generated it. Two news accounts—one in the *Boston Globe*, the other in the *San Francisco Chronicle*—provided balanced and detailed accounts of the conference and its effort in its serious examination of the Panthers and their historical significance. Despite this straight news, two op-ed pieces written by Kate Coleman disparaged the conference she had not attended while reasserting the Panther mythology revolving around Huey Newton. With the title, "Revisionism: Guess Who's Mything Them Now: The Real Black Panthers Were a Bunch of Thugs," one op-ed appeared in the same *San Francisco Chronicle* as the straight news article and opened with the line, "The conference last week at Wheelock College in Boston . . . had all the veneer of a scholarly gathering." Not surprisingly, given the author's absence, only two sentences focused on the conference itself; the rest revived Huey Newton stories and asserted that the "real Panther legacy" was the "leap in drive-by-shooting deaths in Oakland" in the 1990s.[110] The second op-ed piece appeared in the *Los Angeles Times* a week later under the title "Black Panthers: Just a Pack of Predators." In it Coleman expanded to three sentences her discussion of the conference, which she claimed "celebrated" the Panthers, and after revisiting sordid episodes occurring in Oakland in the 1970s and 1980s, repeated the charge about the Panthers' "drive-by-shooting" legacy and briefly asserted that a post-conference dispute with a caller on NPR's *Talk of the Nation* program reaffirmed her account.[111]

The effort to bring a more comprehensive and analytical historical perspective into some level of public awareness is thus likely to become, itself, a target of polemical Panther bashing. Public history, it seems, is meant to be frozen in the images and stories that have survived in media culture's accounts of the Panthers. The backlash against these efforts does not mean that they are futile or should not be pursued; it merely demonstrates the significance of obstacles in a media culture that is so thoroughly permeated with pejorative imagery and hostile propaganda.

What, then, of an effort to resurrect some authentic Panther history through the medium of entertainment film, designed to reach a broader audience more directly? In 1995, a year after *Forrest Gump*, the director Mario Van Peebles converted a screenplay written by his father into the film *Panther*, with the intention of correcting the historical record. Needless to say, the film revealed the pitfalls of using the entertainment media of popular culture as an avenue for historical reconsideration.[112] Van Peebles's partly fictionalized dramatic account revives the story of Panther origins by depicting the graphically violent police abuse to which inner-city youth were repeatedly subjected and by reenacting the Panthers' early strategy of shadowing police cruisers. It also reveals the Panthers' breakfast for children program as well as the FBI campaign to neutralize the program, though it adds an improbable government/organized-crime conspiracy twist to the latter. At the same time, the film pays little attention to the internecine warfare that plagued the Panthers in their later years, and it all but ignores the significant role played by Panther women (as well as their abuse by some Panther men).

In playing up the Panther perspective through provocative and partially fictional dramatization, it was hardly surprising that the film drew considerable media attention and sharp criticism from Panther detractors and ex-Panthers alike. The right-wing Center for the Study of Popular Culture, headed by David Horowitz, took out an advertisement in the 2 May 1995 issue of *Variety*, in which it called the film "a two-hour lie" and repeated the generalization that the Panthers were "cocaine-addicted gangsters who turned out their own women as prostitutes and committed hundreds of felonies." *Time* chimed in with its own remarks, such as "How did Oliver Stone let this one get away? A gang of 60s rebels, an aura of righteous violence, the charge that J. Edgar Hoover and the mafia flooded our nation's cities with cheap drugs — why, it's all so lurid, it must be true. And if it's not, it can still be a movie. . . . In offering the Panthers as idealists and objects of veneration to today's youth, the movie surely stands guilty of criminal naiveté. What's the politically correct term for whitewash?"[113]

At the same time, Bobby Seale issued a statement proclaiming that "ninety percent of what you see on the screen is absolutely not true. It never happened."[114] Some viewed *Panther* more sympathetically; for example, Kathleen Cleaver observed: "I'm not convinced that dramatic films are the place for historical accuracy, but emotionally this film is an accurate portrayal."[115] In effect, Van Peebles was constrained not only by the medium he chose but by the dramatic symbolism used by the original Panthers: the guns, black berets and leather garb, the battles with police—precisely what the mass media preserved of the Panthers and what the Right attacked.

The limitations of popular film as a vehicle for "correcting" distorted history reflect the ways that the market-driven mass media subvert democracy. Even discounting the media's ideological boundaries, the film's market-embellished emphasis on dramatic action, appeal to emotion, vivid images, and provocative personal texts reduces its audiences to spectatorship and imitation. No doubt some audiences were fascinated by *Panther*, which appropriately ends in a "shoot-out." As with the "Malcolm mania" that surfaced with Spike Lee's *Malcolm X*, today's younger inner-city generation is encouraged to emulate the heroic fighting stance of the Panthers. But *Panther*—the entertaining combination of drama, emotion, vivid imagery, and personality—cannot connect the Panthers' story with the community histories of contemporary audiences. It is something to watch or something to imitate.

This dynamic is not new. It characterized some responses to the Panthers when they were accessible through the mainstream media. Presumably, *Panther* emulators today are like those drawn to the magnetism of the black revolutionaries they witnessed in the mass media in the 1960s—most notably, perhaps, the white radicals who were themselves often criticized in the media for their "uncritical adulation" of the Panthers. These are the white "hero-worshippers," as John Fischer put it in his 1970 *Harper's* attack. In effect, however, this adulation was simply the mirror opposite of the mainstream response to the one-dimensional figures that the media advertised. Especially if one had access to other sources of information, or if one had experience with political organizing, one might well be more thoughtful about the Panthers or able to make discriminating judgments about different Panther personalities and strategies. But for those restricted to mass media sources, there was only the one-dimensional figures. One either *felt* sympathetic toward the Panthers and unsympathetic toward the government forces suppressing them, or one felt the opposite.

As it was in our media culture in the 1960s, so it is today. Groups that target the fundamental institutions of American political and social life face a conundrum: they can express their grievances in a voice that society considers legitimate, though it won't be their voice; or they can strive for some form of expression that feels authentic, though society will treat it as illegitimate. The key arbiters in the process, in many cases, are the mass media — and the institutional sources upon which they depend — as they virtually ignore or actively belittle some arguments yet at the same time invite forms of expression that, however illegitimate, feel gratifyingly authentic and thus seem empowering to the participants. The effect of this dynamic is, first, to create a political spectacle that can entertain wide audiences, all of whom can cheer or jeer in their private spaces, and, second, to close off the discourse between those who are drawn to these media expressions and those who are alienated by them.

Ultimately, this produces a political spectacle that is seemingly open to anyone. Yet, the spectacle is far removed from the actual policy-making arenas of material politics, arenas that remain open only to those with legitimate voices. Instead, most are entertained and distracted by the spectacle, quick to form feeling-based opinions about various others in the spectacle yet also increasingly unlikely to engage in any form of political discourse with them. Absent a discourse that engages us with different others, we lack opportunities for the democratic development of the politically relevant self. We embrace expressions we see that resonate as expressions of who we are, and we view those of different others with increasingly rigid distaste. We then become increasingly prone to "express ourselves" in the ways that the media have noticed. Narcissism flourishes. Political discourse and the citizenry atrophy. Such is today's media culture.

Thus, the form, the style, and the expressiveness of the Black Panther Party has replaced the political meaning of the historical Panthers and any critical insight that the Panther experience might have for radical politics today — at least within mainstream discourse. It is a sorry excuse for a public discourse that encompasses the full range of voices and ideas addressing the nation's troubles. Instead, we are encouraged to sit back and observe the spectacle — or perhaps to "participate" in it by embracing either the images of rebellion or their opposite, the political leadership that will ensure that no such threat resurfaces. As the Panthers could tell us, spectator democracy won't empower the people.

Notes

1. *Forrest Gump*, one of the box-office hits of 1994, echoed the "declensionist" theories of the 1960s as a time of grassroots democratic revolt that spiraled out of control into self-destructive excess and dissolution late in the decade. The correspondence between the media "stories" of the 1960s and such renditions of the era is telling. As Alice Echols has argued, these accounts reflect the perspective of white males of the Students for a Democratic Society (SDS), eliding the women's movement and others that survived well after SDS's demise. She links this "ungendered Sixties" to "mythmaking" about the "good" and the "bad" sixties in "'We Gotta Get Out of This Place': Notes Toward a Remapping of the Sixties," *Socialist Review* 22.2 (April-June, 1992): 9–33. Prominent among these works are Todd Gitlin, *The Sixties: Years of Hope, Days of Rage* (New York: Bantam, 1987); James Miller, *Democracy Is in the Streets: From Port Huron to the Siege of Chicago* (New York: Simon and Schuster, 1987); Tom Hayden, *Reunion: A Memoir* (New York: 1988). For an account of the ideological campaign against the 1960s generally, see my "Who Controls the Past? Propaganda and the Demonised Sixties," *Irish Journal of American Studies* 5 (December 1996): 33–57. *Gump*'s "realism" reflects the pervasiveness of media culture's familiar 1960s imagery, which I document in my "Democracy in Eclipse? Media Culture and the Postmodern 'Sixties,'" *New Political Science* 40 (summer, 1997): 5–31. By "mass media culture" or "mainstream media," I am referring to the mass market media that, by virtue of being mass market enterprises, reflect the imperatives and reinforce the ideology of American capitalism.

2. "Echoes of an Empty Decade: The 60s Are Back," *Bethlehem Globe-Times*, 24 July 1987, A7.

3. David Horowitz and Peter Collier, *Destructive Generation: Second Thoughts about the Sixties* (New York: Summit, 1989); David Horowitz, *Radical Son: A Generational Odyssey* (New York: Touchstone, 1997); Hugh Pearson, *The Shadow of the Panther: Huey Newton and the Price of Black Power in America* (Reading, Mass.: Addison-Wesley, 1994).

4. A lengthy 1978 retrospective by Kate Coleman in *New Times* also emphasized the "street gang" thuggery that grew up around Huey Newton in the 1970s (Coleman, with Paul Avery, "The Party's Over: How Huey Newton Created a Street Gang at the Center of the Black Panther Party," *New Times*, 10 July 1978, 23–47).

5. Commonly used as a pejorative label for activists, the term "radical" often means "militant" in public discourse. In this essay, "radical" denotes a critical perspective that views significant social issues as embedded in the "roots" or fundamental institutions and structural imperatives of society rather than their particular manifestations produced by specific political actors. In contrast, "militant" denotes a type of confrontational strategy aimed at producing change. Thus nonradical political actors may adopt highly militant strategies to change a particular public policy or replace a political party. Similarly, radical critics may favor anything from long-term electoral and nonviolent processes to decisive revolutionary action. The distinction is critical, as the mass media culture effectively excludes radical argu-

ments about fundamental institutional flaws, while at the same time gravitating toward militant behaviors.
6. Edward Herman and Noam Chomsky, *Manufacturing Consent: The Political Economy of Mass Media* (New York: Pantheon, 1988).
7. W. Lance Bennett, *News: The Politics of Illusion*, 5th ed. (White Plains, N.Y.: Longman, 2002); Robert McChesney, *The Problem of the Media: U.S. Communication Politics in the Twenty-first Century* (New York: Monthly Review Press, 2004).
8. Some of this dynamic was initially uncovered by Gitlin, *The Whole World Is Watching: Mass Media in the Making and Unmaking of the New Left* (Berkeley: University of California Press, 1980). For an analysis of this phenomenon in entertainment television, see Mark Crispin Miller, *Boxed In: The Culture of TV* (Evanston, Ill.: Northwestern University Press, 1988), especially "The Hipness Unto Death" and "Big Brother Is You Watching." On advertising and consumer culture, see Thomas Frank, *The Conquest of Cool: Business Culture, Counterculture, and the Rise of Hip Consumerism* (Chicago: University of Chicago Press, 1997).
9. William A. Gamson and Gadi Wolfsfeld, "Movements and Media as Interacting Systems," *Annals of the American Academy of Political and Social Sciences* 528 (July 1993): 119.
10. For a discussion of Judith Butler's theory of "performativity" and how it applies to the Black Panthers, see Nikhil Pal Singh, "The Black Panthers and the 'Undeveloped Country' of the Left," in *The Black Panther Party [Reconsidered]*, edited by Charles E. Jones (Baltimore: Black Classic Press, 1998), 57–105, especially n.135; and Tim Lake's essay, this volume. See, too, W. Lance Bennett and Murray Edelman, "Toward a New Political Narrative," in *Journal of Communication* 35. 4 (1985): 156–69.
11. My interest in reviewing the mainstream media representations of the Panthers is in understanding the legacy of these representations for democratic empowerment today, not in extolling or condemning their tactics.
12. "What We Want / What We Believe," in *The Black Panthers Speak*, edited by Philip S. Foner (Philadelphia: J. S. Lippincott, 1970), 3 (italics in original).
13. According to one sympathetic early observer, "the impact of the showdown on the watching crowd was electric. A large group of 'brothers and sisters on the block' had seen something they had never seen before: black men, proud and dignified, daring to meet the white policeman on equal terms and face him down" (Gene Marine, *The Black Panthers* [New York: Signet, 1969], 43).
14. Churchill, "'To Disrupt, Discredit and Destroy': The FBI's Secret War against the Black Panther Party," in *Liberation, Imagination, and the Black Panther Party*, edited by Kathleen Cleaver and George Katsiaficas (New York: Routledge, 2001), 84. See also Ward Churchill and Jim Vander Wall, *Agents of Repression: The FBI's Secret Wars against the Black Panther Party and the American Indian Movement* (Boston: South End Press, 1988).
15. Political Scientist Christian Davenport has assembled a major database of newspaper articles (including the *Black Panther*), and has begun systematic content analysis of these accounts, although his findings remain largely unpublished. See his

"Reading the 'Voice of the Vanguard': A Content Analysis of the Black Panther Intercommunal News Service, 1969–1972," in Jones, ed., *The Black Panther Party*, 193–210; Christian Davenport and Claudia Dahlerus, "Tracking Down the Empirical Legacy of the Black Panther Party; or, Notes on the Perils of Pursuing the Panthers," in Cleaver and Katsiaficas, eds., *Liberation, Imagination, and the Black Panther Party*, 212–26.

16. Staub attributes a 1970 surge of "moral panic" in Panthers stories to two events: (1) the "FBI-instigated police killing" of Fred Hampton and Mark Clark in December 1969 and the "rhetorical battle over whether the U.S. government was indeed targeting a group of its own citizens for assassination"; and (2) the "specter of wealthy white liberal support for black militancy," a "problem" that first appeared in a *New York Times* fashion article about a 14 January fundraiser at the Park Avenue apartment of the composer Leonard Bernstein. As Staub observes, media coverage exploded when Panther activities "appeared to pose the gravest danger to civil stability," as they were simultaneously "announced to be passé" ("Black Panthers, New Journalism, and the Rewriting of the Sixties," *Representations* 57 [winter 1997], 53–72). My own reading of newsmagazine (and some *Times*) coverage suggests greater continuity in the pre- and post-December 1969 articles. While Staub argues that these mass media were not "particularly hostile nor especially sympathetic" in the early years, I have found a systematically unsympathetic media, with concern about the Panther threat growing more intense during 1969. At the same time, Staub's discussion of Tom Wolfe's critical "Radical Chic: That Party at Lenny's" (*New York*, June 1970) is entirely valid; as I document below, both events—the Hampton-Clark killing and liberal support—generated a backlash in the mass media. Moreover, in framing his analysis with a 1995 *New York* feature on "The [Mumia Abu Jamal] Case that Brought Back Radical Chic," and observing how "mobilized memories of the sixties" were being used "for the purpose of ridiculing and neutralizing political activism in the nineties," (53) his analysis parallels mine.

17. Using the electronic "Readers Guide Retrospective," these include the ideologically edged *Ramparts, Nation, National Review*, and *New Republic*, along with the more mainstream *Commonweal, New York Times Magazine, Esquire, New Yorker, America*, and *Christian Century*. Though television offers another important resource, the weekly newsmagazines were, as Richard Lentz has observed, particularly tailored to "making sense of the world" for their national mass publics (Lentz, *Symbols, the News Magazines, and Martin Luther King* [Baton Rouge: Louisiana State University Press, 1990], 4). One would expect comparable ideological framing from television, along with significantly less content on each news story, and, as W. Lance Bennett argues in chapter 2 of his *News*, significantly greater dramatization, personalization, and fragmentation of news coverage.

18. I discuss this "New Journalism" below; it is a term originally applied to nonfiction pieces written with the full character development and range of subjectivity typical of fiction writing in an effort to capture the meaning of tumultuous 1960s events more fully and richly than could be done by traditional mainstream ("objective") journalism.

19. The general pattern of magazine stories is itself instructive. First, while *Time* and *Newsweek* carried the single largest number of articles during this time period—twenty-six and thirty-four, respectively (*U.S. News and World Report* published only seven articles)—there were more articles about the Black Panthers aggregated in the variety of magazines targeting more specialized audiences. Some, such as the *Nation* with fourteen articles, and *Ramparts* with thirteen, were not subject to the same mass market imperative of "balance" and "impartiality" and thus provided their readers with a far more sympathetic view of Panther clashes with the police and other governmental authorities. Many of these magazines provided their far smaller readership with more in-depth analysis of the Panthers and their politics, and they were able to take their readers beyond the number-one preoccupation of the newsmagazines—namely, Panther violence.
20. Yohuru Williams, *Black Politics/White Power: Civil Rights, Black Power, and the Black Panthers in New Haven* (St. James, N.Y.: Brandywine Press, 2000), 114.
21. "EXTREMISTS: The Panthers' Bite," *Time*, 20 September 1968, 29.
22. The showdown, in which a cocky Huey Newton allegedly dared a police officer to draw his gun, reportedly had a powerful impact on observers like Eldridge Cleaver. See Marine, *The Black Panthers*, 53–56.
23. "The story made the front pages of every major daily in the state and the major television networks" (Williams, *Black Politics/White Power*, 113).
24. "Armed Negroes Protest Gun Bill," *New York Times*, 3 May 1997, 23. The *Times*' anti-white framing of the Panthers echoed the perspective of the *Sacramento Bee* and other California papers covering the State Assembly protest. It would appear that predominantly white mainstream reporters responded subjectively to their encounter with the visually threatening group of armed blacks—despite Seale's angry retort, when asked by newsmen if the Panthers hated white people: "We don't hate nobody because of their color; we hate oppression!" (documentary footage in *Eyes on the Prize II: Power! 1967–68*, a Blackside Production, written by Steve Fayer [(Alexandria, Va.: PBS Videos, 1989)].
25. "The Spirit of Lawlessness," *New York Times*, 7 May 1967, 228. Two weeks later, the *Times* ran "A Gun Is Power, Black Panther Says," which featured an interview with Huey Newton explaining the Panthers' embrace of guns, but also included a broader (and rare) glimpse into Panther ideas about self-defense, nonviolence versus violence, and the war in Vietnam (*New York Times*, 21 May 1967, 66).
26. Interestingly, *U.S. News and World Report*, which rarely reported on the Panthers, was the first national newsmagazine to take note of them. A brief report ("Invasion by Armed Black Panthers") on the Sacramento incident appeared in its 15 May edition. A second event that attracted brief attention in the *Times* was the 28 October exchange of gunfire that resulted in the death of the Oakland policeman John Frey Jr. and the wounding, arrest, and incarceration of Huey Newton. Newton's trial and incarceration for manslaughter became the focus of significant media attention.
27. See Gamson and Wolfsfeld, "Movements and Media as Interacting Systems."
28. "Shoot-Out on 281th Street," *Time*, 19 April 1968, 17–18. While police procedure

may indeed have been "routine," it was far more aggressive and brutal than *Time's* choice of terms would suggest to most American readers.

29. In a far more detailed "New Journalism" account, initially published in the *Saturday Evening Post*, Don Schanche included the testimony of "one woman who came upon the scene immediately after Hutton was killed" and observed Hutton's body "sprawled face down with his hands reaching straight above his head, as if they had been raised in surrender when he was shot and instantly killed." Schanche included Cleaver's testimony and the verdict of trial juries (agreeing with the police version) and reported on his follow-up investigation efforts. After noting that "my own examination of the house that was destroyed by police gunfire left me with the distinct feeling that Cleaver, not the police, had truth on his side," Schanche concluded by writing, "I was inclined to side with the Panthers. I remain so inclined" (*The Panther Paradox: A Liberal's Dilemma* [New York: David McKay, 1970], 59, 224).

30. "Panther Hunt," *Newsweek*, 22 April 1968, 38B.

31. Subsequently, Cleaver admitted that the events of 6 August 1968 were part of a Panther ambush of police, a claim verified by David Hilliard in his autobiography. But, there was no way for journalists to know that at the time, and it was true that the Panthers had "cooled" Oakland youth in the immediate aftermath of King's assassination and the virtual national riot that ensued. See Coleman, "Souled Out"; David Hilliard and Lewis Cole, *This Side of Glory: The Autobiography of David Hilliard and the Story of the Black Panther Party* (Boston: Little, Brown, 1993), 182 ff.

32. "EXTREMISTS: The Panther's Bite," *Time*, 20 September 1968, 29.

33. "Waiting for the Verdict," *Newsweek*, 16 September 1968, 35.

34. The second dichotomy was posed as follows: "Did Frey and his colleague in effect provoke the incident in the first place because of the Oakland police force's animosity toward its avowed Black Panther enemies? Did Newton attempt to kill both police officers because there were two matchboxes of marijuana in the car (as well as, perhaps, the pistol the prosecution said the defendant carried), and because the possession of these articles would have meant the automatic revocation of Newton's parole from a 1964 conviction on charges of assault with a deadly weapon?" There is no mention in this questioning that Frey was, according to some accounts, a particularly aggressive and racially hostile policeman. See Gene Marine, *The Black Panthers*, 76.

35. "On the Prowl," *Newsweek*, 23 September 1968, 35–6.

36. "Penning the Panthers," *Time*, 4 October 1968, 20.

37. Williams, *Black Politics/White Power*, 116–7.

38. According to Seale, the "serve the people" programs did not represent a shift to "reformist" strategies but rather were "revolutionary" because they were part of the struggle to "change the system to a better system," rather than being "set up by the existing exploitative system . . . to fool the people and keep them quiet" (JoNina M. Abron, "'Serving the People': The Survival Programs of the Black Panther Party," in Jones, ed., *The Black Panther Party*, 177–92, quoting Seale's *Seize the Time*, 412–13).

39. Abron, "'Serving the People,'" 183–84.
40. Churchill, "'To Disrupt, Discredit, and Destroy,'" 87; FBI air-tel from Director to 27 field offices, 15 May, 1969, quoted in Tracye Matthews, "'No One Ever Asks What a Man's Place in the Revolution Is': Gender and the Politics of the Black Panther Party, 1966–1971," in Jones, ed., *The Black Panther Party*, 292, drawing from Huey P. Newton, "War against the Panthers: A Study of Repression in America," (Ph.D. diss., University of California, Santa Cruz, 1980), 109.
41. "The Left: Guns and Butter," *Newsweek*, 5 May 1969, 40.
42. Churchill, "'To Disrupt, Discredit, and Destroy,'" 87. The FBI concern about Panther propaganda success was later picked up in the 13 January 1970 issue of the *Wall Street Journal*. Titled "Panther Supporters," the front-page editorial reported on a sampling of opinion among black citizens from four cities that found ample support for the Panthers' community activities. The *Journal* commented that "a sizeable number of blacks support the Panthers because they admire other, less-publicized activities of the Party such as its free breakfast program for ghetto youngsters, its free medical care program and its war on narcotics among black youth" (quoted in Foner, ed., *The Black Panthers Speak*, xiii).
43. "A Booklet That Shocked Congress," *U.S. News and World Report*, 7 July 1969, 4. According to Churchill, the coloring book was the creation of an aspiring Panther recruit "eager to impress" Panther leadership. "Upon review of a twenty-five-copy pilot edition, the Party's Central Committee determined that the book's content was inappropriate for young people. Bobby Seale thereupon instructed that the book not be produced, and that the original copies be destroyed" ("'To Disrupt, Discredit, and Destroy,'" 88).
44. Churchill notes that the infiltrator, Larry Powell, testified before Senator John McClellan's Permanent Subcommittee on Investigations—and the national media—that the Panthers were an "organized criminal enterprise" which engaged in extortion of area businesses in order to fund operations like the breakfast program and materials like the coloring book, even though subsequent investigations failed to substantiate such systematic extortion.
45. William Schule, "Intelligence Report on Today's 'New Revolutionaries,'" *Reader's Digest*, October 1969, 11–126.
46. "Radicals: Gathering of the Clans," *Newsweek*, 4 August 1969, 32.
47. Writing of the actual FBI involvement in the "New York 21" and the New Haven murder trials, Churchill and Vander Wall refer to both as "legal travesties" that "ultimately resulted in the acquittal of the defendants," noting that Bobby Seale and Erica Huggins "seem to have been drawn into" the New Haven trial "almost as a 'dividend' or afterthought." They also compare the light plea-bargained sentence given to Sams, charged with murder, to the "heavy sentences" given to the New Haven Panther captain Lonnie McLucas and others convicted as "accessories" to the murder of Rackley (Churchill and Vander Wall, *Agents of Repression*, 52–53).
48. "THE LEFT: Panther Hunt," *Newsweek*, 1 September 1969, 22.
49. Despite the investigative Walker Commission's finding that the Chicago police

"rioted" against the demonstrators, the events of those days are often referred to as "the violent antiwar protest" at the convention.

50. For a detailed discussion of the media handling of Garry's remarks on the number of Panthers killed, see below.
51. "Chicago Exclusive," *Newsweek*, 22 December 1969, 90–91; "Controversial Verdict," *Newsweek*, 2 February 1970, 23; "Second Thoughts: Case of the Chicago Seven," *Newsweek*, 18 May 1970, 46; "Black Panthers: Slap on the Wrist," *Newsweek*, 25 May 1970, 41; "Chicago: Panther Ghost," *Newsweek*, 6 September 1971, 20.
52. The four articles appeared on pages 20, 26, 49–50, and 50 of their respective issues. Churchill and Vander Wall unearth a different perspective on the ("Fast Eddie") Hanrahan acquittal in the Hampton-Clark killings. Reviewing the painstaking investigation of attorneys in Chicago's "People's Law Office," they argue that the acquittal appeared to be a *"quid pro quo"* deal in which "Hanrahan and his raiders would 'walk' in exchange for their continued silence concerning the facts and nature of FBI involvement in the murders." About the latter, they note that the presiding judge John F. Grady, of the U.S. Seventh Circuit Court, ruled in the civil case brought on behalf of Hampton and Clark's families that "there *had* in fact been an active governmental conspiracy to deny Hampton, Clark, and the BPP plaintiffs their civil rights" (*Agents of Repression*, 76–77).
53. "Police in Chicago Slay 2 Panthers," *New York Times*, 5 December 1969, 1.
54. "Inquiry into Slaying of 2 Panthers Urged in Chicago," *New York Times*, 6 December 1969, 29.
55. "Inquiry Is Urged in Slaying of Chicago Black Panther," *New York Times*, 9 December 1969, 40.
56. "Inquiry Is Urged," *New York Times*, 10 December 1969, 50.
57. "Negroes in Chicago Impose a Curfew on Whites," *New York Times*, 16 December 1969, 21.
58. "5 Negroes Start Panther Inquiry," *New York Times*, 21 December 1969, 47.
59. "ACLU Report Says Police Harass the Panthers," *New York Times*, 29 December 1969, 38.
60. "Probing Panther Attack," *New York Times*, 21 December 1969, 15.
61. "Panel to Review Panther Clashes," 16 December 1969, 20.
62. Tom Wicker, "In the Nation: Songmy and the Black Panthers," *New York Times*, 16 December 1969, 46.
63. "Hoover Deplores Attacks on Police," *New York Times*, 3 January 1970, 6.
64. "Police and Panthers," *New York Times*, 17 December 1969, 54. Ten days later, a reader objected to the *Times*' characterization of the Panthers as "neo-fascist," suggesting that the term might be better applied to government repression.
65. Ibid.
66. "Police and Panthers: Growing Paranoia," *Time*, 19 December 1969, 14–16.
67. Ibid., 15.
68. Ibid., 15–16.
69. Ibid., 16.

70. "The Panthers and the Law," *Newsweek*, 13 February 1970, 26.
71. Ibid., 27.
72. One member of Mitchell's task force on extremism was quoted as saying, "I'm no student of revolutionary activity, but I would suppose that Batista didn't regard Castro as a real danger at first. I don't think the government can take the chance of saying, 'There are only 1,000 of them — what can these ding-a-lings do?'" (ibid., 26).
73. Ibid., 30.
74. Distinct themes emerged, of course, during the trials. Judge Murtagh's iron-handed courtroom rule in New York was initially noted in *Time* in his imposing excessive bail against the Panther suspects, who remained incarcerated for months before their trial. Both *Time* and *Newsweek*'s sympathies turned sharply, though, as the Panther defendants became vocally obstreperous and abusive during pretrial hearings ("Glowering, hooting, they yelled and swore, keeping up a desultory cacophony of epithet, calling the judge and [prosecutor] Phillips 'fascists,' 'pigs,' and 'racists'"). Murtagh won praise for simply suspending the hearing until the Panthers apologized; yet a month later *Time* reported more sympathetically that the Panthers languished in jail "unable to raise money for their high bail." Finally, *Newsweek* published a story on the outcome ("Verdict on the Panthers," 24 May 1971) when the jury returned not-guilty verdicts on the remaining conspiracy charge. Similarly the long, drawn-out New Haven trial produced a surprise verdict when Lonnie McLucas was found guilty of conspiracy but not guilty of any of the more serious charges. Also, when the jury members in the Seale-Huggins trial reported that they were unable to reach a verdict (reportedly stuck with ten votes for acquittal and two for conviction), Judge Mulvey dismissed the charges on grounds that the selection of an unbiased jury for any retrial would be impossible. Both *Time* and *Newsweek* gave significant play to the testimony of George Sams, taking as credible the alleged but discredited Panther enforcer who apparently orchestrated the killing of Alex Rackley and then became the prosecution's key witness.
75. "The Persecution and Assassination of the Black Panther Party as Directed by Guess Who," *National Review*, 30 December 1969, 1306–7.
76. As if to dismiss any suggestions that Hampton might have some virtuous qualities, the *Review* noted that he "died in the apartment where police found shotguns, automatic weapons and hundreds of rounds of ammunition" (ibid., 1306).
77. Ibid.
78. Wolfe's piece appeared in *New York*, 8 June 1970.
79. Some of the backlash attacks highlighted the liberals' gullibility toward alleged media distortion. However, more ridiculed what they alleged was misplaced white guilt—misplaced because of the Panthers' culpability. In an August 1970 *Harper's* article, Fischer lamented the Yale students' embrace of Bobby Seale and the Panthers' case in the New Haven trial, suggesting that Seale would not be a "folk hero" to the protesting students if they had only read his book, *Seize the Time*. Fischer then suggested a close parallel between it and Hitler's *Mein Kampf*, though he wryly observed that the latter at least reflected the work of a "formidable," if paranoid,

mind. After reviewing the sins of black militants generally and of Seale and the Panthers in particular, Fischer adopted the now-familiar, patronizing black-friendly stance, quoting "one black businessman" that "the Panthers aren't a party at all. They are just a gang of hoods, a sort of black Mafia who have pretty well succeeded in terrorizing a good part of the black community." Of the police clashes, Fischer noted, "in several cities policemen were killed or wounded in ambushes which they attributed to the Panthers, and in Chicago two Panthers died in a police raid which never has been satisfactorily explained" ("Black Panthers and Their White Hero-Worshipers," *Harper's* 24 [August 1970]: 18–19 ff).

80. "False Note on Black Panthers," *New York Times*, 16 January 1970, 46.
81. "That Party at Lenny's," *Time*, 26 January 1970, 14.
82. "Upper East Side Story," *Time*, 26 January 1970, 14.
83. See note 16, above.
84. See, for example, Stanley Crouch's "Civil Rights Blues" and other works discussed in Elisabeth Lasch-Quinn, "Radical Chic and the Rise of a Therapeutics of Race," *Salmagundi*, no. 112 (fall 1996): 8–25.
85. As Staub noted, "In the immediate wake of the Chicago killings, most of the mainstream media, in a peculiar double maneuver, at one and the same time allowed Garry's statement to stand as a provocative possibility . . . and simultaneously . . . launched a full-scale rhetorical campaign *against* the Panthers" ("Black Panthers, New Journalism, and the Rewriting of the Sixties," 58).
86. Edward Jay Epstein, "The Panthers and the Police: A Pattern of Genocide?" *New Yorker* 46 (13 February 1971): 45.
87. Epstein stressed, moreover, that "over three hundred newspapers and news agencies" subscribed to the *Times* wire service and "about two hundred" subscribed to the *Post*'s wire service.
88. David Burnham, "F.B.I.'s Informants and 'Bugs' Collect Data on Black Panthers," *New York Times*, 14 December 1969, 1. Garry had not used the term "conspiracy"; rather, it was inferred by the media from SCLC leader Ralph Abernathy's charge of a "systematic pattern of genocide."
89. "Mea Culpa," *Time*, 8 March 1971, 45.
90. "RACES: Police and Panthers at War," *Time*, 12 December 1969, 20.
91. Epstein's reading ignores the kind of perceptions that informed an argument made later by a Chicago policeman, Howard Saffold, of the Afro-American Patrolmen's League. Speaking of Hoover's proclamation about the Panther threat, Saffold observed, "the police community is sort of a built-in reward and punishment system of its own, and you get a lot of rewards when you go after who the boss says is the bad guy and you get him. And I think what J. Edgar Hoover was able to do was to give police officers the impression that it was ok, it was open season. You didn't have to worry about the law. I think what he in effect said was, 'It's our ballgame, guys. We've got the authority. We have the capacity. Let's crush 'em'" (*Eyes on the Prize II: A Nation of Law? 1968–71*).
92. Seeking to enlist CBS as an ally in its attack on television, the author concluded by

noting ruefully that the commentator Eric Sevareid's criticism of the highly charged debate about Panther deaths failed to reflect on "television's role in this episode in the politics of hysteria" (Jean Jeffries, "The 'Black Genocide' Myth," *National Review*, 16 February 1973, 206–7).

93. "The Panthers: Their Decline and Fall," *Newsweek*, 22 March 1971, 26–28.

94. While the conflict was real, *Newsweek*'s coverage echoed the COINTELPRO effort to "push ideological disagreements between Party members Huey P. Newton and Eldridge Cleaver into the realm of open hostility" (Churchill and Vander Wall, *Agents of Repression*, 40).

95. "Destroying the Panther Myth," *Time*, 22 March 1971, 19–20.

96. Seale's mayoral campaign, and Elaine Brown's run for city council, reflected a 1972 BPP Central Committee decision to close Panther locals and emphasize the training of Party members in political organizing and campaigning. This decision has been characterized by Ollie Johnson as a "strategic mistake," as it "led to an unfortunate concentration of power in [Huey] Newton's hands (Johnson, "Explaining the Demise," 403). Both Seale and Brown lost, though Seale came in second in the initial three-person race, and then garnered 43,719 votes in the run-off election.

97. "Tame Panthers?" *Time*, 25 December 1972, 13–14.

98. "New Bobby," *Newsweek*, 2 April 1973, 30.

99. "Old Panther with a New Purr," *Newsweek*, 17 March 1975, 40.

100. "Purring Panthers," *Newsweek*, 22 November 1976, 16.

101. "Whatever Happened to . . . the Black Panthers," *U.S. News and World Report*, 16 August 1976, 61.

102. Don Schanche's early articles on the Panthers were published in the *Saturday Evening Post* in 1968 and in the *Atlantic Monthly* in 1970. He collected his reflections on the Panthers, with a heavy emphasis on his considerable time spent with Eldridge and Kathleen Cleaver, in *The Panther Paradox: A Liberal's Dilemma* (New York: David McKay, 1970). At the beginning of his book, he expressed a perception that never appeared in the weekly newsmagazines. "Most of the Black Panthers I have met are naïve, malleable ghetto kids, angry and despairing, but not naturally vicious or mean-spirited men and women. They have been driven by white society to their insanity; they have not marched to it by choice" (ix). However, after intense, up-close experiences with Eldridge Cleaver, and after encountering more "wild" and "terrifyingly heated" Panther rhetoric than he cared to, Schanche described his account as a "narrative of a deeply disappointing acquaintance" (xx). While finding the behavior of the government and its police agents thoroughly reprehensible, Schanche backed away from the "black rage" he witnessed. Not surprisingly, the Panthers' radical critique of the United States is scarcely perceivable in his account.

103. In her book on the New Haven Panther trial (*Panthermania: The Clash of Black against Black in One American City* [New York: Harper and Row, 1971]), Sheehy began by noting that "a year ago I was just as taken up with the Panther cause as anyone else" (ix) and by describing her inclination to "think of all Panthers as

martyrs" after the Hampton-Clark killings. The Panther "mania" in the book's title was, in effect, about this uncritical embrace of everything Panther. Having completed a highly subjective investigation of the Rackley murder, Sheehy's second thoughts led her to an equally uncritical embrace of all the right's denunciation of the Panthers (and their liberal "supporters"). Thus, "the Panther movement was created by and for the media. The more it was publicized by the liberal white media, the greater the imagined ranks of a black army grew. This gave police a massive case of Pantherphobia. And a good excuse to attack" (8). Or, in reflecting the Epstein article, she simply asserted, "Without verification, Garry's body count [of Panthers killed by police] passed like gospel throughout the white media," leading to widespread support for the "beleaguered black revolutionaries" (and presumably helping to fuel Sheehy's charge that the Panthers were a "media creation"). Noting that she, too, rallied and contributed to this "spellbinding cause," Sheehy shared her encounter with the "Panther movement's . . . loss of innocence" in New Haven. Of particular note was her patronizing embrace of middle-class blacks as the group bearing the greatest burden of "Panthermania." Her grounds for criticizing FBI repression, it turned out, were that "J. Edgar Hoover may have been the nation's greatest Panther recruiter" (6).

104. Staub noted that "Wolfe, like Sheehy utilized the narrative freedom of New Journalism in order to move subtly and cleverly from perspective to perspective — none of them completely his own nor identifiably anyone else's. . . . Instead of inviting (though then also blocking) identification with the narrative's characters, as Sheehy did, Wolfe invited identification with, if anyone, his supercilious omniscient narrator." Staub reviewed examples of Wolfe's "suave malice," his mockery of the Bernsteins and their guests, and his "play" with "tense and tone" that "managed to make the sixties themselves seem like they were part of some previous century." He also discerned another tactic common to the Right's ridicule of the 1960s liberal sympathizers: "There was Leonard Bernstein, the host, against whom Wolfe mobilized an always popular resentment against class privilege." Staub pointed out that the Bernstein-Panther get-together became the archetype for subsequent applications of "radical chic" to apparent alliances between loathsome radicals and gullible liberals. (Another example occurred in an 8 March 1970 *New York Times Magazine* article by Gerald Emanuel Stearn, titled, "Rapping with the Panthers in White Suburbia" [15].) Wolfe himself helped to entrench the phrase in his later book *Radical Chic and Mau-Mauing the Flak-Catchers* (New York: Farrar, Strauss, 1970).

105. In its conclusion, the *Esquire* piece offered its readers a typically dichotomized choice: either "the various prosecutions of the Black Panthers are one stage in the extinction of a party which, in the view of J. Edgar Hoover, represents the greatest threat to the internal security of the nation, 'greater even than the Communist Conspiracy' (right on, J. Edgar), *or*: that the Sixties period of 'protest' and 'resistance' is over and the Panthers are the vanguard of the coming, inevitable Revolutionary Liberation." Assuming its hip readers had "chosen to run with the Revolution," *Esquire* offered them a way to do it ("Start helping to raise money for the

Panther defense fund") but concluded by warning, "Bear in mind: from the distance he's at, Huey Newton can't tell *you* from J. Edgar Hoover. If you want to catch up to the new reality, you're going to have to get moving. Feets, do yoah stuff" ("Is It Too Late for You to Be Pals with a Black Panther?" *Esquire* [November 1970], 142–46).

106. Both Pearson and Horowitz professed initial attraction to the Panthers' fighting image—Pearson as a young boy who first became taken with the book *Free Huey* in seventh grade, Horowitz as a New Left radical who became directly involved with Newton and his coterie in the early 1970s. Both became disillusioned, though for different reasons: Pearson because of the sordid violence he uncovered through research interviews (however few), Horowitz because (among other things) he experienced a sense of guilt and angry betrayal, believing that the woman he recommended for the Party's bookkeeping work, Betty Van Patter, had been killed by the Panthers.

107. Stern goes on with some liberal media bashing: "Except, that is, at the *New York Times*, where the obsession with white guilt and black victimhood apparently trumps every standard of journalistic and historical accuracy." The *Times*' crime was a Holland Carter review of an exhibit of Panther photographs, in which he, according to Stern, lectured on the "justice of black violence" ("Soundings: 'Ah, Those Black Panthers! Beautiful!'" *City Journal* 13.3 [summer, 2003]: 12–13).

108. Maurice Isserman and Michael Kazin, *America Divided: The Civil War of the 1960s* (New York: Oxford, 2000), 275. One of the Panther references in the book notes that an "obscure group" called the Black Panther Party for Self-Defense organized by Newton and Seale sold Mao's *Little Red Book* to raise funds to buy guns and ammunition; the other reference occurs in passages about the growth of Christian fundamentalism. While discussing religious millennialism, the authors note how the appeal of "'Jesus freaks' outlasted that of their secular detractors," and they go on casually to mention that "SDS and the Black Panthers expected some kind of socialism would emerge from the ashes of the U.S. empire" (178, 247).

109. "Toward a New Political Narrative," 156–69.

110. *San Francisco Chronicle*, 15 June 2003, D2.

111. *Los Angeles Times*, 22 June 2003, M1.

112. In this, I distinguish *Panther* from efforts to provide documentary analysis of the Panthers' history and politics—ranging from segments of the *Eyes on the Prize* to BET Movies' *The Panther Perspective* or small-budget films like *All Power to the People* and *Public Enemy*.

113. "Power to the Peephole," *Time*, 15 May 1995, 73.

114. Quoted in Richard Leiby, "Black Out: What a New Movie about the Black Panthers Remembers—and What It Forgets," *Washington Post*, 30 April 1995, G1. The *Post* article used the occasion to explore charges and countercharges between former Panthers like Seale, David Hilliard, and Elaine Brown, and Panther detractors like Pearson and Horowitz—a rare mass media retrospective look at the Panthers' place in history.

115. Renee Graham, "An Ex-Panther defends 'Panther,'" *Boston Globe*, 9 May 1963, 63.

Contributors

Bridgette Baldwin is an assistant professor of law at the Western New England School of Law. Her research and teaching interests include criminal law and legal philosophy, critical race theory, and social welfare policy.

Davarian L. Baldwin is an assistant professor of history at Boston College where his research focuses on black cultural studies, the social production of knowledge, critical urban studies, and social and political theory. He has published in *Black Renaissance/Renaissance Noire*, *Journal of Urban History*, *American Studies*, and *Critical Sociology*, and he is the author of *Chicago's New Negroes: Race, Class, and Respectability in the Black Metropolis, 1910–1935*.

David Barber is an assistant professor of history at University of Tennessee, Martin. An early draft of parts of his dissertation, *The Price of the Liberation: The New Left's Dissolution, 1965–1970*, appeared in the spring 2001 issue of the journal *Race Traitor*.

Rod Bush is an associate professor in the department of sociology and anthropology at St. John's University. As a recent Ph.D. recipient after many years in the movement for social change and black liberation, he is the editor of *The New Black Vote: Politics and Power in Four American Cities* and the author of *We Are Not What We Seem: Black Nationalism and Class Struggle in the American Century*.

James T. Campbell is an associate professor of American civilization, Africana studies, and history at Brown University. His publications include *Songs of Zion: The African Methodist Episcopal Church in the United States and South Africa* and the forthcoming *Middle Passages: African American Encounters with Africa*.

Tim Lake is the Visiting Owen Duston Assistant Professor in the English department at Wabash College in Crawfordsville, Indiana. He earned his Ph.D. in American culture studies from Bowling Green State University in Ohio.

Jama Lazerow is a professor of history at Wheelock College. He is the author of *Religion and the Working Class in Antebellum America* and of the forthcoming *The Awakening of a Sleeping Giant: New Bedford, the Black Panthers, and the 1960s*.

Edward P. Morgan is University Distinguished Professor of Political Science at Lehigh University. The author of *The Sixties Experience: Hard Lessons about Modern America*, he is currently writing a book titled *The Twilight of Democracy? Capitalism, Media Culture and the Postmodern Sixties*.

Jeffrey O. G. Ogbar is an associate professor of history at the University of Connecticut. He is the author of *Black Power: Radical Politics and African American Identity*.

Roz Payne is a photographer, filmmaker, and historian, and she teaches at Burlington College. A founding member of the Newsreel film collective, she is currently producing a DVD on the Black Panthers.

Robert O. Self is an assistant professor of history at Brown University. He is the author of *American Babylon: Race and the Struggle for Postwar Oakland*.

Yohuru Williams is an associate professor of history at Fairfield University. He is the author of *Black Politics/White Power: Civil Rights, Black Power, and the Black Panthers in New Haven*, and he is currently working on a book titled *Six Degrees of Segregation: Lynching and Capital Punishment in America*.

Joel Wilson's dissertation, "'Free Huey': The Black Panther Party, the Peace and Freedom Party, and the Politics of Race in 1968" explored the connections between race, progressive electoral politics, and criminal law. In 2002 he received his Ph.D. from the University of California, Santa Cruz; and he is currently pursuing a legal degree at the University of California, Los Angeles.

Index

Abernathy, Ralph, 343
Abrams, Charles, 30
Acoli, Sundiata, 77
Adams, John, 70
Adams, Samuel, 70
African Americans: 16, 26, 198, 264; and class, 4, 41, 200; and employment, 254; and gangs, 266; and ideas of citizenship, 20, 22, 90 n.39, 202; and internationalism, 21, 28, 61; and political struggle, 28, 34, 49, 192, 195–96, 254; and racism, 29, 207, 211–13
African Blood Brotherhood (ABB), 64
African Party for the Independence of Guinea Bissau and Cape Verde (PAIGC), 114
Afro-American Association, 38
Afro-American Patrolmen's League, 341
Ageism, 183, 184
Agnew, Spiro, 351
Al-Amin, Jamil. *See* Brown, H. Rap
Albino, Harry, 126, 128
Algeria, 40, 43, 60, 105, 197
Ali, Muhammad, 68, 302
American Civil Liberties Union, 341, 350
American exceptionalism, 22, 34, 35

American Indian Movement, 158, 299, 339
Americanization, 295
American Revolution, 8, 60, 63, 70, 76, 79, 81, 85
Ann Arbor, 185
Anthony, Earl, 204, 220 n.58
Antiwar movement, 15, 97, 207
Apartheid, 295
Aquash, Anna Mae, 158
Aragon, Louis, 311, 312
Arum, Donald "Dolomite," 126, 128, 132, 147 n.110
Assata, 98
Association for the Reduction of Violence (ARV), 109, 111, 129
Attica Prison, 269
Atzlan, 259
Austin National Council (ANC), 234
Austin, 231, 233, 236
Avakian, Bob, 192, 204, 214, 220 n.69
Axlerod, Beverly, 217 n.17
Aztecs, 260

Baker, Ella, 245 n.1
Baker, Eric "Ricky," 125, 126, 128, 133
Baldwin, Bridgette, 7, 62, 63
Baldwin, James, 215, 297

Ball, Hugo, 311
Ballinger, Howard, 209, 210
Bandung Conference, 74, 296
Bandung World, 301
Baraka, Amiri, 43, 269, 301
Barber, David, 6–7, 187
Barker, Ma, 164
Base of Operation campaign, 41
Bass, Charlotta, 35, 40
Bennett, Fred, 170
Bennett, W. Lance, 357
Bensky, Larry, 248 n.25
Bergman, Arlene Eisen, 235, 237
Berkeley Barb, 204
Berkeley Tribe, 242
Bernstein, Leonard, 347–48, 372 n.104
Bill of Rights. *See* United States Constitution
Binetti, Nicholas, 161
Bingham, Lynette, 112, 128, 151 n.125
Bin Wahad, Dhoruba. *See* Moore, Richard
Biondi, Martha, 25, 26, 34
Birmingham, 17, 35, 99
Black Arts movement, 301
Black Belt, 34, 243
Black Brothers, 120
Black consciousness movement, 113
Black Convention Movement (BCM), 38
Black Liberation movement, 192, 210
Black Metropolis, 31
Black migration, 26, 30
Black Muslims, 5
Black Nationalism, 5, 36, 246 n.1, 250 n.43, 256, 260, 291; and armed protest, 68, 211; and Black Panthers, 214, 220 n.58, 237, 309; and Chicanos, 255, 259, 265; and civil rights movement, 17; and Federal Bureau of Investigation, 248 n.19; and Huey Newton, 40; and New Left, 233; and Progressive Labor Party, 231; and socialism, 33; and Student Nonviolent Coordinating Committee, 225, 229, 244
Black Panther, 4, 5, 41, 43, 80, 99, 193, 204, 213, 242, 257, 259, 267, 268, 273, 277, 327
Black Panther Party (BPP): 38, 104, 119, 255, 292–95; alleged sexism of, 12, 277–78, 285 n.80; and alliance with Peace and Freedom Party (PFP), 204, 205, 209, 213, 215, 216 n.11; and armed militancy, 73, 87, 193–96, 237, 299, 322 n.37; and break with SNCC, 201; and coalitions with whites, 2, 3, 6, 226; and concept of self-defense, 69, 70, 73–76, 80–86, 212, 232; and cultural politics, 290; and development of, 19, 41, 42, 64, 105, 169, 199, 214, 307; and education, 260–61; and FBI, 159, 160–66, 172, 176; and gangs, 266–70; and grassroots activity, 39, 43–45, 98, 262; historiography of, 3, 15–19, 48, 67, 101, 105, 134; and ideological evolution of, 42, 64, 199–208, 235; and internal factionalism, 43, 262; and Latinos, 279; and Martin Luther King Jr., 16; and media depiction, 330, 332; and Panther mimics, 184, 187, 188; and People's Constitutional Convention of 1970, 69; and police, 47, 60, 83, 99, 100, 104, 106, 235, 239, 241, 243, 255–58, 261, 322 n.37, 329, 332; and politics, 6, 185, 199, 200, 328; restructuring of, 83, 169, 353; revolutionary character of, 7–9, 28, 29, 186, 242, 306–9, 312–17; and SDS, 188, 230–35, 245, social programs of, 46–47, 68, 84, 97, 123, 127, 159, 168, 175, 261, 265, 315, 329, 336, 366 n.38; Ten-Point Program, 29, 40, 69, 84–85, 184, 189, 195, 202, 227, 255, 257, 328, 329; and Third World nationalism, 39; and violence,

378 *Index*

7, 15, 42, 44, 59–66, 68, 77, 81, 98, 173, 187, 198; and voter registration, 43, 60
Black Panther Party [Reconsidered], 8
Black Panthers, 67
Black People's Army, 232
Black political economy, 41, 42
Black Power movement: 32, 36–39, 191, 194, 221 n.74, 231, 320; alleged sexism of, 276; and Black Panthers, 1, 3, 15; and Chicanos, 255, 257, 259, 274, 279; and cultural politics, 43, 290–92, 294, 301–2; and Puerto Ricans, 262–65, 269–71, 279; and whites, 17, 208–10
Black Power, 75
Black radicals, 24, 34, 37, 48, 49, 184, 241
Blackstone Rangers, 265
Black United Front, 118
Black Vigilantes, 99
Blair, Ezell, Jr., 107, 108
Blake, Albert, 131
Blake, Herman J., 180
Blight, David, 3
Bloom, Bob, 161
Boggs, Grace Lee, 298
Boggs, James, 298
Bolsheviks, 159
Bond, Julian, 216 n.2, 347
Booth, Paul, 216 n.2
Boston, 106, 118, 119, 120, 121, 127, 134
Boston Panthers, 121
Boumedienne, Houari, 300
Boyle, Robert, 161
Braudel, Fernand, 62
Breton, André, 311, 312
Brewer, Brad, 312
Bridgeport, 99
Bristol Community College (BCC), 118, 119, 135
Brooke, Ed, 122
Brooklyn, 243

Broslawky, Farrel, 207–10
Brotherhood of Sleeping Car Porters, 33
Brown, Elaine, 7, 8, 41, 43, 44, 48, 170, 257, 276–77, 353
Brown, H. Rap, 67, 202, 213, 255, 259
Brown, Jim, 302
Brown, Ralph, 122
Brown, Sam, 347
Brown Berets, 188, 252, 256–58, 260–62, 269, 275, 278, 280, 299; and eight points of attention, 257; and lumpen, 258; and patriarchy of, 274, 278; Thirteen-Point Program, 257, 267, 276; and *vatos locos*, 258
Brown v. Board of Education, 16, 18
Brzezinski, Zbigniew, 341
Bukhari-Alston, Safiya, 276
Bunche, Ralph, 32, 33
Bursey, Charles, 169, 170
Bursey, Shelley, 170
Business Week, 61
Butler, Judith, 319, 323 n.45

Cabral, Amilcar, 114
Caldwell, Earl, 346
California: 40, 83, 117, 192, 214, 253; California Democratic Caucus (CDC), 216 n.2; Constitution of, 81; State Assembly, 193
Cambodia, 61
Cambridge Friends, 134
Cambridge movement, 74
Campos, Pedro Albizu, 267
Cape Verdean Veterans' Association (CVVA), 115, 188
Capitalism: 197, 269, 270–71, 289, 294, 313–14, 317, 320, 326
Captain Crutch, 83
Carlos, John, 302
Carmichael, Stokely: 1, 118, 315; and Black Power, 259; and Black United Front, 118; and ideology of, 75, 191, 297; and SNCC, 201, 213, 225, 244

Index 379

Carter, Alprentice Bunchy, 234
Carter, Rubin "Hurricane," 305 n.26
Casady, Simon, 216 n.2
Castro, Tony, 259
Castro, Vickie, 254
Catlett, Elizabeth, 321 n.25
Cayton, Horace, 31, 32
Center for the Study of Democratic Institutions (CSDI), 216 n.2
Chavez, Cesar, 253
Chicago, 4, 31–33, 45, 105, 160, 167, 177, 192, 193, 234, 238–42, 263, 275, 330
Chicago Conspiracy Trial, 345
Chicago school, 30, 32
Chicano Moratorium Committee, 261
Chicano Power, 262
Chicanos: 41, 270, 272, 274, 275; and health, 254; in East Los Angeles, 254; and nationalism, 253, 258, 259
China, 60, 298
Church Committee, 160, 161, 174
Churchill, Ward, 171, 323 n.41
Civil Rights Act of 1964, 17
Civil rights movement: 3, 8, 17–18, 23, 35, 60–64, 325; and black radicalism, 18; and campaign to suppress black dissent, 158; and liberalism, 18; media coverage of, 16; and Montgomery bus boycott, 16
Civil War, 3, 8
Clark, Gloria, 108–11, 113, 118–19, 129, 135
Clark, Mark, 158, 330
Class, 4, 22, 196, 236, 266, 270, 307
Cleaver, Eldridge: 9, 277, 331, 335, 344; and Black Panther Party, 40, 90 n.39, 194, 200–202, 246 n.1, 315; and exile from the Panthers, 43, 316–17, 330; and Huey Newton, 69, 77, 100, 293, 317–19, 320 n.5; and Peace and Freedom Party, 105, 204, 208, 215, 224, 226–27, 245, 333; and revolutionary politics, 5, 6, 40, 49, 73, 81, 193, 242, 258, and SDS, 228, 229, 232; and *Soul on Ice*, 1, 230; and Stokely Carmichael, 2, 10; and whites, 194, 213, 219 n.43
Cleaver, Kathleen, 170, 194, 199, 233, 277, 336
Clemons, Michael L., 307
Cleveland, 27
Clinton, George, 297
Cockrel, Kenneth, 66 n.10
Cohen, Richard, 352
Cohendet, William A. (WAC), 102, 158–77
COINTELPRO (Counter-Intelligence Program), 160–65, 167, 168, 171, 248 n.19, 262, 323 n.41, 329–30, 335, 339
Cold War, 19–21, 23, 24, 34, 37, 295
Cole, Lew, 237
Coleman, Kate, 6, 174, 358
Colonialism: 70, 73, 294–96; and African American liberation, 35–37, 40–41, 43–45, 197, 297–98; and decolonization, 39, 75; and internal colony, 75, 83, 202; and postcolonial cultural politics, 61, 290–91; and Third World, 69, 76, 78, 252–53, 302; as Western pattern, 22, 63
Columbia University, 243
Combahee River Collection, 300
COMINTERN, 250 n.43
Committee for a Unified Newark, 269
Commonwealth Office, 264
Commonwealth of Massachusetts v. Frank Grace, 138 n.22
Communist International, 243
Communist Party, 25, 33–34, 47, 117, 159–60, 193, 209, 217 n.17, 220 n.58, 230, 241, 270, 294
Community for New Politics (CNP), 192, 221 n.73
Confederate flag, 17, 283 n.51

Confronting the Veil, 32
Congress of Racial Equality (CORE), 37, 61
Consultation of Older and Younger Adults for Social Change, 186
Containment and Change, 227
Cordwell, Robin "Carlene," 131, 132
Council on African Affairs (CAA), 64
Covert Action Quarterly, 176
Cox, Donald, 174, 347
Crow, Jim, 16–18, 20–23, 26, 28, 35, 36, 51 n.9, 60, 63
Cruse, Harold, 297
Cruz, Ronnie, 108
Cuba, 60
Curry, Thomas, 161

Dada, 311, 312
Dar es Salaam, 35
Davis, Angela, 305 n.26
Davis, Benjamin, 33, 34, 40
Days of Rage, 240, 242, 245
Dayton, 301
Deacons for Defense, 74, 265
Debord, Guy, 312, 313, 314, 315
Declaration of Independence, 21, 62, 69, 70, 76, 78, 79, 80
Declaration of Negro Voters, 34
Declensionist history, 3, 245, 246 n.1, 250 n.44, 251 n.44, 362 n.1
Dellums, Ronald, 43
Deloach, Cartha, 158
Democratic Party, 16, 43, 199, 200, 214, 229, 278
Denning, Michael, 294, 295, 305 n.26
Denver, 234
Department of Youth Services, 133
Derrida, Jacques, 315–19
Detroit, 17, 27, 30, 75, 191, 238, 239
Dillinger, John, 164
Dodge Revolutionary Union Movement (DRUM), 66 n.10, 75
Dohrn, Bernardine, 227, 228, 229, 239

Dolan, Elizabeth, 132, 133–34
Doss, Erika, 299, 310
Douglas, Emory, 5, 277, 300, 310, 313, 314, 321 n.25
Douglas, William O., 72
Douglass, Frederick, 247 n.12
Drake, St. Clair, 30, 31, 32
Duarte, Dickie, 132
DuBois, Ellen, 246 n.1
Du Bois, W. E. B., 23, 30–33, 35, 247 n.12, 307
Duchamp, Marcel, 311

East Los Angeles, 253, 254, 256, 261
Edelman, Murray, 355
Education Act of 1965, 46
Edwards, Harry, 302
Eisenstadt, Abraham, 2
El Barrio, 267, 268, 273
Elbaum, Max, 61
Elrod, Richard, 240
Engels, Frederick, 65
Episcopal Church of the Epiphany, 255
Epstein, Edward Jay, 349–51
Epton, Saul, 340
Esparza, Moctesuma, 254
Esquire, 330, 355

Fair Employment Practice Committee (FEPC), 26
Fanon, Frantz, 28, 40, 44–45, 74, 197, 202, 206, 217 n.25, 273, 279, 296–98
Featherston, Daniel, 128, 133
Federal Bureau of Investigation (FBI): 6, 15, 64; and COINTELPRO, 329, 335; and Frank "Parky" Grace, 104, 124, 127, 145 n.103, 146 n.104; and J. Edgar Hoover, 178 n.4, 336; and suppression of BPP, 98–100, 171, 175, 177, 220 n.58, 234, 262; and view of BPP as security threat, 5, 45–46, 55 n.56, 168, 215; and William A. Cohendet, 102, 158

Fink, Elizabeth, 161
Fischer, John, 348
Floyd, Charles "Pretty Boy," 164
Fontanez, Gloria, 275
Forman, James, 201, 213, 219 n.45
Forrest Gump, 324, 359
Fort Dix, 243
Fort Rodman Job Corps, 118
Fort, Jeff, 266
Foucault, Michel, 305 n.26
Franklin, Aretha, 314, 322 n.25
Franklin, John Hope, 2
Frazier, Franklin E., 32, 297
Free Huey, 258–59
Free Speech Movement (FSM), 210
Freedom House, 134
Freedom Summer of 1964, 118
Frey, John, Jr., 217 n.18, 334, 365 n.26, 366 n.34

Gandhi, Mahatma, 16
Gangster Disciples, 265
Garrow, David, 172
Garry, Charles, 339, 341, 345, 349–52
Garvey, Marcus, 41, 64, 159, 309
Gay liberation movement, 188, 277, 299
Gender, 103, 273, 278, 307
Generation X, 289
Ghana, 60
G.I. Bill, 19
Gifford, Kenny, 125
Gil, Gilberto, 301
Giovantti, Louis A., 176
Gitlin, Todd, 246 n.1, 247 n.4
Glover, 128
Goines, Donald, 301
Goldberg, Arthur J., 341, 347
Gonzalez, Corky, 259, 260
Gonzalez, Juan, 271
Grace, Clo, 116, 124, 128
Grace, Frank ("Parky"): 6, 101–2, 104–57, 188; and early life, 113–15; and gang association, 107, n.137; and Marvin Morgan, 124–28, 136 n.2, 144 n.94, 147–56; and prison, 109–12, and Vietnam, 116; and violence, 121–24
Grace, Ross, 108, 125–29, 133, 136 n.6
Gray Panthers, 184–86, 189
Great Depression, 32
Great Migration, 27, 32, 35, 63
Great Proletarian Cultural Revolution, 298
Great Society, 18, 20, 24, 27, 36, 41, 60, 97
Greensboro, 17
Greensboro Four, 107
Griswold v. Connecticut, 72
Guardian, 267
Guevera, Che, 28, 74, 279, 280, 298
Guinea, 60
Guzman, Pablo "Yoruba," 268, 273, 276

Haden, Patricia, 300
Hale and Dorr, 109, 128, 129, 131, 132
Hall, Simon, 192
Hamilton, Charles, 24, 25, 26, 75, 297
Hamilton, Dona, 24–26
Hampton, Fred: 241, 268, 247; and denouncement of Weathermen, 239, 242, 245; slaying of, 45, 158, 330, 339–41, 346, 350, 352, 364 n.16, 371 n.103; and Young Lords, 265, 267
Hancock, John, 70
Hanrahan, Edward V., 340, 342, 343
Harlem, 32, 277
Harlem Renaissance, 33, 64
Harrington, Edward F., 126, 128, 133
Harris, Abram, Jr., 32
Harvard Strike of 1969, 118
Hayden, Tom, 245 n.1
Haymarket Square, 240
Haywood, Harry, 33, 34
Head Start, 46
Healey, Dorothy, 209
Heard, Big Bob, 119

Henson, Larry, 285 n.80
Hewitt, Raymond Masai, 171, 350
Hill, Michael, 170
Hilliard, David, 7, 46, 82, 84, 169, 174, 203, 216 n.15, 330, 335
Hilliard, June Bug, 171
Hirsch, Arnold, 19
Historic memory, 3, 68
Hobbes, Thomas, 76
Holloway, Jonathan, 32
Hoover, J. Edgar, 64, 158, 172, 175, 177, 178 n.4, 359; and idea of BPP as threat, 45, 159–60, 167–68, 215, 342, 370 n.91, 372 n.105; and operations against BPP, 100, 102, 163, 165, 171
Horowitz, David, 7, 325, 355, 359
Houston, 177
Houtmann, Warren, 121
Huggins, Ericka, 277
Huggins, John, 234
Hunton, Alphaeus, 35
Hutton, Bobby, 174, 332, 333, 335, 350

Imperialism, 192, 206, 214, 231, 232, 236, 243, 262, 296, 317, 328, and anti-imperialist revolution, 241; and Europeans, 260
In Defense of Self-Defense, 70
India, 16
Indianapolis, 234
Industrialism, 26, 29, 30, 36, 48, 49
Innis, Richard, 132, 133
Intercommunal Youth Institute, 46
International Law Library, 243
International Section of the Party, 43
Isou, Isidore, 312
Israel, Barbara, 210
Isserman, Maurice, 246 n.1

Jackson, George, 246 n.1
Jackson, Jesse, 190 n.8
Jackson, Phyllis, 170
Jacobs, John, 239

Jaga, Geronimo ji. *See* Pratt, Elmer "Geronimo"
James, C. L. R., 291, 297
Janco, Marcel, 311
Jefferies, Judson, 8, 318
Jennings, Regina, 204
Jimenez, Jose "Cha Cha," 265, 266, 267, 271, 272, 273
Job Corps, 107
Johnson, Lyndon B., 20, 23, 97, 191, 214
Jones, Charles E., 8–9, 307
Joseph, Pauline, 178 n.7
Justice for Parky Coalition (JPC), 129, 131
Justice in the Deep South, 74

Kansas City, 99
Karenga, Maulana, 68, 255, 259, 269
Katsiaficas, George, 84, 307
KcKee, Albert, 44
Kelley, Robin D. G., 18, 21, 34, 292, 306–9, 318
Kennedy, John F., 16, 23
Kennedy, Robert, 214
Kent State University, 61, 129
Kerner Commission of 1968, 121
Kessler-Harris, Alice, 20
Keynes, John M., 19, 20, 296
Khazan, Jibreel. *See* Blair, Ezell, Jr.
Kimbro, 101, 103 n.5
King, B. B., 314
King, Martin Luther, Jr., 10, 15–17, 45, 60, 64, 97, 99, 116, 264, 290, 294, 296, 298, 325, 327, 332
Klonsky, Mike, n.249
Kozol, Jonathan, 130
Ku Klux Klan, 17, 74, 343
Kuhn, Maggie, 183, 184, 185, 189
Kuti, Fela, 301

Labor history, 253, 269, 295
Labor unions, 24, 29
La Causa, 274, 275

Index 383

Lake, Tim, 9, 292, 299
Languth, A. J., 70
La Piranya, 255
Lassiter, Jasper, 125, 126, 127, 129, 132, 133
Latinas/Latinos, 7, 183–222, 252
Latin Kings, 266
Law Enforcement Group (LEG), 187
Lazerow, Jama, 6, 101, 188
League of Latin America Citizens (LLAC), 278
League of Revolutionary Black Workers (LRBW), 66 n.10, 242
Leary, Howard R., 187
Lee, Spike, 360
Leninism, 279, 331
Lester, 233
Lewis, Tommy, 257
Lewlee, Lee, 277
Liberation, 130
Licon, George, 254
Lihares, Matthew, 125
Lima, Lester, 122, 123, 125
Lincoln Park, 240
Lindsay, John, 268
Livramento, Rhoda, 135
Locke, John, 76
Lopez, Omar, 272
Lords and Patriots, 267
Lords, Stones, and Disciples (LDS), 265
Los Angeles, 105, 165, 234
Los Angeles Board of Education, 255
Los Angeles Free Press, 207
Los Angeles Human Rights Commission, 254
Los Siete de La Raza, 259
Lost Cause, 3
Lowe, Mary Johnson, 161
Lowndes County, 38
Lubell, David, 170
Luce, Henry, 60
Luce, John, 255
Lumpen proletariat, 74, 112, 188, 197, 266, 276, 296
Lynching, 73
Lynd, Staughton, 225

Machismo, 274
Madison, James, 71, 85
Magnett, Jimmy, 121
Major, Reginald, 204
Malcolm X: 227, 299, 309, 331; and militancy of, 17, 254, 333; as revolutionary theorist, 28, 38, 40, 61, 64, 255, 256, 307, 328; and self-defense ideology, 74; and separatism, 41, 60
Malcolm X (film), 360
Mansfield, Harvey, 337
Maoism, 18, 37, 331
Mao Zedong, 28, 38, 40, 55, 74, 81, 113, 276, 279, 280, 298
Mapfumo, Thomas, 301
Marine, Gene, 67, 204
Marley, Bob, 301
Márquez, Gabriel García, 298
Martinez, Joe, 267, 268
Marx, Karl, 65, 279
Marxism, 279, 331
Massachusetts, 117, 131
Matza, Michael, 111
May 2nd Movement, 230
McAfee, Thomas, 76, 85
McClellan, John, 337
McGee, Michael, 289
Media, 324–28
Memphis, 112, 119, 131
Messenger, 64
Mexican Americans, 252, 253, 260
Mexican-American War, 253
Mexican-American Youth Leadership Conference, 254
Mexicans, 253
Mexico, 278
Middle class, 220 n.72
Middleton, Donna, 300

Mills, C. Wright, 297
Mitchell, Daniel, 129
Mitchell, John, 344
Mitchell, Roy, 158
Montgomery bus boycott, 25
Month of Soul Dances, 265
Moore, Richard, 102, 161, 162, 168, 171
Morales, Iris, 276
Morgan, Edward, 9
Morgan, Marvin, 106, 107, 124, 128, 134, 135
Morgan, Ted, 292, 299
Moye, Kelly, n.103
Murray, George Mason, 183
Murrell, Virtual, 345
Murtagh, John, 243
Muste, A. J., 16

Nation of Islam, 40, 64, 263, 265
National Association for the Advancement of Colored People (NAACP), 34, 118, 160, 247 n.12, 278, 341, 346
National Center for Attitude Change, 133
National Committee to Combat Fascism (NCCF), 99, 122, 123
National Conference for New Politics (NCNP), 191, 192, 195, 206
National Interim Committee (NIC), 227, 229, 236
National Negro Congress (NNC), 33
National Review, 346, 352
National Urban League (NUL), 27, 347
Negro History Week, 34
Negro Industrial and Economic Union (NIEU), 302
Negro National Congress (NNC), 64
Negroes with Guns, 74
Newark, 17, 30, 191
New Bedford, 99, 105–6, 108, 113–16; as center of unrest, 119–22, 127, 129; and childhood of Frank "Parky" Grace, 101–2

New Deal, 17, 18, 19, 20, 21, 24, 27
New Haven, 100, 101, 160, 177
New Journalism, 354–56, 364 n.18, 372 n.104
New Left: 61, 213, 279, 325; and African American control of, 229, 233, 246 n.1, 247 n.4, 252, 298; and BPP, 234, 235, 333, 357; and decline of, 224, 244; and FBI, 335, 339
New Orleans, 99
Newsweek, 330, 332, 334, 335, 338, 339
Newton, Fredrika, 8
Newton, Huey, 5–6, 42, 67–68, 163, 258, 277, 325, 329–31; and arrest of, 43, 47, 172–74, 194–95, 215, 314, 320 n.5, 333–35; as BPP leader, 9, 46, 200, 218 n.29, 226; and decline of, 98, 309; and Eldridge Cleaver, 68, 77, 100, 170, 293, 317, 319; and idea of self-defense, 70, 80, 82–83; and influences, 38, 40, 44–45; and launch of BPP, 39, 105–6, 165, 184, 193, 328; political philosophy of, 75, 76, 79, 197, 247 n.4, 266, 299, 300, 315–16; and PFP, 198, 203–5, 208–11, 213; and Stokely Carmichael, 201, 213
New York, 9, 17, 25, 26, 34, 100, 102, 105, 130, 187, 234, 243, 263, 275, 300
New York, 330, 347
New Yorker, 330, 349
New York Times, 7, 326, 330, 331–32, 347, 355, 356
Nightingale, Carl, 42
Nixon, Richard M., 61, 97, 109, 268, 341, 350, 351
Njeri, Akua, 277
Nobre, Richard, 128
North American Liberation Front, 317
North Carolina, 74
Notes of a Native Son, 215
Nuyorican Boogaloo, 301

Oakland: and BPP, 7, 36–49, 60, 99, 105, 167, 173–75, 255, 329; and gang warfare, 6; as power base for Huey Newton, 124
O'Brien, Charles, 5
Ochoa, Rachel, 254
Ogbar, Jeffrey, 7, 188
Oglesby, Carl, 224, 227, 228, 229, 239
Ohio, 61
Old Left, 230, 231, 243
Old Mole, 237
Oliver, Denise, 272, 275
Olympic Project for Human Rights (OPHR), 302
O'Neal, William, 167
O'Reilly, Kenneth, 159, 166, 171
Organization of African Unity, 299
Organization of Afro-American Unity, 299
Ortiz, John, 254
Ousmane, Sembene, 301

Palante!, 275
Pan-Africanism, 34–35, 307
Panther, 359, 360
Parker, Mike, 212, 219 n.43, 221 n.77
Parks, Robert, 30–31
Party Membership, 4
Patterson, William, 40
Payne, Roz, 6, 102
Peace and Freedom Party (PFP): and alliance with SDS, 189, 192–99, 200–5, 232; and BPP, 60; and Eldridge Cleaver, 105, 226, 227, 333, 335; and internal strife, 195; and interracial alliance, 196, 224, 228; and Robert Scheer, 209
Pearson, Hugh, 174, 325, 355
People's Free Medical Research Health Institute, 46
People v. Dhoruba Bin Wahad, 161
Pepper, William, 191
Perez, David, 268

Perry, Charlie, 116, 120, 123, 128
Philadelphia, 27, 63, 84
Philadelphia Negro, 31
Phoenix, 111, 128
Plamondon, Lawrence Pun, 185
Plant, Sadie, 311
Police officers, 273
Popular Front, 18, 25, 34, 40, 64
Portelli, Alessandro, 114
Poststructuralism, 315
Poughkeepsie Journal, 130
Poverty, 191, 325, 327
Powell, Adam Clayton, 34
Pratt, Elmer "Geronimo," 105, 308, 309
Preminger, Otto, 348
Presbyterian Church Council, 183
Price, David, 158
Progressive Labor Party (PL), 230, 231, 235, 238
Project for a New American Century, 61
Providence, 107, 124
Provisional Committee to Defend Ethiopia (PCDE), 33
Public Enemy, 9, 289
Puerto Ricans, 252, 268, 269; and gangs, 267; and independence, 268, 272; and interracial alliances, 272; and nationalism, 252, 262; and race, 269, 270, 284 n.63; and social programs, 269
Puerto Rican Student Association at City College, 263
Puerto Rican Student Union (PRSU), 263
Puerto Rican Young Lords Organization, 252, 262
Puerto Rico, 278
Pufendorf, 76

Race and Reunion, 3
Racial Matters, 166
Racism: 16, 22, 23, 37, 45, 184, 191, 194, 197, 214, 225, 317; and class power, 32; and racial prejudice, 169; and

racial privilege, 32; and racial violence, 196, 296
Rackley, Alex, 100, 101, 103 n.5, 338, 345
Radical Republicans, 3
Rainbow Coalition, 190 n.8, 267, 268
Ramirez, Julio, 211
Ramirez, Ralph, 254
Ramparts, 1, 204, 330
Randolph, A. Philip, 33
Rappaport, Stephen J., 128, 129
Reagan, Ronald, 329
Reconstruction, 3, 97
Red Guard, 299
Reed, Adolph, 48
Regional Action Group (RAG), 118, 119, 121
Representations, 330
Republican Party, 44, 200, 278
Republic of New Africa, 74
Revolutionary Action Movement (RAM), 37–39, 42, 64, 75, 265, 298, 299
Revolutionary People's Constitutional Convention (RPCC), 63, 84, 85, 91 n.52
Revolutionary Suicide, 98
Revolutionary War, 73
Revolutionary Youth Movement (RYM), 231–32, 234, 236–38, 243, 244, 245, 248 n.25, 250 n.44,
Revolutionary Youth Movement I 1/2, 248 n.25
Revolutionary Youth Movement II (RYM II), 225, 235, 238, 243, 244, 249 n.30, 250 n.43, 251 n.44
Revolution in the Air, 61
Reyes, Grace, 274
Ribeiro, Bruce, 132
Rice, Jon, 4
Richard Pryor Show, 302
Robbins, Terry, 249 n.30
Robeson, Paul, 35

Robinson, Dean, 198
Robinson, Pat, 300
Robnett, Belinda, 307, 308
Rollins, Phillip A., 123
Roosevelt, Franklin D., 20, 26, 115
Roxbury, 119
Royal Canadian Mounted Police, 176
Rudd, Mark, 239, 249 n.30
Rudolph, Vern, 109, 124, 125, 126, 135, 138 n.21
Rush, Bobby, 340
Rustin, Bayard, 16

Sacramento, 40, 68, 234, 332, 333, 336
Saigon, 75
Salazar, Ruben, 262
Salt Lake City, 234
Sams, George, 100, 101, 103 n.5, 338
San Diego, 234
San Francisco, 39, 105, 159, 162, 163, 165, 168, 175, 234
Sanchez, David, 254, 256, 257, 262
Santos, Ernie, 109
Saturday Evening Post, 330
Savio, Mario, 210
Say, Brother!, 121
Schanche, Don, 355, 371 n.96
Scheer, Robert, 208, 209, 210, 220 n.73
Schneider, Bert, 170
Schon, Michael, 209
Seale, Artie, 170
Seale, Bobby: 174, 309, 345, 359; and Alex Rackley murder, 101; and BPP development, 41–44; as BPP leader, 9, 46, 63, 100, 193, 315, 319, 330–33; and Chicano community, 259; and Huey Newton, 70, 79–81, 105, 120, 165, 184, 258, 314; and launch of BPP, 39, 217 n.15; and media, 334–35; and PFP, 194, 201–4, 208, 214, 219 n.43; and politics, 353–54, 371 n.96; and SDS, 238, 245
Seale, John, 170

Index 387

Seattle, 177
Seberg, Jean, 171, 172, 179 n.16
Segregation, 30, 41, 253
Seize the Day, 98
Selma, 17
Shabazz, Betty, 317, 322 n.37, 331
Shakur, Afeni, 277
Shakur, Tupac, 9
Sheehy, Gail, 348, 355, 372 n.103
Sickle Cell Anemia Research Foundation, 46
Sinclair, John, 183, 185, 186, n.190
Singh, Nikhil Pal, 15, 16, 20, 24, 26, 34, 98, 297
Situationist International, 312, 313
Sixties: Years of Hope, Days of Rage, 246 n.1
Slavery, 22, 55, 77, 230
Slim, Iceberg, 301
Smith, Clinton "Rahim," 170
Smith, Tommie, 302
Social movements, 327; and antecedent tradition, 307; and collective identity, 307, 308, 309; and evaluation of, 306; and theory of, 310, 315
Socialist Workers' Party (SWP), 193, 217 n.17, 270
Sociedad deeAlbizu Campos (SAC), 267–68
Soul on Ice, 1, 98, 105, 217 n.16, 230, 333
Soul Power, 301
South Central Los Angeles, 75, 254
Southern Christian Leadership Conference (SCLC), 17, 35, 343
Soviet Union, 20
Spanish Action Committee, 264
Spanish-Cuban-Filipino-American War, 262
Spanish Harlem, 263
Spencer, Robyn, 10
Stagolee, 68
Stanford, Max, 298
Staub, Michael, 330, 331

Stern, Saul, 355, 356
Stern, Susan, 237, 239, 240
Stone, Oliver, 359
Student Nonviolent Coordinating Committee (SNCC): 17, 38, 234, 251 n.44, 255; and BPP, 39, 197–98, 201–2, 225–26, 233; and coalitions with other groups, 61, 64, 212–13; and fight against segregation, 35, 245 n.1; and NCNP, 216 n.2; and New Left, 333; and SDS, 229–30; and Stokely Carmichael, 1, 213, 244
Students for a Democratic Society (SDS): 60–61, 191, 244; and alliances with other groups, 190 n.8, 228, 230–32, 233–39, 267; and BPP, 187–89, 224, 226–28, 238, 337; and NCNP, 216 n.2; and New Left, 38, 298; and Weathermen, 42, 245, 250 n.44
Suburbanization, 29, 36
Sullivan, Kenneth, 126
Sullivan, William, 158, 172, 336
Surrealism, 311, 312
Swearingen, Wesley, 161, 172
Sylvia, Eileen "Peachy," 126

Tal, Kali, 9
Taste of Power, 98
Third Chicano Moratorium, 261
Third World, 74, 76, 78, 84, 97, 250 n.44, 295, 296, 335; and internationalism, 74, and links with conditions in the United States, 75
Third World Liberation Front, 263
This Side of Glory, 7
Thuotte, Bob, 109, 128–33
Tijerina, Reies, 259
Time, 330, 332, 333, 335
Treaty of Guadalupe Hidalgo, 253
Trouillot, Michel-Rolph, 4
Tse-Tung, Mao, 166, 333
Tulsa, 301

Tupamaros, 185
Ture, Kwame. *See* Carmichael, Stokely

United Auto Workers, 347
United Front Against Fascism (UFAF), 225, 235, 236, 237, 238, 243, 245, 337
United Nations, 21, 40, 201, 299
United States Congress, 25, 43, 160
United States Constitution: 62, 63, 69, 71–72, 74–76, 78, 80, 82, 84–87, 117; Fourteenth Amendment, 72, 77; Ninth Amendment, 69, 70, 71, 73, 76, 77, 78, 79, 80, 82, 83, 85, 86, 87; Reconstruction Amendments, 72; Second Amendment, 68, 81, 82; Tenth Amendment, 76
United States Court of Appeals, 131
United States Secret Service, 124
United States Senate, 45, 122, 185, 208
United States Supreme Court, 16, 72
United States Trust Company, 130
United Presbyterian Church, 185
Universal Negro Improvement Association (UNIA), 159
Urbanism, 29, 33, 35, 37, 48, 184
Urban rioting, 3
Uruguay, 185
U.S. News and World Report, 330, 336
US Organization, 255, 260

Vander Wall, Jim, 171
Vanguard Party, 266
Vann, James, 211
Van Peebles, Mario, 9, 301
Vassar College, 130
Vice Lords, 265
Vietnam, 60, 75, 101, 104, 106, 108, 110, 116, 117, 118, 120–21, 134–35, 167, 191–92, 205–6, 210–11, 230, 238, 261, 325, 327–28
Vietnam's National Liberation Front (VNLF), 244

Von Eschen, Penny, 21, 34
Voting Rights Act of 1965, 17

Walker, Alice, 7–8
Wallace, Lurleen, 332
Walpole, 108
Warden, Don, 38
War on Poverty, 19, 36, 39, 103, 107, 118
Washington, D.C., 17, 110, 119, 175
Waskow, Arthur, 192
Watergate, 130, 160
Watts, 17, 18, 30, 254, 259, 298, 301
Watts Rebellion, 254
Weathermen, 42, 224–27, 235, 237–39, 241–45, 346
Webb, Robert, 353
Wheelock College, 3, 6, 98, 118, 291, 294, 358
White, Charles, 313, n.322
White, Deborah Gray, n.285
White Panthers, 185, 188, 189, 270; and social programs, 190 n.9; and White Panther Manifesto of 1968, 186
Whites: as activists, 225, 226; backlash of, 17, 73; as employers, 33; flight of, 29; and the Left, 48, 187, 203, 206; and liberals, 24, 212, 279; middle-class, 195, 270; of European ethnicity, 264; and poverty, 189; and radical organizations, 188, 204; and rejection of culture, 5; and whiteness, 263; working class, 237, 238, 239, 243, 270
White supremacy, 232, 236, 263
White Tigers, 187
Wicker, Tom, 340, 341
Wilkins, Roy, 160, 341, 347
Williams, Karen, 170
Williams, Landon, 169, 170
Williams, Ora, 170
Williams, Robert F., 41, 74, 296, 298

Index 389

Williams, Yohuru, 100, 101, 176, 330
Wilshire Boulevard Temple's Camp Hess Kramer, 254
Wilson, Joel, 6, 188, 189
Winston-Salem, 176
Wolfe, Tom, 347, 348, 355
Women's movement, 188, 224, 277, 299
World War I, 29, 64, 310, 311
World War II, 19, 25, 27, 29, 30, 115, 159, 165
Wretched of the Earth, 40, 44, 197
Wright, Richard, 21

Yale University, 101
Yardley, Jonathan, 324, 325
Young, Whitney, 43
Young Citizens for Community Action (YCCA), 254–56
Younger, Evelle J., 261
Young Lords Organization, 38, 188, 239, 242, 264–65, 268–69, 270–73, 275, 277, 280, 299
Young Lords Party (YLP), 275, 276
Young Patriots, 189, 266, 270; Eleven-Point Program and Platform, 267
Youth Council, 118

Zeman, Donald, 126
Zevin, Robert, 130
Zimbalist, Efrem, Jr., 175
Zinn, Howard, 176, 177

Library of Congress Cataloging-in-Publication Data
In search of the Black Panther Party : new perspectives on a revolutionary
movement / Jama Lazerow and Yohuru Williams, editors.
p. cm.
Includes bibliographical references and index.
ISBN-13: 978-0-8223-3837-6 (cloth : alk. paper)
ISBN-10: 0-8223-3837-8 (cloth : alk. paper)
ISBN-13: 978-0-8223-3890-1 (pbk. : alk. paper)
ISBN-10: 0-8223-3890-4 (pbk. : alk. paper)
1. Black Panther Party — History. 2. Revolutionaries — United States — History — 20th century. 3. Radicalism — United States — History — 20th century. 4. African Americans — Politics and government — 20th century. 5. African Americans — Civil rights — History — 20th century. 6. Civil rights movements — United States — History — 20th century. 7. United States — Race relations — History — 20th century. 8. United States — Race relations — Political aspects — History — 20th century.
I. Lazerow, Jama. II. Williams, Yohuru R.
E185.6151453 2006
322.4′20973 — DC22   2006010439